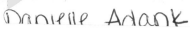

Rap Music and Hip Hop Culture

A Critical Reader
Second Edition

Richard Mook

Arizona State University

Kendall Hunt
publishing company

Kendall Hunt
publishing company

Contents

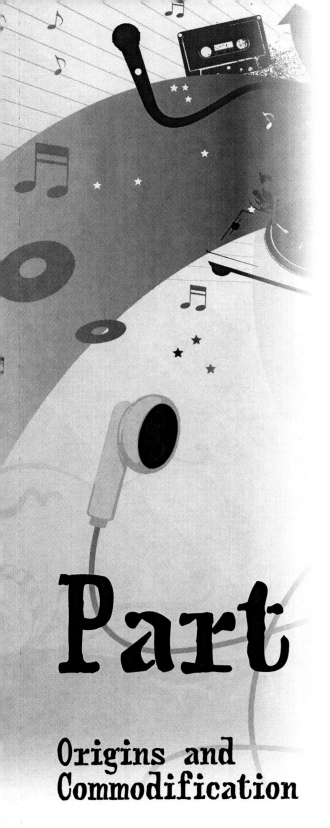

Part 1

Origins and Commodification

The readings in this section examine the creation of rap music and hip hop culture through a variety of sources, including journalism, scholarship, and artist interviews. They offer us a window into how the elements of hip hop connected in the 1970s and early 1980s, the period when hip hop emerged as a commodity in the popular mainstream. We can thereby start to identify key aesthetic principles that unite hip hop elements into a single culture.

Furthermore, these readings show that the popularization of hip hop elements was uneven: graffiti was first to gain notice, followed by the other elements. With all of the elements, however, the shift from local scene to national phenomenon was politically charged. Some segments of society embraced these new art forms, while others fought them as signs of social decay or blight. These debates took place in public, often through mass media.

As breaking, writing, DJing, and MCing appeared in the spotlight, entrepreneurs and established businesses found ways to package and sell these art forms. This process by which something becomes an item or product to be bought and sold is called "commodification." Tracing the history of media interest in hip hop, then, can tell us much about how and when hip hop elements were commodified. Note that this is different from "commercialization."

As you will read, from the very beginning hip hop artists depended on their performances for status, survival, and income (however meager); in this respect, hip hop has always been "Commercial."

In summary, these readings raise some important issues in the history of hip hop including commodification, interaction between hip hop elements, media coverage, and aesthetic principles. As you work through the materials in this section, keep the following questions in mind:

Do these issues also appear in any other assigned materials for this class? How so?

What do these essays tell us about rap music's place in hip hop culture and society at large?

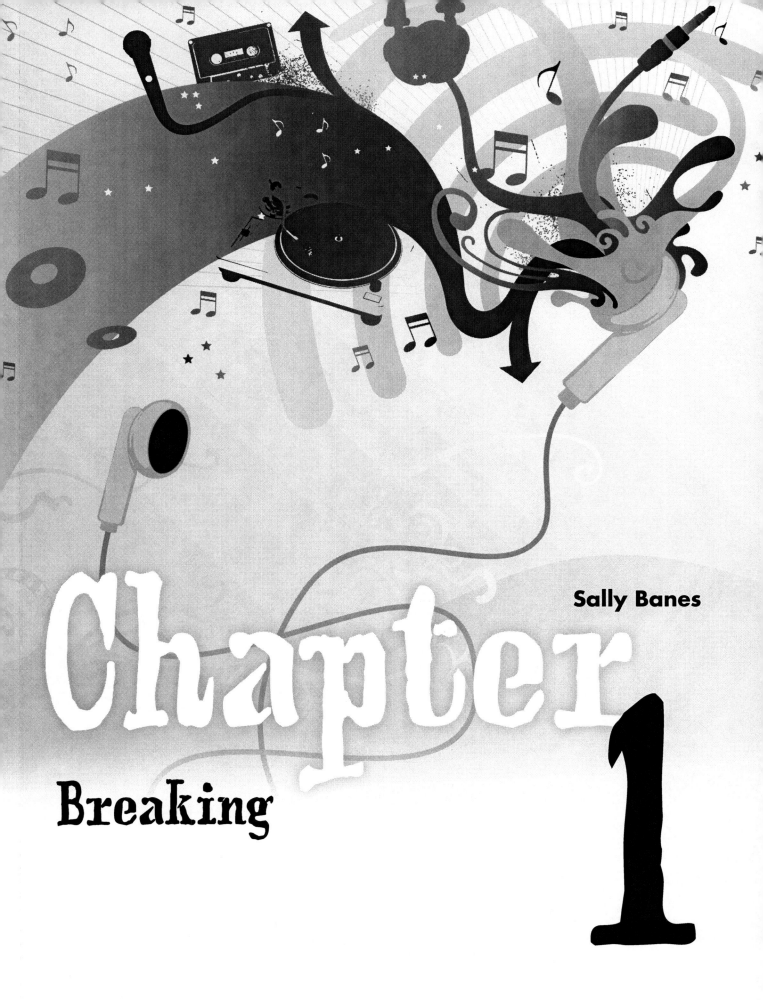

Sally Banes

Chapter 1

Breaking

Break dancing is a style of competitive, acrobatic, and pantomimic dancing. It began as a kind of game, a friendly contest in which black and Hispanic teenagers outdid one another with outrageous physical contortions, spins, and back flips, wedded to a fluid, syncopated, circling body rock done close to the ground. Breaking once meant only dancing on the floor, but now its definition has widened to include electric boogie, up-rock, aerial gymnastics, and all sorts of other fancy variations.

Although breaking is the newest part of hip-hop culture, it's the part that has made hip hop a media obsession. Five years ago the only people who had ever heard of breaking were the kids in New York's ghettos who did it. They didn't even have a definite name for the form—they sometimes called it "breaking," but they also referred to it as "rocking down," "b-boy," or just "that kind of dancing you do to rap music." By 1980—when the form had already been around for a few years—they weren't even very interested in it anymore. This kind of dancing was a passing fad, they felt, that would soon be replaced by roller disco. But history was to prove them wrong. Not since the twist, in the early sixties, has a dance craze so captured the attention of the media.

By 1984 only a hermit could *not* have known about breaking. It had arrived, not only in the United States but also in Canada, Europe, and Japan. Breaking had been featured in the 1983 Hollywood film *Flashdance*, the Independent hip-hop musical film *Wild Style*, and the documentary *Style Wars* (which aired on PBS), served as the inspiration for the 1984 films *Breakin'* and *Beat Street*, and was rumored to be the subject of fifteen forthcoming Hollywood movies. Countless how-to books and videos had hit the market. Breaking had been spotlighted on national news shows, talk shows, and ads for Burger King, Levi's, Pepsi-Cola, Coca-Cola, and Panasonic. One hundred break dancers heated up the closing ceremonies of the 1984 summer Olympics in Los Angeles. And Michael Jackson had given the form national currency.

Breaking made the cover of *Newsweek* in 1984. Newspapers all over the country regularly carried stories on its latest ups and downs. The paradox emerged, as you flipped the pages of the *Washington Post* or the *Los Angeles Times*, that break dancers who'd come up in the ghetto were banned from city streets and shopping malls for causing disturbances and attracting undesirable crowds, while at the same time middle-class housewives and executives could learn to break dance in their spare time at classes proliferating throughout the suburbs. Doctors added to the form's acceptability by giving medical advice on how to survive it unbruised. And the *New York Times* began using breaking as a metaphor even in articles that had nothing to do with hip hop.

By now, break dancing was happening at bar mitzvahs, children's dance recitals, high-school proms, college dances, in prison talent shows, at ballet galas, and on Broadway, as well as in clubs and discos—and, in a second-generation revival, in city parks and on the streets once again. Even President Reagan was delighted by breaking when he saw the New York City Breakers perform in Washington, D.C., at a Kennedy Center gala.

The media hype about break dancing has changed both its form and its meaning. So to talk about break dancing you have to divide it into two stages: before and after media. Before the media turned breaking into a dazzling entertainment, it was a kind of serious game, a form of urban vernacular dance, a fusion of sports, dancing, and fighting whose performance had urgent social significance for the dancers. After media, participation in break dancing was stratified into two levels: professional and amateur. For the pros, break dancing had become a theatrical art form with a technique and a vocabulary that, like ballet's, could be refined and expanded. On this level, competition took on new meaning. It was no longer a battle for control of the streets, for neighborhood fame, or to win your opponent's "colors" (tee-shirt with crew insignia). Now cash prizes, roles in Hollywood movies, and European tours were at stake. For the amateurs, the element of competition had diminished. The appeal was a mixture of getting physically fit, tackling the challenge of breaking's intricate skills, and even becoming more like street kids, who've suddenly become stylish thanks to the meteoric vogue of hip hop.

Breaking first entered media consciousness when Martha Cooper, a photographer who had for years been documenting graffiti, was sent by the *New York Post* to cover "a riot" and found some kids—members of the High Times Crew, friends and relatives from West 175th Street—who claimed they'd been dancing, not fighting, in a subway station. One kid demonstrated some moves to a policeman, who then called in the others one by one. "Do a head spin," he commanded as he consulted a clipboard full of notes. "Do the baby." As each crew member complied, performing on cue as unhesitatingly as a ballet dancer might pirouette across a stage, the police had to admit defeat.

Or so the story goes. But, like ballet and like great battles (it shares elements of both), breaking is wreathed in legends. Since its early history wasn't documented—the *Post* never ran Cooper's photos—it lives on only in memories and has taken on mythological form.

The heroes of these legends are the b-boys, the original break dancers, black and Hispanic teenagers who invented and endlessly elaborate the heady blend of dancing, acrobatics, and warfare that is breaking. Like other forms of ghetto street culture and like the other elements of hip hop, breaking began as a public showcase for the flamboyant triumph of virility, wit, and skill. In short, of style.

The intensity of the dancer's physicality gives breaking a power and energy even beyond the vitality of graffiti and rapping. If graffiti is a way of "publishing," of winning fame by spreading your tag all over the city, breaking is a way of claiming the streets with physical presence, using your body to publicly inscribe your identity on the surfaces of the city, to flaunt a unique personal style within a conventional format. The body symbolism makes breaking an extremely powerful version of two favorite forms of street rhetoric— the taunt and the boast. The razzing takes the form of insulting gestures aimed at your opponent, while the bragging is expressed through acrobatic virtuosity. Breaking is a competitive display of physical and imaginative prowess, a highly codified dance form that in its early stages served as an arena for both battles and artistic invention and that allowed for cracking open the code to flaunt personal inventiveness.

The High Times Crew told the cops they were dancing, not fighting, and as breaking captured mainstream attention it was touted in the media as a transfiguration of gang warfare. Breaking may be a stylized, rhythmic, aesthetically framed form of combat—but it still escalates, at times, into Actual violence. Peace is volatile when honor is at stake, and the physical heat of the form itself makes for situations that are highly combustible, as scenes from both *Breakin'* and *Beat Street* show.

Until breaking became frozen and legitimated by media hype, it was, like much of kids' culture in our cities, self-generated and nearly invisible to outsiders, especially adults—who just didn't want to even think about it or know about it, much less watch it. It was both literally and figuratively an underground form, happening in the subways as well as in parks and city playgrounds, but only among those in the know. Its invisibility and elusiveness had to do with the extemporaneous nature of the original form and also with its social context. Breaking jams weren't scheduled; they happened when the situation arose. You didn't get advance notice of a breaking "performance"; you had to be in the right place at the right time. In other words, you had to be part of the crew system that provided social order among the kids of the Bronx, Manhattan, and Brooklyn ghettos.

Since May 1981, when Henry Chalfant presented the Rock Steady Crew at Common Ground in SoHo as part of a graffiti rock show, breaking has taken to theatrical presentation like a duck to water. The first article on the form, by Sally Banes with photos by Martha Cooper, appeared in the *Village Voice* just before the concert, giving breaking instant visibility. By the end of that summer, break dancers had appeared outdoors at Lincoln Center and at other festivals, and endless filming had begun. The Rock Steady Crew signed up for an appearance in *Flashdance*, and kids were already learning to break not from older brothers and cousins on the Street, but from watching Rock Steady on TV. Breaking had entered the public eye and left the underground for the mainstream, and this new theatrical context, with a style largely disseminated by the Rock Steady Crew, quickly crystallized the form for spectators.

Through breaking, in its original form, all the pleasures, frustrations, hopes, and fears of adolescence were symbolically played out in public spaces. Breaking was inextricably tied to rapping, both in terms of its style and content and because the rap provides the insistent percussion that drives the dance.

The format of the dance was at first quite fixed. The dancers and onlookers formed an impromptu circle. Each person's turn in the ring was very brief—ten to thirty seconds—but packed with action and meaning. It began with an entry, a hesitating walk that allowed him time to get in step with the music for several beats and take his place "onstage." Next the dancer "got down" to the floor to do the footwork, a rapid, slashing, circular scan of the floor by sneakered feet, in which the hands support the body's weight while the head and torso revolve at a slower speed, a kind of syncopated, sunken pirouette, also known as the helicopter. Acrobatic transitions such as head spins, hand spins, shoulder spins, flips, and the swipe—a flip of the weight from hands to feet that also involves a twist in the body's direction—served as bridges between the footwork and the freeze. The final element was the exit, a spring back to verticality or a special movement that returned the dancer to the outside of the circle.

The entry, the footwork, and the exit were all pretty formulaic, with very little room for showing off personal style, although some dancers created special versions of these elements—Frosty Freeze, for instance, often exited "on point," walking on the tips of his sneakers. The entry, the footwork, and the exit were like the stock expressions and nonsense syllables that sandwich narrative content in a rap. They provided a rhythmic frame for the freeze, an improvised pose or movement, which broke the beat. They also provided a nicely textured, comfortably predictable backdrop against which the freeze stood out in bold relief. And besides their aesthetic function, these segments were a way for the dancer to "tread water" between strokes, to free the mind for strategizing while the body went through familiar, uninventive paces.

The simplest combination of a breaking sequence was entry-footwork-spin-freeze-exit. But turns in the center could be extended by inserting more footwork-spin-freeze segments. In other words, you might get: entry-footwork-spin-freeze-footwork-spin-freeze-exit. And so on.

The entry, the footwork, and the exit framed the freeze, a flash of pure personal style, which was the most important part of the dance. The main thing about the freeze was that it should be as intricate, witty, insulting, or obscene as possible. "You try to put your head on your arm and your toenails on your ears," explains Ken of the Breakmasters crew. "When you spin on your head," says another b-boy. "When you take your legs and put them in back of your head out of the spin." A dancer might twist himself into a pretzel, or strike a cocky salute. He would quote the sexy poses of a pinup girl, or perhaps present his ass to his opponent in a gesture of contempt. Through pantomime, he might extend the scatological insult even more graphically, pretending to befoul his opponent. Or he might hold his nose, telling the other guy he stinks. He might put his hand to his spine, signaling a move so good it hurts. Sometimes the dancers in the opposing crew joined in, razzing the performer from the sidelines.

Some of the freeze motifs prophetically rehearsed possible futures for the b-boys. Several images quoted sports actions—swimming, rowing a boat—and even more suggested the military. The freeze celebrated the flexibility and budding sexuality of the gangly male adolescent body, and looked forward to sexual adventures or commemorated past ones. The gun imagery of the military pantomimes doubled as phallic imagery. A dancer would often grab his crotch or hump the floor for a memorable finale.

Another important set of motifs in the freeze section was the exploration of body states in a subjunctive mode—things not as they are, but as they might be—comparing and contrasting youthful male vitality with its range of opposites: women, animals (dogs, horses, mules), babies, old age, injury and illness (e.g., a heart attack à la Richard Pryor's routines), and death.

Various dancers had their specialties, especially in the freeze, but also sometimes in the other sections of the dance. Crazy Legs got his name from his rubber-legged way of walking into the ring, a move descended from the Charleston, and he also takes credit for the W, both face-up and face-down. Kip Dee claims he invented the elbow walk. As breaking moved from the streets to the stage, dancers teamed up to make group freezes, a development that has been elaborately extended over the past two or three years.

In the broadest sense, freezes were improvised. Few were devised on the spot; they were imagined and worked out in advance. But they allowed for the greatest range of individual invention, and the choice of which freeze to use at a given time was often an extemporaneous decision. The b-boys used a variety of methods to create new freezes, including techniques, such as accidents and dreams, preferred by shamans and by the Dadaist and Surrealist painters and poets. Not all freezes have names, but to name your speciality—and to write it as graffiti—was a way of laying claim to it, a kind of common-law copyright.

In breaking as street competition, the freeze was the challenge that incited a virtuosic performance as well as a symbol of identity. As each dancer repeatedly took his turn and, through a series of strategic choices, built excitement with a crescendo of complicated, meaning-packed freezes, he won status and honor for himself and for his group.

The b-boys organized themselves according to neighborhood or family ties into crews, which were networks for socializing, writing graffiti, and rapping, as well as dancing, held together by a strict code of ethics and loyalty. Crews performed in a spirit of friendly competition at jams where the crew leader directed the group's moves. One kid would set up a challenge, and a b-boy from the opposing crew would try to top him, or "burn" him. The crew leader was in charge of sending in new players to spell someone who had run out of moves. Onlookers—more friends, relatives, and neighbors—would judge the contest by consensus. B-boys learned to dance in a system of master-apprentice, referring to each other as father and son—even though the "father" was usually only a few years older than his "son"!—and even chose names that reflected their relationship, like Ty Fly and Kid Ty Fly.

In those days, although there were some girls who joined in, most of the break dancers were boys from the ages of about eight to sixteen. One reason that girls were the exception was that breaking was a specific expression of machismo. Part of its macho quality comes from the physical risk involved—not only the bruises, cuts, scratches, and scrapes, but also the risk of real fighting that might erupt. And part of it is the deliberate attempt to impress the girls.

Breaking was one kind of "rocking," which also included up-rock, a more pantomimic, narrative style of dancing done jumping down and up to standing level, kicking, jabbing, and punching right in a rival's face, without actually touching. In up-rock every move is intended to insult the opponent, and besides actual fighting gestures, a dancer might mime grabbing his rival's private parts, smelling his hand, making a face, and then throwing the offending odor back. Up-rock is funny, but like a rapper's boast it has a mean edge.

The break dancer's "costume" was born of necessity as well as style. Tee-shirts and net over-shirts provide traction on the spins, and sneakers are important to the footwork. Their critical role in the dance is emphasized by making the feet look gigantic and by nearly fetishizing the shoes with embellishments like wide, bright laces loosely tied so that the tongues stick out. The insignia of the crew, as well as colors and outfits that coordinate with those of fellow crew members, play a part in intensifying group solidarity. And the overall look of militarized athleticism creates an image of power and authority. The other accessory for break dancing is a mat, made of cardboard or linoleum, that originally protected the dancers from scraping against concrete.

For the current generation of b-boys, it doesn't really matter that the breakdown is an old name in Afro-American dance for both rapid, complex footwork and a competitive format. Or that a break in jazz means a soloist's improvised bridge between melodies. Or that break is a technical term in Haitian voodoo, referring to both drumming and dancing, that marks the point of possession. Katherine Dunham defines the term as "convulsive movements and sharp temporary changes in a ceremonial…rhythm." Or that in a different Afro-American culture, in French Guiana, there is an old dance called, in Creole, *cassé ko* (translation: breaking the body). All these connections have obvious links with break dancing as we now know it. For the b-boys, memory is short and history is brief; breaking started in the mid-seventies, maybe in the Bronx, maybe in Harlem. It started with Afrika Bambaataa's Zulus. Or with Charlie Rock. Or with Joe, from the Casanovas, from the Bronx, who taught it to Charlie Rock. "Breaking means going crazy on the floor," one b-boy explained back in 1980. "It means making a style for yourself."

As Fab Five Freddy (Fred Braithwaite), the musical director for *Wild Style*, remembers it, breaking began when rapping did, as an intuitive physical response to the music. "Everybody would be at a party in the park in the summer, jamming. Guys would get together and dance with each other, sort of a macho thing where they would show each other who could do the best moves. They started going wild when the music got real funky "—music by groups like SuperSperm and Apache. As the beat of the drummer came to the fore, the music let you know it was time to break down, to freestyle." The cadenced, rhyming, fast-talking epic mode of rapping, with its smooth surface of sexual braggadocio, provided a perfect base for a dance style that was cool, swift, and intricate. The structure of the rap, with its play of quick, varying rhythms going on and off the beat within a steady four-square pulse, is like the off-balance, densely packed, lightning-speed pace of the breaking routine. The sense of inclusiveness, of all being in on a fun time together ("Everybody say ho!" "This is the way we rock the house!" "I am! We are!"), of turn-taking, is there both

Breaking   11

in the rap and in the dance. At times the lyrics of the rap even dictate the break-dancing moves, as the MC calls out the names of the dancers and the steps.

For the current generation of b-boys the history of breaking may reach back only to recent memory—and even those stories conflict—but of course in a broader sense the history of breaking goes back to the slave trade, when Afro-American dancing was born. Breaking is something new and original, born of American ghetto culture in the seventies and (in its latest manifestation) in the eighties, but its basic building blocks are moves from the Afro-American repertory, which includes the lindy and the Charleston and also includes dances from the Caribbean and South America. *Capoeira*, a Brazilian form of martial art that, since slaves were forbidden to practice it, evolved as a dance to disguise itself, bears a striking resemblance to breaking, with its crouching, circling, cartwheeling moves. And, as the Africanist Robert F. Thompson has pointed out, *capoeira* is a pretty direct descendant from Angolan dance. But while breaking is not *capoeira*, but something unique, and while breakers may never have seen *capoeira* until others pointed out to them the similarities of the two forms, the two dance/sport/fight forms have the same roots, just as rapping and the collage of music that comes with it are new and at the same time firmly rooted in a tradition of black and Hispanic music and verbal style.

The main source of the movement in breaking is black dance, but like the rest of hip hop, breaking is an exuberant synthesis of popular culture that draws on everything in its path. Some moves can be traced to the Caribbean, some to the black church, some to the Harlem ball-rooms of the twenties and thirties, some to such dances as the lindy and the Charleston, and others to such diverse sources as kung-fu movies—which were immensely popular in the seventies—*playboy* magazine, French pantomime, cartoons, comics, and TV.

Like any form of dance, breaking is more than the sum of its movements; it is also the way movements are combined, as well as the costumes, music, setting, audience, and the interaction between dancers and spectators. And its context. As an integral part of hip hop, breaking shares many stylistic features with graffiti, rapping, and scratching. Like wild-style graffiti, it emphasizes flamboyance, and the embellishment of the tag finds its parallel in the freeze. The act of writing graffiti is, despite its acceptance on canvas at the Fifty-seventh Street galleries, an act of defacement, and breaking, in its days before media hype, was an act of obscene gestures, a threat. In both graffiti and breaking, each piece or freeze is a challenge, a call to rivals to try to top this, and at the same time a boast that it is unbeatable. Graffiti, rapping, and breaking alike celebrate the masculine heroes of the mass media—Superman and other comic-book heroes, the Saint of detective book and TV fame, athletes, kung-fu masters, and great lovers. The obscure gestural ciphers of breaking find their parallels in the (deliberately) nearly unreadable alphabets of wild-style graffiti, the (deliberately) nearly unintelligible thicket of rap lyrics, and the (deliberately) barely recognizable music that is cut up and recombined in scratching.

Graffiti writers make up new names for themselves, choosing tags partly on the aesthetic grounds that certain letters look good together; break dancers, too, rename themselves, either after their dancing specialty or style—Frosty Freeze, Kid Glide, Spinner, Little Flip—or, like rappers and DJs, with an alliterative name that sounds good—Eddie Ed, Nelly Nell, Kip Dee. And they name their crews in a similar fashion: Break-masters, Rock Steady, Dynamic Breakers, Magnificent Force, Rockwell, Floormasters, Rockers' Revenge, Supreme Rockers, Furious Rockers. Just as graffiti writers mark off city territory and lay title to it with their tags, breakers claim space by tracing symbols on the streets with their dancing and penetrating public space with their ghetto blasters. To write on subway trains, to strike obscene poses, to wear torn clothing, to scratch records, to talk in secret codes, and to sing one's sexual exploits and other praises are transgressive acts. But it is a mark of our times that even such acts, vivid, proud, and aggressive, transmuting destruction into imaginative creation, can be defused as mainstream culture adopts them. Instead of dreaming of becoming revolutionaries, as they might have in the sixties, in the eighties the b-boys aspire to be stars. And at least for some of them, the dream has already come true.

After media exposure, the form of break dancing immediately began to change as theatrical and other experiences—such as a panel at a conference on the folklore of the Bronx—were brought back to "home base." The folklore conference arranged a jam at a roller disco in the Bronx, and soon after, Henry Chalfant and Tony Silver, the directors of *Style Wars*, shot a battle between the Rock Steady Crew and the Dynamic Rockers (later Dynamic Breakers) at a roller disco in Queens. The stage was set for the scene at the Roxy, a roller disco in Chelsea, in Manhattan, that soon replaced the Negril as the venue for Wheels of Steel hip-hop nights. When *Style Wars* was being filmed, the owner of the Queens disco kept clearing out the circle so the cameramen could get in. The next time Rock Steady was break dancing in the park, the crew's president, Crazy Legs, was walking back and forth saying, "Open up the circle."

By now, the circular format has opened up so far it's become linear, for greater theatrical legibility. Less improvisation takes place as well-worn popular moves become standard. As is often the case in the development of a dance form, acrobatic transitions are elaborated, while the freeze, which once concentrated personal expression, competitive gestural dialogue, and group style into a single significant image, has dwindled away to almost nothing and sometimes even merges with the exit. What once was a dance for adolescents is now the terrain of young adults, professionals whose bodies are less gangly and whose higher level of skill is commensurate with their years of practice. Group choreography and aerial spins, reminiscent of the spectacular balancing acts of circus gymnasts, have added to breaking's theatrical brilliance, as has the influx of electric boogie, popping, locking, ticking, King Tut, the float, and other moves that are not break dancing *per se*, into the genre.

Locking is a comic dance that creates the illusion that a person's joints are stuck in one place while his extremities are swinging in wild, rapid circles. It was originally popularized in the early seventies by dancers on the popular black dance television program *Soul Train*, which spawned a dance group called the Lockers, whose flamboyance made locking and the related popping—where one segment of the body moves while others stay still—nationally known. Fred Berry, star of the seventies television comedy series *What's Happening!!*, Jeffrey Daniels, ex-member of the pop-funk vocal group Shalamar, and choreographer Toni Basil were key members of the dance troupe. Berry's bouncy body and beefy face were symbolic of locking's comic appeal. Daniels, a willowy stick figure with an enormous Afro, not only locked and popped, but did a mean robot (the moves look like they sound)—and, along with Michael Jackson, helped spread the moonwalk, a pantomimed illusion of walking backwards, via Shalamar tours and videos. Basil, a choreographer since the sixties, when she worked on the television series *Shindig!* and the legendary film *The T.A.M.I. Show*, worked throughout the seventies and eighties integrating the Lockers' moves into progressive film and video projects, such as her contribution to the Talking Heads' trailblazing "Once in a Lifetime" video. Another noteworthy ex-Locker is the Latin dancer Shabbadoo, who went on to star in the break dance film *Breakin'*.

The electric boogie is a mimelike movement of the entire body, full of wiggles and robotic head turns, that refined the Lockers' movements into a more fluid, less jerky style. It was inspired by moves seen on a summer replacement television show hosted by mimes Shields and Yarnell. Kids picked up on it from TV, as they had locking, and embellished it, though the mime artists' white gloves are often worn by Street dancers. Also via television came the King Tut and its kissing cousin the Egyptian after comedian Steve Martin appeared on *Saturday Night Live* in mock Egyptian garb to perform his hit single "King Tut." With his arms aimed out at sharp right angles, Martin resembled a talking stone carving, and this move was quickly assimilated by youngsters.

All these moves—locking, popping, the electric boogie, the King Tut, and the Egyptian—were similar in that each emphasized arm and upper-body motions, and unlike break dancing, kept the dancers in basically upright positions.

As kids began to learn break-dancing moves by watching the pros on TV or at dance classes, instead of from breakers on the Street, the performance style became homogenized. There's now more of a tendency to copy personal style directly instead of making one's own signature. Amateur breaking still happens—in fact, more than ever, as children as well as adults of all classes and ethnic backgrounds get down at school dances, country clubs, shopping malls, in living rooms, and even on street corners, not in the original competitive mode, but as a moneyearning public performance.

The flexibility and resilience of breaking is evident in the way it incorporated electric boogie and other new moves, rather than letting itself be replaced by them. B-boys vow that it will never die out but, like ballet, become an honored tradition. Interviewed by the *New York Times*, Kid Smooth, sixteen years old, imagined having a son and that son having a conversation someday with his friends: "One kid says, 'My father is a doctor.' The other kid says, 'My father is a lawyer.' And my kid, he says, 'My father spins on his head.' "

At a time when youth culture is again taking center stage in America, the rest of the country is fascinated by black and Latin kids' Street life precisely because of its vivid, flamboyant, energetic *style*. It symbolizes hope for the future—born of a resourceful ability to make something special, unique, original, and utterly compelling out of a life that seems to offer very little. As Fab Five Freddy puts it, "You make a new style. That's what life on the Street is all about, just being you, being who you are around your friends. What's at stake is a guy's honor and his position in the Street. Which is all you have. That's what makes it so important, that's what makes it feel so good—that pressure on you to be the best. Or to try to be the best. To develop a new style nobody can deal with. If it's true that this stuff reflects life, it's a fast life."

Craig Castleman

Chapter 2

The Politics of Graffiti

In 1972 subway graffiti became a political issue in New York City. In that year and the two following, a variety of elected and appointed city officials, particularly Mayor John V. Lindsay, devised and debated graffiti-related policies and programs and issued numerous public statements on the subject.

In examining the progress of subway graffiti as a political issue, New York's newspapers and magazines serve as a revealing and important resource, for not only did they report the graffiti policies of public officials but seemingly played a role in motivating and shaping them as well.

By summer 1971 the appearance of the mysterious message "Taki 183" had sufficiently aroused the curiosity of New Yorkers to lead the *New York Times* to send one of its reporters to determine its meaning. The results of his search, published on July 21, 1971, revealed that Taki was an unemployed seventeen year old with nothing better to do than pass the summer days spraying his name wherever he happened to be. He explained, "I just did it everywhere I went. I still do, though not as much. You don't do it for girls; they don't seem to care. You do it for yourself. You don't go after it to be elected president."[1] The reporter interviewed other neighborhood youths, including Julio 204 and Ray A.O. (for "all over"), who were following in the footsteps of Taki, to whom they referred as the king, and he spoke with an official of the MTA who stated that more than $300,000 was being spent annually to erase graffiti. Patrolman Floyd Holoway, a vice-president of the Transit Patrolmen's Benevolent Association questioned by the reporter as to the legal machinery relating to graffiti writing, explained that graffiti was barred only by MTA rules, not by law. Thus writers under the age of sixteen could only be given a lecture, not a summons, even if they were caught in the act of writing on the walls. Adult writers could be charged with malicious mischief and sentenced to up to a year's imprisonment. Didn't I read this somewhere?

Taki confessed that as he grew older, he worried more about facing adult penalties for writing graffiti but admitted, "I could never retire…besides…it doesn't harm anybody. I work. I pay taxes too. Why do they go after the little guy? Why not the campaign organizations that put stickers all over the subways at election time?"[2]

The *Times* article presented Taki as an engaging character with a unique and fascinating hobby, and this seemed to have a profound effect on the city's youth. Taki became something of a folk hero, and the ranks of the graffiti writers increased enormously. However, though each day brought numerous new writers to the walls and the subways were marked with names from top to bottom, 1971 brought no further press coverage of graffiti.

In spring 1972 another article on graffiti appeared in the press. It was intended not to help familiarize New Yorkers with the writers but to declare war on them. On May 21 city council president Sanford Garelik told reporters, "Graffiti pollutes the eye and mind and may be one of the worst forms of pollution we have to combat." He called upon the citizens of New York to band together and wage "an all-out war on graffiti" and recommended the establishment of a monthly "antigraffiti day" on which New Yorkers, under the auspices of the Environmental Protection Agency, would scrub walls, fences, public buildings, subway stations, and subway cars.[3]

From Castleman, Craig. *Getting Up: Subway Graffitti in New York*, pp. 135–157. © 1982 Massachusetts Institute of Technology, published by The MIT Press.

The *Times*'s management followed up on Garelik's statement by printing an editorial denouncing the "wanton use of spray paint to deface subways." They praised Garelik's "noble concept" of an antigraffiti day but questioned its lasting appeal. Rather than burden the populace with the responsibility for cleaning up graffiti, the *Times* called upon the city administration to ban the sale of spray paint to minors and thus stop graffiti at its source.[4]

Taking his cue from both the *Times*'s and Garelik's suggestions, Mayor Lindsay announced his own antigraffiti program in late June. The mayor's proposal called for the fining and jailing of anyone caught with an open spray can in any municipal building or facility. Lindsay was highly agitated at the time of the announcement, and Robert Laird, his assistant press Secretary, admitted to a Times reporter that "the unsightly appearance of the subways and other public places created by the so-called graffiti artists has disturbed the Mayor greatly."[5]

Lindsay again addressed the graffiti problem in extemporaneous comments before a large crowd at the rededication ceremonies for Brooklyn's Prospect Park boathouse in late August. Standing before the white ceramic exterior of the newly renovated structure, Lindsay noted that he had asked for tighter legislation against graffiti vandalism but said that police action alone would not cure the problem. Pleading for greater public interest in the problem, the mayor exclaimed, "For heaven's sake. New Yorkers, come to the aid of your great city—defend it, support it and protect it!"[6]

Lindsay's graffiti legislation had been referred to the city council's General Welfare Committee in early August, but the members had shown little inclination to deal with it at that time. (The council meets only twice during the summer months, and committee activity is virtually suspended from July to September.) Impatient with the committee's foot dragging, Lindsay insisted that they hold a special meeting on graffiti on August 31. The mayor asked a number of top administration officials, including the deputy mayor, the parks commissioner, and the MTA chief administrator, to testify in favor of the legislation. But only four members of the fifteen-member committee were present at the session, and no action was immediately forthcoming.[7]

Meanwhile MTA chairman Ronan publicly gave his support to Mayor Lindsay's graffiti campaign. On October 28 he told reporters that he had instructed the transit police to charge "such miscreants with 'malicious mischief,' " and he urged the mayor to stress the seriousness of "this blighting epidemic" to the courts.[8] Later that same day Mayor Lindsay held a ceremony in his office at which he officially commended one of Dr. Ronan's transit policemen, patrolman Steven Schwartz, for his "personal crusade" against graffiti. Schwartz alone had apprehended thirteen writers in the previous six months, a record for graffiti arrests unmatched in the department. The mayor followed up the ceremony with a statement that it was the "Lindsay theory" that graffiti writing "is related to mental health problems." He described the writers as "insecure cowards" seeking recognition.[9]

The General Welfare Committee submitted a graffiti bill to the city council in mid-September stating that the use of markers and spray paint to write graffiti has "reached proportions requiring serious punishment for the perpetrators" and that such defacement and the use of "foul language" in many of the writings is "harmful to the general public and violative of the good and welfare of the people of the city of New York."[10] The bill proposed to eliminate graffiti by making it illegal to carry an aerosol can of paint into a public facility "unless it is completely enclosed in a sealed container." It specified that "no person shall write, paint or draw any inscription, figure or mark of any type" on any public property. Judges were given wide latitude in dealing with such offenses, but the law stated that it was the council's intent that any person guilty of writing graffiti "should be punished so that the punishment shall fit the crime." In this spirit the bill recommended that judges sentence writers "to remove graffiti under the supervision of an employee of the public works office, New York City transit authority or other officer or employee designated by the court."[11] The bill also recommended that merchants selling spray paint or markers be required to register with the Police Department and to keep a record of the names and addresses of all persons who purchase such merchandise.[12]

The day after the General Welfare Committee approved the bill, the *Times* published an editorial stating that graffiti "are day-glo bright and multicolored, sometimes obscene, always offensive." The editorial praised the committee for getting tough with "youthful vandals" and announced that "graffiti are no longer amusing; they have become a public menace."[13]

Perhaps intending to spur the full council on to faster action on the graffiti law, Mayor Lindsay on October 5 announced the formation of a graffiti task force under the direction of his chief of staff, Steven Isenberg. The task force, which included among its members the heads of a number of city agencies, was designed to coordinate "tough new programs" for the enforcement of the expected graffiti legislation.[14] The mayor further stated that

the ugliness of graffiti and the ugly message—often obscene or racist—has generated widespread support for the City's campaign to end this epidemic of thoughtless behavior. Even those who once possessed mild amusement about graffiti are becoming increasingly indignant at the damage being done.... I know the problem is complex, but we have to roll up our sleeves and solve it. The assault on our senses and on our pocketbooks as we pay the clean-up costs must be stopped.[15]

The graffiti bill was approved unanimously by the full city council on October 11, minus the section on control of the sale of spray paint, which had aroused opposition from merchants and was considered by the council to be "too controversial."[16] Mayor Lindsay, who signed it into law on October 27, was pleased with the bill but warned merchants to "self-regulate" their sales or he would impose further legislation that would make it illegal to sell spray paint to anyone under eighteen years of age.[17]

There was also antigraffiti action on other fronts. Science came to the aid of graffiti fighters with the invention, by E. Dragza of the Samson Chemical Corporation, of an "artproof acrylic polymer hydron" which he named Dirty Word Remover (DWR).[18] On July 31 Mayor Lindsay announced that Dragza's formula, renamed Hydron 300, was to be sprayed on a library in Queens, another in Brooklyn, and a firehouse in the Bronx, to facilitate the removal of graffiti from their walls. The mayor expressed hopes that use of the "Teflon-like coating" would help to make graffiti removal "easier and less costly." The cost of the experiment was set at $5,000.[19] Results of the test were never made public.

Inspired by the growing campaign against graffiti, private citizens also got involved in the "graffiti war" of 1972. In November the Kings County Council of Jewish War Veterans invited "citizens of good will" to join their bucket brigade to clean graffiti off the monument to President John F. Kennedy in Brooklyn's Grand Army Plaza.[20] The Boy Scouts and Girl Scouts staged their own graffiti cleanup day when more than 400 scouts spent a day partially cleaning six IND trains. Bach participating scout received a citizenship medallion in honor of his or her achievement from the Avon Products Corporation.[21]

Other New Yorkers devised ingenious solutions to the problem. E.A. Sachs, for example, in a letter to the *New York Times* suggested that the MTA paint subway vehicles with a "multi-colored spray" that would "camouflage any attempts at graffiting."[22] M.W. Covington, also in a letter, made the more drastic suggestion that a "massive police assault" be launched against graffitists who deface Central Park monuments.[23] R.H. Robinson of Brooklyn showed great ingenuity in his suggestion that large fines levied on convicted graffitists be divided between the city and persons turning in the graffitists. He noted that he had already assembled a lengthy list of offenders in his own neighborhood.[24] Of more than a dozen letters concerning graffiti that appeared in the *Times* that winter, only one was sympathetic to the writers. The letter writer, P.R. Patterson, hailed youths who paint graffiti for "cheering up the depressing environment in the poorer areas of the city" and accused most people of being "guilty of subduing the desire to mark up subways as a protest against the indignities of the city bureaucracy."[25]

Early in 1973 Steven Isenberg announced that over the year the police had arrested 1,562 youths for defacing subways and other public places with graffiti. Of those arrested, 426 eventually went to court and were sentenced to spend a day in the train yards scrubbing graffiti.[26]

Two weeks after Isenberg's announcement Frank Berry, the executive officer of the transit authority, announced that conventional "quick treatment" graffiti writing had reached the "saturation level" and was being supplanted by "large...multi-colored inscriptions that may cover one-half or more of a subway car's outer surface." The alarming proliferation of such "grand design" graffiti constituted, according to Berry, distinct danger to riders because "they can block the vision of riders preparing to enter or leave through the door." In light of these new developments Berry called for an increase in the number of graffiti arrests to eliminate the possibility of a "grand design" epidemic.[27]

On February 26 the New York City Bureau of the Budget completed a detailed work plan for Mayor Lindsay's graffiti task force. The report began by stating that antigraffiti efforts in 1972 had cost the city $10 million, yet they had not been sufficient to reduce "the city-wide level of graffiti defacement" below "fifty percent surface coverage," a level that it declared "unacceptable."[28] It thus proposed that the city engage in a graffiti prevention project that would seek to reduce the level of defacement to an acceptable 10 to 20 percent. The cost of such a project was estimated to be $24 million.[29]

Under the control of a project management staff team appointed by the mayor, the proposed project would coordinate efforts by various city agencies and private corporations toward four major project elements:

- Technological improvements: Testing and implementing the use of high-performance paints, coatings, and solvents for graffiti-defaced surfaces.

- Security measures: Testing and implementing increased security measures in those areas of the city where security may deter graffiti vandalism.

- Motivation of graffiti vandals: Testing and implementing psychological measures aimed at either inhibiting vandalism or diverting vandals elsewhere.

- Control of graffiti Instruments: Testing and implementing the feasibility of manufacturer and retailer restrictions on packaging and display of graffiti instruments.[30]

Under these categories the report listed nearly one hundred specific tasks, the completion of which would lead to the achievement of the overall objectives. The tasks included "implementing and monitoring psychological field-testing for graffiti vandalism prevention and developing procedures for monitoring of procedures involved in implementation of restrictions." Mayor Lindsay devoted a month to study of the report before releasing it or commenting on it publicly.

Meanwhile on March 26 *New York Magazine* published a long article by Richard Goldstein, "This Thing Has Gotten Completely Out of Hand." His reference was not to the growing graffiti fad but to the city's fight against it. Goldstein, giving the pro-graffiti forces their first published support, stated that "it just may be that the kids who write graffiti are the healthiest and most assertive people in their neighborhoods." He further declared graffiti to be "the first genuine teenage street culture since the fifties. In that sense, it's a lot like rock 'n' roll.[31]

In the same issue the *New York Magazine* management presented a "Graffiti 'Hit' Parade" in which it gave "Taki awards" to a number of graffitists in categories labeled "Grand Design" and "Station Saturation." Award-winning works were reproduced in full color in the magazine. They declared the emergence of grand design pieces a "grand graffiti conquest of the subways" and ridiculed chairman Ronan, Mayor Lindsay, and the *Times* for their attitude toward the new art form. The Taki Awards article also contained a statement in praise of graffiti from pop artist Claes Oldenberg that was reprinted in the catalog for two subsequent UGA exhibitions and was quoted in a number of magazine and newspaper articles about graffiti, as well as Norman Mailer's book, *The Faith of Graffiti*. Said Oldenberg:

> I've always wanted to put a steel band with dancing girls in the subways and send it all over the city. It would slide into a station without your expecting it. It's almost like that now. You're standing there in the station, everything is gray and gloomy and all of a sudden one of those graffiti trains slides in and brightens the place like a big bouquet from Latin America. At first it seems anarchical—makes you wonder if the subways are working properly. Then you get used to it. The city is like a newspaper anyway, so it's natural to see writing all over the place.[32]

The day after the *New York* articles appeared, Mayor Lindsay called a press conference at which he discussed the findings and proposals contained in the graffiti prevention project report. He stated that copies of the work plan would be sent to the heads of the MTA, the Environmental Protection Agency, the board of education, and all other agencies and authorities concerned with graffiti prevention. He ridiculed "those who call graffiti vandalism 'art' " and asked the citizens of New York to join him in denouncing the graffiti vandals. "It's a dirty shame," said the mayor, "that we must spend money for this purpose in a time of austerity. The cost of cleaning up graffiti, even to a partial extent, is sad testimony to the impact of the thoughtless behavior which lies behind…the demoralizing visual impact of graffiti."[33]

As graffiti continued to appear on subways and other city property, Mayor Lindsay became increasingly angry, not only at supporters of graffiti and the writers themselves but at his own staff for their inability to control the problem. In an interview with a *Sunday News* reporter, Steven Isenberg "smiled when he recalled two times when Mayor Lindsay burst into his office and—with four-letter fervor—ordered him to 'clean up the mess.' One time the Mayor had snipped a ceremonial ribbon at the opening of a Brooklyn swimming pool that was already covered with graffiti and the other time he had spotted a graffiti-laden bus in midtown. 'I certainly got reamed out,' Isenberg recalled."[34]

The mayor's anger over the continued appearance of graffiti on the subways exploded publicly on June 30, 1973. Steven Isenberg explained, "When the Mayor went to mid-town to publicize the parking ticket step-up, he took the subway back to City Hall and what he saw made him madder than hell."[35] Immediately upon his return to his office the mayor called a hurried press conference at which he snapped, "I just came back from 42nd Street in one of [MTA chairman] Dr. Ronan's graffiti-scarred subway cars, one of the worst I've seen yet."[36] The mayor stated that the extent of name marking in the trains and stations was "shocking" and pointed out that the antigraffiti force he had organized the year before had come up with a plan to prevent the writing through increased police surveillance of lay-ups, train yards, and stations. "Since the time the plan was sent to the MTA I haven't heard a word," he said. "I don't think they even bothered to look at it. They don't give a damn and couldn't care less about being responsive to elected officials."[37]

A few months later in an interview with Norman Mailer, Lindsay explained that his aggravation with graffiti was due to the fact that it tended to nullify many of his efforts to provide the city's subway passengers with "a cleaner and more pleasant environment" in which to travel. At that time the mayor was also attempting to justify the city's massive expenditures for new subway cars, which, once covered with graffiti, "did not seem much more pleasant" than the old cars.[38]

The graffiti policies that were established during the Lindsay administration are still being pursued. The MTA continues to scrub trains only to find them immediately redecorated. The police continue to apprehend writers only to see them released, unpunished, by the courts. It would seem that the failure of the city's expensive antigraffiti policies should be a matter of great concern to the press and elected officials; however, the management, expense, and overall wisdom of New York City's antigraffiti policies have not been criticized publicly by either politicians or the press and thus continue unchanged.

Norman Mailer attributed Lindsay's attitude toward graffiti to the fact that the mayor had earlier sought the Democratic presidential nomination in 1972 and that graffiti had been

> an upset to his fortunes,... a vermin of catastrophe that these writings had sprouted like weeds over the misery of Fun City, a new monkey of unmanageables to sit on Lindsay's overloaded political back. He must have sensed the Presidency draining away from him as the months went by, the graffiti grew, and the millions of tourists who passed through the city brought the word out to the rest of the nation: "Filth is sprouting on the walls."[39]

It is doubtful that graffiti played as important a role in Lindsay's declining political fortunes as Mailer speculates. Evidently, however, Lindsay believed that graffiti was a problem significant enough to rate a substantial amount of his attention, and thus it became a political issue during his administration.

The fact that there has been very little reduction in the amount of graffiti that has covered the city's subways since 1971 can be seen as proof that the city's antigraffiti policies have failed. John deRoos, former senior executive director of the MTA, has placed the burden of blame for this failure on the city's judicial system: "Almost all graffiti can be traced to people who have been arrested at least once. But the courts let them off. Six, seven, eight, or nine times."[40] In an interview former transit police chief Sanford Garelik also laid the blame for the failure of the MTA's graffiti arrest policies on the courts: "The transit police are doing their job but what's the use of making arrests if the courts refuse to prosecute? Graffiti is a form of behavior that leads to other forms of criminality. The courts have to realize this...anything else is an injustice to the public."

Chief Judge Reginald Matthews of the Bronx Family Court has replied to such criticism of the courts' handling of graffiti: "Graffiti is an expression of social maladjustment, but the courts cannot cure all of society's ills. We have neither the time nor the facilities to handle graffiti cases; in fact, we cannot always give adequate treatment to far more serious crimes. Graffiti simply cannot be treated by the juvenile justice system as a serious thing, not in New York."

Not everyone in the MTA and the transit police blames the courts. Reginal Lewis, a car maintenance foreman at the MTA, puts the blame on the transit police for "not keeping the kids out of the (train) yards." Detective Sergeant Morris Bitchachi, commander of the MTA's ten-member graffiti squad, blamed the city's Department of Social Services for not providing special rehabilitation programs for "known graffiti offenders."

City University professor George Jochnowitz had another idea: "The *New York Times* is...responsible for the prevalence of graffiti. On July 21, 1971, an interview with Taki 183, a previously unknown graffiti dauber, appeared.... The glorification of this vandal by the nation's most prestigious newspaper was not without effect. Within months a minor problem became a major one."[41]

After 1975 there was little press coverage of graffiti, a reflection of the city government's reluctance to publicize the city's continuing failure to control the graffiti phenomenon This, combined with the seeming unwillingness of the press to bring criticism upon itself through the publication of Taki-style reports, led to a near press blackout on the subject of graffiti.

In 1980 the blackout ended when the *New York Times Magazine* published a long article about three graffiti writers: NE, T-Kid, and Seen. Other newspapers followed suit, featuring articles on other writers and on the current state of the graffiti phenomenon.

In September 1981 the mayor's office broke its silence when Mayor Koch declared that "New Yorkers are fed up with graffiti," and announced a 1.5 million dollar program to provide fences and German Shepherd watchdogs for the Corona trainyard. MTA chairman Richard Ravitch had at first rejected the idea, stating that, "fences are not going to work. It is likely that they would be cut and the dogs would get out and perhaps injure someone in the neigh-boring community."[42] Ravitch quickly gave in to pressure from the mayor, however and a double set of razor wire-topped fences were quickly installed, between which six dogs patrolled the perimeter of the yard. Mayor Koch and the press were present on the day the dogs were released and the mayor declared, "We call them dogs, but they are really wolves. Our hope is that the vandals will ultimately get the message."[43]

To test the effectiveness of the fences and dogs, all of the trains stored at the yard were painted white and the mayor asked the MTA to inform him immediately if any graffiti was painted on them. For the following three months the trains were watched closely and no graffiti appeared on the outsides of the trains. Declaring the Corona experiment a success, the mayor announced on December 14 that the city would increase its contribution to the MTA by $22.4 million to fund the installation of similar fences at the other eighteen train yards operated by the authority. The mayor stated that the new security installations would not feature attack dogs because, at $3,000 per year apiece, their maintenance had proved too expensive. Instead, coils of razor wire would be placed between the fences. Said Koch "I prefer to think of these as steel dogs with razor teeth. And you don't have to feed steel dogs."[44] Ravitch said that he was pleased by the mayor's decision to increase transit financing and that the MTA would attempt to complete construction of the new fences within six months.

Privately, MTA officials expressed doubts that the fences would, ultimately, be effective. Graffiti writers did so as well. Said Ali, "We haven't gone over the fences at Corona because it's on a lousy subway line. If they fence a popular yard like Pelham or Coney Island, the writers won't be stopped by razor wire, dogs, or laser towers. We'll get past the fences. Wait and see." Daze said, "All the fences will do is keep most of us out of the yards. We'll still be able to hit the trains in the lay-ups, and we'll bomb the insides and the outsides of in-service trains with tags—big spray-paint tags like nobody's ever seen. The MTA can't stop us from doing that unless they put a cop on every car." Bloodtea continued, "AU they're doing is moving graffiti from the outsides of the trains to the insides. It's the inside graffiti—the tags—that the public hates. All the mayor is doing is getting rid of the outside pieces that the public likes, the big colorful pieces."

According to mayoral aide Jack Lusk, the yard-fencing program is the first step in a long-range antigraffiti program. Said Lusk;

"The public hates graffiti and it's up to us to do something about it. Fencing the yards will take care of some of it. Beyond that we're planning a series of antigraffiti television, radio, and print advertisements featuring the slogan. 'Make your mark in society, not on it.' We're also considering sponsoring antigraffiti citizens' groups; legislation banning the sale of spray paint and markers to minors; and possibly the establishment of a special transit court that will handle crimes like graffiti and other forms of vandalism. Even though the mayor does not have direct authority over the MTA, the public holds him responsible for the state of the subways. The public is frightened and disgusted by graffiti and they want us to do something about it. We're going to do whatever is necessary to wipe it out."

NOTES

1. " 'Taki 183' Spawns Pen Pals," *New York Times*, July 21, 1971, p. 37.
2. Ibid.
3. "Garelik Calls for War on Graffiti," *New York Times*, May 21, 1972, p. 66.
4. "Nuisance in Technicolor," *New York Times*, May 26, 1972, p. 34.
5. "Fines and Jail for Graffiti Will Be Asked by Lindsay," *New York Times*, June 26, 1972, p. 66.
6. "Lindsay Assails Graffiti Vandals," *New York Times*, August 25, 1972, p. 30.
7. Edward Ranzal, "Officials Testify in Favor of Mayors Graffiti Bill," *New York Times*, September 1, 1972, p. 25.
8. Edward Ranzal, "Ronan Backs Lindsay Antigraffiti Plan," *New York Times*, August 29, 1972, p.66.
9. Ibid.
10. "Stiff Antigraffiti Measure Passes Council Committee," *New York Times*, September 15, 1972, p. 41.
11. New York Administrative Code,Section 435-13.2 (1972).
12. "Stiff Administrative Measure Passes Council Committee," *New York Times*, September 15, 1972, p. 41.
13. "Scratch the Graffiti," *New York Times*, September 16, 1972, p. 28.
14. "Lindsay Forms 'Graffiti Task Force,'" *New York Times*, October 5, 1972, p. 51.
15. Office of Mayor John V. Lindsay, press release, October 4, 1972.

16. "Antigraffiti Bill One of Four Gaining Council Approval," *New York Times*, October 11, 1972, p. 47.

17. "Lindsay Signs Graffiti Bill," *New York Times*, October 28, 1972, p. 15.

18. "New Chemical May Curb Graffiti," *New York Times*, April 22, 1972, p. 35.

19. Office of Mayor John V. Lindsay, press release, July 31, 1972.

20. "Antigraffiti 'Bucket Brigade' Planned," *New York Times*, November 13, 1972, p. 41.

21. "Boy Scouts Scrub Graffiti Off Walls of Subway Cars," *New York Times*, February 25, 1973, p. 35.

22. E. H. Sachs, Jr., letter, *New York Times*, December 24, 1972, Sec. 8, p. 2.

23. M. W. Covington, letter, *New York Times*, December 26, 1972, p. 32.

24. R. H. Robinson, letter, *New York Times*, June 5, 1972, p. 32.

25. P. R. Patterson, letter, *New York Times*, December 14, 1972, p. 46.

26. *New York Times*, January 14, 1973, p. 14.

27. "Fight against Subway Graffiti Progresses from Frying Pan to Fire," *New York Times*, January 26, 1973, p. 39.

28. Bureau of the Budget of the City of New York, *Work Plan—Graffiti Prevention Project* (February 26, 1973), p. 2.

29. Ibid., p. 3.

30. Ibid., p. 2.

31. Richard Goldstein, "This Thing Has Gotten Completely Out of Hand," *New York Magazine*, March 26, 1973, pp. 35-39.

32. "The Graffiti 'Hit' Parade," *New York Magazine*, March 26, 1973, pp. 40-43.

33. Murray Schumach, "At $10 Miliion, City Calls It a Losing Graffiti Fight," *New York Times*, March 28, 1973, p. 46.

34. James Ryan, "The Great Graffiti Plague," *New York Daily News Sunday Magazine*, May 6, 1973, p. 33.

35. James Ryan, "The Mayor Charges MTA Is Soft on Graffiti" *New York Daily News*, July 1, 1973, p. 2.

36. Alfred E. Clark, "Persistent Graffiti Anger Lindsay on Subway Tour," *New York Times*, July 1, 1979, p. 47.

37. Ibid.

38. Norman Mailer, *The Faith of Graffiti* (New York: Praeger/Alskog Publishers, 1974).

39. Ibid.

40. Owen Moritz, "The New Subway," *New York Daily News*, December 5, 1978, p. 37.

41. George Jochnowitz, "Thousands of Child-hours Wasted on Ugly Daubings," *New York Post*, October 20 1978, p. 43.

42. Ari L. Goldman, "Dogs to Patrol Subway Yards," *New York Times*, September 15, 1981, p. 1.

43. Ibid.

44. Ari L. Goldman, "City to Use Pits of Barbed Wire in Graffiti War," *New York Times*, December 15, 1981, p. B-1.

Nelson George

Chapter 3

Hip-Hop's Founding Fathers Speak the Truth

Kool DJ Herc. Afrika Bambaataa. Grandmaster Flash. Old School, you say? Hell, these three are the founding fathers of hip-hop music—the progenitors of the world's dominant youth culture. For them, hip-hop is not a record, a concert, a style of dress or a slang phrase. It is the constancy of their lives. It defines their past and affects their view of the future. As DJs in the '70s, these three brothers were the nucleus of hip-hop—finding the records, defining the trends, and rocking massive crowds at outdoor and indoor jams in parts of the Bronx and Harlem.

What hip-hop was and has become is the subject of the first collective interview involving Herc, Bambaataa and Flash—the first time, in fact, that Herc has spoken on record in over ten years. One late summer evening they sat together, first in a Broadway photography studio and later at The Source's offices, telling stories, laughing at old rivalries and setting history straight.

Kool DJ Herc (aka Clive Campbell) used the sound systems of the Caribbean as the model for his mammoth speaker setup. But the sensibility that led him to scout for obscure records and mesh beats from blaxploitation soundtracks with Caribbean dance hits, soul grooves and novelty records was born of the hectic world that was the Bronx during the Carter administration. Hip-hop's sonic montage was conceived by him in city parks and school yards, where crowds flocked to hear him play, grooving to the beats he unearthed. Fact is, there were no B-boys until Herc labeled them so.

If Kool Herc is the base, then Bambaataa and Flash are twin pillars who complemented and extended the original vision. Bam came through New York's early '70s gang banging era unharmed but wiser. Seized by an enormous musical curiosity and a communal vision of African-American empowerment, he founded the Zulu Nation, the single most enduring institution in hip-hop. While labels and clubs have come and gone, the Zulu Nation emerged from the Bronx River Community Center into a collective with adherents around the world. At its center all these years is Bambaataa, who found musical inspiration in rock, Third World music and, most crucially, the electronic instrumentation that would support his breakthrough group, the Soul Sonic Force.

Grandmaster Flash (Joseph Saddler) was a teenager fascinated by records and audio circuitry. Aside from having a wide musical interest, Flash became intrigued with the possibilities the technology surrounding music suggested for innovation. The concept of scratching—now the backbone of hip-hop DJing—came out of his laboratory (with an assist from his friend Grand Wizard Theodore). Flash's introduction of the "beat box" turned DJs from beat mixers to beat makers. And the building blocks of rapping as we know it were laid by the crew that gathered around Flash—initially, Kid Creole, his brother Melle Mel and the late Cowboy.

The conversation that evening was wide ranging, including issues of historical detail and philosophy. Who was the first to scratch a record? Was DJ Hollywood the first hip-hop rapper? What was the relationship between break dancing and rapping? Who first played "Apache"? These and other often-debated questions are addressed by the people who were in the eye of the cultural hurricane.

In a broader sense, Herc, Bambaataa and Flash talk at length about the all-embracing musical curiosity that inspired hip-hop's creation and how debates about "hardcore" and "sell-out" records run contrary to the scene's roots. The wholesale dissing of women, the increasing violence between rival rap posses and the control of rap's manufacture by major corporations troubles them. The [camaraderie] of these rivals-turned-griots, the good humor in their remembrances and the vivid descriptions of epic park parties are a powerful contrast to the Black-on-Black crime that scars much contemporary hip-hop.

Because of their shared affection and respect, this conversation is not mere nostalgia—it is a testament to why mutual respect is integral to hip-hop's future.

Afrika Bambaataa: *Most people today, they can't even define in words, hip-hop. They don't know the whole culture behind it.*

Grandmaster Flash: *You know what bugs me, they put hip-hop with graffiti. How do they intertwine? Graffiti is one thing that is art, and music is another.*

Kool DJ Herc: *I was into graffiti. That's where Kool Herc came from.*

The Source: *Were people doing [tags] and shit when you were playin'?*

Bam: *No, they did tags on the wall. See before the whole word hip-hop, graffiti was there before that. But really when the Zulu Nation pulled the whole thing together and we laid down the whole picture. You know, the graffiti and the breakdancers.*

Herc: *That's where the graffiti artists were congregating at. Going to the Factory West, or going to the Sand Pad, or going down to the Nell Guen on 42nd Street, or going to the Puzzle up there on 167th street, or to the Tunnel. That's where the graffiti guys used to hang out. That's how hip-hop came a long way.*

Bam: *It was there with the street gang movement. The gangs would've started dying down, but you still had the graffiti crews coming up into the hip-hop culture. Once everything started coming into place, we started doing shows and traveling into different boroughs. Then we started traveling to different states and that's when we threw everything together.*

Herc: *And the thing about graffiti was, I was the guy with the art. I liked graffiti flyers. My graffiti friend used to do my flyers.*

Bam: *Sometimes we didn't need flyers, we just say where we gonna be and that's where we at.*

Herc: *Block party, we gonna be over there, be there! That was it.*

Flash: *Or what might happen is, if I'm playin', I'll say "Herc's givin' a party tomorrow in the street," or if Bam's playin', Bam will say, "Flash will be here."*

The Source: *Ok, how does breakdancing, or breaking fit into all that?*

Flash: *It was basically a way of expressing how the music sounds. Early breakdancing you hardly ever touched the floor. I would say, maybe this is a bad comparison, but it was more like a Fred Astairish type of thing—stylin', the hat, you know, touchin', white laces, finesse, that's where the two intertwined. It was like just one particular couple would draw a crazy crowd in the street. Stylin', nothing sweaty, they wouldn't break a sweat. Just fly. Like Eldorado, like Mike, Sasa, Nigger Twins, Sister Boo.*

Bam: *You had Mr. Rock, the Zulu Queens, the Zulu Kings.*

The Source: *So when did it get involved with guys getting' on the floor?*

Bam: *Well the first form of break dancing started with the Street gangs with a dance called "Get on the Good Foot" by James Brown. There were a lot of women who was really into the break dancing too that would tear the guys up in the early stages. But then it all came together.*

Herc: *They started to bet money.*

Bam: *The first era lasted for a while then it died down. And then the second generation came.*

Herc: *The Puerto Ricans carried breakdancing.*

Flash: *They took it to the next level for sure.*

Herc: *They carried all forms of hip-hop music with dancing.*

Flash: *It died for a while then it came back and it was this new acrobatic, gymnastic type of style.*

Bam: *And really with some of them, they had been doing this since '77 and it never really died with them. Especially with the Rock Steady Crew, the New York City Breakers, and a couple of those crews.*

The Source: *OK, the phrase B-boy. What does that mean to you?*

Herc: *The boys that break. When somebody go off in the neighborhood, "Yo, I'm ready to break on somebody," so we just say B-boys, you know, breakers.*

The Source: *So it doesn't necessarily mean, he's a dancer? It's an attitude or somebody who does something?*

Flash: *You don't have to be a dancer!*

Herc: *B-boys, these are the boys, these are the boys that break. So we call 'em B-boys.*

The Source: *Let me ask you, is there a time where you remember the whole style of the hat sideways attitude coming in? Where you said this is a new style as opposed to what had gone before? Is there a point where you said, "Oh he's a B-boy. This is new."*

Flash: *I think when actually dancers started making contact, like doing jump kicks and kicking people on the floor, that's when the hat started going like this [Flash turns his hat sideways]. It was like, "I ain't dancing with you, I'm gonna try to hurt you." That's when the hat went to the side.*

Bam: *With some of them, they did hurt some. Some people got hurt. When they danced against each other, or especially if they had different crews. All through the time there was a struggle. You had your peaceful moments and you had your straight-up battles.*

Herc: *After a while guys would start to say, "Well you gonna have to pay to see me dance." Or, "If you want to take me out or discredit me you have to put some money up."*

The Source: *Like Basketball. What were the records that made them do that?*

ALL: *James Brown, "Give It Up, Turn It Loose."*

Bam: *"Apache" was the national anthem.*

Herc: *"Just Begun."*

Flash: *"Black Heat," remember that one?*

Bam: *"Family..." by Sly and the Family Stone.*

The Source: *To find these beats, you would go to Downstairs Records and just find a ton of records?*

All: *No we didn't just go to Downstairs!*

Flash: *That was one of Herc's spots.*

Herc: *That spot to me was where I find shit that wouldn't be nowhere else, or I found something that I could say, "Hey this is good." I'd go to somebody's house and they'd say, "Herc, I know you like records, run through my records. I got a whole lot of stuff there."*

Flash: *Or girls' houses for sure. Dope.*

Herc: *Or going to one of Bam's parties and I hear something and I say, "I could use this with this."*

Bam: *I took music from around the whole world. I was playin' so much crazy shit, they called me the master of records.*

Flash: *He was the man. He was the king of the records.*

Herc: *When I go to his party, I'm guaranteed to be entertained by some shit I don't hear other people play. Then I step to Mr. Bam, "What's that one?"*

The Source: *Tell me five records you might play in a row back in the day?*

Bam: *Well you would hear something from the Philippines by a group named Please which did a remix for "Sing a Simple Song."*

Flash: *You might hear "Fernando" by Bob James, I might play that with a...*

Herc: *You might hear "Fat Sap from Africa" or "Seven Minutes of Funk." "Babe Ruth."*

Flash: *Or how about on the back side of the Incredible Bongo Band, the other one, "Bongolia."*

Bam: *You could hear "The Return of Planet Rock" by the Incredible Bongo Band. "Sing, Sing, Sing," "Sex" by Bobby Knight.*

The Source: *Who was the first person to take the record in the bathtub and wipe the labels off?*

Flash: *That was me. People were getting too close, you know. I will give all due respect to my boys right here, but you know, other people.*

Herc: *He put us on a wild goose chase [everyone laughs].*

Bam: *I had a way of telling things from the color of the album. I could know if it was Mercury or Polygram. Then I would try to see who it sounded like.*

Flash: *Hey Bam, I followed you on a Saturday with glasses on. I seen one bin you went to, pulled the same shit you pulled, took that shit home—and the break wasn't on the mutha-fucka [everyone is hysterical].*

Bam: *I used to tell people, "Do not follow me and buy what I buy," and I went into a record store and everyone was waitin' around to see what I pulled. So I pulled some Hare Krishna records [everyone laughs]. It had beats but...*

Flash: *You couldn't play that bullshit. I got a crate full of bullshit.*

Herc: *If I go somewhere and I hear something, I give the DJ respect. I don't try to say, "I played it." 'Cause the first time I heard "Seven Minutes of Funk," I was with this girl I used to talk to, and we were at this place called The Point, and it was like a movie. The minute we hit the door, people knew who we were, and we didn't know people knew who we were. All we heard was…[Herc hums the "Seven Minutes of Funk" baseline which was used on EPMD's "It's My Thing"] The further we walk in the party the record was still going. I was like, "That shit is ruff."*

The Source: *Who discovered "The Mexican"?*

Bam: *Herc got "The Mexican."*

The Source: *What kind of equipment did you have in the late '70s, early '80s?*

Flash: *I had six columns and maybe two bullshit bass bottoms. I didn't have much of a system. I was going to school and I had a messenger job. I also had electronic experience though, so a lot of the stuff I make-shifted. I didn't really hear a real heavy, heavy, heavy system until I heard this man [Herc] out in the park. It was incredible.*

The Source: *Where did you get your equipment?*

Herc: *My old man bought a Sure P.A. system for his band he used to be with. The band fell off and the speakers wound up in my room. My pops was a little strict and told me to not touch 'em. I never did play 'em but another kid in the neighborhood had the same system and played his. So I asked him how to hook up the Sure P.A. to the system. They wouldn't tell me. So I borrowed one of my father's friend's systems 'cause I wouldn't touch the Sure stuff in the house. What they was doing was using one of the channels from the turntables and using the brain itself to power the whole thing. My shit was, I used the pre-amp, used the speakers wires put into a channel, and used the two knobs to mix. I got more sound than they ever got.*

The Source: *What kind of turntables were you using?*

Herc: *At first I started with Gerards [laughs]. Then from there I went downtown and I seen two Technics 1100As and I went and got 'em.*

Flash: *They're still the best turntables in the world right now, the 1100A, but you can't find 'em. Because of the tork and the pick-up. You could have the hand the size of a monkey and that thing would still turn. The actual design of that turntable was incredible. I was never able to afford 'em so I had to adjust my touch to cheaper turntables.*

The Source: *But the questions is, who started it?*

Flash: *There was this __family__ called the Livingstons, OK. There was Gene, Claudio, and this little kid named Theodore. Now, before we actually became Grandmaster Flash and the Furious Five, I kept my equipment at Gene Livingston's house. What he would tell me is because his little brother was so interested was, "Don't let Theodore in the room, don't let Theodore on the turntables!" Now when he went to work, I would tell Theodore to come on in and let me see what you can do. Now, he had an ability to take the needle and drop it and just keep it going. He had such a rhythm that was incredible. I begged Gene for like a year and a half to take this little kid out in the park with us as the team to get larger notoriety. He didn't like* *the idea of it. After a while this little kid kinda outshined his big brother. So what Theodore did for scratchin' is this—where I had expertise on the back-spin or fakin' the faze, what Theodore would do with a scratch was make it more rhythmical. He had a way of rhythmically taking a scratch and making that shit sound musical. He just took it to another level.*

The Source: *People don't appreciate how much technical knowledge went into the creation of music. You had to really study turntables and speakers and the entire thing.*

Flash: *Break-up plenty of equipment to get what it was.*

The Source: *So you had to custom-make everything.*

Flash: *I had to custom-make my cue system also. I couldn't afford a mixer with a built-in cue system where you could hear turntable one or two in advance. I had to actually get a single pole-double throw switch, crazy glue it to the top of my mixer, build an external mix on the outside just strong enough to drive a headphone, so when you clicked it over you would hear the other turntable in advance. But this whole idea of hearing the cut ahead of time took three years to come into being.*

The Source: *How did you create the beat box?*

Flash: *For some reason the world seems to think the beat box is something you do with your mouth. The beat box was an attempt to come up with something other than the techniques I created on the turntables to please the crowd. There was this drummer who lived in the Jackson projects who had this manually operated drum box he used to practice his fingering. I begged him to sell it to me. Then I found a way to wire it into my system and called it the beat box. The drummer taught me how to use it. When my partner Disco Bee would shut the music off, I would segue into it, so you couldn't tell where the music stopped and I started.*

The Source: *Bam, where do you trace your interest in music to?*

Bam: *I'll give credit to my mother. When I was growing up in the '60s, I used to hear a lot of the Motown sounds, James Brown sounds, the Stax sounds, Isaac Hayes and all of them. As well as Edith Piaf, Barbra Streisand, the Beatles, the Who, Led Zeppelin. From there I started knowing about a lot of different music and that's when I first heard African music from Miriam Makeeba. I was listening to this sister talk about things about South Africa which I didn't really understand at the time. One movie that grabbed my attention was this movie called Zulu. At the time when you were seeing Black people on TV, you would see us in degrading roles. So to see this movie with Black people fighting for their land was a big inspiration for me. Then here comes this guy that I used to not like at first, I though he was weird and crazy, which was Sly Stone. But once I heard "Sing a Simple Song," "People," and "Stand," I switched totally to this sound of funk. Then I seen the whole Motown start changing. The Temptations started getting psychedelic. I was a gang member by that time. From '69 to about '75 I was in the Black Spades but, like a lot of these young great Black musicians, I was a visionary. I said to myself, "When I get older, I'ma have me a Zulu Nation." I just waited for the right time.*

The Source: *You went from gangs to doing parties—how did you make that transition to being a DJ?*

Bam: *Well before Flash, Herc, all of us, there was Disco DJs happening in the areas. Flowers, Kool DJ Jones, Lovebug Starski, and Kool DJ Dee. Those were who I follow at one time. Then you* started hearing the sound that was coming from my brother Kool DJ Herc. Then when I came out with my system, Herc was like an angel looking over me. Then when I changed over to giving my big party, I didn't have to worry about having it packed 'cause I was in control of all the gangs out there anyway. So when I changed over and brought everybody from the street gangs into the Zulu Nation, when I gave the first big function, everyone knew who I was and backed me up.

The Source: *People have always speculated that the rise of hip-hop caused the gangs to disappear in New York or changed them over. What would you say the relationship was to the rise of hip-hop parties to the gangs of New York?*

Bam: *Well, I would say the women were more important. The women got tired of the gang shit. So brothers eventually started sliding slowly out of that 'cause they had people that got killed. Cops were breakin' down on people. The cops actually had a secret organization called the "purple mothers" that were ex-Vietnam veterans that would roll on gang members. There was a lot of crazy shit going on in the struggle of the gangs and the transition from the gangs dying down and the women putting their foot down. Drugs helped destroy the gangs too. Now one thing people must know, that when we say Black we mean all our Puerto Rican or Dominican brothers. Wherever the hip-hop was and the Blacks was, the Latinos and the Puerto Ricans was, too.*

The Source: *What do you think now when people say that there's a certain style of music that's considered hip-hop, and a certain style that's not considered hip-hop? Claims that some records are fake hip-hop records and some are real?*

Bam: *They're ignorant. They don't know the true forms of hip-hop. Just like I tell 'em, you got all styles of hip-hop, you gotta take hip-hop for what it is. You got your hard beats, you got your gangsta rap, you got your electro-funk sound which came from the party rock sound, you got your Miami bass, you got the go-go from DC. We was playin' go-go years ago. If you really with Teddy Riley, he came to Bronx River parties and heard go-go music and just flipped it up and now you got new jack swing. All of this was all part of hip-hop.*

Flash: *It's all about different tastes. It could be hard drums like a Billy Squire record. It could be the bass hitting and drums soft like "Seven Minutes of Funk." It could have the hallway echo effect of "Apache."*

Herc: *We can't let the media define this for us. Someone says it's got hardcore beats and talkin' about bitches sucking dick, thats hardcore. That same person says that Jazzy Jeff & the Fresh Prince are soft, it's not hip-hop. It is hip-hop. It's just another form. It's about experimenting and being open.*

Bam: *Different generations have lost the true meaning. We were teaching the public when we did parties in the park.*

The Source: *Tell me about doing parties in the park.*

Herc: *See, the park playin' is like playin' for your people. You give them something free. Sometimes it's hot and a lot of the clubs didn't have no air conditioner. So I gave parties out in the park to cool out while summer's there. To play in the park is to give the fans and the people something.*

Bam: *We'd play for everybody. You'd play certain records that grabbed the old, you played the straight up hip-hop records...*

Flash: *You can actually experiment 'cause now you have a wider audience coming. You have like mothers and fathers and a wide spread of people. You can actually test your new-found jams to see how they work on the public right then and there. You'll know right then and there if you got something, as soon as you play it.*

Bam: *We were selling cassettes of our mixes that were really our first albums. We had luxury cabs like OJ and the Godfathers and Touch of Class that would buy our tapes.*

Flash: *How it worked was people would call for a car, and if they had a dope Herc tape, or a dope Bam tape, or a dope Flash tape, that particular customer might stay in the cab all day long. So these cab drivers were making extra money and at the same time they were advertising us. Like Bam said, it was like cuttin' an album, but it was on tape.*

The Source: *The first hip-hop I ever heard was on a tape that was sold in Brooklyn. I saw it on Fulton Street, and that's first time I realized it was being passed around the city.*

Bam: *Circulating. If you look at it, everything's repeating itself now. Look at all the DJ tapes now. You have Ron G, Kid Capri, Doo Wop. All these kids are doing the same things we did twenty something years ago. It's like life is returning back to the surface. Just like your hearing a new rebirth of funk. All of the stuff is coming back, like Pumas...*

Flash: *Bell bottoms, teardrops, the big high-heel shoes.*

The Source: *Talking about style, your two groups were both stylistically influenced by funk groups.*

Bam: *I could tell you about that. A lot of the rappers used to dress regular and then we got more into presenting people with something. You know, when you're payin' five, ten dollars to come in, you want to see people dressed up.*

Flash: *You know what, we was like businessmen. In a very simplistic sort of fashion. It was like three corporations and we carefully did things without realizing it.*

Bam: *We was businessmen at like thirteen, fourteen. Making our own parties. We had payrolls. Picking the venues or the streets or the centers. Dealing with the politics, or deciding whether you needed police. We dealt with so much business at such a young age.*

The Source: *One of the things you hear is that battling the essence of hip-hop. But you're saying that that was something that came afterwards. At the root of it was some kind of fellowship.*

Flash: *Yeah. Experimental musically, but it was a fellowship.*

The Source: *Would guys roll up who were tryin' to make a rep and challenge you one-on-one?*

Flash: *You can't take away three or four years of establishment in one night. You can't do that. You'll just be a statistic. Bam, Herc and myself already had a science on how to control our crowd. At that time you definitely had to earn it. Not in days, weeks, months—it took years to get a little bit of respect. Then you had to pass through one of the three of us.*

Bam: *You couldn't even come in our areas to play or else you dealt with us with respect. We would make sure you couldn't play one of the clubs or even come into the community.*

The Source: *I remember a club called 371. This was DJ Hollywood's club. What did you guys think about that whole scene?*

Bam: *Hollywood, himself, was more like disco oriented.*

The Source: *I've heard Hollywood was the first hip-hop rapper.*

Flash: *No, the first people I heard talk on the microphone and do it extremely well and entertain the crowd and wasn't talkin' to the beat of the music, was Herc's people. Coke La Rock. He would just talk while Herc was cuttin'.*

Herc: *Little phrases and words from the neighborhood that we used on the corner is what we would use on the mic. Like we talkin' to a friend of ours out there in the crowd.*

Bam: *And when they got rhymin' it came from the Furious when they added Melle Mel.*

Flash: *It was Cowboy, then it was Kid Creole, and Melle Mel. There were these dancers Debbi and Terri who used to go through the crowds shouting "Ho!" and people picked up on that. Cowboy came up with a lot of phrases and had a powerful voice that just commanded attention. "Throw your hands in the air!" "Clap to the beat!" "Somebody scream!" all came from Cowboy. Kid Creole and his brother Melle Mel were the first to really flow and have a poetic feel to their rhymes. They were the first rhyme technicians. They were the first to toss a sentence back and forth. Kid would say, "I," Mel would say, "was," Kid would say, "walking," Mel would say, "down." They just tossed sentences like that all day. It was incredible to watch, it was incredible to hear. Along with Coke La Rock with Herc, they were the root. It was Cowboy, Kid Creole and Melle Mel for quite a while before it became the five of us. Like syncopating to the beat of music was incredible. You just didn't get it overnight. You had to play with it, develop it, break things, make mistakes, embarrass yourself. You had to earn it.*

The Source: *Is it a real important distinction between Hollywood and what you were doing?*

Flash: *He did come in around the same era. He was there and made a mark. It was just he was a softer side of music. Something we might not play, he would jam and kill it. He was a disco rapper. He'd rap over things like "Love is the Message" which I would never play. Things that were on the radio he'd do for the crowds at after-hours clubs.*

The Source: *For a lot of people, Disco Fever was the first place where they heard hip-hop.*

All: *No.*

The Source: *OK, then what was that place's significance.*

Flash: *There was a lot of clubs between Flash, Bam, and Herc. But the clubs started diminishing slowly but surely. Fatalities were happening there, there, and there. Things got a little bad for everybody. This guy Sal at the Fever resisted at first, but then decided to take a chance on it. What happened was the Fever became a later meeting point for a lot of mobile jocks and new stars at the time. At any given time Camacho would walk in there, Herc would walk in there, Kurtis Blow, Sugarhill Gang, a member of the Commodores. I mean it was like this place was quite well known.*

Herc: *What the Fever did was give hip-hop a place with disco lights, fly, you could come nice. It had a prime location next to the Concourse. It had a downtown atmosphere uptown.*

The Source: *When the Sugar Hill Gang made "Rapper's Delight," hip-hop was now on record. You guys were the founders of this style, yet it was a while before you guys got involved with making records. Did you discuss recording in the mid-'70s?*

Flash: *I was approached in '77. A gentleman walked up to me and said, "We can put what you're doing on record." I would have to admit that I was blind. I didn't think that somebody else would want to hear a record re-recorded onto another record with talking on it. I didn't think it would reach the masses like that. I didn't see it. I knew of all the crews that had any sort of juice and power, or that was drawing crowds. So here it is two years later, and I hear "To the hip-hop, to the bang to the boogie," and it's not Bam, Herc, Breakout, A J. Who is this?*

Herc: *And when I heard [Big Bank] Hank [of the Sugar Hill Gang], I was like, what? I knew Hank. I didn't really appreciate that Hank knew me personally, had been to my house, was from the neighborhood, and never once said, "Herc, I'm doing something." Never, until this day.*

Bam: *'Cause he never gave credit to Grandmaster Casanova Fly, who is called Grandmaster Caz these days from the Cold Crush Brothers, for the rhymes.*

The Source: *Now did he literally write them and Hank took them?*

Herc: *Caz used to come to the Sparkle where Hank was a doorman. He used to get on the mic and Hank heard him. That's when Hank saw the scene growing. I went to New Jersey—my girlfriend knew him—and he was working in a pizza shop down there. I just said, "When Sylvia [Robinson, of Sugar Hill Records] hear the real deal, she gonna know." And I was happy to be in the Fever when she seen the truth. And it was hell with them after that. To see Melle Mel and them on stage.*

Flash: *'Cause the cream of the crop like Caz, The Fantastic Five was in there.*

The Source: *Again, you guys did eventually make records. You got with Bobby Robinson who had Enjoy Records in Harlem for years.*

Flash: *Yeah we got with Bobby. We was playin' at a club on 125th Street. All I know was he made me very nervous 'cause I knew what my age bracket was, and here was this old man who came in at about 11:00, and he stayed to the end of the party. So I said to myself, "Either he's the cops, he's somebody's father looking for his daughter, or something's gonna go down here." So then when we were breaking down the equipment at the end of the night, he stepped me and said, "Flash, do you think it's possible that we can get together and possibly put together a record." You know, I went back to the folks, talked about it, and we did it.*

The Source: *How much did he pay you?*

Flash: *Maybe a thousand a man. Not bad.*

The Source: *Almost all the people who came at this point were still Black though, am I right?*

Bam: *Record companies, yeah they were still Black.*

The Source: *It was still a Black thing in the sense that to find out about it you had to be near the grass roots.*

Flash: *These were little record companies that were selling records out the trunk of their car. They were only looking for cream of the crop rappers to do this. At that time, all they wanted was what Sylvia was doing.*

The Source: *A lot is going on right now. We're talking about '80, '81. We have the first rap records. The music is starting to spread in terms of your appearances outside of the Bronx. Did you get the sense that it was getting out of control?*

Flash: *I wanted to push it.*

Herc: *I was mad when Sugar Hill came first and did their thing.*

Bam: *I was the one who was always more independent. I would just sit back and watch to see where things were going before I stepped into it. 'Cause I was watching Flash be successful moving his stuff, I was happy. Then this white guy came down and checked us out named Malcolm MacLaren. And Tom Silverman came down and checked me out in Bronx River with Arthur Baker. First Malcolm MacLaren came, 'cause he said, "There's this Black kid playin' all this rock and other type of music to a Black and Spanish audience." When he seen this, he invited me to come play at the Ritz with Bow Wow Wow. So when I came and did that show, I brought everybody together like Rock Steady and all the groups. That's where I first met them and we all came under the Zulu Nation. There was this guy Michael Holman who used to invite me down to DJ at the Mudd Club, then to Negril with my son Afrika Islam, D.St., Whiz Kid.*

Then we used to get too big for that so we went to Danceteria and got too big for that until finally the Roxy became our home. Then Flash and them came and played the Ritz on the Sugar Hill tour with Sequence and the West Street Mob. With the Roxy it became like an international world club. Everyone was coming to the Roxy. Then you had the clubs that didn't want hip-hop nowhere down there like the Limelight. They would make a dress code 'cause there were too many Blacks and Puerto Ricans coming into the neighborhood. That's when I started fighting racism down in the club scene. I would say, "If you don't let my Blacks or Puerto Ricans in, I'm gonna leave." That's when we started gettin' power in the clubs.

The Source: *How did you feel about the whole process of going from having parties to doing records?*

Flash: *I'd have to say, I wasn't ready. I was content with what I was doing. I think what happened was when Herc stopped playing eight hours a night. Flash stopped playing, Bam stopped playing, the street thing flipped. Like one DJ would play eight different clubs in one night and not really have an audience anymore. You lost your home champion because there was nobody there. I would have personally like to stay away from records a little longer. Not to say that I wouldn't want to make records 'cause records was the next plateau for spreading the musical word.*

Bam: *Everyone was nervous. It took the excitement away. We didn't have the parties. Everyone would go out and buy the record.*

Flash: *It was a thing to me coming into the place at six and taking two-and-a-half hours to set up the sound system and make sure the EQs were right and the crates were right. It was fun.*

Bam: Plus a lot of people in the early records were gettin' robbed. That's something a lot of people don't want to talk about it. A lot of people now who know they can make money have to know what the Old School went through.

Flash: You know what's really sad to know and see, is that these people have never really seen a block party—like a block party that goes ten or twelve hours. Starting at noon and ending at midnight. I mean you have to really be in a party for hours to watch a DJ expand on what he would play. That would separate the men from the boys as far as the DJ is concerned. The way I see it, the less times he repeats something in a ten hour period, the more qualified he is. That's why we would come up with ten-fifteen crates of records. So we wouldn't have to play anything twice.

The Source: You all seem to feel there's a sense of community about the hip-hop scene during the party era that's never really been recaptured.

Bam: Today it gets sickening with the disrespecting of self. To me a lot of brothers and sisters lost knowledge of self. They're losing respect of the "us syndrome" and getting into the "I syndrome." You can't build a nation with an "I" you got to build a nation with a "us." The disrespecting of the Black women—you got some sisters that go into the category "bitches," although you got a lot of the Black women that don't deserve that.

The Source: I want to get into the whole area of the media and rap's evolution. How do you feel the history rap has been told? Do you think it has been distorted in any way?

Flash: There are those out there that made a great attempt to accuracy. Then there are those who are just doing it to make a dollar. I think to this point it hasn't been really told. I'm not going to try to toot my own horn, but I think the only ones that can really tell you the story are Herc, Bam, Breakout and myself. Either you can hear his-story or history, and the only way you gonna hear the real historical views on it is by the people who were actually there—who actually took it from nothing and built into whatever it became to be. Some people don't dig deep enough to find out what happened back then. They just fix it so it's comfortable for the reader, which is really dangerous.

Bam: My thing from studying history and listening to great leaders like Elijah, Malcolm, and Minister Farrakhan, I see that everything is planned by design. Even in the industry, nobody talked to the Black and Latino and said, "Do y'all want to get rid of vinyl?" They never had no survey. But the next thing you know vinyl is out the door and CDs are in. I always told people that there was people in the industry that was tryin' to destroy hip-hop. They couldn't do it. That's why Zulu Nation, TC Islam and all of us are pushing a united hip-hop front. Cause you got a lot of people from the Old School who are really mad. Melle Mel, Kurtis Blow, Kevi Kev, a lot of old timers who didn't get their due respect or even the money that they should have made. You got people who are opening the door that are out of there now who ain't paying no mind where the history come from.

The Source: When you say Old School guys are mad, who owes them? Where did the point come where they were left behind?

Bam: A lot of the companies, a lot of friction happened between the companies. You had companies that was robbing people by not telling them about publishing. Some artists' albums went gold but they didn't give them no money. You know, here's a leased car instead of royalties.

The Source: *Well let me ask you something—who owns hip-hop now?*

Bam: *White industry.*

Herc: *Whites.*

Bam: *The white industry owns it now because they control all the record companies. And all our people that make money worry about Benz's and big houses and fly girls instead of being Black entrepreneurs. You need to take the business back.*

The Source: *Herc, you're one of the people that there's a great mystique or mystery about. Tell us about the decisions you made during the period when rap came out on records.*

Herc: *I was maintained as far as running the sound system and giving parties. The mic was always open for the MCs. My thing was just playin' music and giving parties. I wasn't interested in making no records.*

The Source: *What do you most like about hip-hop culture today?*

Flash: *Contrary to the media and to the powers that be, hip-hop has a vibe. Under all the crush and blows, being called a fad, it now has its own category and is stronger than ever. I thank God that I'm here to see it. It's quite a compliment to walk down the street and be told, "Flash do you realize you're a legend?" But a lot of times legends die young and don't get to see what they seeded. I'm glad to see it.*

The Source: *What about hip-hop culture at this point do you dislike the most?*

Flash: *I think that somebody went around and said that in order to cut a hit record, we have to disrespect our brothers, sisters, mothers and children. What people don't realize here is that hip-hop has a large influence on people. What you say maybe just frivolously, somebody can seriously go out and go do. I'm not sayin' that what we're doing is not right, but it shouldn't be the only way that a record is made. Like if you listen to ten records, seven of them is either disrespecting our sisters, or hurting people.*

The Source: *Bam, what do you like most about what's going on now?*

BAM: *I love that hip-hop has become international. I love when I go to France and hear French hip-hop groups. I love when I go to England and hear British hip-hop groups. I love to see hip-hop groups all through Africa. Hip-hop has taken a lot of brothers and sisters who might be doing negative things and have gotten into the rap world to see other people's way of life. Hip-hop has also had a force to unite people together. You have all people of color trying to understand what's happening with the Black problem. Some are getting educated about negative and positive things.*

Nelson: *Herc, what aspect of hip-hop culture do you like the most?*

Herc: *That it's still here. It's giving youth a chance to pay for education if they want to. Giving 'em a chance to go overseas. It's here, it ain't going nowhere. Music was always our way of information—it was the drums. They took it away from us in Africa, now we found it again. The music is our fuckin' drums man. All I could say right now as far as rappers out here today is: be true to the game.*

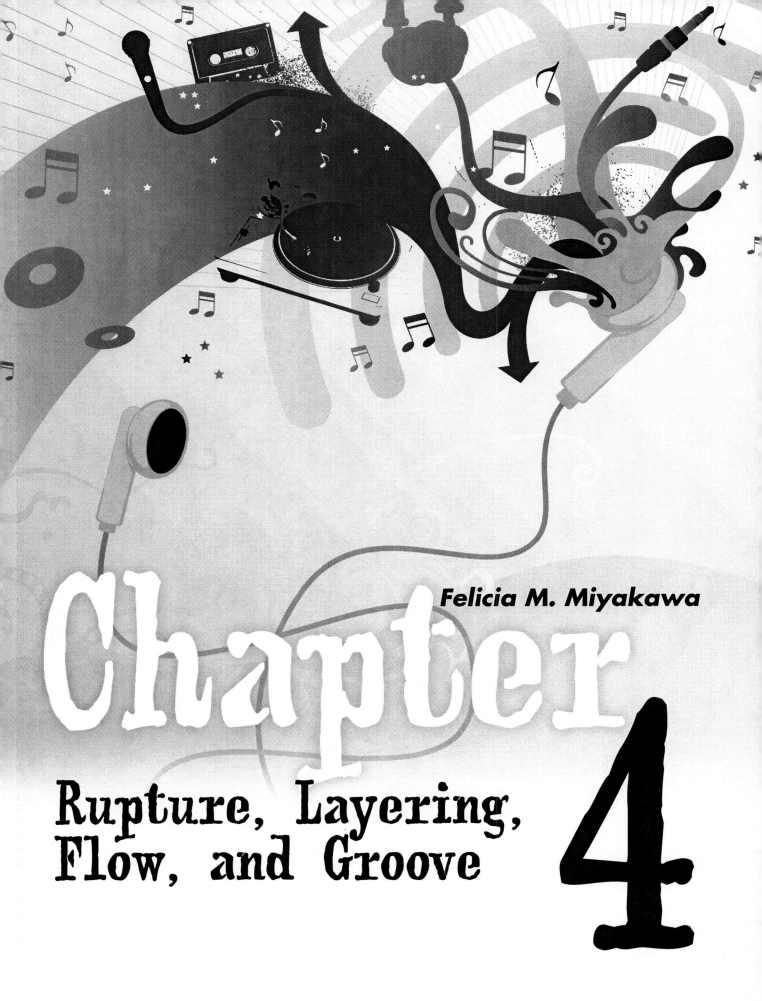

Felicia M. Miyakawa

Chapter

Rupture, Layering, Flow, and Groove

4

```
              1 – * – 2 – * – 3 – * – 4 – * –
    m 88                              x x x x
    m 89    x   x x x x x   x   x x x x
    m 90    x   x x x x   x   x   x x x x
    m 91    x   x x x   x x x x   x x x x x
    m 92    x   x x x x   x x
```

Then they give us *church*, a trick to try to *ease* this, thought I'd check it *out*, had to learn about *Jesus*. Told them he was *black* and they called me a *hater*, then he's on a church *wall*, yeah like a slave *trader*.

Figure 1. Poor Righteous Teachers, "Ghetto We Love," mm. 88–92.

As Figure 1 illustrates, Wise Intelligent creates his own form from these lines, a form built around regular patterning. First, he finishes each line of poetry not within beat 4 of each measure, but within beat 3, leaving beat 4 open to begin the next line of text before the new measure of music begins. In so doing, he also places the rhyming words of each line—"ease this," "Jesus," "hater," and "trader"—on beat 3 of their respective measures and allows himself a breath, a sixteenth-or eighth-note rest before beginning the next line. Furthermore, he accents the syllables that fall on the first sixteenth notes of beats 1 and 3 of every measure (italics indicate accented text and beats). Between his textual accents and the snare drum hits on the backbeats (beats 2 and 4), every beat is clearly delineated. His flow in this example is also marked by speed: the high number of syllables in these lines demands quick delivery and Wise must use consistent sixteenth-note divisions in order to fit his couplets within the four measures. In short, Wise Intelligent's flow transforms his text from mundane rhyming couplets to rapidly delivered, rhythmic syllables that both help define the meter and fill up the meter's subdivisions.

As Adam Krims has pointed out, flow styles mark both geographic and personal styles, and also help define generic boundaries. Rap fans recognize MCs by their rhyme patterns, syncopations, textual accents, triplets, timbre, and poetic enjambment. Describing flow is therefore an essential element of rap analysis.[5] Krims admits that fans recognize many flow styles, but for purposes of his discussion he distinguishes three types: "sung" flow, "percussion effusive" flow, and "speech effusive" flow, each of which is marked by a characteristic rhyme scheme, patterns of beat accentuation, and timbral delivery.[6] According to Krims, sung style features rhythmic repetition, on-beat accents, regular on-beat pauses, and strict couplet groupings. The effusive flows, on the other hand, "spill over the rhythmic boundaries of the meter, the couplet, and, for that matter, of duple and quadruple groupings in general."[7] Whereas sung flow tends to be squarely placed within the given duple meter, effusive flows work against duple division and produce polyrhythms and subdivisions. In the passage shown in figure 1, Wise Intelligent's delivery may therefore be referred to as a kind of effusive flow.

Krims's terms are merely his way of dividing what are known more generally in rap circles as "old school" flow (Krims's "sung" flow) and "new school" flow (Krims's effusive flows). The transition between "old school" and "new school" flow happened gradually around 1990, and since most of the songs analyzed for this study date from 1990 or later, it makes sense that their MCs would make use of modern, faster, percussive, syncopated, or speech-like styles.[8] Whereas the term "flow" is used in the rap community, Krims's terms for flow styles are not. Hip-hop publications tend instead to use adjectival descriptions of flow; distinct categories have not been fixed. In a single issue of the *Source*, for example, Project Pat (of the Three 6 Mafia) has a flow style described as "leisurely" and "choppy"; unsigned artist Saigon has a "clear, forceful flow"; and Aceyalone has a "mind-blowing," "multilayered," "bouncy," and "Dirty-Dirt-type flow."[9]

```
                    1 – * – 2 – * – 3 – * – 4 – * –
         m 29     x x x x x x x x x x x      x x
         m 30     x                x x  xx    x  xx
         m 31     x x x x x x x x x x x x x
         m 32     x    x x x    x x x x x      x x x
```

Ten percent of *us* can help but *don't* feel a *need*/they lot *greed*, and *this* really *bothers* me/*Eighty*-five *percent* of us are *totally* *ig*norant/*Walk*in' a*round* with the *nigger* mentality/

Figure 2. Lakim Shabazz, "The Lost Tribe of Shabazz," mm. 29–32.
Courtesy of Tufamerica.Inc. Used with permission.

Krims's categories may not be as vivid as these journalistic flow descriptions, but they are a useful starting point, a simplified way to understand basic differences in flow styles.

Understanding and mapping flow styles also helps us to visualize the moments when MCs effectively break flow patterns to emphasize a key word or concept. Lakim Shabazz's exegesis of Lost-Found Lesson no. 2, questions 14–16 in "The Lost Tribe of Shabazz," for example, makes the most of a varied flow pattern, particularly in the passage describing the 10 percent (see figure 2). His strongest indictment is of the 10 percent's greed (m. 30), and this he highlights with poetic enjambment, space, and dotted rhythms. Instead of splitting the text of measures 29–30 into two equal phrases (after "need"), he deliberately places "greed" on the downbeat—a heavily accented beat—of measure 30. Further more, the lines surrounding measure 30 fill up the sixteenth-note space, but after "greed" falls on the downbeat of measure 30, Lakim rests until the final sixteenth note of the second beat, leaving time for his message to sink in. The syncopated figures for the text "this really bothers me," illustrated in the flow map of figure 2 by closely packed Xs in measure 30, aptly depict his agitation.

Even these few examples illustrate a point raised by Robert Walser (echoing Tricia Rose) in his seminal article on the music of Public Enemy: "the music is not an accompaniment to textual delivery; rather, voice and instrumental tracks are placed in a more dynamic relationship in hip hop, as the rapper interacts with the rest of the music."[10] In short, there must be a medium to deliver the message. Or, to paraphrase Walser, without the groove under the flow, the lyrics are simply poetic utterances with little rhetorical power.[11] To understand the rhetorical power of these songs, then, we must also look to the musical layers under the text and the overall groove that music and text together produce.[12]

Layering and Form

The way in which rap music is produced demands specific attention to musical layers. DJs and producers lay down (create) tracks one line at a time, thereby building texture not in vertical stacks, but in horizontal layers. Each layer is then coaxed into appropriate interaction with the other tracks. When arranging tracks, producers pay attention not only to timbral variation, but also to the overall form of the song.[13] Indeed, each section of a song has a signature sound created through the manipulation of musical layering.[14] Therefore, as a prelude to describing specific approaches to musical layering, the following paragraphs provide a brief description of the typical form of a rap song.[15]

Modern rap (that is, rap of the 1990s and beyond) relies heavily on verse/chorus form, a form common to American popular music of many genres. But this form has not always dominated rap composition. Many early rap songs simply strung together enough verses to account for each MC of a crew, as in the Sugarhill

Gang's "Rapper's delight". It has been argued that modern rap's dependence on catchy "hooks" (choruses) reflects rap's crossover into mainstream popular music.[16] According to this argument, hip-hop musicians began to include R&B-style melodic choruses to appeal to a wider audience as a response to naysayers who found no melodic value in rap. Music critic Nelson George suggests that the commercial value of the melodic hook increased after prosecution for sampling heated up in the early 1990s, noting that after the through-composed, complexly interwoven sample-based production of groups such as Public Enemy, rap production turned to "often simpleminded loops of beats and vocal hooks from familiar songs."[17] George's critique shares the familiar criticism that hooks signify the act of "selling out," turning away from "pure" hip-hop aesthetic values. Verse/chorus form may currently dominate rap production, but the form itself occupies contested terrain in the hip-hop community, a community deeply concerned with issues of authenticity.

Songs which do fall into verse/chorus form often begin with a brief introduction, typically of four, eight, twelve, or sixteen measures.[18] The first verse or the first chorus follows the introduction. Verses are nearly always rapped and verse lengths typically range from sixteen to thirty-six measures.[19] Likewise, choruses (or refrains) are usually four to eight measures long, but need not be standardized, even within a single song. Choruses may be rapped, sung, or instrumental, but they share repeated musical or textual material with each statement, thereby unifying the song through repetition.[20] Verses and choruses alternate throughout the songs, and most songs end with either a final chorus or a coda.[21] Finally, codas—called "outros" in hip-hop speak, since they lead out from the song in the same way that "intros" lead in to the song—share musical tracks from the song and are typically places for the MC to speak, not rap, over the music, often to give "shout-outs" to friends and compatriots.

In order to illustrate the centrality of layering in rap's formal construction, I have charted the following examples onto a new form of transcription, a "groove continuum." The groove continuum separates the many sounds of a single rap composition into two large groupings—melodic layers and percussive layers—in order to tease out the interplay between groove and melodic ornamentation, a figure/ground relationship common to black musical genres.[22] Melodic layers tend to be those pitched instruments and timbres not included in a rhythm section of a live band: reeds, brass, and strings, for example. I also include some sung vocals within melodic layers in order to differentiate their function from that of rapped sections of a song. The percussive layers of my groove continuum chart the activity of instruments typically considered part of a rhythm section: drums of all sorts (such as the typical rap complement of kick drum, snare drum, and hi-hat) and bass line, produced either by keyboard or guitar. But keyboards and guitar occupy liminal space: at times these instruments act like part of a rhythm section and keep time, while at other moments they carry a song's only melodies, revealing an inherent flexibility in hip-hop musicality and necessitating an individual approach to each song rather than a fixed methodology. The ultimate purpose of my groove continuum therefore is not only to graphically illustrate individual timbral moments but also to demonstrate the forward-moving nature of layering techniques and the interplay between layering and song form. In other words, both melodic and percussive layers contribute to a song's groove, a continuously unfolding, participatory musical experience.

Consider figure 3, a groove continuum analysis of Digable Planets' tour de force "Dial 7 (Axioms of Creamy Spies)." The graph itself should be read from left to right. Under the measure numbers four lines follow the composition layer by layer: the top two lines track the activity of melodic and percussive layers by measure, and the bottom two lines track the formal divisions of the text. (Note that this groove continuum does not graph every musical event of "Dial 7" but attends specifically to the interplay of musical layers.) "Dial 7" is built from four primary melodies—labeled 1, 2, 3, and 4 and written for synthesized sax, voice, keyboard, and keyboard respectively—and two percussive patterns—labeled 1a and 1b because they are similar.[23] The key below the graph explains and notates what each number in the graph represents.

The graph helps to illuminate several points. First, the layers I have classified as melodic confine themselves to non-verse sections of the song. In other words, during the verses Digable Planets carefully pare down the texture to only a percussive groove in order to clear textural space for the rapped text. Conversely, the group seems to prefer a thicker bass sound (percussion pattern 1a) for the majority of the song, including the verses, excepting the second half of Doodlebug's verse. The second percussion pattern, essentially the same as the first but without the added depth of keyboard bass, is otherwise held in reserve for transitional moments just before and after verses. The looped sax riff is also confined to Sara Webb's sung choruses and the final four measures of the song. The Planets also vary their melodic layering, introducing a secondary synthesizer melody nearly halfway into the song (m. 45), lightly sprinkling their composition with the looped sax riff, and freely mixing all four melodic layers in different combinations throughout the song. Clearly, Digable Planets valued the interplay of musical layers and formal structure in the "composition" of "Dial 7."

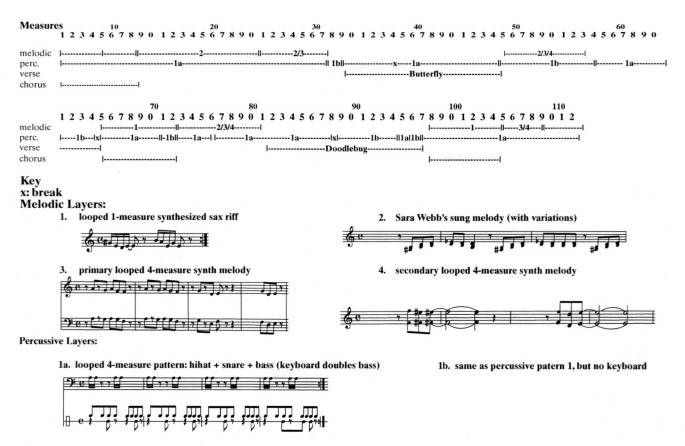

Figure 3. "Dial 7 (Axioms of Creamy Spies)" Groove Continuum

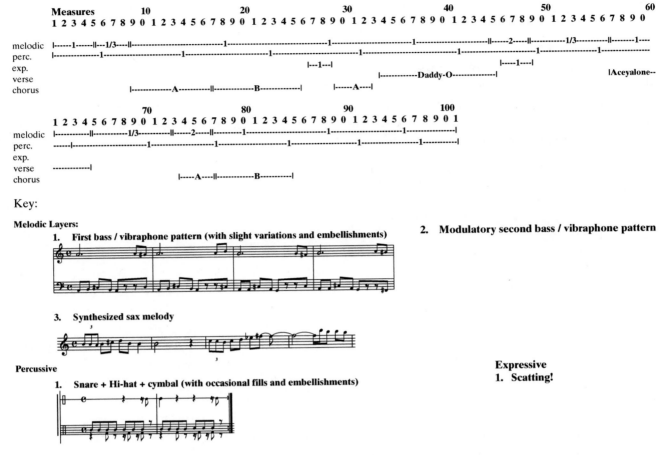

Figure 4. "Innercity Boundaries": Groove Continuum

Whereas the groove continuum for "Dial 7" illustrates the interaction of layering changes and form, Freestyle Fellowship's "Innercity Boundaries" emphasizes the continuity of layers over an extended musical structure (see figure 4). Here the percussive groove of hi-hat, snare, and cymbal remains consistent throughout the song (with the exception of occasional fills and embellishments) while variable bass, vibraphone, and sax melodies weave over and through the percussive layer. I include the bass and vibes in the melodic layer in this example because of their prominent melodic patterns and soloistic treatment as they vary slightly with occasional embellishments throughout the song. Unlike most hip-hop songs, in which performers rhyme over pre-recorded music, "Innercity Boundaries" uses a live band. The embellishments and variations are therefore more frequent and flexible than usual. But again, the producer—Daddy-O, formerly of Stetsasonic— reserves certain instrumental layers for key structural moments: the sax riff, for example, marks only the second half of the introduction (mm. 5–8) and the instrumental breaks before and after Aceyalone's verse (mm. 49–56 and 65–72). And whereas a primary bass and vibraphone duet pattern play for most of the song, a modulatory secondary bass and vibraphone duet take over in transitional moments: during the harmonically unstable scatting just after Daddy-O's verse (mm. 45–48) and again against the final statement of chorus A (mm. 73–76) as a Freestyle Fellowship member expressively expands the original melody of chorus A, neatly imitating a saxophone in the process.[24]

Rupture

Both "Dial 7" and "Innercity Boundaries" illustrate the interlocking nature of form and layering: on a large scale, layering produces a continuous groove, an unfolding and repetitive musical structure over which MCs deliver their flow of words. But just as layering helps delineate form, so, too, do moments of discontinuity, moments when effective producers and DJs manipulate musical layers to interrupt—or rupture, as Rose would have it—the musical groove and continuity for a variety of expressive and formal purposes. Rose's discussion of rupture points especially to rhythm:

> the flow and motion of the initial bass or drum line in rap music is abruptly ruptured by scratching (a process that highlights as it breaks the flow of the rhythm), or the rhythmic flow is interrupted by other musical passages. Rappers stutter and alternatively race through passages, always moving within the beat or in response to it, often using the music as a partner in rhyme.[25]

Here Rose distinguishes between three forms of rupture: the rhythmic rupture produced by scratching; the rhythmic rupture that occurs when musical patterns interrupt each other (perhaps a description of sampling); and the rupture produced when MCs change their flow patterns over the musical tracks. Given the percussive and polyrhythmic nature of rap, it is not surprising that Rose focuses primarily on rhythmic rupture. But her treatment of rupture downplays melodic layers, subtly agreeing with (and perpetuating) the canard that rap has no melody worth discussing. Therefore, instead of describing rupture as a predominantly rhythmic process, I prefer to see rupture as textural change, as manipulation (whether subtle or abrupt) of both melodic and percussive layers. Seen in this way, rupture can emphasize formal design, outlining, for example, the boundaries between verses and choruses. Rupture can also highlight structural repetition, helping to delineate four-and eight-bar phrasing. And finally, rupture in the form of textural changes can be used for expressive purposes in order to stress specific moments of text.

Percussive Ruptures

For percussive ruptures to be effective, the discrete drum layers must be recognizable and their functions understood. Rap percussion instruments typically include a hi-hat or ride cymbal, often relegated to the function of outlining straight or swung eighths; a snare drum, typically given the backbeats; and a kick (bass) drum, often heard in one-, two-, or four-measure patterns. Thus, each of these instruments—whether acoustic or produced with drum machines—not only performs a different timekeeping function, but also occupies distinct timbral space. Indeed, every layer of rap music relies heavily on differentiated timbral spaces, what Olly Wilson calls the "heterogeneous sound ideal," a key element of black diasporic and African American music-making.[26] Producers attend to even the smallest details when manipulating percussive layers, and their compositional choices are broad. The most common strategy used to rupture percussive layers is dropping one or more drum layers out of the musical texture to mark formal and structural divisions or expressive details of the text. Rupture can also take the form of complete musical breaks under the text. Less frequently, producers rupture not textures but specific rhythms. Detailed examples of all three techniques follow.

In order to mark formal divisions of the text, the bass drum pattern of Poor Righteous Teachers' "Conscious Style" changes significantly between the introduction and verse 1 and between the last line of each verse and the following chorus. The snare drum pattern also adjusts in these measures: it is absent at the ends of the introduction and the first two verses, and only sounds on beat 2 of the last measure of verse 3. For the rest of the song, however (with a few exceptions to be discussed below), the snare and bass drum fall into a two-measure pattern, as in Figure 5.

Rakim's "The Mystery (Who Is God)" reveals a similar strategy. Naughty, Shorts, the producer, varies the percussive textures to mark the formal divisions between the introductory chorus and verse 1, the second chorus and verse 2, and the third chorus and verse 3. In the last two measures before verse 1 (mm. 14–15), Naughty Shorts strips the texture down to only synthesized horn and kick drum, adding hi-hat in the second measure. He then elongates the pattern into four measures between the third chorus and verse 3: measures 63–64 have only kick drum and synthesized horn, measure 65 adds the hi-hat on beats 1 and 3, and measure 66 repeats the pattern found in measure 15. Between the second chorus and verse 2, however, he keeps the kick drum intact and gives the hi-hat a new rhythmic pattern; only the snare drum is absent.[27]

Subtle changes in percussive textures can also mark elements of large-scale and small-scale structural repetition. Poor Righteous Teachers' "Conscious Style," for example, shows changes in percussive texture at similar points in each verse. Whereas the hi-hat articulates each eighth note for the majority of the song, it drops out in the sixteenth measure of each verse for either the entire line (verses 1 and 2) or a single beat (beat 4 in verse 3). The kick drum and snare drum patterns are also altered in the same measure of each verse: in the first two verses the kick is absent on beats 2 and 3 while the snare hits only on beat 4, and in the third verse no percussion sounds on beat 4 (compare these exceptions to Figure 5).

Poor Righteous Teachers use a different approach in "Word Iz Life." For most of the song, the drums fulfill typical rap drum roles: the snare hits the backbeats, the hi-hat outlines every eighth, and the kick drum provides structure with the two-measure pattern seen in Figure 6. At regular intervals throughout the song, however, this percussion pattern is disrupted. The first measure of verse 1 (m. 9) has no kick drum, no snare on beat 2, and no hi-hat until beat 4. In other words, until beat 4 we are left with only melodic instruments (bass guitar, lead guitar, and synthesizer) and voice. Exactly eight measures later (m. 16), the same pattern occurs; however, whereas measure 9 is the first measure of the two-measure kick drum pattern outlined above, measure 16 is the second measure of this pattern. Measure 16, then, completes a cycle of four kick drum statements. Verse 2 uses the same reduced texture with two small differences: this time the first measure of the pattern is the second measure of the verse (m. 38), and the second measure with this texture occurs only five measures later (m. 42). Here both affected measures are the second measure of the kick drum pattern.

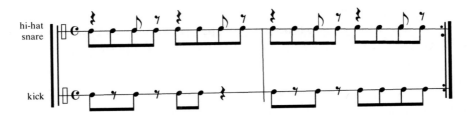

Figure 5. "Conscious Style," typical 2-measure percussion pattern

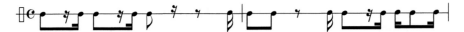

Figure 6. "Word iz life" bass drum pattern

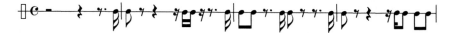

Figure 7. "We Dat Nice," bass drum pattern

Figure 8. "The Long Run," percussion

The kick drum pattern is again a determining structural element in Poor Righteous Teachers' "We Dat Nice." Father Shaheed uses a four-measure pattern, and throughout the song, percussive textures change primarily within the fourth measure of the pattern (see Figure 7). Although the verses are of different lengths (25, 25, and 21 measures respectively), they all end with measure 4 of this pattern, and within each verse, a variety of subtleties mark the fourth measure of this pattern. In measure 18 (the twelfth measure of verse 1, and hence the last measure of the third four-measure kick pattern in the verse), the kick drum is silent for the second half of the measure and the snare hits not the back beats, but beats 2 and 3. In measures 26, 54, and 86 (all of which are, again, measure 4 of the kick pattern), however, the kick pattern is intact, and the snare hits beats 2, 3, and 4. Changes of percussive texture in this song are thus linked at the levels of both the verse and the four-bar phrase.[28]

DJ Khalil of Self Scientific uses a similar strategy in "The Long Run" but organizes his four-bar phrases around the hi-hat, the percussive layer that is entrusted with timekeeping in the vast majority of rap songs. There is, in fact, no kick drum in "The Long Run": all drumming is left to the snare, which takes a typical backbeat pattern, and the hi-hat, which elaborates slightly on the common eight-to-the-bar timekeeping pattern. The first three measures of the hi-hat pattern are identical; the only change in this pattern comes in the second half of beat 4 of the fourth measure (see Figure 8). Just as the majority of changes in percussive textures in "We Dat Nice" come in measure 4 of the kick drum pattern, in "The Long Run" most textural changes happen in measure 4 of the hi-hat pattern. The hi-hat's pattern shifts in the final measure of each verse and each statement of the chorus, coinciding with both with the fourth measure of the hi-hat's pattern and with the end of formal sections. DJ Khalil varies the percussive textures in a variety of ways, although he seems to prefer emptying the first two or three beats of a measure and retaining beat 4's activity as a pick-up to the next measure. More isolated moments of change happen for expressive purposes: in measures 14, 38, 40, and 44 Khalil makes room for Chace Infinite as the MC names himself (m. 38), speaks of the power of his rhymes (mm. 38 and 40), and explains his purpose: "living my life hoping that the youth remember us" (m. 44).

DJ Khalil's preference for four-bar patterning and subtle text accentuation reflects his obvious concern for structure. His attention to even momentary effects results in compelling and effective musical structures, artfully ruptured here and there to give life to Chace Infinite's rhymes. And Khalil is just one example of a meticulous producer at work. Indeed, as this section illustrates, close inspection of rap's percussive ruptures reveals a wealth of constantly shifting, obviously intentional details programmed by producers who understand the impact of their every musical decision.

Complete Ruptures: Breaks in the Musical Texture

Complete breaks in the musical texture, just like changes in percussive layers, often serve as markers of key formal or structural divisions.[29] The only complete breaks of musical texture in Poor Righteous Teachers' "We Dat Nice," for example, occur within measure 4 of the song's four-measure kick drum pattern, emphasizing the song's four-bar phrasing. Two of these breaks, those in measures 14 and 78, occur within the eighth measure of their respective verses, but the third break (m. 89) occurs in the last full measure of verse 3, helping to delineate the song's form. Likewise, in "Gods, Earths and 85ers" breaks occur either as divisional markers (as at the beginning of verse 1, the end of verse 1, and the end of verse 2), or as an element of structural repetition within the fourth measure of the song's four-measure kick drum pattern (as in mm. 16, 47, and 83). "Miss Ghetto" shows a similar interest in aligning breaks with formal and structural elements. Two breaks separate verses from choruses (mm. 36 and 60, the last lines of verses 1 and 2 respectively), but these and the remaining three breaks come in the fourth measure of the kick drum's four-measure pattern. On the other hand, breaks and other percussion changes in Poor Righteous Teachers' "Holy Intellect" have little to do with the kick drum pattern, since the drum pattern here is only one measure long. Instead, breaks tend to occur at similar places in each verse: at the fourth measure of verses 1, 2, and 4.

"Allies," the joint effort of Poor Righteous Teachers and the Fugees, features three breaks, one in Culture Freedom's verse and two in Pras's verse. But in this song, breaks are not aligned with percussion patterns, as the drums are relatively skittish and often deviate from their primary one-measure patterns. Instead, breaks in "Allies" come in the first measure of a four-measure synthesizer and sax riff (see Figure 9). Because these melodic lines are so spare, all that is necessary to produce a break in the first measure of the pattern is to leave out percussion between beats 1 and 4, which is indeed what happens in all three breaks. Pras further emphasizes the breaks in his verse by delaying his triplet-driven flow (indicated by brackets) until after the downbeats of measures 49 and 53 (see figure 10; underlined text falls within the break), each of which coincides with the first measure of the four-measure pattern. Pras's words thus fall between beats 1 and 4, making the most of the measure's momentary break.

A similar break caused by textural change comes in measure 64 of Eric B. and Rakim's "In the Ghetto." Eric B. constructed the song over three samples: 24 Carat Black's "Ghetto: Misfortunes Wealth" (from *Misfortune's Wealth*, 1973); Donny Hathaway's "The Ghetto" (from *Live*, 1971); and Bill Withers's "Kissin'

Figure 9. Synth and Sax riff from "Allies"

```
          1 –  *  – 2 –  *  – 3 –  *  – 4 –  *  –
m 49          x x x     x    x x x    x    x x
m 50      [ x x x ] [ x x x ] [ x x x ]  x
m 51      [ x x x ] x       x [ x x x ]  [ x x x ]    Catch the midnight train to Georgia as my tongue does a drop-
                                                       kick like Sgt. Slaughter New world order, you lions who trying
m 52      x    x x x x    x x [ x x x ]  x             to Roar, I'll silence your lambs like Jodie Foster  There's no
                                                       need to feel sentimental ...
m 53          x   x x    x    x    x x    x    x
```

Figure 10. "Allies," flow and breaks, mm. 49–53 (brackets indicate triplets).

Figure 11. "In the Ghetto," bass and keyboard

```
                1 – * – 2 – * – 3 – * – 4 – * –
m 61        x x x x x x x x x x x x x x
m 62              x x x x x x x    x x x x
m 63        x  x    x x x   x x    x    x x x       Reaching for the city of Mecca, visit Medina/Visions of Neff-
                                                    ertiti, then I seen her/Mind keeps traveling/I'll be back after I
m 64        x x x x x x x x x x x x    x x          stop and think about the brothers and sisters in Africa/
```

Figure 12. Rakim's flow from "In the Ghetto" (mm. 61–64)

My Love" (from *Still Bill*, 1971). The drum line from "In the Ghetto" comes from "Kissin' My Love," but over the sampled drum layer Eric B. foregrounds a jangly hi-hat line playing heavily swung eighth notes. For measures 61 through 64 Eric B. takes away the added hi-hat for the first time, and this reduced texture continues for four measures. The only break in this song comes during beat 3 of the fourth measure of this four-measure textural change (m. 64), a brief pause between the bass and keyboard lines that would not be as audible with the hi-hat line (see Figure 11 and figure 12).[30]

Breaks in the music can also serve purely expressive purposes; that is, breaks leave a brief window of silence that allows the MC a moment of textual clarity and emphasis. For example, the only break to occur in GZA's "B.I.B.L.E." comes at a textually significant moment. As GZA explains his struggle out of Christianity toward "true knowledge of self," he and the producer for this song, 4th Disciple, silence the music under the text "religion did nothing" (m. 47), thereby not only providing space for textual emphasis, but also illustrating the text "did nothing" by doing nothing.[31] Similarly, both breaks that occur with text in Grand Puba's "Soul Controller" dramatize Grand Puba's text. The first comes in measure 13, after Grand Puba has posed a question to his crew: "You mean to tell me that we're still not a slave / in the land of free and the home of the brave?" Their collective thoughtful response, "mmm," comes at a break. The song's second break with text falls in measure 62 as Grand Puba compares churches to liquor stores, claiming that if churches were good for the black population they would not be on every block. He and DJ Alamo underscore his comparison by placing a break under the statement that church is "no good (no goddamned good), they represent the 10 percent."

Likewise, the only break in the Wu-Tang Clan's "Impossible" comes in the last line of the song. Raekwon, a Wu-Tang member who does not perform in the main body of the song (the three verses are rapped by RZA, U-God, and Ghostface Killah respectively) enters in the coda to present the "moral" of the song. He condemns worldwide violence and especially black-on-black crime, and ends this cautionary tale with the lines "'cause this is only a story, from the real." The final clause, "from the real," is unaccompanied, producing an unexpected irony in Raekwon's warning. The verses preceding his coda may be only stories, but they are drawn form everyday life events and should not be taken lightly or dismissed as fiction. RZA, the producer, here manipulates musical texture to add depth to the Wu-Tang's anti-violence message.

Big Daddy Kane uses complete breaks in the musical texture for a different expressive purpose in "Mortal Combat." He chooses not to highlight doctrine or a moral center through his breaks, but to put down his lyrical competitors. The break during the final line of his final verse makes way for a shout-out to the Nation of Islam, but the six earlier breaks in his song, falling in measures 30, 52, 60, 68, 96, and 104, each involve elaborate challenges to other MCs, claiming his competitors' rhymes are "old as Pro-Keds" (m. 96), avowing he will play other MCs "like a game of Nintendo" (m. 60), and making general deprecatory accusations such as "rappers are so full of shit they need Ex-Lax" (m. 52). Although the song is not built on repeated patterns of eight measures, the breaks themselves create such a pattern, falling primarily eight measures apart. In this way, Big Daddy Kane, both MC and producer of this song, uses silence as both an expressive and structural element; silence here does not respond to other structural patterns, but creates the pattern.

A few songs, such as Brand Nubian's "Ragtime," take advantage of breaks for both formal and expressive reasons. Two breaks occur in the last measure of each statement of "Ragtime's" chorus, introducing the next MC and separating the verses, but three breaks highlight significant moments. Sadat X's statement in measure 14, "In fact, they failed the test," is a subtle rebuke of his unnamed challengers. And two breaks come in Grand Puba's verse to emphasize boasts of his rhyming abilities (m. 74) and, ironically, his humility (m. 90). Likewise, the single break in the Micranots' "Culture" serves both expressive and formal ends. The break happens on the downbeat of measure 45, the first line of I Self Devine's second verse, thereby clearly delineating the end of the previous chorus and the beginning of the verse, but the text over the break, "pain," is clearly meant to be heard. Breaking here, even for just the downbeat, draws attention to I Self Devine's struggle through the maze of the record industry and his nostalgia for unsullied hip-hop culture.

On the other hand, in Digable Planets' "Dial 7 (Axioms of Creamy Spies)" the reason for the three breaks is somewhat ambiguous. Although the melodic patterns change frequently, the percussion groove provided by the keyboard, bass guitar, hi-hat, and snare remains steady. A four-measure snare and hi-hat pattern provides the underlying phrase structure of the song, and two of the breaks coincide with the fourth measure of this pattern (mm. 64 and 88). But the break in measure 64 comes at the end of Ladybug Mecca's verse and therefore also delineates a formal division. Furthermore, the text of this line, "you subtract the devils that get smoked," reinforces the message of resistance to white oppression throughout the song. The break in measure 34, however, is clearly expressive. Coming in the second measure of the snare/hi-hat pattern and in the middle of Butterfly's verse, this break happens under Butterfly's text "true black man that I am."

As "What Cool Breezes Do" illustrates, Digable Planets use musical breaks eclectically. Two breaks come in Ladybug Mecca's verse, the first as she states her name for the first time (downbeat of m. 13) and the second as Butterfly addresses her by name in beat 4 of measure 19. In measure 58, Butterfly "disses" his competition with a reference to his Muslim dietary restrictions, claming that even if critics find their competition "phat," "we just ignore it like it's pork." But the remaining breaks, in measure 34 and measures 61–62 of "What Cool Breezes Do," have no easy explanation. The groove of this song is continuous: neither melodic nor percussive lines work in cycles larger than a single measure.[32] The break in measure 34 comes at the halfway point of Doodlebug's sixteen-measure verse, and thus could be of structural importance, linking two sections of eight measures, but no other musical layers privilege a division here. On the other hand, the break in measures 61–62 comes in the fifteenth and sixteenth measures of Butterfly's twenty-four-measure verse, suggesting that structure is not the dominant impulse. But Butterfly's verse is a study in textural change. Of the entire song, Butterfly's verse uses call-and-response most extensively as Ladybug Mecca responds to his statements and questions throughout the verse. Furthermore, the fifth through eighth measures of Butterfly's verse feature a drastic textural change: here all melody instruments drop out, leaving only the percussion groove. The full texture then returns for three measures, but a break under measure 58 interrupts what would be a fourth measure for this phrase. Textural variety continues after this break: for two measures the full texture returns, followed by two measures of break in measures 61–62. The Planets round out Butterfly's verse with a return to the song's full texture for his final eight measures. The breaks in Butterfly's verse, then, reinforce a key point: in addition to their structural and expressive uses, breaks generally serve as another textural tool in the hands of a good producer.

Rhythmic Changes

Shifting rhythmic patterns is another common rhetorical strategy. Like textural changes, subtle modifications in rhythmic patterns can play key structural or expressive roles, as is true in Poor Righteous Teachers' "We Dat Nice." Like the changes in percussive texture in this song described above, key rhythmic variations are made in the final line of each verse. The default pattern for the snare in this song is accenting backbeats, but in measures 30 and 62 (the last measures of verses 1 and 2 respectively) new, syncopated patterns are introduced (see Figure 13). Additionally, measure 89, the last measure of verse 3, features a complete break. In this way, major adjustments in both rhythm and texture mark the end of each verse. These changes are clearly meant to delineate formal divisions, yet the text at these points of rhythmic transformation is key. Each verse ends with the same text, beginning with beat 4 of the previous measure and extending to the downbeat of the following measure: "take/flight, make ice of any MCs you like, I'm dat/nice." In other words, Father Shaheed under-girds Wise Intelligent's boasts of lyrical prowess with complicated rhythmic flexibility, musically "showing and proving" that Wise Intelligent and his crew are capable of creativity and ingenuity.

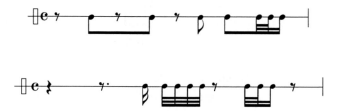

Figure 13. "We Dat Nice," approximations of snare drum patterns for measures 30 and 62

"We Dat Nice" is a study in frequent rhythmic changes: snare and kick drum patterns change throughout the song, and in most cases these variations occur within the fourth measure of the kick drum pattern. But "Word from the Wise," also by Poor Righteous Teachers, shows yet another approach to rhythmic change. Here rhythmic patterns coincide with melodic textures. A two-measure saxophone riff plays intermittently throughout the song: in the second half of the introduction, throughout the choruses, and during the coda. Both the hi-hat and the kick drum have two primary rhythmic patterns: when the sax plays, the hi-hat, kick, and cymbal play the rhythmic groove seen in figure 14. When the sax drops out, however, the drums play a different pattern, as seen in figure 15. Rhythmic modifications here are subtle but also involve a change in timbre; whereas the first pattern includes an open cymbal, the second pattern does not.

In some cases, such as in "Conscious Style," a given rhythm is altered in order to emphasize changes in the MC's flow. In this song, both the otherwise-steady kick drum and snare patterns change throughout guest MC KRS-One's verse, making way for his unusually asymmetrical, almost ametrical, flow. This strategy is likely a deliberate production choice: KRS-One is not only the guest MC, but also the producer of this song, and his production style here makes the most of his guest verses.

Rhythmic changes are also sometimes due to intertextual references, as we see in Brand Nubian's "The Godz Must Be Crazy." The only rhythmic disruption in this song occurs at the text "Punks jump up to get beat down" (m. 76), which happens to be the title of another song on the same album. The full text phrase is "Cee-Cypher-Punks jump up to get beat down," a practical example of using the Supreme Alphabet to create acronyms and new meanings from old words: "Cee-Cypher-Punks" here spells out the word COP, in keeping with Sadat X's verse, which calls for self-defense and decries corruption in American governmental systems. For this single measure, Brand Nubian samples the rhythmic pattern of its own song "Punks Jump Up to Get Beat Down" to draw attention to this line of text.

Rhythmic change can also take the form of the DJ's scratching, the act of moving a record back and forth under the stylus to produce rhythmic or melodic sounds. Although scratching adds rhythmic complexity to percussive layers, there is little variation with respect to where scratching takes place within songs. Scratching is generally limited to choruses, and is sometimes found also in introductions and codas, but a few songs depart from scratching conventions and illustrate other possibilities for this rhythmic layer. The

Figure 14. First drum pattern of "Word from the Wise"

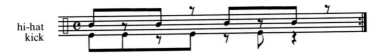

Figure 15. Second drum pattern of "Word from the Wise"

producers of "Soul Controller," "Wake Up (Reprise in the Sunshine)," and "Return" include scratching intermittently throughout the songs for no obvious structural, formal, or expressive purpose. In Rakim's "The 18th Letter," however, scratching partners an eight-measure bass guitar ostinato to delineate Rakim's otherwise unchanging forty-measure verse. Both "Anger in the Nation" and "Culture" feature scratching in the chorus, but the producers of these songs (Pete Rock and Kool Akiem respectively) also use scratching to segue smoothly from the last line of the previous verse into the chorus, thus anticipating the textural change the chorus will bring. Poor Righteous Teacher' "Pure Poverty" features moments of percussive scratching within beat 4 of measures 12 and 58 in addition to scratching throughout the choruses; these two moments of scratching coincide with the fourth measure of both the kick drum and bass guitar patterns and therefore serve structural functions similar to those of other changes in percussive texture. And in "Allies," the only scratching happens in measure 22 for text painting as Wyclef Jean issues the challenge "play it on your turntable, scratch it if you're able." In short, like other layers of rap production, rhythmic changes play a significant role in formal, structural, and expressive design.

Rupturing Melodic Layers

Ruptures in melodic layers are made in the same way as their percussive equivalents: through the manipulation of individual musical tracks. Typical melodic ruptures can involve adding new melodic instruments over the current texture, alternating melodic instruments, or lifting all melodic instruments from the musical texture, leaving only voice and percussion. Furthermore, producers use melodic and percussive ruptures for similar purposes: to outline formal and structural design and to highlight expressive moments. GZA's "B.I.B.L.E.," for example, shows attention to both formal and structural details through manipulation of melodic layers. All melody instruments drop out after the downbeat in the measure before verse 2 (m. 56), and all other changes in melodic texture—curiously only found in verse 2—occur only within the second measure of the kick drum's two-measure pattern. Producers also frequently limit certain melodic layers to specific formal sections of the song, as illustrated in both "The Lost Tribe of Shabazz" and "Dance to My Ministry": the former features a pipe or flute only in the introduction, choruses, and coda, and the latter introduces a wordless vocal refrain only in the introduction and choruses.[33] Poor Righteous Teachers' "Holy Intellect" shows a different approach. Wise Intelligent and Culture Freedom begin verse 3 in call-and-response fashion over a sort of stop-time texture: all melodic instruments drop out of the texture here, and only the kick drum keeps time under these four measures.

Melodic changes in these examples seem linked to song form, but in other examples melodic changes merely provide a shifting palette of timbres and harmonies. Nas's "Affirmative Action," for example, strays far from verse/chorus form and instead is simply a strung-together collection of verses from the featured MCs—Nas, AZ, Cormega, and Foxy Brown—between an introduction and a brief instrumental coda.[34] Under the various vocal flows, the production team (Dave Atkinson, Poke, and Tone from Trackmasters) repeats three two-measure synthesized melodies (with a harpsichord timbre) in various repetition schemes (see figure 16). Each melodic pattern forms an antecedent/consequent phrase. The first measure of all three patterns emphasizes A-flat, while the second measure of each pattern revolves around E-flat, creating a consistent tonic-dominant movement throughout the song. A single two-measure bass pattern provides the harmony for all three melodies. Since the bass's harmonic underpinning is consistent throughout the song, the melodic patterns can be mixed and matched with the appropriate corresponding bass measure. Thus, the second measure of the first melody (1b) follows the first measure of the first melody (1a)—as

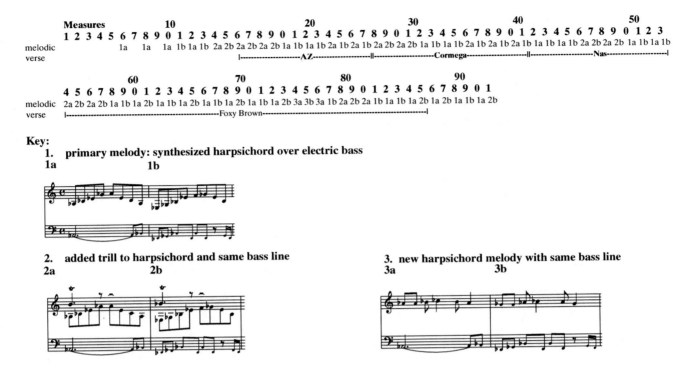

Figure 16. Melodic layers and progression of Nas's "Affirmative Action"

for example in measures 10–14—but it could just as easily follow the first measure of the second pattern (2a)—as in measures 24–27. And indeed, the production team mixes up melody halves throughout the song to provide variety (see, for example, mm. 70–77).

As figure 16 illustrates, melodies 1 and 2 are closely related and clearly dominate the song. The only difference between these melodies is the layering of trilled notes in an upper voice over the arpeggiated melody 1 to form melody 2. The third melody, however, moves away from this arpeggiation for the first time, bringing a new character to the synthesizer, if only for three measures: melody 3 enters only in Foxy's verse (mm. 74–76) and only one and a half statements of this melody are heard. Why the melody changes at this particular point in the song is unclear. Foxy's text in these measures, which concerns a drug sale, does not warrant a new musical sound to attract attention ("flippin' the bigger picture, the bigger nigga with the cheddar / Was mad dripper, he had a fuckin' villa in Manila / We got to flee to Panama, but wait it's half and half") and the measures do not occur at a formally significant moment of the song. Ultimately the melodic variations of this song seem calculated to provide musical interest, to keep the song moving forward as the MCs spin out their drug-sale tale.

But significant changes in a song's melodic layers can also have a more profound effect, such as in the Wu-Tang Clan's "Wu-Revolution," a primer of Five Percent doctrine for the uninitiated (see chapters 2 and 3 for a discussion of these lessons). The song opens as a dialogue between two men, the first (Poppa Wu) "lost" and looking for redemption, and the second (Uncle Pete) comforting. The lyrics below come from the first twenty-one measures of "Wu-Revolution" (each line represents one measure of music). Both voices of the dialogue are in the left-hand column of the example; the second voice is differentiated with italics. These voices are spoken, not rapped.

These things just took over me,

Just took over my whole

body, so I can't even see no

more. I'm calling my black woman a

bitch, I'm calling my peoples all

kinds of things that they not

I'm lost brother, can you help me? Can you

help me brother, please?

You see what we did, we lost the love

I'm talking 'bout the love

The love of your own. But brother, but brother, but brother, check this out. I still don't

understand man, I'm all high off this shit man

Well, what I'm trying to say my brother

Why, why do we kill each

other? Look at our children,

what kind

of a future? This is the training that's gonna be

given to you by the Wu, brothers   [The revolution, the revolution will be
and sisters. It's time to rise, and take   televised, televised, televised]
our place so we can inherit the universe.

The bracketed text in the right-hand column beginning in measure 18 is also spoken, but simultaneously rather than in dialogue (later in the song this voice sings). Low in the mix, behind the two initial voices, a woman's voice weaves in and out of the texture, improvising countermelodies over the relatively spare musical tracks, which consist of only snare drum, hi-hat, bass guitar, and the synthesized melodic layers shown in figure 17. For the rest of the song Poppa Wu delivers doctrine drawn from Lost-Found Lessons nos. 1 and 2, English Lesson no. C1, and the Student Enrollment Lessons, aided by sung and spoken responses from Uncle Pete and other singers, as well as by patterns of tension and release created by RZA's manipulation of melodic layers.

Three synthesized melodic layers (in addition to the voices) are at work in this song: two keyboard melodies (one with a clear electronic, synthesizer timbre and the other resembling a harpsichord) and a dramatic riff of octave Ds made up of synthesized horns and strings. Figure 17 illustrates the complex alternation of these layers. RZA, the song's producer, uses the primary synthesizer melody (labeled "1") most often, and rarely overlaps the horn and string riff (labeled "3"). The synthesizer melody tends to give way to the harpsichord melody, overlapping its beginning at several points (mm. 19–21, 41–44, 49–51, 67–68, 87, 100, and 107). For the first half of the song the horn and string riff does not segue directly back to the synthesizer melody but instead buffers statements of the harpsichord melody. Yet after setting up these

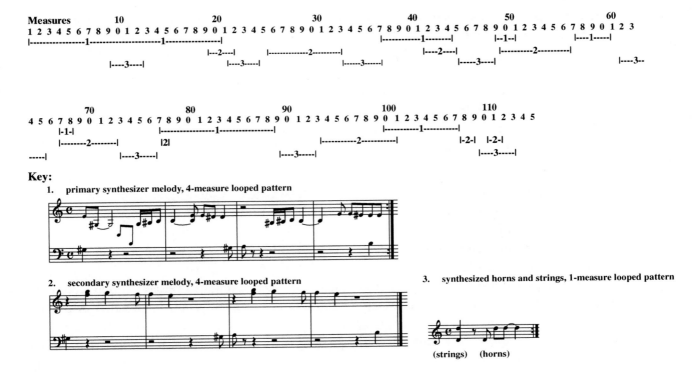

Figure 17. "Wu-Revolution," Instrumental Melodic Layers

expectations, RZA compresses the lag time between melodies 1 and 3, so that by measure 109—nearly the end of the musical portion of this song—the horn and string ensemble interrupts the harpsichord melody and overlaps the synthesizer melody, bringing the music to a climax as Poppa Wu describes the 85 percent. Throughout this alternating pattern, the song's entire texture slowly thickens: handclaps enter on the back-beats and more background singers add their voices one by one. Thus, three separate melodic layers, each occupying a different timbral space, together propel the drama of the song forward and provide the expressive and affective foundation for Poppa Wu's sermon.

"Wu-Revolution" illustrates several of the many tools God Hop producers bring to their musical proselytism. Repetition and shifting melodic textures, both hallmarks of rap's musical style, here provide the continuous groove for Poppa Wu's delivery of lessons all Five Percenters know. Yet RZA, Poppa Wu, and Uncle Pete also reach out to the uninitiated through the dramatic and emotional call-and-response style of traditional African American sermons. The doctrine here may have originated with the Nation of Islam and the Five Percent Nation, but its packaging has an altogether different religious context, a context familiar to the African American audience the Wu-Tang hopes to reach.

Groove

The doctrine in "Wu-Revolution" could just as easily have been distributed in sermons or pamphlets, yet the music brings a crucial unifying device and rhetorical figure of diasporic black cultural production: repetition. James Snead, one of the many scholars to comment on repetition, speaks of repetition in terms of circulation and flow, of continuous presence: "the thing (the ritual, the dance, the beat) is 'there for you to pick it up when you come back to get it.'"[35] Snead also describes what he calls the "cut," a "seemingly unmotivated break" in the midst of repetition.[36] Although his study appears in a volume on black literature and he speaks generally of music, dance, and language, his descriptions of repetition and cuts could very well serve as an interpretation of rap. Bringing the study of repetition directly to hip-hop, Tricia Rose notes not only the power of repetition, but also the effects of momentary disruptions of repeated patterns: "In hip hop, visual, physical, musical, and lyrical lines are set in motion, broken abruptly with sharp angular breaks, yet they sustain motion and energy through fluidity and flow."[37]

Both Rose and Snead describe the same musical phenomenon without going so far as to name it: groove. As defined by Steven Feld, who, with Charles Keil, opened the way to our understanding of groove, music that grooves is "regular and somewhat sustainable, identifiable and repetitive."[38] Later in the same study, Feld elaborates on his definition, emphasizing the processual, yet cyclic nature of groove: "In the vernacular, a 'groove' refers to an intuitive sense of style as process, a perception of a cycle in motion, a form or organizing pattern being revealed, a recurrent clustering of elements through time."[39] For Feld, repetition is the glue holding together form, content, and groove; without repetition, music ceases to groove. Keil, on the other hand, holds hat variations on a groove are just as significant as the repetition itself.[40] Although not intended specifically as descriptions of rap music, the definitions of groove provided by Keil and Feld are highly appropriate to rap. As the musical examples in this chapter illustrate, rap works rhetorically because it grooves. Rap musicians unfold repeated cycles, processes, and patterns over time, occasionally rupturing—or varying—the groove's melodic and percussive layers.

Keil also emphasizes that active participation among musicians, music, and listeners is an essential part of grooved.[41] Participation in a musical experience is certainly not limited to musicians, as Christopher Small has reminded us.[42] Feld, too, understands that "getting into the groove" can describe "how a socialized listener anticipates pattern in a style, and feelingfully participates by momentarily tracking and appreciating subtleties vis-à-vis overt regularities."[43] In other words, it is groove that propels God Hop's music and messages into the ready ears of listeners as they participate in the musical experience. Rap audiences socialized to formal, textural, textual, and expressive rap norms will be aware of changes in melodic and percussive textures; will feel expressive and formal breaks; will take note of subtle interactions between music and text, and will respond to affective musical and textual flows. Simply by hearing and responding to a song's groove, fans of God Hop "feelingfully" participate in music intended to introduce them to the Five Percenter way of life.

As these examples of flow, layering, and rupture illustrate, Five Percenter rap musicians use a spectrum of expressive strategies to underpin their messages. But the expressive strategies outlined in this chapter are not specific to God Hop. Flow, layering, rupture, and groove are essential elements of all rap production; God Hop musicians have simply adopted these common practices for specific rhetorical ends. Producers and MCs alike are keenly aware of the rhetorical power their musical choices can have. In a 1999 interview, I Self Devine, MC of the Micranots, spoke deliberately of the coloristic *affect* of compositional choices, the ability of musical programming to ready the ears of a listener:

Whatever has been built can be destroyed. With that in mind, it is our goal to be able to reprogram people through visual stimulus as well as audio stimulus. You know, colors do affect the way that you think and feel—certain soundwaves, certain vocals, subliminal programming, mental programming and whatnot.[44]

I Self Devine's awareness of the close connection between musical sound and spiritual/social consciousness is commonplace in God Hop, as this chapter reveals.

Counting on their audience's familiarity with rap's genres, styles, forms, and structures, Five Percenter musicians subtly manipulate formal, structural, and expressive details, thus carefully crafting fertile rep soundscapes from haunting melodies, shifting textures, and inviting, infectious grooves in order to capture the attention of their audience and plant seeds of doctrine. Audiences may not understand the specifics of the doctrine in these songs, but that is not necessarily the point of the musical exercise. Musical communication in God Hop is above all intended to invite understanding through active participation. Indeed, Feld's concept of feelingful participation, which he defines as "a form of pleasure that unites the material and mental dimensions of musical experience as fully embodied,"[45] appropriately describes the type of interaction God Hop musicians can expect from their fans. And as Feld understands, feelingful participation produces "a special way of experiencing, knowing, and feeling value, identity, and coherence."[46] By uniting music and message in rap (a practice furthered by sampling and intertextuality, as we shall see in the next chapter), Five Percenter musicians construct a compelling musical voice with which to "civilize the uncivilized."

Since their emergence in the 1970s, rap music and hip hop culture more generally have often been represented as "black" and masculine. The historical record documents some ties between rap music and black culture: as we have learned, the roots of hip hop aesthetics and artistic practice can be linked to the African diaspora. And hip hop culture itself emerged from a population that, relative to the United States as a whole, was disproportionately black.

Meanwhile, debates continue today over representations of women in rap music, and the persistence of misogyny and sexism in rap. In some cases, these debates are cast in racial terms: addressing negative representations of women in gangsta rap, Jesse Jackson was recently quoted as saying that "anyone, white or black, calling our [black] women bitches and our people niggers, will have to face the wrath of our indignation."

Yet, as first-person accounts and early hip hop videos like "Wild Style" attest, the notion that hip hop was originally or exclusively black or male is false.

The readings for this section examine the roles of women, Puerto Ricans, and whites in the creation and development of rap music. They all critique, though in different ways and with different agendas, the commonly-held notion that rap was originally or even primarily black and masculine.

As you study these readings, notice how their different approaches (journalistic and scholarly) affect what the authors are able to say. Also, keep in mind that you are not supposed to believe what these writings say just because they're in this book—quite the opposite! It's important that we interrogate how an author's conclusions follow logically from the evidence that they present. All of these articles have flaws and weaknesses—see if you can find them.

Part 2

Race and Ethnicity

Also, think about these questions as you complete the readings:

Flores' article mentions almost no female MCs. Does he re-create the problems identified by Rose?

Compare and contrast the view of gender in Rose and Chang. What common gender issues emerge in these readings? Do the authors view gender in hip hop differently?

Compare the readings by Flores and Ramsey. How does hip hop function differently in these communities? How does it signify different identities?

Tricia Rose

Chapter 5

Never Trust a Big Butt and a Smile

If you were to construct an image of rap music via accounts of rap in the established press, you would (besides betraying limited critical instincts about popular culture) probably perceive rap to reflect the violent, brutally sexist reality of a pack of wilding "little Willie Hortons."[1] Consequently, you would wonder what a group of young black women rappers were doing fraternizing with these male rappers and why they seemed to be having such a good time. If I were to suggest that their participation in rap music produced some of the most important contemporary black feminist cultural criticism, you would surely bemoan the death of sexual equality. As Public Enemy's Chuck D has warned regarding the mainstream press, "Don't believe the hype." Sexism in rap has been gravely exaggerated by the mainstream press. Rap is a rich, complex multifaceted African–American popular form whose male practitioners' style and subject matter includes the obsessive sexism of a 2 Live Crew, the wacky parody of Biz Markie, the "edutainment" of Boogie Down Productions, the gangster-style storytelling of Ice Cube, the gritty and intelligent speed rapping of Kool Moe Dee, and the explicit black nationalism of X-Clan. Women rappers are vocal and respected members of the Hip Hop community, and they have quite a handle on what they are doing.

Fortunately or unfortunately (I'm not sure which), most academics concerned with contemporary popular culture and music have avoided sustained critical analysis of rap. A few literary scholars and theorists have explained the historical and cultural heritage of rap as an African–American form, while others have made passing reference to it as an important site of postmodernist impulses or as the prophetic voice of an angry disenfranchised group of young African–Americans.[2] The work on women rappers (while making claims that women rappers are pro-women artists) has been published in popular monthly periodicals and consequently has been limited to short but provocative inquiries.[3]

While any positive, critical attention to rap comes as a welcome relief, almost all of these accounts observe rap music outside of its socio-historical framework, as texts suspended in time. Such distanced readings, especially of a musical form to which it is difficult to gain direct and sustained access, leave open the possibility of grave misreadings regarding meanings and context. Women rappers are especially vulnerable to such misreadings precisely because their presence in rap has been consistently ignored or marginalized, even by those social critics who have published some of the most insightful analyses of rap. This essay, which is part of an extended project on rap music, will try to correct some of these misunderstandings, or as Chuck D states, "give you something that I knew you lacked. So consider me a new jack."[4] Better yet, here's Queen Latifah:

> Some think that we can't flow (can't flow)
>
> Stereotypes they got to go (got to go)
>
> I'm gonna mess around and flip the scene into reverse
>
> With what?
>
> With a little touch of ladies first.[5]

The summer of 1989 marked the tenth anniversary of rap music's explosive debut in the recording industry. In honor of its unexpected longevity, Nelson George, a pro-Hip Hop music critic and Village Voice columnist, published a sentimental rap retrospective in which he mourned rap's movement from a street subculture into the cold, sterile world of commercial record production. George points out that, until recently, music industry powers have maintained a studied indifference to rap music, but now that rap's "commercial viability has been proven" many major recording companies are signing any half way decent act they can find. What worries George, and rightly so, is that corporate influence on black music has led, in the past, to the dissolution of vibrant black cultural forms and that rap may become the latest victim. The problem is complex, real and requires analysis. However, Nelson George, like media critics generally, imbeds his descriptions of "authentic rap" and fears of recent corporate influence on it in gender-coded language that mischaracterizes rap and silences women rappers and consumers. In his tenth anniversary piece, George traces major shifts in rap, naming titles, artists and producers. He weaves over twenty rap groups into his piece and names not a single female rapper. His retrospective is chock-full of prideful, urban black youth (read men), whose contributions to rap reflect "the thoughts of city kids more deeply than the likes of Michael Jackson, Oprah Winfrey et al." His concluding remarks make apparent his underlying perception of rap:

> To proclaim the death of rap, is to be sure, premature. But the farther the control of rap gets from its street corner constituency and the more corporations grasp it—record conglomerates, Burger King, Minute Maid, Yo! MTV Raps, etc.—the more vulnerable it becomes to cultural emasculation.

For George, corporate meddling not only dilutes cultural forms, it also reduces strapping testosterone-packed men into women! Could we imagine anything worse? Nelson George's analysis is not unusual; his is merely the latest example of media critics' consistent coding of rap music as male in the face of a significant and sustained female presence.

Many social critics who have neglected to make separate mention of women rappers would probably claim that these women are in many ways just "one of the boys." Since they are as tough as male rappers, women rappers fit into George's mind-boggling yet emblematic definition of rap as an "ultra-urban, unromantic, hyperrealistic, neo-nationalist, antiassimilationist, aggressive Afrocentric impulse." For George, and for media critics generally, it is far easier to re-gender women rappers than to revise their own gender-coded analysis of rap music.[6]

Since the summer of 1989, there has been a marked increase in media attention to women rappers. Most of the articles have been written by women and have tried to shed some light on female rappers and offer a feminist analysis of their contributions. I would like to extend some of the themes presented in these pieces by showing how women rappers participate in a dialogue with male rappers and by revising some of the commonly held assumptions about what constitutes "feminist" expression.

As Nancy Guevara notes, the "exclusion and/or trivialization of women's role in Hip Hop" is no mere oversight.[7] The marginalization, deletion, and mischaracterization of women's role in black cultural production is routine practice. Angela Davis extends this criticism by stating that this is "an omission that must be attributed to the influence of sexism." In her article, "Black Women and Music: An Historical Legacy of Struggle," Davis makes three related arguments that are of particular importance here. First, she contests the marginal representation of black women in the documentation of African–American cultural developments and suggests that these representations do not adequately reflect women's participation. Second, she suggests that music (song and dance) are especially productive sites for examining the collective consciousness of black Americans. And third, she calls for a close reexamination of black women's musical legacy as a way to understand black women's consciousness. She writes:

> Music has long permeated the daily life of most African-Americans; it has played a central role in the normal socialization process; and during moments characterized by intense movements for social change, it has helped to shape the necessary political consciousness. Any attempt, therefore, to understand in depth the evolution of women's consciousness within the Black community requires a serious examination of the music which has influenced them—particularly that which they themselves have created.[8]

She continues by offering a close reading of Gertrude "Ma" Rainey's music as a step toward redressing such absences. Dealing with similar issues, Hazel Carby charges that white dominated feminist discourse has marginalized (and I would add often ignored) non-white women and questions of black sexuality. She further argues that representations of black women's sexuality in African–American literature differs significantly from representations of sexuality in black women's blues.[9]

Carby and Davis, while concerning themselves specifically with women's blues, are calling for a multi-faceted analysis of black women's identity and sexuality as represented by their musical production. Stating that "different cultural forms negotiate and resolve different sets of social contradictions," Carby suggests that black women writers have been encouraged to speak on behalf of a large group of black women whose daily lives and material conditions may not be adequately reflected in black women's fiction. For example, the consumption patterns and social context of popular music differ significantly from those of fiction. The dialogic capacity of popular music, especially that of rap music, engages many of the social contradictions and ambiguities that pertain specifically to contemporary urban, working-class black life.

George Lipsitz, applying Mikhail Bakhtin's concept of "dialogic" criticism to popular music, argues that:

> Popular music is nothing if not dialogic, the product of an ongoing historical conversation in which no one has the first or last word. The traces of the past that pervade the popular music of the present amount to more than mere chance: they are not simply juxtapositions of incompatible realities. They reflect a dialogic process, one embedded in collective history and nurtured by the ingenuity of artists interested in fashioning icons of opposition.

Lipsitz's interpretation of popular music as a social and historical dialogue is an extremely important break from traditional, formalist interpretations of music. By grounding cultural production historically and avoiding the application of a fixed inventory of core structures, dialogic criticism as employed by Lipsitz is concerned with how popular music "arbitrates tensions between opposition and co-optation at any given historical moment."[10]

This notion of dialogism is especially productive in the context of African–American music. The history of African–American music and culture has been defined in large measure by a history of the art of signifying, recontextualization, collective memory and resistance. "Fashioning icons of opposition" that speak to diverse communities is part of a rich black American musical tradition to which rappers make a significant contribution. Negotiating multiple boundaries, black women rappers are in dialogue with each other, male rappers, other popular musicians (through sampling and other revisionary practices), and with Hip Hop fans.

Never Trust a Big Butt and a Smile   79

Black women rappers are integral and resistant voices in Hip Hop and in popular music generally. They sustain an ongoing dialogue with their audiences and male rappers about sexual promiscuity, emotional commitment, infidelity, the drug trade, racial politics and black cultural history. Rappers interpret and articulate the fears, pleasures and promises of you black women and men whose voices have been relegated to the silent margins of public discourse. By paying close attention to rap music, we can gain some insight into how young African–Americans provide for themselves a relatively safe free-play zone where they creatively address questions of sexual power, the reality of truncated economic opportunity, the pain of racism and sexism and, through physical expressions of freedom, relieve the anxieties of day-to-day oppression.

If you have been following the commercial success of rap music, it is difficult to ignore the massive increase in record deals for women rappers following Salt-N-Pepa's double platinum (two million) 1986 debut album *Hot, Cool and Vicious*. Such album sales, even for a rap album by a male artist, were virtually unprecedented in 1986. Since then, several female rappers, many of whom have been rapping for years (some since the mid-1970s), have finally been recorded and promoted.[11] Says female rapper Ms. Melodie:

> It wasn't that the male started rap, the male was just the first to be put on wax. Females were always into rap, and females always had their little crews and were always known for rockin' house parties and streets or whatever, school yards, the corner, the park, whatever it was.[12]

In the early stages, women's participation in rap was hindered by gender considerations. M.C. Lady "D" notes that because she didn't put a female crew together for regular performances, she "didn't have to worry about getting [her] equipment ripped off, coming up with the cash to get it in the first place, or hauling it around on the subways to gigs—problems that kept a lot of other women out of rap in the early days."[13] For a number of reasons (including increased institutional support and more demand for both male and female rappers), such stumbling blocks have been reduced.

MC Lyte's 1988 release, "Paper Thin," sold over 125,000 copies in the first six months with virtually no radio play. Lady B, who became the first recorded female rapper in 1978, was Philadelphia's top rated D.J. on WUSL and is founder and Editor-in-Chief of *Word Up!*, a tabloid devoted to Hip Hop.[14] Salt-N-Pepa's first single, "Expressions," from their latest album release *Black's Magic*, went gold in the first week and stayed in the number one position on *Billboard*'s Rap Chart for over two months.

But these industry success-markers are not the primary focus here. I intend to show that the subject matter and perspectives presented in many women's rap lyrics challenge dominant notions of sexuality, heterosexual courtship, and aesthetic constructions of the body. In addition, music videos and live performances display exuberant communities of women occupying public space while exhibiting sexual freedom, independence and, occasionally, explicit domination over men. Women's raps grow more and more complex each year and, with audience support, many rappers have taken risks (regarding imagery and subject matter) that a few years ago would have been unthinkable. Through their lyrics and video images, black women rappers—especially Queen Latifah, MC Lyte and Salt-N-Pepa—form a dialogue with working-class black women and men, offering young black women a small but potent culturally-reflexive public space.

In order to understand the oppositional nature of these women rappers, it is important to have at least a sketch of some of the politics behind rap's battle of the sexes. Popular raps by both men and women have covered many issues and social situations that pertain to the lives of young, black working-class teens in urban America. Racism, drugs, police brutality, sex, crime, poverty, education and prison have been popular themes in rap for a number of years. But raps about celebration, dance, styling, boasting and just "gittin' funky" (in Kid-N-Play's words) have been equally popular. Raps about style and prestige sometimes involve the possession of women as evidence of male power. Predictably, these raps define women as commodities, objects and ornaments. Others are defensive and aggressive raps that describe women solely as objects of male pleasure. In rap music, as in other popular genres, women are divided into at least two categories—the "kind to take home to mother" and the "kind you meet at three o'clock in the morning." In Hip Hop discourse, the former is honest and loyal—but extremely rare (decidedly not the girl next door). The latter is not simply an unpaid prostitute, but a woman who only wants you for your money, cars and cash, will trap you (via pregnancy or other forms of manipulation), and move on to another man (probably your best friend). It would be an understatement to suggest that there is little in the way of traditional notions of romance in rap. Sexist raps articulate the profound fear of female sexuality felt by these young rappers and by many young men.

In a recent *Village Voice* interview with ex-NWA member Ice Cube, notorious not only for harsh sexist raps but for brilliant chilling stories of ghetto life, Greg Tate (one of the best Hip Hop social critics) tries to get "some understanding" about the hostility toward women expressed in Ice Cube's raps:

Tate: *Do you think rap is hostile toward women?*

Ice Cube: *The whole damn world is hostile toward women.*

Tate: *What do you mean by that?*

Ice Cube: *I mean the power of sex is more powerful than the motherfuckers in Saudi Arabia. A girl that you want to get with can make you do damn near anything. If she knows how to do her shit right, she can make you buy cigarettes you never wanted to buy in life.... Look at all my boys out here on this video shoot, all these motherfuckers sitting out here trying to look fly, hot as a motherfucker, ready to go home. But there's too many women here for them to just get up and leave. They out here since eight o'clock in the morning and ain't getting paid. They came for the girls.[15]*

Ice Cube's answer may appear to be a non sequitur, but his remarks address what I believe is the subtext in rap's symbolic male domination over women. Ice Cube suggests that many men are hostile toward women because the fulfillment of male heterosexual desire is significantly checked by women's capacity for sexual rejection and/or manipulation of men. Ice Cube acknowledges the reckless boundaries of his desire as well as the power women can exercise in this sexual struggle. In "The Bomb," Ice Cube warns men to "especially watch the ones with the big derriers" because the greater your desire, the more likely you are to be blinded by it, and consequently the more vulnerable you are likely to be to female domination. From the perspective of a young man, such female power is probably more palpable than any woman realizes. Obviously, Ice Cube is not addressing the institutional manifestations of patriarchy and its effects on the social construction of desire. However, he and many black male rappers speak to men's fears and the realities of the struggle for power in teenage heterosexual courtship in a sexist society.

During the summer of 1990, Bell Biv Devoe, a popular R&B/Rap crossover group, raced up the charts with "Poison," a song about women whose chorus warns men not to "trust a big butt and a smile." The song cautions men about giving in to their sexual weaknesses and then being taken advantage of by a sexy woman whose motives might be equally insincere. The degree of anxiety expressed is striking. "Poison" explains both their intense desire for and profound distrust of women. The capacity of a woman to use her sexuality to manipulate his desire for her purposes is an important facet of the sexual politics of male raps about women Bell Biv Devoe are telling men: "You may not know what a big butt and a smile really means. It might not mean pleasure; it might mean danger—poison."

All of this probably seems gravely sexist—so much so that any good feminist would reject it out of hand. However, I would like to suggest that women rappers effectively engage with male rappers on this level. By expressing their sexuality openly and in their own language, yet distinguishing themselves from poisonous and insincere women, black women rappers challenge men to take women more seriously. Black women rappers might respond by saying: "That's right, don't automatically trust a big butt and a smile. We've got plenty of sexual power and integrity, but don't mess with us." I am not suggesting that women have untapped power that once accessed will lead the way to the dismantling of patriarchy. Ice Cube and Bell Biv Devoe's expressions of fear must be understood in the context of their status as men and the inherent social power such a gender assignment affords. But, understanding the fear of female sexuality helps explain the consistent sexual domination men attempt to sustain over women. Without such fears, their efforts would be unnecessary.

Women's raps and my interviews with female rappers display similar fears of manipulation, loss of control, and betrayal at the hands of men. What is especially interesting about women rappers is the way in which they shift the focus of the debate. Male rappers focus on sexually promiscuous women who "want their money" (in rap lingo they are called skeezers) and almost never offer a depiction of a sincere woman. Female rappers focus on dishonest men who seek sex from women (much like the women who seek money from men), and they represent themselves as seasoned women with sexual confidence and financial independence.

During my interview with Salt (one half of the female rap duo Salt-N-Pepa), I pressed her about how she could envision a committed relationship without some degree of emotional dependence. She replied:

> I just want to depend on myself. I feel like a relationship shouldn't be emotional dependence. I, myself, am more comfortable when I do not depend on hugs and kisses from somebody that I possibly won't get. If I don't get them then I'll be disappointed. So if I get them, I'll appreciate them.[16]

Salt's lyrics reflect much of how she feels personally: "You know I don't want to for your money"; "I'm independent, I make my own money, so don't tell me how to spend it"; "You can't disguise the lies in your eyes, you're not a heartbreaker"; "You need me and I don't need you."[17]

Women rappers employ many of the aesthetic and culturally specific elements present in male rap lyrics while offering an alternative vision of similar social conditions. Raps written by women which specifically concern male/female relationships almost always confront the tension between trust and savvy, between vulnerability and control. Women rappers celebrate their sisters for "getting over" on men. Some raps by women such as Icey Jaye's "It's a Girl Thang" mock the men who fall for their tricks. But for the most part, women rappers promote self-reliance and challenge the depictions of women in male raps, addressing the fears about male dishonesty and infidelity that most women share.

Raps written and performed by women regarding male/female relationships can be divided into at least three categories: (1) raps that challenge male dominance over women within the sexual arena, (2) raps, that by virtue of their authoritative stance, challenge men as representatives of Hip Hop, and (3) raps that explicitly discuss women's identity and celebrate women's physical and sexual power. Across these three categories, several popular female rappers and their music videos can serve as illuminating examples.[18]

MC Lyte and Salt-N-Pepa have reputations for biting raps that criticize men who manipulate and abuse women. Their lyrics tell the story of men taking advantage of women, cheating on them, abusing them, taking their money and then leaving them for other unsuspecting female victims. These raps are not mournful ballads about the trials and tribulations of being a woman. Similar to women's blues, they are caustic, witty and aggressive warnings directed at men and at other women who might be seduced by men in the future. By offering a woman's interpretation of the terms of heterosexual courtship, these raps cast a new light on male/female sexual power relations and depict women as resistant, aggressive participants.

Salt-N-Pepa's 1986 single, "Tramp," speaks specifically to black women, warning us that "Tramp" is not a "simple rhyme," but a parable about relationships between men and women:

> Homegirls attention you must pay to what I say
>
> Don't take this as a simple rhyme
>
> 'Cause this type of thing happens all the time
>
> Now what would you do if a stranger said "Hi"
>
> Would you dis him or would you reply?
>
> If you'd answer, there is a chance
>
> That you'd become a victim of circumstance
>
> Am I right fellas? Tell the truth
>
> Or else I'll have to show and prove
>
> You are what you are I am what I am
>
> It just so happens that most men are TRAMPS.

In the absence of any response to "Am I right fellas?" Salt-N-Pepa "show and prove" the trampings of several men who "undress you with their eyeballs," "think you're a dummy" and "on the first date, had the nerve to tell me he loves me." Salt-N-Pepa's parable, by defining promiscuous *men* as tramps, inverts the social construction of male sexual promiscuity as a status symbol. This reversal undermines the degrading "woman as tramp" image by stigmatizing male promiscuity. Salt-N-Pepa suggest that women who respond to sexual advances are victims of circumstance. It is the predatory, disingenuous men who are the tramps.

The music video for "Tramp" is a comic rendering of a series of social club scenes that highlight tramps on the make, mouth freshener in hand, testing their lines on the nearest woman. Dressed in Hip Hop street gear, Salt-N-Pepa perform the song on television, on a monitor perched above the bar. Since they appear on the television screen, they seem to be surveying and critiquing the club action, but the club members cannot see them. There are people dancing and talking together (including likeable men who are coded as "non-tramps"), who seem unaware of the television monitor. Salt-N-Pepa are also shown in the club, dressed in very stylish, sexy outfits. They act as decoys, talking and flirting with the tramps to flesh out the dramatization of tramps on the prowl, and they make several knowing gestures at the camera to reassure the viewer that they are unswayed by the tramps' efforts.

The club scenes have no dialogue. The tramps and their victims interact only with body language. Along with the music for "Tramp," we hear Salt-N-Pepa's lyrics, which serve respectively as the club's dance music and the video's voice-over narration. Viewing much of the club action from Salt-N-Pepa's authoritative position through the television monitor, we can safely observe the playful but cautionary dramatization of heterosexual courtship. Rapping to a woman, one tramp postures and struts, appearing to ask the stock pick-up line, "What is your zodiac sign, baby?" When she shows disgust and leaves her seat, he repeats the same body motions on the next woman who happens to sit down. Near the end of the video a frustrated "wife" enters the club and drags one of the tramps home, smacking him in the head with her pocketbook. Salt-N-Pepa stand next to the wife's tramp in the club, shaking their heads as if to say "what a shame." Simultaneously, they point and laugh at him from the television monitor. At the end of the video, a still frame of each man is stamped "tramp," while Salt-N-Pepa revel in having identified and exposed them. They leave the club together without men, seemingly enjoying their skill at exposing the real intentions of these tramps.

Salt-N-Pepa are clearly "schooling" women about the sexual politics of the club scene. They are engaged in and critiquing the drama of heterosexual courtship. The privileged viewer is a woman who is directly addressed in the lyrics and can fully empathize with the visual depiction and interpretation of the scenes. The video's resolution is a warning to both men and women. Women: Don't fall for these men either by talking to them in the clubs or believing the lies they'll tell you when they come home. Men: You will get caught eventually and you'll be embarrassed. The "Tramp" video also tells women that they can go to these clubs and successfully play along with the game as long as the power of female sexuality and the terms of male desire are understood.

In her video, MC Lyte has a far less playful response to her boyfriend Sam, whom she catches in the act of flirting with another woman. MC Lyte's underground hit, "Paper Thin," is one of the most scathing raps about male dishonesty/infidelity and the tensions between trust and vulnerability. Lyte has been burned by Sam, but she has turned her experience into a black woman's anthem that sustains an uncomfortable balance between brutal cynicism and honest vulnerability:

> *When you say you love me it doesn't matter*
> *It goes into my head as just chit chatter*
> *You may think it's egotistical or just very free*
> *But what you say, I take none of it seriously.*
>
> *I'm not the kind of girl to try to play a man out*
> *They take the money and then they break the hell out*
> *No that's not my strategy, not the game I play*
> *I admit I play a game, but it's not done that way*
> *Truly when I get involved I give it my heart*

I mean my mind, my soul, my body I mean every part

But if it doesn't work out—yo, it just doesn't

It wasn't meant to be, you know it just wasn't

So, I treat all of you like I treat all of them

What you say to me is just paper thin.

Lyte's public acknowledgment that Sam's expressions of love were paper thin is not a source of embarrassment for her, but a means of empowerment. She plays a brutal game of the dozens on Sam while wearing her past commitment to him as a badge of honor and sign of character. Lyte presents commitment, vulnerability and sensitivity as assets, not indicators of female weakness. In "Paper Thin," emotional and sexual commitment are not romantic Victorian concepts tied to honorable but dependent women; they are a part of her strategy, part of the game she plays in heterosexual courtship.

The high energy video for "Paper Thin" contains many elements present in Hip Hop. The video opens with Lyte (dressed in a sweatsuit and sneakers) abandoning her new Jetta because she wants to take the subway. A few members of her male posse follow along behind her, down the steps to the subway tracks. Once in the subway car, her D.J. K-Rock, doubling as the conductor, announces that the train will be held in the station due to crossed signals. While they wait, Milk Boy (her body guard) spots Sam at the other end of the car, rapping heavily to two stylish women. Lyte, momentarily surprised, begins her rhyme as she stalks toward Sam. Sam's attempts to escape fail; he is left to face MC Lyte's wrath. Eventually, she throws him off the train to the tune of Ray Charles's R&B classic, "Hit the Road Jack," and locks Sam out of the subway station, symbolically jailing him. The subway car is filled with young black teenagers, typical working New Yorkers and street people, many of whom join Lyte in signifying on Sam while they groove on K-Rock's music. MC Lyte's powerful voice and no-nonsense image dominate Sam. The tense, driving music—which is punctuated by sampled guitar and drum sections as well as an Earth Wind and Fire horn section—complement Lyte's hard, expressive rapping style.

It is important that "Paper Thin" is set in public and on the subway, the quintessential mode of urban transportation. Lyte is drawn to the subway and obviously feels comfortable there. She is also comfortable with the subway riders in her video; they are her community. By setting her confrontation with Sam in the subway, in front of their peers, Lyte moves a private problem between lovers into the public arena and effectively dominates both spaces.

When her D.J., the musical and mechanical conductor, announces that crossed signals are holding the train in the station, he frames the video in a moment of communication crisis. The notion of crossed signals represents the inability of Sam and Lyte to communicate with one another, an inability that is primarily the function of the fact that they communicate on different frequencies. Sam thinks he can read Lyte's mind to see what she is thinking and then feed her all the right lines. But what he says carries no weight, no meaning. His words are light, they're paper thin. Lyte, who understands courtship as a game, confesses to being a player, yet expresses how she feels honestly and in simple language. What she says has integrity, weight, and substance.

After throwing Sam from the train, she nods her head toward a young man standing against the subway door, and he follows her off the train. She will not allow her experiences with Sam to paralyze her, but she does have a new perspective on dating. As she and her new male friend walk down the street, she raps the final stanza for "Paper Thin," which sets down the ground rules:

So, now I take precautions when choosing my mate

I do not touch until the third or fourth date

Then maybe we'll kiss on the fifth or sixth time that we meet

'Cause a date without a kiss is so incomplete

And then maybe, I'll let you play with my feet

You can suck the big toe and play with the middle

It's so simple unlike a riddle....

MC Lyte and Salt-N-Pepa are not alone in their critique of men's treatment of women. Neneh Cherry's "Buffalo Stance" tells men: "You better watch, don't mess with me / No money man can buy my love / It's sweetness that I'm thinkin' of"; Oaktown 3–5–7's "Say That Then" lashes out at "Finger poppin', hip hoppin', wanna be bed rockin' " men; Ice Cream Tee's "All Wrong" chastises women who allow men to abuse them; and MC Lyte's "I Cram to Understand U," "Please Understand" and "I'm Not Havin' It" are companion pieces to "Paper Thin."

Women rappers also challenge the popular conception that male rappers are the only M.C.s who can "move the crowd," a skill that ultimately determines your status as a successful rapper, Black women rappers compete head-to-head with male rappers for status as the preeminent M.C. Consequently, rhymes that boast, signify and toast are an important part of women's repertoire. Antoinette's "Who's the Boss," Ice Cream Tee's "Let's Work," MC Lyte's "Lyte as a Rock," Sait-N-Pepa's "Everybody Get Up," and Queen Latifah's "Dance for Me" and "Come Into My House" establish black women rappers as Hip Hop M.C.s who can move the crowd, a talent that is as important as writing "dope" rhymes. Latifah's "Come into My House" features Latifah as the dance master, the hostess of physical release and pleasure:

Welcome into my Queendom

Come one, come all

'Cause when it comes to lyrics I bring them

In Spring I sing, in Fall I call

Out to those who had a hard day

I've prepared a place on my dance floor

The time is now for you to party....

I'm on fire the flames too high to douse

The pool is open

Come Into My House.[19]

As rap's territory expands, so does the material of female rappers. Subjects ranging from racism, black politics, Afrocentrism and nationalism to homelessness, physical abuse of women and children, drug addiction, AIDS and teen pregnancy can all be found in female rappers' repertoire. "Ladies First," Queen Latifah's second release from her debut album, *All Hail the Queen*, is a landmark example of such expansions. Taken together, the video and lyrics for "Ladies First" is a statement for black female unity, independence and power, as well as an anti-colonial statement concerning Africa's southern region. The rap recognizes the importance of black female political activists, offering hope for the development of a pro-female, problack, diasporatic political consciousness. A rapid-fire and powerful rap duet between Queen Latifah and her "European sister" Monie Love, "Ladies First" is thus a recital on the significance and diversity of black women. Latifah's assertive, measured voice in the opening rhyme sets the tone:

> *The ladies will kick it, the rhyme it is wicked*
>
> *Those who don't know how to be pros get evicted*
>
> *A woman can bear you, break you, take you*
>
> *Now it's time to rhyme, can you relate to*
>
> *A sister dope enough to make you holler and scream?*

In her almost double-time verse, Monie Love responds:

> *Eh, Yo! Let me take it from here Queen*
>
> *Excuse me but I think I am about due*
>
> *To get into precisely what I am about to do*
>
> *I'm conversatin' to the folks who have no whatsoever clue*
>
> *So, listen very carefully as I break it down to you*
>
> *Merrily merrily, hyper happy overjoyed*
>
> *Pleased with all the beats and rhymes my sisters have employed*
>
> *Slick and smooth—throwing down the sound totally, a yes*
>
> *Let me state the position: Ladies First, Yes?*

Latifah responds, "YES!"

Without attacking black men, "Ladies First" is a wonderful rewriting of the contributions of black women into the history of black struggles. Opening with slides of black female political activists Sojourner Truth, Angela Davis and Winnie Mandela, the video's predominant theme features Latifah as Third World military strategist. She stalks an illuminated, conference table-size map of Southern Africa and, with a long pointer, shoves large chess-like pieces of briefcase carrying white men off white dominated countries, replacing them with large black power style fists. In between these scenes, Latifah and Monie Love rap in front of and between more photos of politically prominent black women and footage of black struggles that shows protests and acts of military violence against protestors. Latifah positions herself as part of a rich legacy of black women's activism, racial commitment and cultural pride.

Never Trust a Big Butt and a Smile   87

Given the fact that protest footage rap videos (which have become quite popular over the last few years) have all but excluded scenes of black women leaders or foot soldiers, the centrality of black women's political protest in "Ladies First" is refreshing. Scenes of dozens of rural African women running with sticks raised above their heads toward armed oppressors, holding their ground alongside men in equal numbers and dying in struggle, are rare media images. As Latifah explains:

> I wanted to show the strength of black women in history. Strong black women. Those were good examples. I wanted to show what we've done. We've done a lot; it's just that people don't know it. Sisters have been in the midst of these things for a long time, but we just don't get to see it that much.[20]

After placing a black power fist on each country in Southern Africa, Latifah surveys the map, nodding contentedly. The video ends with a still frame of the region's new political order.

Latifah's self-possession and independence is an important facet of the new cultural nationalism in rap. The powerful, level-headed and black feminist character of her lyrics calls into question the historically cozy relationship between nationalism and patriarchy. The legendary Malcolm X phrase, "There are going to be some changes made here," is strategically sampled throughout "Ladies First." When Malcolm's voice is introduced, the camera pans the faces of some of the more prominent female rappers and D. J.s including Ms. Melodie, Ice Cream Tee and Shelley Thunder. The next sample of Malcolm's memorable line is dubbed over South African protest footage. Latifah evokes Malcolm as part of a collective African–American historical memory and recontextualizes him not only as a leader who supports contemporary struggles in South Africa, but also as someone who encourages the imminent changes regarding the degraded status of black women and specifically black women rappers. Latifah's use of the dialogic processes of naming, claiming and recontextualizing is not random; nor is it simply a "juxtaposition of incompatible realities." "Ladies First" is a cumulative product that, as Lipsitz would say, "enters a dialogue already in progress." It affirms and revises African–American traditions at the same time that it stakes out new territory.

Black women rappers' public displays of physical and sexual freedom challenge male notions of female sexuality and pleasure. Salt-N-Pepa's rap duet, "Shake Your Thang," which they perform with the prominent go-go band E.U., is a wonderful verbal and visual display of black women's sexual resistance. The rap lyrics and video are about Salt-N-Pepa's sexual dancing and others' responses to them. The first stanza sets them in a club "shakin' [their] thang to a funky beat with a go-go swing" and captures the shock on the faces of other patrons. With attitude to spare, Salt-N-Pepa chant: "It's my thang and I'll swing it the way that I feel, with a little seduction and some sex appeal." The chorus, sung by the male lead in E.U., chants: "Shake your thang, do what you want to do, I can't tell you how to catch a groove. It's your thang, do what you wanna do, I won't tell you how to catch a groove."[21]

The video is framed by Salt-N-Pepa's interrogation after they have been arrested for lewd dancing. New York police cars pull up in front of the studio where their music video is being shot, and mock policemen (played by Kid-N-Play and their producer Herbie Luv Bug) cart the women away in handcuffs. When their mug shots are being taken, Salt-N-Pepa blow kisses to the cameraman as each holds up her arrest placard. Once in the interrogation room, Kid-N-Play and Herbie ask authoritatively, "What we gonna do about this dirty dancing?" Pepa reaches across the table, grabs Herbie by the tie and growls, "We gonna do what we wanna do." Outdone by her confidence, Herbie looks into the camera with an expression of shock.

The mildly slapstick interrogation scenes bind a number of other subplots. Scenes in which Salt-N-Pepa are part of groups of women dancing and playing are interspersed with separate scenes of male dancers, co-ed dance segments with Kid-N-Play, E.U.'s lead singer acting as a spokesman for a "free Salt-N-Pepa" movement, and picketers in front of the police station calling for Salt-N-Pepa's release. When he is not gathering signatures for his petition, E.U chants the chorus from a press conference podium. The camera angles for the dance segments give the effect of a series of park or block parties. Salt-N-Pepa shake their butts for the cameras and for each other while rapping, "My jeans fit nice, they show off my butt" and "I Like Hip Hop mixed with a go-go baby, it's my thang and I'll shake it crazy. Don't tell me how to party, it's my dance, yep, and it's my body."

A primary source of the video's power is Salt-N-Pepa's irreverence toward the morally-based sexual constrictions placed on them as women. They mock moral claims about the proper modes of women's expression and enjoy every minute of it. Their defiance of the moral, sexual restrictions on women is to be distinguished from challenges to the seemingly gender neutral laws against public nudity. Salt-N-Pepa are eventually released because their dancing isn't against the law (as they say, "We could get loose, but we can't get naked"). But their "dirty dancing" also teases the male viewer who would misinterpret their sexual freedom as an open sexual invitation. The rappers make it clear that their expression is no such thing: "A guy touch my body? I just put him in check." Salt-N-Pepa thus force a wedge between overt female sexual expression and the presumption that such expressions are intended to attract men. "Shaking your thang" can create a stir, but that should not prevent women from doing it when and how they choose.

At the video's close, we return to the interrogation scene a final time. Herbie receives a call, after which he announces that they have to release the women. The charges will not stick. Prancing out of the police station, Salt-N-Pepa laughingly say, "I told you so." The police raid and arrests make explicit the real, informal yet institutionally-based policing of female sexual expression. The video speaks to black women, calls for open, public displays of female expression, assumes a community-based support for their freedom, and focuses directly on the sexual desirability and beauty of black women's bodies. Salt-N-Pepa's recent video for "Expression" covers similar ground but focuses more on fostering individuality in young women.

Salt-N-Pepa's physical freedom, exemplified by focusing on their butts, is no coincidence. The distinctly black, physical and sexual pride that these women (and other black female rappers) exude serves as a rejection of the aesthetic hierarchy in American culture that marginalizes black women. There is a long black folk history of dances and songs that celebrate big behinds for men and women (e.g., the Bump, the Dookey Butt, and most recently E.U. and Spike Lee's black chart topper, "Da Butt"). Such explicit focus on the behind counters mainstream definitions of what constitutes a sexually attractive female body. American culture, in defining its female sex symbols, places a high premium on long thin legs, narrow hips and relatively small behinds. The vast majority of white female television and film actresses, musicians and even the occasional black model fits this description. The aesthetic hierarchy of the female body in mainstream American culture, with particular reference to the behind and hips, positions many black women somewhere near the bottom. When viewed in this context, Salt-N-Pepa's rap and video become an inversion of the aesthetic hierarchy that renders black women's bodies sexually unattractive.

Obviously, the common practice of objectifying all women's bodies complicates the way some might interpret Salt-N-Pepa shaking their collective thangs. For some, Salt-N-Pepa's sexual freedom could be considered dangerously close to self-inflicted exploitation. Such misunderstanding of the racial and sexual significance of black women's sexual expression may explain the surprisingly cautious responses I have received from some white feminists regarding the importance of female rappers. However, as Hortense Spillers and other prominent black feminists have argued, a history of silence has surrounded African–American women's sexuality.[22] Spillers argues that this silence has at least two faces; either black women are creatures of male sexual possession, or else they are reified into the status of non-being. Room for self-defined sexual identity exists in neither alternative. The resistant nature of black women's participation in rap is better understood when we take the historical silence, sexual and otherwise, of black women into consideration. Salt-N-Pepa are carving out a female-dominated space in which black women's sexuality is openly expressed. Black women rappers sport Hip Hop clothing and jewelry as well as distinctively black hairstyles. They affirm a black, female, working-class cultural aesthetic that is rarely depicted in American popular culture. Black women rappers resist patterns of sexual objectification and cultural invisibility, and they also resist academic reification and mainstream, hegemonic, white feminist discourse.

Given the identities these women rappers have fashioned for themselves, it is not surprising that they want to avoid being labeled feminists. During my conversations with Salt, MC Lyte and Queen Latifah, it became clear that these women saw feminism as a signifier for a movement that related specifically to white women. They also thought feminism involved adopting an anti-male position, and they did not want to be considered or want their work to be interpreted as anti-black male.

In MC Lyte's case, she remarked that she was often labeled a feminist even though she did not think of herself as one. Yet, after she asked for my working definition of feminist, she wholeheartedly agreed with my description, which was as follows:

> I would say that a feminist believed that there was sexism in society, wanted to change and worked toward change. [She] either wrote, spoke or behaved in a way that was pro-woman, in that she supported situations [organizations] that were trying to better the lives of women. A feminist feels that women are more disadvantaged than men in many situations and would want to stop that kind of inequality.

MC Lyte responded, "Under your definition, I would say I am." We talked further about what she imagined a feminist to be, and it became clear that once feminism was understood as a mode of analysis rather than as a label for a group of women associated with a particular social movement, MC Lyte was much more comfortable discussing the importance of black women's independence: "Yes, I am very independent and I feel that women should be independent, but so should men. Both of us need each other and we're just coming to a realization that we do."[23] For MC Lyte, feminists were equivalent to devoutly anti-male, white middle-class members of the National Organization of Women.

Queen Latifah was sympathetic to the issues associated with feminism, but preferred to be considered pro-woman. She was unable to articulate why she was uncomfortable with the term "feminist" and preferred instead to talk about her admiration for Faye Wattleton, the black president of Planned Parenthood, and the need to support the pro-choice movement. As she told me:

> Faye Wattleton, I like her. I look up to her. I'm pro-choice, but I love God. But I think [abortion] is a woman's decision. In a world like we live in today you can't use [God] as an excuse all the time. They want to make abortion illegal, but they don't want to educate you in school.[24]

Salt was the least resistant to the term feminism yet made explicit her limits:

> I guess you could say that [I'm a feminist] in a way. Not in a strong sense where I'd want to go to war or anything like that [laughter].... But I preach a lot about women depending on men for everything, for their mental stability, for their financial status, for their happiness. Women have brains, and I hate to see them walking in the shadow of a man.[25]

For these women rappers, and many other black women, feminism is the label for members of a white woman's social movement, which has no concrete link to black women or the black community. Feminism signifies allegiance to historically specific movements whose histories have long been the source of frustration for women of color. Similar criticisms of women's social movements have been made vociferously by many black feminists who have argued that race and gender are inextricably linked for black women—and I would add, this is the case for both black and white women.[26] However, in the case of black women, the realities of racism link black women to black men in a way that challenges cross-racial sisterhood. If a cross-racial sisterhood is to be forged, serious attention must be paid to issues of racial difference, racism within the movement, and the racial blind spots that inform coalition building. In the meantime, the desire for sisterhood among and between black and white women cannot be achieved at the expense of black women's racial identity.

If feminist scholars want to contribute to the development of a women's movement that has relevance to the lives of women of color (which also means working-class and poor women), then we must be concerned with young women's reluctance to be associated with feminism. We should be less concerned with producing theoretically referential feminist theories and more concerned with linking these theories to practices, thereby creating new concrete ways to interpret feminist activity. This will involve broadening the scope of investigations in our search for black women's voices. This will involve attending to the day-to-day conflicts and pressures that young, black working-class women face and focusing more of our attention on the cultural practices that are most important to their lives. Academic work that links feminist theory to feminist practice should be wholeheartedly encouraged, and an emphasis on making such findings widely available should be made. For feminist theorists, this will not simply entail "letting the other speak," but will also involve a systematic reevaluation of how feminism is conceptualized and how ethnicity, class and race seriously fracture gender as a conceptual category. Until this kind of analysis takes place a great deal more often than it does, what any of us say to MC Lyte will remain paper thin.

One of the remarkable talents black women rappers have is their capacity to attract a large male following and consistently perform their explicitly pro-woman material. They are able to sustain dialogue with and consequently encourage dialogue between young men and women that supports black women and challenges some sexist male behavior. For these women rappers, feminism is a movement that does not speak to men; while on the other hand, they are engaged in constant communication with black male audiences and rappers, and they simultaneously support and offer advice to their young, black female audiences. As MC Lyte explains, "When I do a show, the women are like, 'Go ahead Lyte, tell 'em!' And the guys are like, 'Oh, shit. She's right.' "[27] Obviously, such instances may not lead directly to a widespread black feminist male/female alliance. However, the dialogues facilitated by these female rappers may well contribute to its groundwork.

In a world of worst possibilities, where no such movements can be imagined, these black female rappers provide young black women with a small, culturally-reflexive public space. Rap can no longer be imagined without women rappers' contributions. They have expanded rap's territory and have effectively changed the interpretive framework regarding the work of male rappers. As women who challenge the sexist discourse expressed by male rappers yet sustain dialogue with them, who reject the racially-coded aesthetic hierarchies in American popular culture, who support black women and black culture, black female rappers constitute an important voice in Hip Hop and contemporary black women's cultural production generally. As Salt says:

> The women look up to us. They take us dead seriously. It's not a fan type of thing; it's more like a movement. When we shout, "The year 1989 is for the ladies," they go crazy. It's the highlight of the show. It makes you realize that you have a voice as far as women go.[26]

NOTES

I would especially like to thank MC Lyte, Queen Latifah, and Salt for their generosity and for their incredible talents. I would also like to thank Stuart Clarke for his thoughtful comments and criticism on earlier versions of this article and its title.

1. For a particularly malicious misreading of rap music see David Gates, "The Rap Attitude," *Newsweek Magazine* 19 March 1990: 56–63. While "The Rap Attitude" is an outrageous example, the assumptions made about the use and intent of rap are quite common. Exceptions to misreadings of this nature include Michael Dyson, "The Culture of Hip Hop," *Zeta Magazine* (June 1989): 45–50 and the works of Greg Tate, a *Village Voice* staff writer, who has been covering rap music for almost a decade.

2. See Henry Louis Gates, Jr., "Two Live Crew De-Coded," *The New York Times* 19 June 1990: 31; Bruce Tucker, "Tell Tchaikovsky the News: Postmodernism, Popular Culture and the Emergence of Rock n Roll," *Black Music Research Journal* (Fall, 1989): 271–295; Anders Stephanson, "Interview with Cornell West," *Universal Abandon?: The Politics of Postmodernism*, ed. Andrew Ross (Minneapolis: U of Minnesota P, 1989): 269–286.

3. See the special issue entitled "The Women of Rap!" *Rappin Magazine* (July 1990); Dominique Di Prima and Lisa Kennedy, "Beat the Rap," *Mother Jones* (Sep./Oct. 1990): 32–35; Jill Pearlman, "Rap's Gender Gap" *Option* (Fall 1988): 32–36; Marisa Fox, "From the Belly of the Blues to the Cradle of Rap," *Details* (July 1989): 118–124.

4. Public Enemy, "Don't Believe The Hype," *It Takes a Nation of Millions to Hold Us Back*, Def Jam Records, 1988.

5. Queen Latifah, "Ladies First," *All Hail the Queen*, Tommy Boy Records, 1989.

6. Nelson George, "Rap's Tenth Birthday," *Village Voice* 24 Oct. 1989: 40.

7. Nancy Guevara, "Women, Writin', Rappin', Breakin'," *The Year Left 2*, ed. Mike Davis, et al. (New York: Verso, 1987): 160–175.

8. Angela Davis, "Black Women and Music: A Historical Legacy of Struggle," *Wild Women in the Whirlwind: Afro–American Culture and the Contemporary Literary Renaissance*, ed. Joanne M. Braxton and Andree Nicola McLaughlin (New Jersey: Rutgers UP, 1990): 3.

9. Hazel V. Carby, "It Jus Be's Dat Way Sometime: The Sexual Politics of Women's Blues," *Radical America* 20.4 (1986): 9–22.

10. George Lipsitz, *Time Passages: Collective Memory and American Popular Culture* (Minneapolis: U of Minnesota P, 1990): 99.

11. Roxanne Shante was the first commercial breakthrough female artist. Her basement-produced single was "Roxanne's Revenge" (1985).

12. Pearlman 34.

13. Di Prima and Kennedy 34.

14. Pearlman 34.

15. Greg Tate, "Manchild at Large: One on One with Ice Cube, Hip Hop's Most Wanted," *Village Voice* 11 Sept. 1990: 78.

16. Salt (Cheryl James from Salt-N-Pepa), personal interview, 17 Aug. 1990.

17. Salt-N-Pepa, *Black's Magic*, Next Plateau Records, 1990.

18. Salt-N-Pepa, "Tramp," *Cool, Hot and Vicious*, Next Plateau Records, 1986; Salt-N-Pepa, "Shake Your Thang," *A Salt With a Deadly Pepa*, Next Plateau Records, 1988; Queen Latifah, "Ladies First," *All Hail the Queen*, Tommy Boy Records, 1989. As you will see, none of my analysis will involve the music itself. The music is a very important aspect of rap's power and aesthetics, but given my space limitations here and the focus of my argument, I have decided to leave it out rather than throw in "samples" of my own. For an extended cultural analysis of rap's music see Tricia Rose, "Orality and Technology: Rap Music and Afro. American Cultural Theory and Practice," *Popular Music and Society* 13.4 (1989): 35–44.

19. Queen Latifah, "Come Into My House," *All Hail the Queen*, Tommy Boy Records, 1989.

20. Queen Latifah (Dana Owens), personal interview, 6 Feb. 1990.

21. The melody and rhythm section for "Shake Your Thang" is taken from the Iseley Brothers single "It's Your Thang," which was on *Billboard's* Top Forty charts in the Winter of 1969.

22. Hortense Spillers, "Interstices: A Small Drama of Words," *Pleasure and Danger: Exploring Female Sexuality*, ed. Carol Vance (Boston: Routledge and Kegan Paul, 1984): 73–100.

23. MC Lyte, personal interview, 7 Sep. 1990.

24. Queen Latifah, personal interview.

25. Salt, personal interview.

26. See Carby, Davis and Spillers cited above. Also see bell hooks, *Ain't I a Woman: Black Women and Feminism* (Boston: South End Press, 1982) and *Feminist Theory: From Margins to Center* (Boston: South End Press, 1984); Barbara Smith, ed., *Home Girls: A Black Feminist Anthology* (New York: Kitchen Table, 1983); Cheryl A. Wall, ed., *Changing Our Own Words: Essays on Criticism, Theory and Writing by Black Women* (New Jersey: Rutgers UP, 1989).

27. MC Lyte, personal interview.

28. Salt, personal interview.

Jeff Chang

Chapter 6

Can't Stop
Won't Stop

When he returned to South Central to film the movie, he met Craig "Kam" Miller, a rapper and a former gang member who was in the process of becoming Craig X at the Compton Mosque #54. Cube was soon meeting with Khallid Abdul Muhammad, the charismatic firebrand who had organized Muhammad Mosque #27. The bald-domed Muhammad called himself a "truth terrorist and knowledge gangsta, a Black history hit man and an urban guerilla," and his mosque expanded its ministry into the broadening gang peace movement, becoming a national model for Farrakhan's gang outreach work.[5] Cube shaved off his jheri-curl and took refuge in the Nation of Islam. Full of new ideas, he was confident his next album, *Death Certificate*, would be his masterpiece.

The Image of Revolution

Angela Y. Davis had grown up in the South in an activist household, and proved an intellectual prodigy. At Brandeis University, where she was one of a handful of African-American students, she was enthralled by a speech given by Malcolm X. Later, while studying in Germany with Theodor Adorno, she had come upon a picture of the Black Panthers in the Sacramento Assembly chambers. She returned to South Central Los Angeles to join the Revolution. After checking out the various political organizations, she rejected Karenga's US Organization as anti-feminist, and joined both SNCC and the Black Panther Party. Soon after, she would note, the Panthers published an essay by Huey Newton in its newspaper that called for solidarity with the emerging gay liberation movement.

After George and Jonathan Jackson were killed and her trial ended in acquittal, she had emerged as an international hero and a leading light in the anti-prisons movement. She became a professor in women's studies and African-American Studies, finally landing at the University of California at Santa Cruz.

As the 1990s opened, she had become painfully aware of how images of her youthful life-and-death struggles were being revived to signify an all-too-vague oppositional style. In a speech she mused, "On the one hand it is inspiring to discover a measure of historical awareness that, in our youth, my generation often lacked. But it is also unsettling. Because I know that almost inevitably my image is associated with a certain representation of Black nationalism that privileges those particular nationalisms with which some of us were locked in constant struggle."[6]

She said, "The image of an armed Black man is considered the 'essence' of revolutionary commitment today. As dismayed as I may feel about this simplistic, phallocentric image, I remember my own responses to romanticized images of brothers (and sometimes sisters) with guns. And, in actuality, it was empowering to go to target practice and shoot—or break down a weapon—as well, or better, than a man. I can relate to the young people who passionately want to do something today, but are misdirected..."[7]

These youths still saw Angela Y. Davis's afro and her Black fist frozen in time. But she had moved on, and she hoped to engage them as an elder would.

The Gangsta Meets the Revolutionary

It had been publicist Leyla Turkkan's idea to sit Angela Davis and Ice Cube together. Turkkan had grown up on New York's Upper East Side, a bohemian "parkie" hanging out with graffiti writers like ZEPHYR and REVOLT. In college, she became a promoter for Black Uhuru on their breakthrough *Red* tour, then moved into publicity, always looking for ways to bring together her P.R. skills, her extensive industry contacts and her progressive politics. Like Bill Adler, she was particularly ready for the rise of Black radical rap. But after the success of the Stop the Violence Movement, she had felt sideswiped by Public Enemy's Griff debacle. At one point, David Mills forced her to deny that she and Adler had ever tried to build up Public Enemy as politicians or social activists. Turkkan felt she had another chance with Ice Cube. By sitting Cube with Davis, he could be presented as an inheritor of the Black radical tradition.

The interview was a provocative idea—one that both Davis and Cube welcomed. But none of them had any idea how the conversation would turn when they got together in Cube's Street Knowledge business offices.

To begin with, Davis only heard a few tracks from the still unfinished album, including "My Summer Vacation," "Us" and a track called "Lord Have Mercy," which never made it to the album. She did not hear the song that would become most controversial—a rap entitled "Black Korea." In another way, she was at a more fundamental disadvantage in the conversation.

Like Davis, Cube's mother had grown up in the South. After moving to Watts, she had come of age as a participant in the 1965 riots. While Cube and his mother were close, they often argued about politics and his lyrics. Now it was like Cube was sitting down to talk with his mother. Davis was at a loss the way any parent is with her child at the moment he is in the fullest agitation of his becoming.

Cube sat back behind his glass desk in a black leather chair, the walls covered with framed gold records and posters for *Boyz N The Hood* and his albums. Copies of *URB*, *The Source* and *The Final Call* were laid out in front of him. Davis asked Cube how he felt about the older generation.

"When I look at older people, I don't think they feel that they can learn from the younger generation. I try and tell my mother things that she just doesn't want to hear sometimes," he answered.

"We're at a point where I hear people like Darryl Gates saying, 'We've got to have a war on gangs.' And I see a lot of Black parents clapping and saying: 'Oh yes, we have to have a war on gangs.' But when young men with baseball caps and T-shirts are considered gangs, what you doing is clapping for a war against your children."[8]

When the conversation swung from generation to gender, Cube's discomfort was palpable:

Ice Cube: What you have is Black people wanting to be like white people, not realizing that white people want to be like Black people. So the best thing to do is to eliminate that type of thinking. You need Black men who are not looking up to the white man, who are not trying to be like the white man.

Angela: What about the women. You keep talking about Black men. I'd like to hear you say Black men and Black women.

Ice Cube: Black people.

Angela: I think that you often exclude your sisters from your thought process. We're never going to get anywhere if we're not together.

Ice Cube: Of course. But the Black man is down.

Angela: Well, the Black woman's down, too.

Ice Cube: But the Black woman can't look up to the Black man until we get up.

Angela: Well why should the Black woman look up to the Black man? Why can't we look at each other as equals?

Ice Cube: If we look at each other on an equal level, what you're going to have is a divide. It's going to be divided.

Angela: As I told you, I teach at the San Francisco County Jail. Many of the women there have been arrested in connection with drugs. But they are invisible to most people. People talk about the drug problem without mentioning the fact that the majority of crack users in our community are women. So when we talk about progress in the community, we have to talk about progress in the community, we have to talk about the sisters as well as the brothers.

Ice Cube: The sisters have held up the community.

Angela: When you refer to "the Black man," I would like to hear something explicit about Black women. That will convince me that you are thinking about your sisters as well as your brothers.

Ice Cube: I think about everybody.[9]

When Davis tried to suggest the power of building alliances with women, Latinos, Native Americans, and others, Cube was dismissive. He said, "You have people who fight for integration, but I'd say we need to fight for equal rights. In the schools, they want equal books, they don't want no torn books. That was more important than fighting to sit at the same counter and eat. I think it's more healthy if we sit over there, just as long as we have good food."

Davis replied, "Suppose we say we want to sit in the same place or wherever we want to sit, but we also want to eat food of our own choosing. You understand what I'm saying? We want to be respected as equals, but also for our differences. I don't want to be invisible as a Black woman."

Cube answered, "It's all about teaching our kids about the nature of the slave master. Teaching them about his nature, and how he is always going to beat you no matter how many books you push in front of him, no matter how many leaders you send to talk to him. He's always going to be the same way. We've got to understand that everything has natural energies."

Then he cited Farrakhan's analogy: "There's the chicken and the chicken hawk. The ant and the anteater. They are enemies by nature. That's what we've got to instill in our kids."[10]

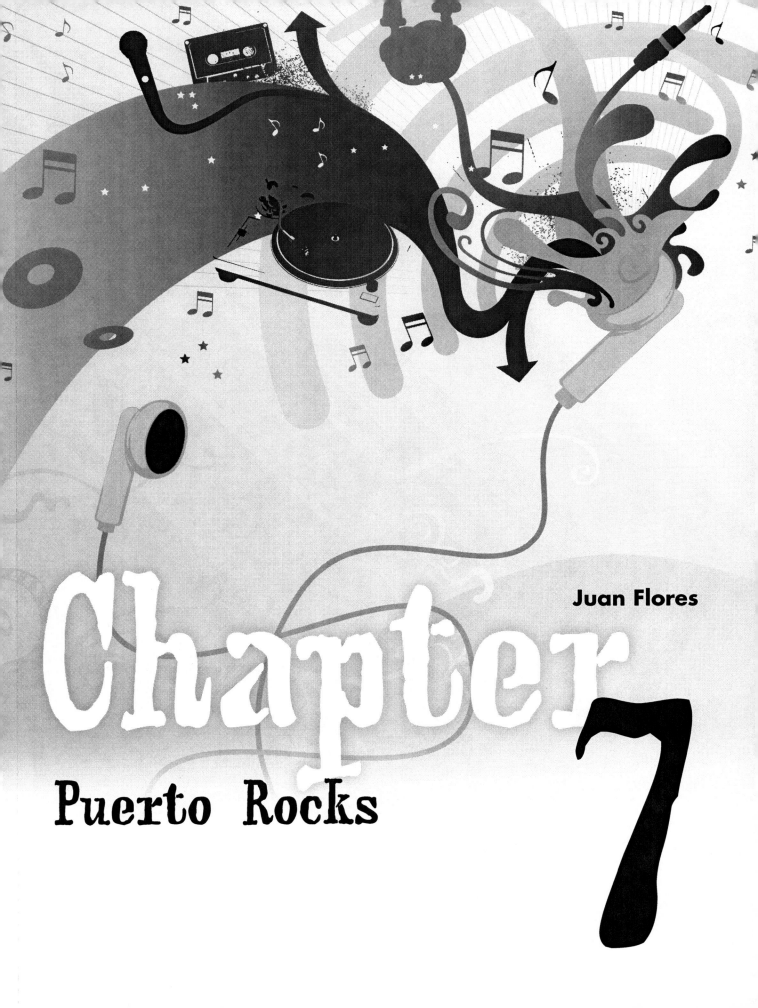

Juan Flores

Chapter 7

Puerto Rocks

By the early 1990s, hip-hop had finally broken the language barrier. Though young Puerto Ricans from the South Bronx and El Barrio have been involved in breakdancing, graffiti writing, and rap music since the beginnings of hip-hop back in the 1970s, it was only belatedly that the Spanish language and Latin musical styles came into their own as integral features of the rap vocabulary. By the mid-nineties, acts like Mellow Man Ace, Kid Frost, Gerardo, and El General became household words among pop music fans nationwide and internationally, as young audiences of all nationalities came to delight in the catchy Spanglish inflections and the *guaguancó* and merengue rhythms lacing the familiar rap formats. Mellow Man Ace's "Mentirosa" was the first Latino rap record to go gold in the summer of 1990; Kid Frost's debut album *Hispanic Causing Panic* instantly became the rap anthem of La Raza in the same year; Gerardo as "Rico Suave" has his place as the inevitable Latin lover sex symbol; and El General has established the immense popularity of Spanish-language reggaerap in the Caribbean and Latin America.

Who are these first Latin rap superstars and where are they from? Mellow Man Ace was born in Cuba and raised in Los Angeles, Kid Frost is a Chicano from East L.A., Gerardo is from Ecuador, and El General is Panamanian. But what about the Puerto Ricans, who with their African American homeboys created hip-hop styles in the first place? They are, as usual, conspicuous for their absence, and the story is no less startling for all its familiarity. Latin Empire, for example, the only Nuyorican act to gain some exposure among wider audiences, is still struggling for its first major record deal. Individual emcees and deejays have been scattered in well-known groups like the Fearless Four and the Fat Boys, their Puerto Rican backgrounds all but invisible. Even rap performers from Puerto Rico like Vico C, Lisa M, and Rubén DJ, who grew up far from the streets where hip-hop originated, enjoy greater commercial success and media recognition than any of the Puerto Rican b-boys from the New York scene.

This omission, of course, is anything but fortuitous and has as much to do with the selective vagaries of the music industry as with the social placement of the Puerto Rican community in the prevailing racial-cultural hierarchy. As the commercialization process involves the extraction of popular cultural expression from its original social context and function, it seems that the "Latinization" of hip-hop has meant its distancing from the specific national and ethnic traditions to which it had most directly pertained. But instead of simply bemoaning this evident injustice, or groping for elaborate explanations, it is perhaps more worthwhile to trace the history of this experience from the perspectives of some of the rappers themselves. For if New York Puerto Ricans have had scant play within the "Hispanic rap market," they have one thing that other Latino rappers do not, which is a history in hip-hop since its foundation as an emergent cultural practice among urban youth.

Such an emphasis is not meant to imply any inherent aesthetic judgment, nor does it necessarily involve a privileging of origins or presumed authenticity. Yet it is easy to understand and sympathize with the annoyance of a veteran Puerto Rican deejay like Charlie Chase when faced with the haughty attitudes he encountered among some of the rap superstars from the Island. "The thing about working with these Puerto Rican rappers," he commented, reflecting on his work producing records for the likes of Lisa M and Vico C, "they are very arrogant! You know, because they are from Puerto Rico, and I'm not, right? I feel kind of offended, but my comeback is like, well, yeah, if you want to be arrogant about that, then what are you doing in rap? You're not a rapper. You learned rap from listening to me and other people from New York!"[1] Actually this apprenticeship was probably less direct than Charlie Chase claims, since they more likely got to know rap through the recordings, videos, and concert appearances of Run DMC, LL Cool J, and Big Daddy Kane than through any familiarity with the New York hip-hop scene of the early years.

Where did those first platinum-selling rappers themselves go to learn the basics of rap performance? Again, Charlie Chase can fill us in, by remembering the shows he deejayed with the Cold Crush Brothers back in the early 1980s.

> When we were doing shows, you know who was in the audience? The Fat Boys. Whodini. Run DMC, L.L. Cool J, Big Daddy Kane. Big Daddy Kane told me a story one time, he said, "You don't know how much I loved you guys." He said, "I wanted to see you guys so bad, and my mother told me not to go to Harlem World to see you guys perform because if she found out I did she'd kick my ass!" And he said, "I didn't care, I went. And I went every week. And I wouldn't miss any of your shows." That's how popular we were with the people who are the rappers today.

To speak of Puerto Ricans in rap means to defy the sense of instant amnesia that engulfs popular cultural expression once it is caught up in the logic of commercial representation. It involves sketching in historical contexts and sequences, tracing traditions and antecedents, and recognizing hip-hop to be more and different than the simulated images, poses, and formulas the public discourse of media entertainment tends to reduce it to. The decade and more of hindsight provided by the Puerto Rican involvement shows that, rather than a new musical genre and its accompanying stylistic trappings, rap constitutes a space for the articulation of social experience. From this perspective, what has emerged as "Latin rap" first took shape as an expression of the cultural turf shared, and contended for, by African Americans and Puerto Ricans over their decades as neighbors, coworkers, and "homies" in the inner-city communities. As vernacular cultural production prior to its commercial and technological mediation, hip-hop formed part of a more extensive and intricate field of social practice, a significant dimension of which comprises the long-standing and ongoing interaction between Puerto Rican and Black youth in the shared New York settings. Not only is the contextual field wider, but the historical reach is deeper and richer as well: the Black and Puerto Rican conjunction in the formation of rap is prefigured in important ways in doo-wop, Latin boogaloo, Nuyorican poetry, and a range of other testimonies to intensely overlapping and intermingling expressive repertoires. Thus when Latin Empire comes out with "I'm Puerto Rican and Proud, Boyee!" they are actually marking off a decisive moment in a tradition of cultural and political identification that goes back several generations.

I have gained access to this largely uncharted terrain by way of conversations and interviews with some of the protagonists of Puerto Rican rap. Early hip-hop movies like *Wild Style* and *Style Wars*, which documented and dramatized the prominent participation of Puerto Ricans, sparked my initial interest and led to a burst of research (which hardly anyone took seriously at the time) and a short article published in various English and Spanish versions in the mid-1980s. At that time, the only adequate written consideration of Puerto Ricans had to do with their role in the New York graffiti movement, as in the excellent book *Getting Up* by Craig Castleman and an important article by Herbert Kohl. Steven Hager's *Hip-Hop* includes a valuable social history of youth culture in the South Bronx and Harlem at the dawn of hip-hop, with some attention to the part played by Puerto Ricans in graffiti, breakdance, and rap music.[2] Otherwise, and since those earlier accounts, coverage of Puerto Rican rap has been limited to an occasional article in the *Village Voice* or *Spin* magazine, generally as a sideline concern in discussions of wider style rubrics like "Hispanic," "Spanish," or "bilingual" rap. Primary evidence of a historical kind is even harder to come by, since Puerto Rican rhymes were never recorded for public distribution and many have been forgotten even by their authors.

Chasin' the Flash

Charlie Chase calls himself "New York's Number One Puerto Rican DJ," and that's how he's been known since back in the seventies when he was blasting the hottest dance music on the waves of WBLS and in the early eighties when he was deejay for the legendary Cold Crush Brothers. When he says "Number One," he means not only the best but also the first: "When I started doing rap, there were no Hispanics doing it. If there were I didn't know about it. Anyway, I was the first Hispanic to become popular doing what I did. I was a deejay."

Charlie was born in El Barrio in the 1950s, and though his family moved a lot it was always from one Puerto Rican and Black neighborhood to another.

> I grew up in Williamsburg from the age of two to nine. I moved to the Bronx, on Brook Avenue and 141st, ¡que eso por allí es candela! I grew up there from ten to about thirteen, then I moved back to Brooklyn, over in Williamsburg, Montrose Avenue, por allá on Broadway. Then we moved back to the Bronx again, 161st and Yankee Stadium. From there we went to 180th and Arthur, and from there it was Grand Concourse and 183rd, then Valentine and 183rd, then back to 180th. I mean, we moved, man! I've been all over the place, and it's like I've had the worst of both worlds, you know what I mean?

Charlie's parents came from Mayagüez, Puerto Rico. Though family visits to the Island were rare, that Puerto Rican background remained an active influence throughout his upbringing. At home he was raised on Puerto Rican music. "You see I always listened to my mother's records. She was the one who bought all the Latin records. She bought them all. She bought Tito Puente, she was into trios, el Trio Los Condes." Even his career in music seems to have been handed down to him as part of that ancestry.

> I come from a family of musicians. My grandfather was a writer and a musician; he played in bands. So did my father; he played in trios. So I kind of followed in their footsteps. My father left me when I was ten and I never learned music from him; he didn't teach me how to play instruments. For some reason or other, it must have been in the blood, I just picked up the guitar and wanted to learn.

Charlie makes clear that he didn't start off in rap or as a deejay. "I'm a bass player. I played in a Spanish ballad band, merengue band, salsa band, rock band, funk band, Latin rock band. I produced my first album at the age of sixteen and it was a Spanish ballad album. We played with the best, Johnny Ventura, Johnny Pacheco, Los Hijos del Rey, Tito Puente. The name of the group was Los Giramundos." So it turns out that Charlie Chase, famed deejay for the Cold Crush Brothers, started off gigging in a Latin band when he was fifteen years old and could have had a whole career in salsa. "Yeah," he recalls, "but there was no money in it. There were a lot of people being ripped off.... I said, man, I want to do something else." Fortunately, he did have somewhere to turn, for alongside his inherited Latin tradition there was his dance music and R&B. Talking about his transition to deejaying he remembers:

I was a music lover. I grew up listening to WABC, Cousin Brucie, Chuck Leonard, all of these guys, and I was always into music. In school I would always have the radio on. It was always a big influence in my life and then I turned into a musician. I started playing with the band, and then a few years later I got into deejaying, and then the deejaying was making more money for me than the band.

It all seems to make sense, I thought, but what about that name? What's a Puerto Rican doing with a name like Charlie Chase? "My name was Carlos," he said. "Charlie is a nickname for Carlos." Fine, I said, but what about Chase? "Chase?" he repeated, hesitantly. "There is a story behind that which I never told anybody, and I don't know if I want to say it. Because when this person reads this, he is going to be so souped." (Little was I to know how much this little story has to say about the situation of young Puerto Ricans in the early days of rap.)

I made up my name because of Grandmaster Flash. Flash is a friend of mine. I first saw Flash doing this, cutting and all of this, and I saw that and I said, aw, man, I can do this. I was deejaying at the time, but I wasn't doing the scratching and shit and I said, I can do this, man. I'll rock this, you know. And I practiced, I broke turntables, needles, everything. Now "Chase" came because I'm like, damn, you need a good name, man. And Flash was on top and I was down here. So I was chasing that niggah. I wanted to be up where he was. So I said, let's go with Charlie Chase.

There's no telling how "souped" Grandmaster Flash will get when he finds out, but his friend and main rival (along with Grandmaster Theo) back in the days, grew up as Carlos Mandes. "It's Mandes," Charlie emphasized, "m-a-n-d-e-s. Not Méndez." Whatever the origin of his Puerto Rican name, ever since he started chasing the Flash Carlos Mandes has been known, by everyone, as Charlie Chase. He doesn't even like it when "Mandes" appears on the records he wrote. "Nobody knows my name was Carlos Mandes. They'd laugh. They'd snap on me."

Charlie might think that Mandes sounds corny now, but at the time the problem was that it didn't fit. He never tires of telling about how difficult it was to be accepted as a Puerto Rican in rap, especially as a deejay, and because he was so good. "A lot of Blacks would not accept that I was Spanish. You know, a lot of times because of the way I played they thought I was Black, because I rocked it so well." As a deejay he was usually seated in back, behind the emcees and out of sight. In the beginning, in fact, his invisibility was a key to success. "I became popular because of the tapes, and also because nobody could see me. Since they thought I was Black, you know, because I was in the background." Even when they saw him, he says that "they still wouldn't believe it. They are like, 'no, that's not him! That's bullshit! That's not him!' A few years went by and they accepted it, you know. I was faced with a lot of that. You know, being Hispanic you're not accepted in rap. Because to them it's a Black thing and something that's from their roots and shit."

"What the fuck are you doing here, Puerto Rican?" Charlie remembers being faced with that challenge time and again when he went behind the ropes, among the rappers, at the early jams. He had to prove himself constantly, and he recalls vividly the times when it took his homeboy Tony Tone from DJ Breakout and Baron to step in and save his skin. "I turn around and see him breaking on them and I hear what he's saying and I'm like, oh shit!" As tough as it got, though, Charlie knew very well that he wasn't out of place. "I was the type of kid that, you know, I always grew up with Black people.... My daughter's godfather is Black. He's like my brother, that guy."

But the best proof was that Charlie was with the Cold Crush Brothers, who were all Black. "We all grew up in the streets, man. It's like a street thing. Once you see that the guy is cool, then you're accepted, everything flows correctly." And it's not that Charlie just did everything like the other brothers, to fit in. Aside from his "mancha de plátano," those indelible earmarks of the Puerto Rican, he had his own personal style about him that he wasn't about to give up just to be one of the boys. He remembers about Cold Crush that "the only thing was, it was a trip when it came to the dressing bit. You see, I don't dress like the average hip-hopper and never did. They wanted to wear Kangols, Martin X, and these British walkers and all that stuff at the time, and I was like, that's not me, fellas. That's not me, man. At that time, I combed my hair back in a DA." Not only did he refuse to fit the mold, but Charlie's insistence helped the group arrive at the look that helped to establish their immense popularity in those years. "We came up with a look that everybody copied afterwards, which we all felt comfortable with. It was the leather and stud look, which we popularized in rap and through that look we became hard."

Besides, as alone as he was sometimes made to feel, Charlie knew that he wasn't the only Puerto Rican who was into rap. "Hispanics always liked rap, young Puerto Ricans were into it since the beginning. I wasn't the only one who felt the same way about music like that. There were plenty of them, but they didn't have the talent, they just enjoyed it. Me, I wanted to do it, you know. Forget it, there were plenty of people. I mean, when you grow up in the streets, it's a street thing, man." In its street beginnings, Puerto Ricans were an integral part of the rap scene, and not only as appreciative fans. Though their participation in production and performance was submerged (far more so than in breaking and graffiti), they were an essential and preponderant presence in the security crews that, in the gang environment, made the whole show possible. "It was rough, man," Charlie recalls.

All of my crew, the whole crew, were Spanish, maybe two or three Black guys. They were all Spanish, and when we jammed we had bats. If you crossed the line or got stupid, you were going to get batted down, alright? And that was that. That was my crew, they would help me with records, they were security. The guys in my group were Black, but the rest of the guys, security, were Hispanic.... People'd be like, yo, those are some wild Spanish motherfuckers. Don't mess with them, man.

But with a little coaxing Charlie will even call to mind some other Puerto Rican rappers from those days. There was Prince Whipper Whip and Ruby D (Rubén García) from the Fantastic Five, OC from the Fearless Four with Tito Cepeda, Johnny who was down with Master Don and the Def Committee. "Then there was this one group," Charlie recalls, "that wanted to do Latin rap songs, way back. And they had good ideas and they had great songs, but they just didn't have enough drive, you know? They had a great idea, they had a routine. They had these crazy nice songs, but they just weren't ambitious enough.... Robski and June Bug, those were the guys." Years before anybody started talking about "Latin rap," Robski and June Bug were busy working out Spanglish routines and even rendering some of the best rhymes of the time into Spanish. "They took our songs and translated them into Spanish. They blew our heads, man! It was weird, because they actually took everything we said and turned it into Spanish and made it rhyme. And they did a good job of it."

But in those days using Spanish in rap was still a rarity, especially in rhymes that were distributed on tapes and records. It wasn't only lack of ambition that prevented Robski and June Bug from making it, "'cause at that time," Charlie says, "a lot of people were doing it underground, but they couldn't come off doing it, they couldn't make money doing it. The people that did it, did it in parties, home stuff, the block, they were the stars in their ghetto." But Charlie himself, "chasing the Flash," was with the first rap group to be signed by CBS Records, the first rap group to tour Japan, the group that played in the first hip-hop movie, Wild Style. At that level, rapping in Spanish was still out of the question. Charlie explains what it was like for him to face this constraint, and gives a clear sense of the delicate generational process involved in the entry of bilingualism into commercially circumscribed rap discourse.

I always stressed the point that I was Hispanic doing rap music, but I couldn't do it in Spanish, you understand? But that was my way of opening the doors for everybody else to do what they're doing now. You see, there are certain degrees, certain levels and steps that you have to follow. And being that I was there at the very beginning, that was the I way I had to do it, That was my contribution. I feel sorry that I couldn't do it then, but I want to do it now and I'm making up for it, because now I can.... I wanted everybody to know that I was Spanish, rocking, ripping shit up. In a Black market.

At that early stage in negotiating Puerto Rican identity in rap, the key issue was not language but what Charlie calls "the Latin point of view"; pushing rhymes in Spanish was not yet part of the precarious juggling act.

For me it's the Latin point of view. You see, what I emphasize is that I'm Hispanic in a Black world. Not just surviving but making a name for myself and leaving a big impression. Everything that happened to me was always within the Black music business, and I always was juggling stuff all of the time, because I had to be hip, I had to be a homeboy. But I also had to know how far to go without seeming like I was trying to kiss up or something, or "he's just trying to be Black." When you deal with the people I deal with, especially at a time when rap was just hard core and raw, you're talking about guys who were títeres, you know, tough guys. I had to juggle that. I had to play my cards correct.

If Spanish wasn't yet part of the "Latin point of view," the music was, especially the rhythmic texture of the songs, which is where as the deejay Charlie was in control. He remembers sneaking in the beat from the number "Tú Coqueta," right "in the middle of a jam. I'm jamming. I throw that sucker in, just the beat alone, and they'd go off. They never knew it was a Spanish record. And if I told them that they'd get off the floor." Even the other rappers couldn't tell because the salsa cuts seemed to fit in so perfectly. "It was great! I would sneak in Spanish records. Beats only, and if the bass line was funky enough, I would do that too. Bobby Valentín stuff. He played bass with the Fania All-Stars, and he would do some funky stuff." As a bassist in Latin bands, Charlie knew the repertoire to choose from.

But he also knew that he had to walk a fine line and that he was ahead of his time, not only for the R&B-sawy rappers but for Latin musical tastes as well. In fact it was because of the resistance he faced from the Latin musicians, and not only the better pay, that Charlie decided to leave Los Giramundos and go into rap full time.

> Sometimes I'd go to gigs and in between songs I'd start playing stuff from rap music and the drummer would like it too, and he'd start doing some stuff. And sometimes people would get up to dance to it and the rest of the guys in the band would get furious at us, and they would say, "What are you doing? If you're not going to play a song, don't do it." They would break on me. They didn't want that stuff.

Not that Charlie didn't try to interest Latin musicians in mixing some elements of rap into their sound. He especially remembers working on a record concept with Willie Colón.

> He could have had the first Latin hip-hop record out and it would have been a hit. It was a singing rap. He was singing, right, there was a little bit of rap, and I was scratching. I did the arrangements. What happened was, the project was being held and held and held. What happened? He put out the record, an instrumental! He took out all the raps, then he overdubbed. Killed the whole project. He slept on it.

But as Charlie learned early on, when it comes to the emergence of new styles in popular music it's all a matter of timing. He himself had trouble relating to the use of Spanish in rap when he first heard it on record. Back in 1981 the group Mean Machine came out with the first recorded Spanish rhymes in their "Disco Dream," a side that deeply impressed some of the present-day Latino rappers like Mellow Man Ace and Latin Empire when they first heard it, though that was some years after it was released. But Charlie knew Mean Machine when they started and recalls his reaction when "Disco Dream" first came out. "It was strange, and it was new. At first I didn't jive with it because I was so used to it and I myself got so caught up in that whole R&B thing that when I heard that, it didn't click with me. And I was like, 'Naw, this is bullshit!'" But with time tastes changed, as did Charlie's understanding of himself and his own role. "And then," he goes on, "something made me realize one day that, wait a minute, man, look at you, what are you? You don't rap like they do, but you're Hispanic just like them, trying to get a break in the business. And I said, if anything, this is something cool and new."

Seen in retrospect, Mean Machine was only a faint hint of what was to become Latino rap in the years ahead. The Spanish they introduced amounted to a few party exhortations rather than an extended Spanish or bilingual text. Charlie draws this distinction, and again points up the changing generations of Latino presence in rap.

"The way that they did it was not like today. Today it's kind of political, opinionated, and commercial, and storytelling. What they did was that they took a lot of Spanish phrases, like 'uepa' and 'dale fuego a la lata, fuego a la lata,' stuff like that, and turned them into a record." However perfunctory their bilingualism and fleeting their acclaim, Mean Machine's early dabbling with Spanglish rhymes did plant a seed. Puerto Rock of Latin Empire attests to the impact "Disco Dream" had on them:

> They didn't continue. After one record, that was it. I know them all, we keep in contact. Mr. Schick came out with, "Tire su mano al aire / Yes, means throw your hands in the air / y siguen con el baile means / dance your body till you just don't care." And then it ended up with, "Fuego a la lata, fuego a la lata / agua que va caer." So we were like bugging! We were more or less doing it but in English and got crazy inspired when we heard that record. We was like, Oh, snap! He wrote the first Spanish rhyme! We was skeptical if it was going to work, and when we heard the record we were like, it's going to work).[3]

The disbelief and strategic invisibility that surrounded Latino participation in rap performance in the early years gave way to a fascination with something new and different. Charlie sees this process reflected in the changing fate of his own popularity among hip-hop audiences. "It was kind of complicated," he recalls. If at first he became popular because "nobody could see me," he later became even more popular because "everyone found out I was Hispanic. And it was like, 'yo, this kid is Spanish!' and 'What? Yo, we've got to see this!'" Once he began to feel this sense of curiosity and openness, a new stage appeared in rap history, and Charlie was quick to recognize its potential, commercially and politically. He tells of how his enthusiasm caught the attention among some of the Latin musicians, especially his friend Tito Puente, who seemed to be fondly reminded of their own breakthrough a generation before.

> These guys, they love it. Because for one, it's for them getting back out into the limelight again, you know, in a different market…. The musicians are very impressed to see that somebody like me wants to work with them in my style of music. And when I tell them about my history they are very impressed because in their day, when they came out, they were the same way. When Tito Puente came out, he was doing the mambo and it was all something new. It was all new to him, too. So he can relate to what I'm doing. And for him it's almost like a second coming.

After the decade it has taken for Puerto Rican rap to come into its own, Charlie now feels that the time is right for the two sides of his musical life to come together, and for full-fledged "salsa-rap" to make its appearance.

> For this next record I want to do a project, where I want to get all the East Coast rappers together, I want to get POW, I want to get Latin Empire, I want to get a few other guys that are unknown but that are good. I want to join them, I want to bring in Luis "Perico" Ortiz, I want to bring Tito, I want to bring Ray Barretto, you know. Bring them to handle all the percussion stuff and then my touch would be to bring in the rap loops, the beats, the bass lines, the programming. I'll program and also arrange it. And they will come in, Luis "Perico" would do the whole horn section, Tito would come in and handle all the percussion section, and Ray Barretto would handle the congas. And I would get my friend Sergio who is a tremendous piano player, a young kid, he's about twenty-four, twenty-five now, he works for David Maldonado. I just want to kick this door wide open, once and for all, and that's the way I'm going to do it.

As ambitious as such a project may sound, bringing together Puerto Rican musicians across musical traditions is only half of Charlie's strategy for promoting Latino unity. For "if any Hispanics want to make it in this business," he claims, "they've got to learn to pull together, no matter where you're coming from, or it's not going to work. It's not going to work, man. Kid Frost on the West Coast right now, he's got a little thing going. He and I are working around a few things. He's got his Latin Alliance on the West Coast. I've got a lot of Latin people who work with me on this. I'm trying to form something here where we can merge, cover the whole United States. That's the best way we can do it, if we unify."

Yet with his repeated emphasis on Latino unity, Charlie has more than commercial success in mind. His own experience, he now feels, leads him to set his sights on the political and educational potential of his musical efforts.

Because what I did, I had to unite with Black people to get my success and become Charlie Chase, "New York's Number One Puerto Rican DJ." Ironically, I did it with Black people. Which proves, man, that anybody can get together and do it. If I did it with Black people, then Hispanics can do it with Hispanics and do a much better job. That's my whole purpose right now. I mean, I have made my accomplishments, I have become famous doing my thing in rap, I have respect. Everybody knows me in the business. I have all of that already, man. I've tasted the good life, I've toured the world, I've done all of that. Now I want to do something meaningful and helpful. Hopefully, because a lot of kids are being steered the wrong way.

Puerto Rocks

Moving into the 1990s, then, the prospects and context have changed for Latino rap. Hugely popular albums like *Latin Alliance, Dancehall Reggaespañol* and *Cypress Hill* have been called a "polyphonic outburst" marking the emergence of "the 'real' Latin hip-hop." Kid Frost's assembly of Latin Alliance is referred to as "a defining moment in the creation of a nation-wide Latino/Americano hip-hop aesthetic." Unity of Chicanos and Puerto Ricans, which has long eluded politicos and admen, is becoming a reality in rap, and its potential impact on the culture wars seems boundless: "Where once the folks on opposite coasts were strangers, they've become one nation 'kicking Latin lingo on top of a scratch', samplin' substrate.... There is no question that we are entering an era when the multicultural essence of Latino culture will allow for a kind of shaking-out process that will help define the Next Big Thing."[4] Not only is the use of Spanish and bilingual rhyming accepted, but it has even become a theme in some of the best-known rap lyrics, like Kid Frost's "Ya Estuvo," Cypress Hill's "Funky Bi-lingo," and Latin Empire's "Palabras." Latino rappers are cropping up everywhere, from the tongue-twisting, "trabalengua" Spanglish of one Chicago-Rican group to the lively current of Tex-Mex rap in New Mexico and Arizona.[5] And it's not only the rappers themselves who have been building these bicultural bridges: Latin musical groups as varied as El Gran Combo, Wilfredo Vargas, Manny Oquendo's Libre, and Los Pleneros de la 21 have all incorporated rap segments and numbers into their repertoires.

But while he shares these high hopes, a seasoned veteran of "the business" like Charlie Chase remains acutely aware of the pitfalls and distortions involved. After all, he had witnessed firsthand what was probably the first and biggest scam in rap history, when Big Bad Hank and Sylvia Robinson of Sugar Hill Records used a rhyme by his close friend and fellow Cold Crush brother Grandmaster Cas on "Rapper's Delight" and never gave him credit. The story has been told elsewhere, as by Steven Hager in his book, but Charlie's is a lively version.

This is how it happened. Hank was working in a pizzeria in New Jersey, flipping pizza. And he's playing Cas' tape, right? Sylvia Robinson walks in, the president of Sugar Hill. She's listening to this, it's all new to her. Mind you, there were never any rap records. She says, "Hey, man, who's this?" He says, "I manage this guy. He's a rapper." She says, "Can you do this? Would you do this on a record for me?" And he said, "Yeah, sure. No problem." And she says, "Okay, fine." So he calls Cas up and says, "Cas, can I use your rhymes on a record? Some lady wants to make a record." You see what happened? Cas didn't have foresight. He couldn't see down the road. He never imagined in a million years what was going to come out of that. He didn't know, so he said, "Sure, fine, go ahead." With no papers, no nothing. And it went double platinum! Double platinum! "Rapper's Delight." A single. A double platinum single, which is a hard thing to do.

Charlie doesn't even have to go that far back to reflect on how commercial interests tend to glamorize and, in his word, "civilize" rap sources. He tells of his own efforts to land a job as an A&R (artist and repertoire) person with a record label. "All of this knowledge, all of this experience. I have the ear, I'm producing for all of these people. I mean, I know. You cannot get a more genuine person than me. I can't get a job." The gatekeepers of the industry could hardly be farther removed from the vitality of hip-hop. "I go to record labels to play demos for A&R guys that don't know a thing about rap. They talk to me and they don't even know who I am. White guys that live in L.A. Forty years old, thirty-five years old, making seventy, a hundred thousand a year, and they don't know a thing! And they're picking records to sell, and half of what they're picking is bullshit. And I'm trying to get somewhere and I can't do it."

As for promoting bilingual rap, the obstacles are of course compounded, all the talk of "pan-Latin unity" notwithstanding. "Not that long ago," Charlie mentions, "Latin Empire was having trouble with a Hispanic promoter at Atlantic Records who wouldn't promote their records. You know what he told them? (And he's a Latino.) He told them, 'Stick to one language.' And that's negative, man. You're up there, man, pull the brother up." And of course it's not only the limits on possible expressive idioms that signal a distortion but the media's ignorance of rap's origins. *Elle* magazine, for example, announced that Mellow Man Ace "has been crowned the initiator of Latin rap," their only evident source being Mellow Man himself: "I never thought it could be done. Then in 1985 I heard Mean Machine do a 20-second Spanish bit on their 'Disco Dream.' I bugged out." And the Spanish-language *Más* magazine then perpetuated the myth by proclaiming that it was Mellow Man Ace "quien concibió la idea de hacer rap en español" ("whose idea it was to do rap in Spanish").[6]

The problem is that in moving "from the barrio to *Billboard*," as Kid Frost puts it, Latino rappers have faced an abrupt redefinition of function and practice. The ten-year delay in the acceptance of Spanish rhymes was due in no small part to the marketing of rap, through the eighties, as a strictly African American musical style with a characteristically Afrocentric message. Charlie Chase confronted this even among some of his fellow rappers at the New Music Seminar in 1990 and appealed to his own historical authority to help set the record straight.

> I broke on a big panel. Red Alert, Serch from Third Base, Chuck D, the guys from the West Coast, these are all my boys, mind you, these are all of my friends. So I went off on these guys because they were like "Black this, and Black music," and I said "Hold it!" I jumped up and I said, "Hold up, man. What are you talking about, a Black thing, man? I was part of, the Cold Crush Brothers, man. We opened doors for all you guys." And the crowd went berserk, man. And I grabbed the mike and I just started going off. I'm like, "Not for nothing, man, but don't knock it. It's a street thing. I liked it because it came from the street and I'm from the street. I'm a product of the environment." I said that to Serch, I pointed to Serch, 'cause that's his record from his album. And I said, "Yo, man, rap is us. You're from the street, that's you man, that's rap. It ain't no Black, White or nothing thing, man. To me, rap is colorblind, that's that!" The niggahs were applauding me and stuff. I got a lot of respect for that.

Latin Empire has had to put forth the same argument in explaining their own project. As Rick Rodríguez aka "Puerto Rock" puts it, "When it comes to hip-hop I never pictured it with a color." They too are a "product of the environment" and see no need to relinquish any of their Puerto Rican background. "Our influence," Puerto Rock says, "is the stuff you see around you. Things you always keep seeing in the ghetto. But they don't put it in art. It's streetwise. The styles, the fashions, the music is not just for one group.

Everybody can do it. But too many Puerto Ricans don't understand. There's a big group of Latinos that's into hip-hop, but most of them imitate Black style or fall into a trance. They stop hanging out with Latin people and talking Spanish. I'm proving you can rap in Spanish and still be dope." Puerto Rock's cousin and partner in Latin Empire, Anthony Boston aka MC KT, has had to deal even more directly with this stereotype of rap, as he is often mistaken for a young African American and was raised speaking more English than Spanish. KT's rhymes in "We're Puerto Rican and Proud!" serve to clarify the issue:

> I rarely talk Spanish and a little trigueño
> People be swearin' I'm a moreno
> Pero guess what? I'm Puertorriqueño.
> Word'em up.
> All jokes aside, I ain't tryin' to dis any race
> And
>
> Puerto Rock
> He'll announce everyplace...
>
> M.C. KT
> That I'll perform at, so chill, don't panic
> It is just me, Antonio, another deso Hispanic.

To drive the point home, the initials KT stand for "Krazy Taino": "It's fly," Puerto rock comments. "With a 'K,' and the 'r' backwards like in Toys-"R"-Us. In our next video he's going to wear all the chief feathers and that. Nice image. With all the medallions and all that we've got. Like in Kid Frost in his video, he wears the Mexican things. That's dope, I like that. Tainos have a lot to do with Puerto Ricans and all that, so we're going to boost it up too. Throw it in the lyrics."

But KT didn't always signal the Puerto Rican cultural heritage, and in fact the derivation of their names shows that their struggle for identity has been a response against the stereotyped symbolism of rap culture. "MC KT is his name because before Latin Empire we were called the Solid Gold MCs. KT stood for karat, like in gold." The group gave up the faddish cliche Solid Gold because they had no jewelry and didn't like what it stood for anyway. When they started, in the early eighties, "We worked with a few different trend names. We started off with our name, our real names, our nicknames. Like Tony Tone, Ricky D, Ricky Rock, all of that. Everything that came out, Rick-ski, every fashion. Double T, Silver T, all of these wild Ts." After trying on all the conformist labels, Rick finally assumed the identity that was given him, as a Puerto Rican, in the African American hip-hop nomenclature itself; he came to affirm what marked him off. "And then I wound up coming up with Puerto Rock," he explains, "and I like that one. That's the one that clicked the most. The Puerto Ricans that are into the trend of hip-hop and all that, they call them Puerto Rocks. They used to see the Hispanics dressing up with the hat to the side and all hip-hop down and some assumed that we're supposed to just stick to our own style of music and friends. They thought rap music was only a Black thing, and it wasn't. Puerto Ricans used to be all crazy with their hats to the side and everything. So that's why they used to call the Puerto Ricans when they would see them with the hats to the side, 'Yo, look at that Puerto Rock, like he's trying to be down.' They used to call us Puerto Rocks, so that was a nickname, and I said, 'I'm going to stick . with that. Shut everybody up.' "

The name the group's members chose to replace Solid Gold was arrived at somewhat more fortuitously, but equally reflects their effort to situate themselves in an increasingly multicultural hip-hop landscape.

> Riding around in the car with our manager, DJ Corchado, we were trying to think of a Latin name. We was like, the Three Amigos, the Latin Employees, for real, we came up with some crazy names. We kept on, 'cause we didn't want to limit ourselves, with Puerto Rican something, yeah, the Puerto Rican MCs. We wanted Latin something, to represent all Latinos. So we was the Two Amigos, the Three Amigos, then we came up with many other names, Latin Imperials, Latin Alliance. And then when we were driving along the Grand Concourse my manager's car happened to hit a bump when I came out with the Latin Employees. Joking around, we were just making fun and when the car hit the bump my manager thought I said Empire." I was like, what? Latin Empire! I was like, yo, that's it! As soon as they said it, it clicked. It's like a strong title, like the Zulu Nation.

Groping for names that click, of course, is part of the larger process of positioning themselves in the changing cultural setting of the later eighties. The decision to start rhyming in Spanish was crucial and came more as an accommodation to their families and neighbors than from hearing Mean Machine or any other trends emerging in hip-hop. "In the beginning it was all in English and our families, all they do is play salsa and merengue, they thought you were American. They considered it noise. "'Ay, deja ese alboroto,' 'cut out that racket,' you know. We said, 'Let's try to do it in Spanish, so that they can understand it, instead of complaining to us so much.' They liked it. They was like, 'Oh, mi hijo.'" And when they tried out their Spanish with the mostly Black hip-hop audiences, they were encouraged further. "We used to walk around with the tapes and the big radios and the Black people behind us, 'Yo, man, that sounds dope, that's fly!' They be like, 'yo, I don't understand it, man, but I know it's rhyming and I hear the last word, man, that's bad' they be telling us. We was like, oh, snap! Then I used to try to do it in the street jams and the crowd went crazy."

Acceptance and encouragement from the record industry was a different story, especially in those times before Mellow Man Ace broke the commercial ice. Atlantic did wind up issuing "We're Puerto Rican and Proud," but not until after "Mentirosa" went gold, and then they dragged their feet in promoting it. Since then, aside from their tours and the video "Así Es la Vida" which made the charts on MTV International, Latin Empire has been back in the parks and community events. They believe strongly in the strong positive messages of some rap and have participated actively in both the Stop the Violence and Back to School campaigns. They pride themselves on practicing what they preach in their antidrug and antialcohol rhymes. They continue to be greeted with enthusiastic approval by audiences of all nationalities throughout New York City, and on their tours to Puerto Rico, the Dominican Republic, and, most recently, Cuba.

Their main shortcoming, in the parlance of the business, is that they don't have an "act," a packaged product. As the author of "The Packaging of a Recording Artist" in the July 1992 issue of *Hispanic Business* suggests, "To 'make it' as a professional recording act, you must have all the right things in place. Every element of what a recording act is must be considered and exploited to that act's benefit. The sound, the image, the look—all these factors must be integrated into a single package and then properly marketed to the public." In the packaging and marketing process, the artists and the quality of their work are of course secondary; it's the managers, and the other gatekeepers, who make the act. The article ends, "So while quality singing and a good song are the product in this business, they don't count for much without strong management."[7]

The pages of *Hispanic Business* make no mention of Latin Empire, concentrating as they do on the major Hispanic "products" like Gerardo, Expose, and Angelica. What they say about Kid Frost is most interesting because here they are dealing with a Latino rapper who is "on his way to stardom in the West Coast Hispanic community" and cannot be expected to "lighten up on who he is just to get that cross-over audience." Clearly the main danger of the artist crossing over is not, from this perspective, that he might thereby sacrifice his focus and cultural context, but that he could lose out on his segment of the market. "It's so tempting for an artist to do that once they've gained acceptance. But you risk losing your base when you do that and you never want to be without your core audience. That's why we work as a team and always include our artists and their managers in the packaging and marketing process."[8]

Latin Empire's members can't seem to get their "act" together because they remain too tied to their base to endure "strong management." Their mission, especially since rap "went Latin," is to reinstate the history and geography of the New York Puerto Rican contribution to hip-hop and counteract the sensationalist version perpetrated by the media. In some of their best-known numbers like "El Barrio," "Mi Viejo South Bronx" and "The Big Manzana," they take us deep into the Puerto Rican neighborhoods and back, "way back, to the days of *West Side Story*" when the New York style originated. Tracing the transition from the gang era to the emergence of the "style wars" of hip-hop, they tell their own stories and dramatize their constant juggling act between Black and Latino and between Island and New York cultures. In another rhyme, "Not Listed," they "take hip-hop to another *tamaño* [level]" by emphasizing the particular Puerto Rican role in rap history and countering the false currency given new arrivals. They end by affirming these ignored roots and rescuing the many early Puerto Rican rappers from oblivion:

> Y'all need to see a médico
> but we don't accept Medicaid
> we don't give no crédito
> we only give credit where credit is due
> we got to give it to the Mean Machine
> and the other brothers who were out there
> lookin' out for Latinos
> some kept it up, some chose other caminos
> but we can't pretend that they never existed
> cause yo, they were out there, just not listed.

In another of their rhymes Latin Empire's members address the music business itself, lashing out at the counterfeits and subterfuges facing them in their "hungry" battle for a fair record deal. Some of "Kinda Hungry" sounds like this:

Yeah that's right I'm hungry,

in other words, yo tengo hambre.

Those who overslept caught a calambre.

Fake mc's hogging up the posiciones,

but all we keep hearing is bullshit canciones.

Don't be feeding mis sueños.

You might be the head of A&R but I want to meet the dueños.

So I can let 'em know como yo me siento

and update 'em on the Latino movimiento

'cause I'm getting tired of imitadores

that shit is muerto, that's why I'm sending you flores,

En diferentes colores.

I'm like an undertaker...

I still don't understand how they allowed you to make a

rap record que no sirve para nada.

I'll eat 'em up like an ensalada.

Speakin' about food you want comida?

Na, that's not what I meant,

what I want is a record deal en seguida

so we can get this on a 24 track

put it out on the market and bug out on the feedback.

Huh, tú no te debas cuenta,

a nigga like me is in effect en los noventas.

Straight outta Vega Baja

the other candidates?

I knock 'em out the caja, knock 'em out the box

because I'm not relajando I truly feel it's time

I started eliminando mc's givin' us a bad nombre.

I can't see TNT nor my righthand hombre

the Krazy Taino sellin' out,

there's no way, there's no how,

that's not what we're about.

We're all about looking out for my gente,

here's some food for thought, comida para la mente.

With all their "hunger" for recognition, members of Latin Empire also feel the burden of responsibility for being the only Nuyorican rap group given any public play at all. They realize that, being synonymous with Puerto Rican rap, they are forced to stand in for a whole historical experience and for the rich variety of street rappers condemned to omission by the very filtering process that they are confronting. A prime example for them of the "not listed" is the "righthand hombre" mentioned here, MC TNT. Virtually unknown outside the immediate hip-hop community in the South Bronx, TNT is living proof that hardcore, streetwise rhyming continues and develops in spite of the diluting effects and choices of the managers and A&R departments. Frequently, Puerto Rock and KT have incorporated TNT into many of their routines, and his rhymes and delivery have added a strong sense of history and poetic language to their presentations.

Like Puerto Rock, TNT (Tomás Robles) was born in Puerto Rico and came to New York at an early age. But in his case, childhood in the rough neighborhoods on the Island figures prominently in his raps, as in this autobiographical section interlaced with samples from Rubén Blades's salsa hit "La Vida Te Da Sorpresas":

Este ritmo es un invento

Cuando empiezo a rimar le doy el roo por ciento

No me llamo Chico, o Federico

Dónde naciste? Santurce, Puerto Rico

Cuando era niño no salía'fuera

porque mataban diario en la cantera

Esto es verdad, realidad, no un engaño

mi pae murió cuando yo tenia seis años

La muerte me afectó con mucho dolor

pues mi mae empaquetó y nos mudamos pa' Nueva York

cuando llegué era un ambiente diferente

pero no me arrepentí, seguí para frente

y por las noches recé a Dios y a la santa

porque en mi corazón el coquí siempre canta.

[This rhyme is an invention / When I start to rhyme I give it 100 percent / My name isn't Chico or Federico / Where were you born? / Santurce, Puerto Rico / When I was a boy I didn't go out / 'cause there were killings / in the quarry every day / This is true, reality, not a hoax / my father died when I was six / his death caused me a lot of pain / well my mother packed up and we moved to New York / when I arrived it was a very different atmosphere / but I didn't regret it, I moved ahead / and at night I prayed to God and the holy mother / because in my heart the coquí frog always sings.]

By the late 1970s, as an adolescent, TNT was already involved in the gang scene in the South Bronx and took part in the formation of Tough Bronx Action and the Puerto Rican chapters of Zulu Nation. By that time he was already playing congas in the streets and schoolyards and improvising rhymes. When he first heard Mean Machine in 1981, he recalls, he already had note-books of raps in Spanish, though mostly he preserved them in his memory.

TNT also goes by the epithet "un rap siquiatra" ("a rap psychiatrist"): in his lively, story-telling rhymes he prides himself on his biting analysis of events and attitudes in the community. He responds to the charges of gangsterism by pointing to the ghetto conditions that force survival remedies on his people. "Livin' in a ghetto can turn you 'to a gangster" is one of his powerful social raps, and in "Get Some Money" he addresses the rich and powerful directly: "he threw us in the ghetto to see how long we lasted / then he calls us a little ghetto bastard." His "Ven acá tiguerito tiguerito," which compares with anything by Kid Frost and Latin Alliance in sheer verbal ingenuity, captures the intensity of a combative street scene in El Barrio and is laced with phrases from Dominican slang. His programmatic braggadocio is playful and ragamuffin in its effect, yet with a defiance that extends in the last line to the very accentuation of the language:

> Soy un rap siquiatra un rap mecánico
>
> óyeme la radio y causo un pánico
>
> te rompo el sistema y te dejo inválido
>
> con un shock nervioso te ves bien pálido
>
> no puedes con mi rap
>
> aléjate aléjate
>
> tómate una Contact y acuéstate
>
> o llame a los bomberos que te rescaten.
>
> [I'm a rap psychiatrist, a rap mechanic hear me on the radio and I cause a panic / I break your system and I leave you an invalid / with a nervous shock you look pretty pale / you can't deal with my rap / go away, go away / take a Contac and go to bed / or call the firefighters to come rescue you.]

By the mid-1990s, at twenty-five, MC TNT was already a veteran of Spanish rap battles, still "unlisted" and awaiting his break, yet constantly working on his rhymes and beats every moment he can shake off some of the pressure. He is the closest I have run across to a rapper in the tradition of Puerto Rican plena music, since like that of the master *pleneros* his work is taking shape as a newspaper of the barrios, a running, ironic commentary on the untold events of everyday Puerto Rican life. When all the talk was of referendums and plebiscites to determine the political status of Puerto Rico, TNT had some advice for his people to contemplate:

> Puerto Rico, una isla hermosa,
>
> donde nacen bonitas rosas,
>
> plátanos, guineos y yautía,
>
> Sasón Goya le da sabor a la comida.
>
> Y ¿quién cocina más que la tía mía?

Pero el gobierno es bien armado,

tratando de convertirla en un estado.

Es mejor la dejen libre (asociado?).

Cristóbal Colón no fue nadie,

cruzó el mar con un bonche de salvajes.

Entraron a Puerto Rico rompiendo palmas,

asustando a los caciques con armas.

Chequéate los libros, esto es cierto.

pregúntale a un cacique pero ya está muerto.

¿Cómo él descubrió algo que ya está descubierto?

Boricua, ¡no te vendas!

[Puerto Rico, a beautiful island / where there are pretty roses, / plantains, bananas, and root vegetables, / Goya seasoning gives the food flavor / And who cooks better than my own aunt? / But the government is well armed, / trying to convert it into a state / It's better to leave it free (associated?) / Christopher Columbus was nobody, / he crossed the sea with a bunch of savages, / they entered Puerto Rico destroying the palm trees, / terrifying the Indian chiefs with their weapons. / Check out the books, this is true, / ask one of the Indian chiefs but they're already dead. / How could he discover something already discovered? / Puerto Rico, don't sell yourself!]

Like other Latino groups, Puerto Ricans are using rap as a vehicle for affirming their history, language, and culture under conditions of rampant discrimination and exclusion. The explosion of Spanish-language and bilingual rap onto the pop music scene in recent years bears special significance in the face of the stubbornly monolingual tenor in today's public discourse, most evident in the crippling of bilingual programs and services and in the ominous gains of the "English Only" crusade. And of course along with the Spanish and Spanglish rhymes, Latino rap carries an ensemble of alternative perspectives and an often divergent cultural ethos into the mainstream of U.S. social life. The mass diffusion, even if only for commercial purposes, of cultural expression in the "other" language, and above all its broad and warm reception by fans of all nationalities, may help to muffle the shrieks of alarm emanating from the official culture whenever mention is made of "America's fastest-growing minority." Latin rap lends volatile fuel to the cause of "multiculturalism" in our society, at least in the challenging, inclusionary sense of that embattled term.

For Puerto Ricans, though, rap is more than a newly opened window on their history; rap is their history, and Puerto Ricans are an integral part in the history of hip-hop. As the "Puerto rocks" themselves testify in conversation and rhyme, rapping is one of many domains within a larger field of social and creative practices expressive of their collective historical position in the prevailing relations of power and privilege. Puerto Rican participation in the emergence of hip-hop music needs to be understood in direct, interactive relation to their experience in gangs and other forms of association among inner-city youth through the devastating blight of the seventies. "Puerto rocks" are the children of impoverished colonial immigrants facing even tougher times than in earlier decades. They helped make rap what it was to become, as they played a constitutive role in the stylistic definition of graffiti writing and breakdancing.

In addition to these more obvious associations, the formative years of rap follow closely the development of both salsa and Nuyorican poetry, expressive modes which, especially for the young Puerto Ricans themselves, occupy the same creative constellation as the musical and lyrical project of bilingual and bicultural rap. Musically, rap practice among Puerto Ricans is also informed by the strong antecedent tradition of street drumming and, at only a slight remove, their parallel earlier role in styles like doo-wop, boogaloo, and Latin jazz. In terms of poetic language, Spanglish rap is embedded in the everyday speech practices of the larger community over the course of several generations, and even echoes in more than faint ways the tones and cadences of lyrics typical of plena, bomba, and other forms of popular Puerto Rican song.

Like these other contemporaneous and prefiguring cultural practices, the active presence of Puerto Ricans in the creation of rap bears further emphatic testimony to their long history of cultural interaction with African Americans. Hip-hop emerged as a cultural space shared by Puerto Ricans and Blacks, a sharing that once again articulates their congruent and intermingling placement in the impinging political and economic geography. It is also a sharing in which, as the story of rap reveals, the dissonances are as telling as the harmonies, and the distances as heartfelt as the intimacy. The Puerto Ricans' nagging intimation that they are treading on Black turf and working in a tradition of performative expression most directly traceable to James Brown and Jimmy Castor, the dozens and the blues, makes rap into a terrain that is as much contested as it is coinhabited on equal terms. Jamaican dubbing, with its strong Caribbean resonance, serves as a bridge in this respect, just as reggae in more recent years is helping to link rap to otherwise disparate musical trends, especially in its reggaespañol dance-hall versions. In the historical perspective of Black and Puerto Rican interaction, rap is thus a lesson in cultural negotiation and transaction as much as in fusions and crossovers, especially as those terms are bandied about in mainstream parlance. If multiculturalism is to amount to anything more than a wishful fancy of a pluralist mosaic, the stories of the "Puerto rocks" show that adequate account must be taken of the intricate jostling and juggling involved along the seams of contemporary cultural life.

What is to become of Latino rap, and how we appreciate and understand its particular messages, will depend significantly on the continuities it forges to its roots among the "Puerto rocks." Recuperating this history, explicitly or by example, and "inventing" a tradition divergent from the workings of the commercial culture, makes for the only hope of reversing the instant amnesia that engulfs rap and all forms of emergent cultural discourse as they migrate into the world of pop hegemony. Charlie Chase, TNT, and the other "Puerto rocks" were not only pioneers in some nostalgic sense but helped set the social meaning of rap practice prior to and relatively independent of its mediated commercial meaning. That formative participation of Latinos in rap in its infancy is a healthy reminder that the "rap attack," as Peter Toop argued some years ago now, is but the latest outburst of "African jive," and that the age-old journey of jive has always been a motley and inclusive procession. And as in Cuban-based salsa, the Puerto Rican conspiracy in the present volley shows how creatively a people can adopt and adapt what would seem a "foreign" tradition and make it, at least in part, its own. To return to the first "Puerto rock" I talked with in the early 1980s, I close with a little rhyme by MC Rubie Dee (Rubén García) from the South Bronx:

> Now all you Puerto Ricans you're in for a treat,
> 'cause this Puerto Rican can rock a funky beat.
> If you fall on your butt and you start to bleed,

Rubie Dee is what all the Puerto Ricans need.

I'm a homeboy to them 'cause I know what to do,

'cause Rubie Dee is down with the black people too.[9]

NOTES

1. Quotes of Charlie Chase are from my interview with him, "It's a Street Thing!" published in *Calalloo* 15.4 (Fall 1992): 999–1021.

2. See my article, written in 1984, "Rappin', Writin' and Breakin': Black and Puerto Rican Street Culture in New York City" *Dissent* (Fall 1987): 580–84 (also published in *Centro Journal* 2.3 [Spring 1988]: 34–41). A shortened version of the present chapter appeared as " 'Puerto Rican and Proud, Boy-ee!': Rap, Roots, and Amnesia," in Tricia Rose and Andrew Ross, eds., *Microphone Fiends: Youth Music and Youth Culture*, pp. 89–98 (New York: Routledge, 1994). Other references are Craig Castleman, *Getting Up: Subway Graffiti in New York* (Cambridge: MIT Press, 1982); Herbert Kohl, *Golden Boy as Anthony Cool: A Photo Essay on Naming and Graffiti* (New York: Dial, 1972); Steven Hager, *Hip-Hop: The Illustrated History of Break Dancing, Tap Music, and Graffiti* (New York: St. Martin's, 1984). See also David Toop, *The Rap Attack: African Jive to New York Hip-Hop* (Boston: South End, 1984).

3. Quotes from Latin Empire are from my interview with them, "Puerto Raps," published in *Centro Journal* 3.2 (Spring 1991): 77–85.

4. Ed Morales, "How Ya Like Nosotros Now?" *Village Voice*, November 26, 1991, 91.

5. For an overview of Latino rap, see Mandolit del Barco, "Rap's Latino Sabor," in William Eric Perkins ed., *Droppin' Science: Critical Essays on Rap Music and Hip-Hop Culture* (Philadelphia: Temple University Press, 1996), 63–84.

6. Elizabeth Hanley, "Latin Raps: Nuevo ritmo, A New Nation of Rap Emerges," *Elle*, March 1991, 196–98: C.A., "El rap latino tienetumbao" *Más* 2.2 (Winter 1990): 81.

7. Joseph Roland Reynolds, "The Packaging of a Recording Artist," *Hispanic Business* 14.7 (July 1992): 28–30.

8. Ibid.

9. Cited in Flores, "Rappin', Writin', and Breakin'."

Guthrie P. Ramsey, Jr.

Chapter

8

Scoring a Black Nation

We make our lives in identifications with the texts around us everyday.

**—Anahid Kassabian Hearing Film:
Tracking Identifications in Contemporary
Hollywood Film Music**

The 1990s will be remembered as a boom decade for black popular culture. One might say that like New Negroes in the 1920s, African American performers were in vogue. By the century's end, black expressive culture had become a pervasive factor in American society, fixed indelibly to the country's cultural profile. African American entertainers of all stripes are a commanding presence in the culture. In the post–*Cosby Show* era, cable television serves up a steady diet of situation comedies starring African American casts, whose exaggerated performances sometimes come dangerously close to worn-out, reliable stereotypes. Trumpeter and composer Wynton Marsalis, whose tireless efforts to put jazz on an equal social standing with Western art music, has been recognized with the most important distinctions and awards, including the prestigious Pulitzer Prize for composition in 1997.

We celebrate and reward black sports figures such as basketball player Shaquille O'Neal with huge sala-ries, unprecedented media visibility, prestige, iconic status, and power. The talk show diva Oprah Winfrey reigns over daytime programming. She attracts a diverse international audience and commands a paycheck that surpasses even NBA MVPs.[1] Whether executing a virtuoso instrumental passage, or dunking basket-balls, or chatting it up through tears and self-help philosophies, or slapsticking through formulaic situa-tion comedies, the early-twenty-first-century black performer is visible and getting paid.[2]

Of all these entertainment activities, the musical arts is perhaps the one in which African Americans ex-acted the greatest influence by century's end. The importance of their music can be felt in many realms of American society as well as globally. For one, music scholars no longer have to apologize or hide their passion for this music; they can earn academic credentials and advance professionally by writing about this topic. Furthermore, scholars in other disciplines have also found these musical genres rich in what they teach us about larger issues in culture and society. And African American musicians are a commanding presence in the marketplace: top-selling artists routinely sign multimillion-dollar contracts, and their fans fill stadiums and consume heavily promoted CDs by their favorite artists.

Black musical styles show up routinely as topics in the culture wars. Politicians of all persuasions have used the music to score rhetorical points with their various constituencies. Some comment on rap music's nihil-ism or debate whether it is music at all. Critics haggle over whether jazz is enjoying a renaissance or is a dead art. The demise of the American family, the angst of black middle-class citizens, juvenile delinquency, inner-city decline, the commodification of Jesus' gospel on *Billboard*'s rhythm and blues charts, and many other indictments have been saddled to the back of black popular music.

While many of the progeny of race music styles continued to flourish throughout the latter half of the century, certainly, the most prominent and controversial of these musical expressions in the 1990s proliferated under the cultural umbrella called hip-hop. If the 1920s were dubbed the Jazz Age and the 1960s marked the as-cendancy of rock, then a strong case can be made for calling the last decades of the twentieth century the Age

---

of Hip-Hop. Hip-hop culture is virtually everywhere: television, radio, film, magazines, art galleries, and in "underground" culture. It has even surfaced in congressional hearings. And even where hip-hop culture is not found, its absence may also be understood as a reaction against it. Wynton Marsalis and a host of other critics, for example, have positioned their musical work against hip-hop's musical and thematic conventions.

In the next two chapters, I explore two very important sites of cultural memory: the medium of film and the dynamic and contested cultural space we refer to as the black church. Rather than solely providing the typical biographical profiles and extensive discussions of hip-hop's canonical figures and musical works that one expects in a musicological study, I approach musical practice in the Age of Hip-Hop from a slightly different angle. I am interested in exploring not only what a musical performance means but also how it achieves a particular signifying inflection. Thus, in the same way that I used family narrative and the theater of the literary, I explore film and the church as two community theaters in which music or discourse about music inform the social reality of historical actors. Within these cultural contexts and social settings lies one of the keys to unlocking the door to meaning.

Although film and the black church may seem unrelated, they both provided twentieth-century African American culture with important contexts for the working out of cultural representation, social class debates, gender performance, spirituality, and various other issues associated with identity. Musical practice operates as an important medium for the circulation of social energy in film and in the church world. Below, I discuss how this is achieved in the content and context of hip-hop culture.

What Is Hip-Hop Culture and Practice?

Hip-hop culture, according to Tricia Rose, one of the foremost scholars to address the topic, consists of three modes of expression: rap music, graffiti writing, and break dancing. It emerged, she writes, "as a source for youth of alternative identity formation and social status."[3] Disenfranchised youth created fashions, language, and musical and bodily performance styles and formed elaborate networks of posses (or crews) that expressed their local identities and affiliations through these modalities. While the origins of hip-hop expressions can be traced to specific locations, its mass-media coverage and broad-based consumption made it one of the most widely known popular musics of the late twentieth century.[4]

Rapping itself denotes a vocal performance in which a rapper uses spoken or semispoken declamations, usually in rhyming couplets. The "rap" is revolutionary: rather than a singing or instrumental performance, in this genre the rap is the emotional focal point of the presentation. The idea of rapping has deep roots in African American culture. Its stylistic and thematic predecessors are numerous: the dozens and toasting traditions from America and Jamaica; sing-song children's games; double-dutch chants; black vernacular preaching styles; the jazz vocalese of King Pleasure, Eddie Jefferson, and Oscar Brown, Jr.; the on-the-air verbal virtuosity of black DJs; scat singing; courtship rituals; the lovers' raps of Isaac Hayes, Barry White, and Millie Jackson; the politicized storytelling of Gil Scott-Heron and the Last Poets; and the preacherly vocables of Ray Charles, James Brown, and George Clinton, among many others. Historians of rap music trace its present-day form, however, to the mid-1970s hip-hop culture of African American and Afro-Caribbean youth living in the South Bronx and upper Manhattan neighborhoods of New York City. The commercial origins of rap began in earnest with the 1979 hit recording "Rapper's Delight," by the Sugarhill Gang.[5]

In the early days of contemporary rap, DJs working in clubs, parks, and local parties would establish reputations by mixing the beats and snippets of sound from various recordings to encourage their audiences to dance. Some of these DJs would perform simple "raps," a practice that soon became more and more complex. MCs (taken from the term *master of ceremonies*) or rappers specializing in the vocal performance of this convention emerged. Within this division of labor, the MCs became the focus of the performance, and they raised the artistic stakes in this realm by creating very elaborate lyrical feats. DJs also elevated the artistic demands in their performance realm: as technology became more sophisticated, DJs began to create stunning rhythm tracks by taking recorded "samples" from a variety of sources, mixing them in inventive ways over which rappers would perform dense, lyrical narratives. Over the last twenty years, rappers and producers (DJs) have developed many satellite idioms, each having specific stylistic traits that signify meaning in particular ways. Changes have occurred in all realms of rap music: in the lyrical focus, body languages, rhythm tracks, slang, and fashions. Regional styles emerged in much the same way as they did in other forms of black popular music of the twentieth century. Rap music and its attendant expressions became so prominent that by the mid-1980s they captured the imaginations of filmmakers.

Film, Music, and Hip-Hop Culture

The medium of film has communicated, shaped, reproduced, and challenged various notions of black subjectivity in twentieth- and twenty-first-century America since D. W. Griffith's *Birth of a Nation* appeared in 1915. Writing in 1949, Ralph Ellison argued that *Birth of a Nation* "forged the twin screen image of the Negro as bestial rapist and grinning, eye-rolling clown—stereotypes that are still with us today."[6] Such depictions in cinema had already existed in print media; and they persisted in all mass-media contexts in varying degrees throughout the twentieth century.

Film, however, has provided a most salient medium for the visual representation of African American subjects. Cultural critic James A. Snead has written persuasively about the power of film and how it helps to shape both social reality and personal experience in this regard. "Even in the infancy of motion pictures, it was obvious that film, as a way of perceiving reality, opened up entirely new perceptual possibilities, giving the eye an augmented sense of visual mastery over its surroundings, preserving events in motion for a seemingly unlimited number of future replays, performing a wide variety of functions: education, propagandistic, recreational, aesthetic." If, as Manthia Diawara has argued, the camera is "the most important invention of modern time," then it becomes an even more powerful tool when its technology is combined with the powers of music. Indeed, when filmmakers combine cinematic images and musical gestures, they unite two of our most compelling modes of perception: the visual and the aural.

Below I consider three films produced during the Age of Hip-Hop: Spike Lee's *Do the Right Thing* (1989), John Singleton's *Boyz N the Hood* (1991), and Theodore Witcher's *Love Jones* (1997).[7] These films form a suggestive, if uneven, trio. *Do the Right Thing* takes place on the East Coast, in the multiethnic Bedford-Stuyvesant neighborhood of Brooklyn, New York. *Boyz N the Hood* paints a poignant picture of the emergence of "gangsta' land" South Central Los Angeles. *Love Jones* is situated in the heartland, in upwardly mobile Chicago. On an immediate level, I am interested in how music shapes the way we perceive these cinematic narratives individually; how music informs the way audiences experience their characters, locations, and plots. But I am also making a larger argument for how the musical scores of these films are sites for the negotiation of personal identity and self-fashioning, on the one hand, and the making and negotiation of group identity, on the other. Both of these activities inform "meaning" in important ways. Finally, I use this analysis to learn more about the process of "making" meaning in hip-hop musical practice generally.

Below, I address several questions with regard to this cinematic function of music in hip-hop film. What role does musical discourse play in cinematic representation? If one of the primary thrusts of black cultural production has been the resistance to and countering of negative black stereotypes forwarded since *Birth of a Nation*, how does the musical score of the film participate in this agenda? How does the music score or artistically (re)invent a black cinematic nation? The musical scores of *Do the Right Thing*, *Boyz N the Hood*, and *Love Jones* provide excellent examples of the fluidity and contestation embedded in the notion of black identity, a topic that became very compelling for theoretical, political, and artistic reflection in the late twentieth century. Before moving to the music in these films, I need to address an important topic raised in most discussions of them: the degree to which they accurately portray an "authentic" black cultural experience.

Keeping It Reel: Diversity, Authenticity, and the Hip-Hop Muze

Hip-hop culture has taken on the profile of a cottage industry because of aggressive corporate commodification. The postindustrial decline of United States urban centers, a downward turn that ironically spawned hip-hop's developments, has been co-opted by corporate America and represented as a glossy, yet gritty, complex of music idioms, sports imagery, fashion statements, racial themes, danger, and pleasure. While history shows us the persistence of the exploitation of African American culture in the United States, hip-hop represents an exemplary case in this regard. As the historian Robin D. G. Kelley argues:

> Nike, Reebok, L.A. Gear, and other athletic shoe conglomerates have profited enormously from postindustrial decline. TV commercials and print ads romanticize the crumbling urban spaces in which African American youth must play, and in so doing they have created a vast market for overpriced sneakers. These televisual representations of "street ball" are quite remarkable; marked by chain-link fences, concrete playgrounds, bent and rusted netless hoops, graffiti-scrawled walls, and empty buildings, they have created a world where young black males do nothing *but* play.[8]

The omnipresence of such imagery in the media has made a strong impact on notions of "authenticity" in African American culture. And moreover, music and musical practices continue to play a crucial role in the creation, renegotiation, and critique of the authenticity trope.

The intersection of hip-hop musical practices and film serves as a cogent example. Hollywood in the early 1990s presented young fans with films like *New Jack City*, *Boyz N the Hood*, *Strictly Business*, and *juice*, among others. Taken together, these films have helped to create a highly recognizable hip-hop mode of representing a one-dimensional black youth culture. As filmmaker Spike Lee notes, these "inner-city homeboy revues" created a world in which "all black people lived in ghettos, did crack and rapped."[9] As thematic heirs of the 1970s blaxploitation genre of film, the 1990s version has been dubbed "rapsploitation," or, as Henry Louis Gates, Jr., has labeled it, "guiltsploitation." Gates uses the latter term to characterize what he sees as a key message underlying many of these films: ambiguity about upward mobility. His observations about class status and black mobility are worth noting: "The politics of black identity, and the determined quest to reconcile upward mobility with cultural 'authenticity,' is a central preoccupation of these films. If genuine black culture is the culture of the streets, a point on which the blaxploitation films were clear, how can you climb the corporate ladder without being a traitor to your race? What happens when homeboy leaves home? A new genre—guiltsploitation—is born."[10] Gates sees this trend as directly linked to the attitudes and backgrounds of the filmmakers. Rapsploitation of the early 1990s occurred, in part, because of an emergence of young, black, college-educated, and middle-class directors. Gates argues that these auteurs did not choose to close "the gulf between the real black people behind the camera and the characters they've assembled in front of it."[11]

Critics have also raised questions beyond this underlying class-status tension, questions with respect to gender issues in these films. Feminist critics such as Valerie Smith, Michele Wallace, bell hooks, Wahneema Lubiano, and Jacquie Jones, among others, have noted that the perceived "realness" of the rapsploitation film genre is also real hostile to black women. But the class-based and feminist critiques of these films are sometimes difficult to articulate because of the compelling nature of the film experience itself and what Smith has identified as a documentary impulse. Wallace, for example, admitted: "The first time I saw John Singleton's *Boyz N the Hood*, I was completely swept away by the drama and the tragedy. It was like watching the last act of *Hamlet* or *Titus Andronicus* for the first time. When I left the theater, I was crying for all the dead black men in my family."[12] Upon subsequent viewings, however, Wallace noticed the strain of misogyny running throughout much of the film. She perceived that *Boyz* and other films like it seemed to be saying that the dismal social conditions depicted in these films were due to character flaws in the women.

Feminist critic Valerie Smith has argued that a documentary impulse authenticates these films with claims that they represent the "real." They achieve this documentary aura through an uncritical use of various aural and visual markers of "real" black living conditions, reproducing stereotypical ideas about African Americans. The boundaries separating fact and fiction, truth and artistic invention, become blurred. Smith notes that critics, reviewers, and press kits assure audiences that these black male directors were "endangered species" themselves and are thus "in positions of authority relative to their material."[13]

While the importance of film cannot be dismissed, we should be careful to recognize the difference between cinematic entertainment and the "truth" of lived experience. There does not exist a one-to-one homology between lived experience and representations of such in film. At the same time, we should keep in mind that the same social energy that sustains ideologies like misogyny and other forms of discrimination also circulates in the narratives of these films. In other words, these directors didn't invent the misogyny, but they help to reproduce it. In this sense, they—perhaps unconsciously—kept it real, as the saying goes.

Writer Lisa Kennedy has argued that the complex of money, narrative, and pleasure bound up in film experiences makes them "extraordinarily powerful." Film, she writes, "is how America looks at itself." Nonetheless, she warns us against confusing the "individual vision" of an artist like a filmmaker with "the" collective reality of a group of people. Despite this warning, the dialogic interplay between "real" lived experience and film narratives (and for that matter, television shows, news programs, independent documentaries, print media, and music) remains an important fact of early twenty-first century life. In the case of film, "the real lives of people are substantiated by their reel lives."[14]

And as I will argue over the next few pages, the nexus of "reel life" and music and musical practices has import on the topic of black music and meaning. What interests me here is not so much the critique of monolithic representations of black class status and life expectations represented in these films. Nor do I want to question Hollywood's capital-driven fixation to exploit these topics. Rather, I want to explore film as one way to enter into an analysis of the intersection of black identity and musical practice. When writers, directors, producers, and composers work together to create convincing characters and story worlds for audiences, they do so with the help of musical codes that circulate and in some ways create cultural knowledge, in the present case about how "blackness" is experienced in the social world at the historical moment in question.

What's the Score?: Defining the Parameters and Functions of Music in Film

Before turning to the specific films in question, it is necessary to provide a brief overview of how music in cinema works generally. Broadly speaking, music works to enhance the story world of the film; it deepens the audience's experience of the narrative and adds continuity to the film's scene-by-scene progression, providing what Claudia Gorbman calls the "bath of affect."[15] Anahid Kassabian argues that the study of music in film should not be an afterthought to what might be considered the more important areas of plot and characterization: "Music draws filmgoers into a film's world, measure by measure. It is . . . at least as significant as the visual and narrative components that have dominated film studies. It conditions identification processes, the encounters between film texts and filmgoers' psyches."[16]

The music in contemporary Hollywood films divides into two broad categories. The first is the composed score, which consists of music written specifically for the film. The second category is the compiled score: songs collected from sources that often preexisted the film. According to Kassabian, these two modes of musical address are designed to generate different responses from the perceiver. The composed score, she argues, is usually associated with the classical Hollywood score and encourages "assimilating identifications"; that is, it helps to "draw perceivers into socially and historically unfamiliar positions, as do larger scale processes of assimilation."[17]

The scoring techniques of the classical Hollywood cinema can achieve this end because of their unconscious familiarity to filmgoers: They have become naturalized through constant repetition. With few exceptions, the musical language of nineteenth-century Romanticism forms the "core musical lexicon" of American films. Music's cultural and cinematic work depends on its ability to signify an emotion, a location, a personality type, a frightening situation, and so on. The specific musical language of nineteenth-century Romanticism works well in this function, because it has been used in this way repeatedly since the 1930s. This repetition has produced a desired result in film scores, since, as Gorbman notes, "a music cue's signification must be instantly recognized as such in order to work."[18]

We can experience the hallmarks of these scoring techniques in the classic Hollywood film *In This Our Life*.[19] As the opening credits roll in this black-and-white film, we hear Max Steiner's familiar orchestral strains, typical of films during this era. The string section bathes the soundscape with sweeping melodies and a Wagnerian orchestral lushness that signals to the audience intense emotion and melodrama. Throughout the film, orchestral codes sharpen our perception of characters' interior motivations, propel the narrative forward, and help to provide smooth transitions between edits. During the plot exposition of the film, for example, we met the vixen Stanley, played by the inimitable queen of melodrama Bette Davis. Although the other characters' dialogues have revealed some of her less than desirable personal qualities, the orchestral strains of the score reveal to the audience much more than mere plot exposition could ever suggest. In her first appearance, Stanley drives up to the house with a male passenger. Viewers hear an ominous-sounding minor chord that is scored in the lower registers of the sounding instruments. As it turns out, the male passenger is her sister's husband, a man with whom Stanley is having a torrid affair. After a brief dialogue between the two reveals Stanley's manipulative personality—emphasized, of course, with melodramatic orchestral passages—the score transitions into animated rhythmic gestures that dissolve into an ascending pizzicato string passage as Stanley leaves the car and bounds up the steps into the family's spacious Victorian home. The music has helped to situate us in the plot and to identify with its characters despite our own subject positions, which may be quite different from those depicted in the film.

The compiled score, a staple feature of many Hollywood films since the 1980s, brings with it "the immediate threat of history."[20] It encourages perceivers to make external associations with the song in question, and these associations become part of the cultural transaction occurring between the film and its audience. Compiled scores produce what Kassabian calls "affiliating identifications." The connections that perceivers make depend on the relationship they have developed with the songs outside the context of the film experience. "If offers of assimilating identifications try to narrow the psychic field," Kassabian argues, "then offers of affiliating identifications open it wide."[21] The discussion that follows will explore how such distinctions bear on the interpretation of music in hip-hop film, a body of cinema having obvious and strong associations with a genre of music that has a discrete history.

Both the classic score's and the compiled score's relationship to the story world of the film can be divided into two primary modes of presentation: diegetic and nondiegetic music. Diegetic (or source) music is produced from within the perceived narrative world of the film. By constrast, nondiegetic music, that is, music produced from outside the story world of the film, serves the narration by signaling emotional states, propelling dramatic action, depicting a geographical location or time period, among other factors. Most of the music in a film fits into this category. Another kind of musical address in film blends the diegetic and nondiegetic. Earle Hagen calls this type of film music source scoring. In source scoring the musical cue can start out as diegetic but then change over to nondiegetic. This often occurs with a shift in the cue's relationship to onscreen events, usually when the narrative world and the musical score demonstrate a much closer fit.[22] With these ideas about music in film in mind, I turn to Spike Lee's now classic film *Do the Right Thing*.

Do the Right Thing

As I stated above, Griffith's *Birth of a Nation* stands as the symbolic, beginning of American cinema, providing a grammar book for Hollywood's historical (and unquestionably negative) depiction of black subjects. Likewise, Spike Lee's *Do the Right Thing* (hereafter *DTRT*) may be viewed as a kind of Ur-text for black representation in the so-called ghettocentric, New Jack flicks of the Hip-Hop Era. This film is important for a number of reasons. Lee succeeded in showing powerful Hollywood studios that this new genre of comparatively low-budget films could be profitable to the major studios. *DTRT*'s popular and critical reception (it earned millions and an Academy Award nomination) caused Lee's star to rise to such a degree that he became the most visible black filmmaker of the past decade. Hollywood studios tried to duplicate *DTRT*'s success, thus allowing other black directors access to the Hollywood production system, albeit within predictably prescribed limits.[23] Lee's use of rap music (and some of the musical practices associated with it) demonstrated how it could be used to depict a range of associations. Some of these include black male and female subjectivity, ethnic identity, a sense of location, emotional and mental states, a specific historical moment, and the perspectives of age groups. In these realms, *DTRT* cast a long shadow over the repertory of acceptable character types, plots, and themes in subsequent ghettocentric films during the Age of Hip-Hop.

Scoring the Right Thing

DTRT conforms to some of the conventions of classical Hollywood cinema discussed above but with marked differences. Victoria E. Johnson has recognized the importance of music in *DTRT*, calling it Lee's most musical film.[24] Johnson identifies two primary modes of musical rhetoric in the score. What she calls the "historic-nostalgic" strain encompasses, for the most part, orchestral music written by Lee's father, Bill Lee. The sound is reminiscent of some of the chamber music by African American composer William Grant Still—quaint, genteel, and staid. Interestingly, Branford Marsalis's jazz-inflected saxophone and Terrance Blanchard's trumpet perform the melodies.[25] This music is always nondiegetic and, in Johnson's view, serves to convey a romanticized vision of community in the ethnically mixed neighborhood in which the story takes place. This use of music corresponds to the classical approach.

Rap music rests at the other end of the aesthetic continuum in this film. The group Public Enemy's rap anthem "Fight the Power" (1989) is heard diegetically at various points in the film as it pours out of the boom box of the character Radio Raheem. Johnson argues that the other musical styles heard in the film, which include jazz, soul, and R&B, mediate the two extremes represented by rap and Bill Lee's original score. (There is one exception to this observation, however. Jazz is also used nondiegetically to help depict flaring tempers between characters.)

While I generally agree with Johnson's reading, I depart from it on several points. Johnson stresses that Lee is conversant with classical scoring conventions and that he "manipulates convention in a traditional manner to orient spectators within the film story."[26] I experience *DTRT* somewhat differently here. The somewhat unconventional approach of the score disorients the audience in my view. This musical strategy is joined to unusual cinematic techniques such as unrealistic visual angles that call attention to the camera and a use of music that moves back and forth between "bath of affect" and "listen to me" narrative positions.

The three modes of musical language in the film—the orchestral music of the Natural Spiritual Orchestra (nondiegetic), the popular music played by WLOV radio station (diegetic), and the rap music from Radio Raheem's boom box (diegetic)—create a rather hectic and conflicted semiotic field. Consider, for example, the first five scenes in which we hear the orchestral music that Johnson believes signals a romanticized community. During a monologue in front of the Yes, Jesus Light Baptist Church, the speech-impaired character Smiley talks about the futility of hate in society while holding up a small placard of Malcolm X and Martin Luther King, Jr. Smiley's stammering seems somewhat at odds with the placid musical gestures heard in conjunction with it.

The next time we hear this mode of music, the Italian pizzeria owner, Sal, and his sons, Vito and Pino, drive up to their shop, which sits on a garbage-strewn corner of a primarily black neighborhood. (Ironically, other scenes in the film portray the neighborhood as whistle clean.) In this scene we learn of the deep hatred

Vito harbors for this neighborhood and for the people who live there. Although Sal admits with glib resolution that the air-conditioner repairman has refused to come around without an escort, he can barely contain his anger over Vito's attitude about working in the neighborhood. This scene does not, in my view, conjure a romanticized community. Again, the placid strains of the score seem strangely at odds with the narrative world on the screen.

When the character Mookie (played by Spike Lee) exits his brownstone into the morning sun, the neighborhood is stirring with Saturday-morning activity. The orchestral strains do portray a cozy, communal feeling in this third instance of hearing this mode of music. But in the very next scene in which music of this type is heard, the characters Mother-Sister and Da Major, the neighborhood's matriarch and patriarch, respectively, trade insults with one another. The fifth time the orchestra is heard, Jade, a young woman who is Mookie's sister, is lovingly combing Mother-Sister's hair on the sun-baked front stoop of a brownstone. The communal feeling created by the music and the scene quickly dissipates, however, as Mother-Sister deflects a compliment from Da Major, responding to his polite advance by hurling more insults. Thus, I see the score not so much signaling community as functioning to highlight conflict and tension in the narrative world of the film. This strategy sets the viewer on edge and frustrates any settled feeling that might be forwarded in the scene.

But the music that Mister Señor Love Daddy plays on radio station WLOV *does* seem to signal community. It marks the geographic space of the neighborhood and underscores his references to love and the importance of community togetherness. In the early scenes of the film, the radio music, which consists of various styles of R&B—replete with gospel singing and funk beats—is heard in sundry settings. We hear it in Da Major's bedroom as he rises, in Mookie and Jade's apartment, in a Puerto Rican home, and in a Korean-owned grocery store—in every cultural space except Sal's Famous Pizzeria. This compiled score inspires the idea of a community, one created by the spatial boundaries of the radio station's broadcast span.

Nonetheless, WLOV's programming inspires one instance of community conflict. When Mookie, an African American, dedicates a song (Rubén Blades's "Tu y Yo") to his Puerto Rican girlfriend, Tina, a group of Puerto Rican young men enjoy the tune on a front stoop. As Radio Raheem passes by playing "Fight the Power," a battle of decibels ensues. "Fight the Power" wins the bout when Radio Raheem's boom box overpowers the scene with one turn of the volume knob. This confrontation contrasts with the first meeting of Radio Raheem's music and that of WLOV. (I discuss this brief meeting below.) Community alliances, like Lee's cinematic uses of various musical styles, are fluid and situational. Why, one might ask, didn't the Puerto Ricans identify with the "Fight the Power" message?

Gorbman writes that "music is codified in the filmic context itself, and assumes meaning by virtue of its placement in the film."[27] Because of the audience's familiarity with rap music and the dynamic formal qualities of the music, Lee is able to highlight its "difference" from other musical styles in *DTRT*'s score. As the film progresses, however, the audience experiences a level of familiarity with "Fight the Power" because of its persistent use. Lee is able to reencode rap music's signifying effect during the film's narrative.

Lee can achieve this because he capitalizes on the history of Public Enemy's reputation outside the use of "Fight the Power" in this film. Clearly, this use fits into the affiliating identifications category. At the same time, repetitively hearing the piece also allows us to spill over into the assimilating identifications arena. I argue this because the repetitive use of "Fight the Power" allows Lee to manipulate audience members of different subject positions to relate to the musical conventions and political message of the piece through their understanding of what it means cinematically. Thus, they have been assimilated into a particular reaction or identification with the music and, perhaps, the story world and its characters as well.

If the typical classic Hollywood film score renders the audience "less awake," as Gorbman contends, then Lee's use of rap music breaks that pattern. He positions it as an intrusive, embodied presence in the film. We see Lee setting the tone for this cinematic treatment during the opening scene of the film, which features a dance sequence by the actress Rosie Perez.

Doin' the Outside Dance!: "Fight the Power" and the Body Politic DTRT's unusual opening has received attention from other scholars, but I want to respond to a critique by the feminist critic bell hooks. Hooks has leveled scathing criticism at this scene, and I quote her at length:

> The long beginning sequence of the film (rarely mentioned by critics) highlighting an unidentified black woman [Perez] dancing in a manner that is usually a male performance is a comment on gender and role playing. Positively, she has "mastered" an art form associated primarily with male performance. Yet to do so, she must stretch and distort her body in ways that make her appear grotesque, ugly, and at times monstrous. That she is attempting to appropriate a male style (we can see the "female" version of this dance in the Neneeh [sic] Cherry video "Kisses on the Wind") is emphasized by her donning the uniform for boxing, a sport most commonly associated solely with males, even though there are a few black female boxers. By evoking the boxing metaphor, this scene echoes Ishmael Reed's new book of essays, *Writin' Is Fightin'*, with its exclusive focus on black males, associating the pain of racism primarily with its impact on that group. Alone, isolated, and doing a male thing, this solitary dancer symbolically suggests that the black female becomes "ugly" or "distorted" when she assumes a role designated for males. Yet simultaneously the onlooker, placed in a voyeuristic position, can only be impressed by how well she assumes this role, by her assertive physicality.[28]

Hooks's discussion does not mention several issues with regard to the expressive practice at the heart of the scene and thereby misses some of its signifying potential. While it is true that boxing is an important metaphor in the performance, I see the role of *dance* as even more significant. If we begin, as hooks does, with the correct observation that the brand of black nationalism echoed in *DTRT* downplays the role of women in that struggle, then one is tempted to read everything in the film through that particular lens. But this performance is first and foremost a dance—the kind of social dancing that has been labeled "the vernacular." Perez moves with agility and authority through many of the hip-hop-inspired dance moves that appeared during the 1980s. We see her moving between the Womp, the Charleston, the Running Man, the Cabbage Patch, the Kid 'n Play, the Fight, the Roger Rabbit, the Elvis Presley, and various other highly stylized pelvic thrusts, shuffles, jumps, and "up-rocking" movements that are closely associated with break dancing and other hip-hop-inspired movements.[29]

Perez is quite simply working it. At no time during this sequence, in my view, did Perez assume the ugly or monstrous bearing noted by hooks. She looks totally engaged, especially near the end of the performance, when she appears to be smiling—as if to say, "I *know* I'm working it!" Although this sequence is not, as hooks points out, in the film narrative proper, it does serve the film's narrative.

When we identify this dancer as a black Puerto Rican in the film, I cannot help but collapse this knowledge into the history of break dancing itself. This important art form has had its Puerto Rican origins erased or at best eroded in the popular imagination, although research is beginning to correct this cultural amnesia.[30]

That Perez went on to be the choreographer of the black-variety television show *In Living Color* in the early 1990s is also significant to the multiethnic, hybrid landscape of what has been called the hip-hop nation. We must take seriously the historical role of black vernacular dancing. To say that in Western discourse issues pertaining to the body have been valued less than those of the mind is an understatement. One example of this is hooks's failure to see the political dimensions of Perez's performance. Although there is no doubt that Spike Lee possessed a good deal of control over the representation of that performance, we cannot discount the historical, signifying, and liberating tradition of black dance, a tradition in which Perez is expertly participating and upon which she is non-verbally commenting.

Black social dancing circulates social energy. Females have played and continue to perform key historical roles in the creation and dissemination of these dances. For this reason, I see Perez as doing a very female thing rather than an exclusively male one. While it is true that at points in the dance sequence, which consists of a series of jump cuts, Perez wears boxing gloves and shorts, her costumes in other frames are more typical of the late-1980s fashions. Since the boxing movements (mostly jabs, uppercuts, and shuffles) are so similar to hip-hop dance movements, especially the upper-body gestures, I experience a strong political connection among the lyrical and instrumental import of "Fight the Power," the sport of boxing, and Perez's expression of hip-hop dance.

The lyrics of "Fight the Power" are given life by Perez's kinetic narrative. In fact, at one point during the dance she mimes the lyrics of a particularly salient political statement. Perez's lip-synching, together with her gestural emphasis on the words, unlike any other sequence in the dance, connects her unquestionably to the song's overtly political sentiments. Moreover, this recognition of "self-consciousness" invites the viewer to make an explicit connection between the flowing words and the moving body. Thus, rather than seeing Perez's performance as extratextual or as merely objectified by the camera's lens, I believe she "subjectifies" a distinctly female presence into Public Enemy's somewhat phallocentric nationalism.

I want to point out that cultural memory also plays a strong role in my reading of this scene. Because she is alone, as hooks points out (alone with an audience, I might add), Perez's performance recalls for me a line from James Brown's "Lickin' Stick."[31] In the song's lyrics, Brown comments that "sister's out in the backyard doing the outside dance." Presumably, sister's "outside dance" takes place beyond the gaze of parental judgment and censure.

During Perez's "outside dance," her body's center and extremities provide a catalog of 1980s hip-hop body attitudes. Viewing this scene in the late 1990s makes this point even more salient, since hip-hop's body grammar has changed significantly over the years. The dance is performed against the backdrop of classic brownstones, and we conclude from this forecasting that the film's story world will somehow be linked to urban America generally and to New York City specifically. The lyrics of "Fight the Power" scream 1989! at the beginning of the piece. The immediacy of Perez's dance "says" the same thing. We are in the present, a present that has urgency, particularity, politics, *and* pleasure.

This interpretation of Perez's performance supports an important observation by feminist salsa scholar Frances R. Aparicio. She argues: "Latinas who are active listeners and consumers of salsa music continuously rewrite patriarchal and misogynist salsa texts. They engage in 'productive pleasure,' which allows them as culturally bound receptors the opportunity to produce meanings and significations that are relevant to their everyday lives."[32]

The fact that Lee does not sustain within the film's narrative all of the political force that my interpretation lends to this opening does not weaken the dance's import, nor does it strip Perez of all her agency and its implications. Much of the power that I perceive in the dance is unquestionably derived from Perez's creativity and the histories it invokes. One might associate this move with affiliating identifications in the same sense that Kassabian uses the term to describe the effective result of a compiled score.

As myriad black cheerleading squads, drill teams, and popular dance troupes do, Perez probably choreographed and improvised (some of) the sequences herself. Lee's choice to introduce in the context of a dance an entire song that will be central to the film's story line works well. Because music with lyrics (not to mention a rap performance with numerous lyrics) would lose some of its communicative effect if it were heard within filmic dialogue or action, the "wordless" (yet very semantic) dance allows viewers to experience the full impact of the sentiments of "Fight the Power." When we do hear this song (nine other times) during the film, we can then focus almost exclusively on the *cinematic* meanings it generates.

Radio Raheem: Bigger with a Boom Box

With respect to filmic association, Perez's body is replaced during the film by Radio Raheem, a key character who speaks sparingly but signifies much. In the climatic scene of *DTRT* Raheem is killed by police officers trying to quell a riot outside Sal's Famous Pizzeria. Radio Raheem, a Bigger Thomas with a boom box, is represented almost in shorthand by Lee. He rarely speaks and doesn't have to. The song "Fight the Power" "speaks" for him. And what is more, his body is objectified as an imposing presence that is to be taken seriously, if not feared. The sonic force of producer Hank Shocklee's innovative and explosive rhythm track combines with the lyrics to create a palpable and, if you love this groove, pleasurable tension. More so than any other musical form heard in the film, rap music stands alone because of its singular cinematic treatment. In fact, because Radio is associated with rap music, no other character measures up to the intensity that his presence achieves.

A good deal of the dramatic thrust of Radio Raheem's character is due to how he is framed musically. When we first meet him, no music has underscored the two previous scenes. This strategy works well in establishing Radio Raheem as an important presence in the film. Radio never responds to the tune by dancing or even moving to its rhythm. Yet because of Perez's opening dance performance, I believe that its bodily connection is never lost on the audience. After we meet Radio Raheem, he has a brief but very important interaction with one of the characters that symbolizes an important message in the narrative.

Earlier in the film we have met Mister Señor Love Daddy, the DJ at the neighborhood's radio station, which programs various popular musical styles throughout the day (one assumes no rap music is programmed). It is important that the music of the station, as I have already mentioned, is for the most part heard diegetically, situating this neighborhood in a specific cultural space, not a universal one. The radio station and the music it plays show the degree to which mass media can unify and demarcate a sense of the local for listeners. The music and the ethos it creates in the film's narrative point to a community with a common past and present. Love Daddy's on-the-air patter, for example, belongs to a long tradition of black radio jocks.

When Love Daddy and Radio Raheem share a scene, one would expect the stationary and mobile DJs to have an unpleasant confrontation. But as he passes the control booth's exterior window, Radio Raheem salutes Mister Señor Love Daddy. Love Daddy responds in kind with a verbal on-the-air greeting. This exchange, together with the opening scene, connects rap music to the cultural orbit of other black vernacular traditions.

At the same time, its cinematic use singles rap out in this story as hyper-political, especially when compared with the treatment of other musical styles in the soundtrack. I argue that this discourse spilled out of the reel world and into the real world, proving that expressive culture has the power to make worlds and worldviews, even as it is shaped by the social world. The singularity of this artistic and political construction by Lee insists on the silencing of rap music, a move that, in turn, depends on the death of Radio Raheem's body for the sake of narrative closure.

The political insurgency of Public Enemy's lyrics encouraging listeners to stand up to hegemonic forces in society and the dense musical play in the rhythm track that makes use of sampled excerpts from black music history (most prominently James Brown) signify profoundly. If you silence this music, you have effectively silenced the past, present, and future of the community. Despite numerous critiques that Radio Raheem's character is too simplistic, I see the cultural work he symbolizes as complex and significant.[33] The cinematic and, most important to my discussion, the *musical* construction of this character provides an important commentary on race, class, and gender in American society.

Boyz 'n the Hood: The West Coast Responds

The film *Boyz N the Hood* (1991), written and directed by John Singleton, appeared in 1991 and earned over fifty million dollars at the box office, making it one of the top-grossing films of its kind. Critically acclaimed, the film was received as a convincing portrait of urban black America. *Boyz* (hereafter *BNTH*) tells the story of three young black men coming of age in South Central Los Angeles. Just as Lee did in *DTRT*, Singleton uses the opening of the film to create a specific ethos.

As the film begins we hear, against a black screen, the audio of an activity for which South Central had become known in recent years: the drive-by shooting. A cacophonous mixture of angry male voices, gunshots, police helicopters, sirens, chaos, and violence assaults the viewers and thrusts them into a 1990s version of a high-noon Wild West showdown. And just in case we don't connect inner-city "blackness" to this violent scenario, these words appear across the screen: "One out of every twenty-one Black American males will be murdered in their lifetime. Most will die at the hands of another Black male." Thus, with these sentiments and the opening drive-by voiceover, "black on black" crime, "black men as endangered species," senseless violence, and youthful nihilism foreground important themes of the plot, setting, and characters we will experience in the film.

The film's narrative proper begins in 1984 South Central with a group of young black children walking to school along garbage-lined streets. The historical and physical settings of this film allow us to speculate that we are also experiencing the "coming of age" of one of the most controversial idioms of hip-hop: gangsta rap. This leap is not a large one, for, as Valerie Smith notes, the directors of rapsploitation "position themselves in a common enterprise with black musicians in the frequent use of rap and hip hop in soundtracks, and with the visible presence of rappers on screen as actors."[34] During the opening scene we meet

Tre, one of three preadolescent boys around which most of this story revolves. We also hear for the first time Stanley Clarke's original score, which plays an important role in *BNTH*'s dramatic thrust.

One of the schoolchildren announces that he wants to show the others something. The something turns out to be a blood-soaked walkway riddled with bullet holes. Somebody got "smoked." Clarke underscores nondiegetic suspenseful-sounding music in the spirit of the classic Hollywood film tradition: minor mode, synthesized strings, percussion, and soprano saxophone. We also hear gunshots during these passages. Serving as metacommentary on the world outside the film, the gunshots and the holes they make are experienced as the camera scans their target: Ronald Reagan reelection campaign posters. The musical score connects us emotionally to the children and their plight.

Singleton's and Stanley Clarke's scoring is somewhat more traditional than Lee's in *DTRT*. Nondiegetic music functions as a bath of affect, drawing us into the spell of the film's narrative, and heightens its dramatic import in a time-proven, "unheard" way. Such moments occur during scenes in which Tre's parents are interacting with him. We are to relate to them as working- to middle-class subjects who are doing the best they can to make it in the world.

The music—often scored with strings or harp as background and simplistic melodies usually played by a single saxophone, trumpet, or flute—sounds like soft pop ballads. It conjures the innocence of childhood, parental love, feelings of neighborhood and friendship. One notable exception in the film, however, occurs in a scene in which an intruder has broken into the house and is shot at by Tre's father, the provocatively named Furious Styles. The music underscoring the scene features a jazz tenor saxophone soloist playing agitated, wailing passages in the upper register. As Furious protects his home and family, the music causes the viewer to identify with the former's state of fear and adrenaline-induced excitement. That this particular style of music could serve in this way demonstrates the degree to which some African American styles have become naturalized—they can assimilate the viewer in much the same way as classic Hollywood scoring can.

If the nondiegetic music is used to represent work ethics, family values, and civic pride in *BNTH*, then the diegetic music articulates more specific ethnic and class affiliations. The scene in which Tre's mother drives him to his father's home near the beginning of the film demonstrates this usage. As they arrive in the sun-drenched neat neighborhood, we hear Clark's nondiegetic scoring of sentimentality and nostalgia. At other moments, we hear diegetic soul music in the distance, marking this as a working-class African American neighborhood. When Tre and his father bond during a "birds and the bees" discussion while fishing, the sentimental scoring returns. The composed and compiled scores together with the narrative work to create an African American community, albeit a male-dominated one, with the typical challenges facing working- and middle-class families: how to maintain or better their status and pass these values along to their offspring.

When Tre and Furious drive home from the fishing trip we experience what is perhaps the most complex use of music in the film. Kassabian writes that film music has three primary purposes: identification, mood, and commentary. All three are achieved in these next scenes. During the ride, a 1970s hit by the R&B group the Five Stair Steps is heard diegetically from the car's radio. "Listen to this song," Furious entreats his son. "I love this song." The song, "Ooo, Ooo Child," a medium-tempo ballad features a soul singer and oooing and ahhhing background vocals in the same stylistic vein as the music first heard from the radio station WLOV in *DTRT*. We witness father and son interacting through this mass-media music. Furious is enjoying his son's company; he hums and sways to "his" music, celebrating soul music's conventions and, no doubt, finding pleasure in the personal and cultural memories they evoke. Tre seems comfortable and amused.

The song performs two other cinematic functions. As Furious and Tre drive past Doughboy's house they see him and another boy being escorted by police into a waiting squad car. At this point, the lyrics of "Ooo, Ooo Child" become a compelling commentary on the unfolding drama:

> Ooo, ooo child, things are gonna get easier
>
> Ooo, ooo child, things'll get brighter
>
> *
>
> Someday, yeah, we'll walk in the rays of a beautiful sun
>
> Someday, when the world is much brighter

By the end of the scene, as the squad car disappears into the distance with Tre watching intently from the curb, the song is no longer diegetic; it is heard only by the audience as its strains fade into the sound of a police siren. This poignant scene ends the depiction of Tre's young life. The remainder of the film, which takes place seven years later, deals with the lives of Tre, Doughboy, and Ricky (Doughboy's brother) as young men coming of age.

BNTH provides a cinematic mediation on how various rap idioms signify in the real world. Two styles are heard in the soundtrack: New Jack Swing and gangsta rap.[35] Each is heard diegetically and shapes the viewer's perceptions of setting and characterization. Immediately following Doughboy's childhood arrest scene, the film cuts to the story world's present.

The adult Doughboy has been given a homecoming cookout to celebrate his release from his latest prison stint. The party takes place in his mother's backyard. An upbeat New Jack Swing recording (featuring female rapper Monie Love) frames the scene; it is heard diegetically from a very large speaker system. (The recording is "Work It Out," written by Jazzy Jeff and Monie Love.) Animated African American teenaged bodies crowd the space with youthful exuberance and bravado. Some are playing dominoes and card games; others drink malt liquor out of forty-ounce bottles. Many of the teenagers dance to the infectious rhythms of the song, executing individualized versions of some of the dances performed by Perez in *DTRT*. The young men and the women verbally tease one another with the dozens; at the same time, they scope the backyard for potential romantic interests.

Through the cultural practices taking place at the party—and music plays a central role here—Singleton creates a sense of community in the scene. Despite Doughboy's troubles with the law, we empathize with him and situate him into this web of culture and the communal feeling evoked. Like Radio Raheem, Doughboy never *moves* to the music, but he obviously relates to it strongly. He is the only character, for example, that comments verbally about the diegetic hip-hop music in the film, taking note of the music emanating from a passing car: "Damn, that shit [is] bumpin'." This gesture may be interpreted as a kind of metanarrative comment on Ice Cube's primary career in gangsta rap, a connection that the primary audience of the film would easily make and identify with strongly.

Hip-hop music, as I mentioned, is always heard diegetically in the film. When the less dance-oriented forms of gangsta rap are heard, they denote the menacing aspects of male nihilist culture, including threats of drive-by shootings or other "hard-core" youth cultural spaces. In one scene, for example, Tre is almost hit by a passing car as he crosses a residential street. When he gathers himself to fashion a response, without ceremony one of the male passengers points a shotgun barrel at his face at point-blank range. In another scene, gangsta rap plays diegetically in Compton, depicted here as a "rough" neighborhood. The sparse, funky, and at once ominous-sounding strains of gangsta rap signify in this film the destruction of a community.

Singleton uses jazz in *BNTH* to signify class status in Tre's mother, Reva Styles, who becomes solidly middle-class by the end of the film. During one scene, Tre is on the telephone with his girlfriend when his mother calls. As the dialogue switches back and forth between the bachelor's quarters he shares with his father and his mother's very chic dwelling, the music moves between R&B for the men's space and urban contemporary jazz for Reva's. This particular use of jazz-related practices will be extended into the next film under discussion: *Love Jones*.

Musical Constructions of Black Bohemia in Love Jones

The film *Love Jones* expands the hip-hop lexicon of acceptable black subjects and their corresponding musical associations. The film is an urban, Afro-romantic comedy, written and directed by Theodore Witcher, and set in contemporary Chicago. Darryl Jones, a bassist and native Chicagoan, scored the original music. *Love Jones*'s eclectic soundtrack and the "musicking" practices associated with the music distinguish the film from run-of-the-mill romantic comedies.

Consider the first few minutes of the film, in which Witcher (like Lee and Singleton before him) sets the tone for the story that follows. During the opening, Witcher strings together a jumble of short urban scenes, including the Chicago skyline, the El train, a run-down neighborhood, a modest storefront shop, trash-lined railroad tracks, a Baptist church, the hands of a shoeshine man, and the faces of black people— old, young, some profiling, others showing no awareness of the camera at all. But all of them striking. Filmed in black and white, Witcher's stylish montage forecasts an approach to the presentation of inner-city blackness that departs from and is, in my view, more expansive than the two previous films I have discussed.

The music underscoring the opening features the genteel song "Hopeless," performed by singer Dionne Farris. The tune borders on soft rock and has virtually none of the hip-hop conventions heard in *Do the Right Thing* and *Boyz N the Hood*. The lyrics of "Hopeless" play a slight trick on the viewer, because we hear the lyric "hopeless" against the first few scenes in the montage, which at first appear to paint a somewhat bleak depiction of inner-city life. But as the visual sequences progress, smiles begin to spread across the subjects' faces. And as the musical narrative spins out, we learn that Farris is singing about romantic love and not social commentary: she's as "hopeless as a penny with a hole in it."

Love Jones features an attractive posse of educated, well-spoken, widely read, comfortably middle-class twenty-something Generation X-styled characters. Their hairdos (always a political statement with regard to African American culture) cover the spectrum: close-cropped, dreadlocks, braids, chemically straightened. They live in tastefully appointed homes, lofts, and apartments that are lined with books and stylishly decorated with modern and African art. They are dressed for success and "wearing the right thing," if I might borrow Lee's title for the moment. Intrablack diversity is the feeling. The characters listen to jazz, the Isley Brothers, and urban contemporary music. Their calculated and robust funkiness translates into frank talk about sensuality. They read Amiri Baraka, smoke, drink, swear, play cards, and talk a boatload of shit in grand style. Like carefree adolescents, they delight in playing the dozens with each other. And with fluency they pepper their musings on poetry, sexuality, Charlie Parker, gender relations, religion, and art with spicy, up-to-the-minute "black-speak" rhetoric. Witcher apparently wants us to recognize these verbal exchanges and their accompanying body attitudes with a contemporary performance-oriented African American culture.

Love Jones's characters portray a hip "big shoulders" black ethnicity that insiders recognize as realistic in cultural spaces like contemporary black Chicago. In this setting, the film's narrative winds through various venues and situations wherein acts of ethnic performance can take place. One such space is a nightclub called the Sanctuary. Modeled after a jazz club, the Sanctuary features spoken-word poetry and live music. The Sanctuary appears to cater to black Generation X-ers. Its audience respects the performers, paying rapt attention to the time, timbre, lyric, and substance of each poet's offering. Quiet diegetic music from the bandstand and jukebox envelopes the Sanctuary with the soundtrack of hip, polite society.

The film tells a love story between Darius Lovehall, an aspiring novelist and spoken-word poet, and Nina Mosley, an ambitious freelance photographer. Darius is a regular performer at the Monday-night open-mike session; Nina, who is on the rebound from a bad relationship, is there relaxing with a female friend. Nina and Darius meet. Nina initiates a conversation, following their exchange of curious glances. Shortly thereafter, an emcee invites Darius to the stage, and he performs a sexually explicit poem, which he titles at the last moment (in true "Mack Daddy" fashion) "A Blues for Nina."

The performance itself is, in fact, not blues or jazz performance but what might be described as easy-listening funk: an ostinato bass pattern in D-minor splashed with subdued colors from a saxophone's soulful riffing. References from black music history inform the poetry; in one line Darius says that he's "the blues in your left thigh, trying to become the funk in your right." The audience, which is depicted in a series of very flattering close-ups that are reminiscent of the opening montage, responds with sporadic declamatory affirmations. These vocables provide an obligatory bow to the southern past, even if they may no longer signify that history solely.

Music in *Love Jones* works overtime. Its characters are more fully constructed, engaging in more musical practices and cultural spaces than in the previous two films discussed. Music in the pool hall, the nightclub, the house party, the WVON "stepper's set," the reggae club, and the residences expands the representations of Hip-Hop Era blackness on screen. While this depiction of black bohemia may be a caricature itself, when compared with contemporaneous visions of black life in America (like *DTRT* and *BNTH*, for example), *Love Jones* can be viewed only as a counterweight to those characterizations.

Although contemporary R&B forms the core musical lexicon of *Love Jones*, jazz references surface in the Sanctuary's performance space and as a way to show how "enlightened" the characters are. In one case, the jazz/blues piece "Jelly, Jelly, Jelly" becomes the soundtrack of sexual frustration as Darius and Nina try to suppress their lust for each other. Important to note, rap music is heard only one time in the film: during a car scene in which one of Darius's friends is courting Nina behind his back. In this very brief scene, rap music becomes quickly associated with a questionable character trait.

Interestingly, in all three films, music is linked to other black cultural practices such as the dozens, dance, card playing, and so on. Music is central to constructing black characters within these films' narratives. Rap music, for example, helps to create specific kinds of character traits in (male) subjects: politicized, nihilistic, or underhanded. Various styles of jazz are used for their identifications with middle-class culture or to enhance the audience's experience of emotional states. R&B styles, for the most part, are used to depict communal associations. The quasi-orchestral music linked most closely to the sound of classic Hollywood scoring, when it does appear in these films, is used in traditional ways: to assimilate audiences into a particular mode of identification with characters and plot situations.

During the Age of Hip-Hop, filmmakers such as Spike Lee and John Singleton worked to create what they thought were realistic portraits of urban life. While their portrayals were popular, many critics believed that they helped to erect harmful stereotypes. Witcher, director of *Love Jones*, for example, had trouble convincing Hollywood executives that his kind of story could find a niche in the market or was even plausible because of the ghettocentric focus of so many black films of the early 1990s.[36] Thus, despite the way in which directors might have positioned their work as countering hegemony in Hollywood, their approaches and the repetition of them became conventions against which those interested in other kinds of representations would have to struggle.

The juxtaposition of different black musical styles in these films demands that audiences grapple with the ways in which numerous musical developments have appeared under the cultural umbrella of hip-hop. How these styles relate to one another cinematically represents only one arena of interest. These expressions have enlarged the boundaries of hip-hop, and this expansion has inspired celebration, dissent, and, of course, debate on exactly where these boundaries lie. Because of the persistence of older styles of black music and their continual evolution of meanings during the Age of Hip-Hop, filmmakers are able to use these external associations as part of the way in which audiences experience these scores, and thus their cinematic representations.

The music, modernism, and modernization processes discussed earlier in the book provided the historical, social, and cultural foundations for what has developed during the Age of Hip-Hop. If we consider, for example, the way in which jazz in the 1940s represented the quintessential Afro-modernist expression of black urbanity, we can better understand how the musical styles most closely associated with hip-hop represent "the urban contemporary" for the present generation. If the blues muse of the World War II years existed as a basic ingredient in various styles, then we need to try to identify, codify, and theorize the elements that make up the decidedly hybrid hip-hop sensibility and "worldview." One might learn, for example, that the idea of Afro-modernism might be extended into the late twentieth century. Indeed, the question might be posed: Does Afro-modernism exist as an unfinished project?

The three urban landscapes portrayed in *Do the Right Thing, Boyz N the Hood*, and *Love Jones* are meditations on how modern blackness is experienced in cities that in the 1940s represented the promised land—the cultural spaces to which black humanity flocked in order to participate fully in modern America. The urban conditions recently called postindustrial and the artistic responses to these conditions reflect the changing social configuration of the late-twentieth-century American city. Just as Dizzy Gillespie's Afro-Cuban experiments participated in a new demographic shift in the 1940s, today's musicians mix hip-hop conventions with other expressions to reflect the configuration of their own social worlds and the statements they want to make in them.

If it is indeed true that contemporary people fashion their lives with the texts around them, as this chapter's epigraph proposes, then the study of hip-hop film provides a fruitful site of inquiry in this regard. In the three films discussed in this chapter, directors and composers worked together to create narratives in which audience members can engage and with which they can form identifications. These texts become ways through which some understand themselves and others in the social world. Music forms an important component in these narratives, serving to order the social world in both the cinematic and real-life domains.

Notwithstanding the scene in *Do the Right Thing* in which Smiley performs his opening dialogue in front of a Baptist church, the black church is invisible in the three films I have discussed. No one appears to go to church, and this is unfortunate, because in reality the black church has been a central institution in the development of African American culture. The ring shout rituals that produced the spirituals of the "invisible institution," the independent mainline denominations that published their own hymnal traditions, and the storefront Pentecostal denominations that infused their services with fervor and dramatic worship patterns point to a vibrant and varied legacy of culture building. Have these practices become outdated in today's social environment?

Musical practice has been central to the formation and relevance of the black church. Innumerable African American performers, for example, have noted their debt to singing in or playing for choirs and the foundational role that these experiences played in their musical development. Just as hip-hop culture's voracious muse has reshaped the contemporary music scene, black gospel music has proven to be just as permeable, flexible, and defiant, despite conservative ideologues who have defended its borders. In the next chapter, I examine, among other things, how the collision of these sensibilities encourages new ways of thinking about the late-twentieth-century black church as a vibrant community theater of African American culture. This cultural space is not, as many believe, any more a "folk" world closed off to commercial and artistic interests than any other music in the marketplace is. On the contrary, contemporary gospel musicians may well be at the fore-front of innovation and artistic risk, even as they ground themselves firmly in history and tradition.

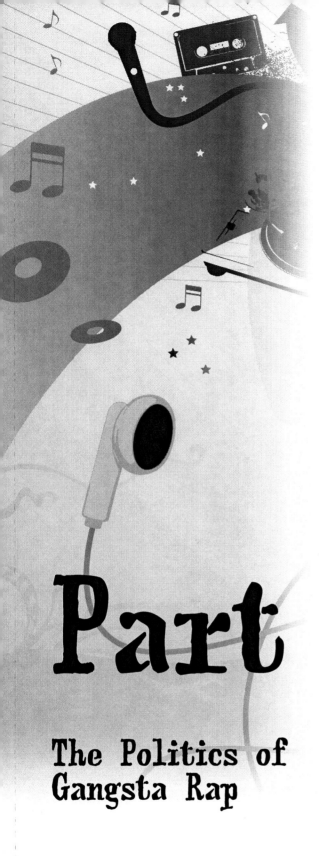

With the arrival of gangsta rap in the American mainstream in 1989, scholars, critics, community leaders, and legislators began to focus attention on this new and self consciously controversial style. Many both inside and outside the black community reacted with shock to the apparent cynicism and individualism of gangsta lyrics. What happened, they wondered, to the "conscious" rap voices, like Public Enemy, that had flourished a few years earlier? Where did gangsta rap come from, and does it signal the death of the civil rights struggle as a larger movement? Some went so far as to call for censorship: Dan Quayle declared that Tupac Shakur's album *2pacalypse Now* "has no place in our society."

Gangsta rap artists countered that their style reflected their authentic experiences of poverty, crime, and the struggle to survive in "the ghetto." As Tupac Shakur noted, "I was raised in this society, so there's no way you can expect me to be a perfect person." Such a reply raises questions about authenticity. For example, if this music was intended to reflect a ghetto experience, then why was it so successful in the popular mainstream? And how could artists like Ice Cube and Dr. Dre claim authentic "ghetto" status while making millions of dollars as rap artists?

The articles in this section, all scholarly, consider the roots of gangsta rap and the struggle for the political soul of rap between 1987 and 1994. The first two reexamine the ties, both real and imagined, between west-coast gangsta rap and an "authentic," black ghetto experience. The second two consider how some rap artists have developed alternatives to the west-coast gangsta image, first by creating politically conscious alternatives, and second by basking in the opulence of the "playa" identity. Keep the following questions in mind while studying these readings:

Do these authors agree about how authenticity figures in message rap? In gangsta rap?

Does Boyd's analysis of Ice Cube's political positions conflict with Kelley's emphasis on the "pleasure principle" in gangsta rap?

Do representations of gangsta rap in today's media, or by rappers themselves, still exhibit the problems identified by these articles? How is this good or bad?

Part 3

The Politics of Gangsta Rap

Raegan Kelly

Chapter 9

Hip-Hop Chicano

What's up Homie? Don't you know me?

Si mon.

Ain't you the brother of the mas chingon?

Straight up, and I'm down with the Raza

Kid Frost got my back

Boo Yaa's en la casa

Cause every day things get a little crazier

As I step to the microphone area

First I call my city

Puro Los Angeles

[lights up & cops a hit] Yeah homes

That's what the ganga says...

— Cypress Hill, "Latin Lingo"

Laying claim to the gangsta persona is a favorite theme in hiphop. Reading the wax, Toddy Tee, Schooly D, and NWA get major props...but for the concepts of *carnelismo, calo* terminology (homeboy, OG, etc.), the pachuco/cholo/gangsta style of dress, and the lowered ride, proper respect is due the *varrio.*

Chicano gangs, or "street syndicates," have been a fact of life in LA since the early 1930s (some claim earlier); accordingly their history, memory, and culture are long and strong. Defined by Martin Sanchez Jankowski as (roughly) adaptational organizations whose primary goal is survival through self-reliance,[1] "gang youth," while always a target of the media and law enforcement, have become, in LA at least, social pariahs without peer. To take pride visibly in this position is one way of inverting it, but the presence of colors, oversized Dickies, pendeltons, street lingo and fire power within the language and style of hiphop is only in small part fantasy-fulfillment—many of those who talk the talk have walked the walk.

Paralleling the development of gang culture were the rise of the lowrider and the zoot suiter in LA. In the *varrio,* self-reliance and brown pride go hand in hand, and a large percentage of brown hiphop integrates commentary on race and cultural difference into straightforward narratives of life on the streets. Sen Dogg of Cypress Hill exemplifies the West Coast B-boy in "Latin Lingo"—he declares his homies, his Paza, his hood, LA hiphop (and, of course, a phat blunt) in a particularly West Coast combination of English, *pachuquismo,* and hiphop slang. Both linguistically and stylistically, aspects of the West Coast gangsta, whether it be Kid Frost, Ganxsta Ridd (of the Boo Yaa Tribe) or Ice Cube in a pendelton, Dickies and a lowered "63 S.S., originated with *pachucos* and Zoot Suiters of 1940s *varrios* of east Los Angeles.

Like the "Teddy Boy" of Harlem, the *pachuco* was the ultimate expression of cultural resistance, anarchy, and (in)difference in the North American south west of the 1940s. Generally identified as Chicano gang

From *It's Not About a Salary: Rap, Race + Resistance in Los Angeles* by Raegan Kelly. Copyright 1993 by Verso. Reprinted by permission.

Hip-Hop Chicano   157

members (although most were not)[2] *pachucos* sported pompadours, wide-shouldered extra-long fingertip coats, high-waisted "drape" pants with pegged ankles and reat pleats, wide-brimmed hats, long watch chains, and *fileros.* Much has been written in detail about the "Zoot Suit Riots" that took place in Los Angeles in 1943, but what matters is precisely what caused civilians and sailors to roam the streets in mobs looking for young Chicanos to beat down. In *The Zoot-Suit Riots*, Mauricio Mazon describes their hatred as being comprised of a mixture of patriotic fervour and fear (mixed with envy) of difference, and of themselves.

To the good citizens of LA, "[Zoot Suiters] seemed to be simply marking time while the rest of the country intensified the war effort."[3] *Pachucos* openly smoked marijuana, spoke their own tongue, had their own style of music, dance and dress. Most infuriating, however, was that *pachucos* and zoot suiters spent so much time developing their own insular culture while good "patriotic" Americans built bombers 9-to-5 and went off to war. *Pachucos* didn't have a good "work ethic." They didn't seem to care, had their own set of priorities, and this pissed people off. (The attacks weren't completely symbolic, of course—it was around this time that the California Youth Authority camps were established, and an increasingly militant approach to law enforcement in Los Angeles was adopted.[4]

The Lowered Ride

Although the east side of Los Angeles was generally regarded as being overrun by gangs, violence, and an undocumented workforce,[5] what was to become one of the largest varrios in the south west had its own fast developing political, musical and street culture. In the early fifties a "basic car plan" was initiated by the First Street Merchants and the sheriff's department, and the tradition of car clubs began among east Los Angeles youth.[6] Originally designed to provide an alternative to gangs, car clubs became a focal point for social life in the *varrio*, providing a place to work, hang out, listen to music, gain knowledge of self-expression and cultural identity through the art of car customizing.

Chicanos have been customizing cars since the forties. The concept of a fully customized car, top to bottom, front to back, inside and out, took years to develop, but from the very beginning it was treated as an art form. Generally starting with a used American standard, a clay model, and much ingenuity and love, customizers take bits and pieces off different automobiles out of scrap yards, alter them and put them together to create a totally new and unique car. Bill Hines is one of *Lowrider* magazine's "Legends of Lowriding"; his first custom was a '41 Buick convertible with "chopped top" and a Cadillac front end. Known to some as the "King of Lead" for his ability totally to rework a body with a lead paddle and a spray gun, he was also one of the first to design a hydraulic lift system for raising and lowering custom cars (using modified aircraft landing gear parts), California-style, in 1964. (The first lifted custom was purportedly done by the Aguirres of San Bernardino, California, on a 1956 Corvette).[7] Hydraulics served a dual function—to raise a lowered vehicle for driving long distances (protect the underside), and to keep the cops away (riding too slow was a ticketable offense). "I remember a guy with this candy turquoise '63 Ford…that wanted to fool the cops. So, he had me juice it in front and back. He'd cruise with it laid until the cops spotted him. They couldn't figure it out. They didn't know what a lift was."[8]

To drive a beautifully customized ride low and slow down one of LA's main thoroughfares is an expression of pride, pride in being different, taking one's time, being Chicano. Jesse Valdez, another of the original lowriders and former leader of one of LA's best-known car clubs, The Imperials, remembers the heyday of lowriding: "In '66, '67, '68—we'd cruise Downey, Paramount, Whittier. That's when everybody was low-riding; Chicanos, black guys, white guys."[9] Whittier Boulevard, a unifying site for east LA through to the mid-seventies, was the site of the Eastside Blowouts, the Chicano political protests of '71–72; it provided a focal point for the *muralista* movement of the same time and Luis Valdez's 1979 movie *Boulevard Nights*. (Valdez's film, a classic Hollywood document of *varrio* street life in LA, opened ironically just after the boulevard was permanently closed to cruisers.) Favorites of the car culture tended to be instrumentals with sparse lyrics and heavy basslines—"Whittier Boulevard" by Thee Midniters, "Lowrider" by WAR (previously Senor Soul), "More Bounce" by Zapp.

Latin Lingo

Calo is the privileged language of the Mexican-American barrio…(It) was neither a pachuco nor a new world contribution. Calo has its ancient roots buried deeply in the fertile gypsy tongue (Calé, Romano, Zincalo and Calogitano…) …fractured in spelling, crippled in meaning; mutilated French, English, Italian, and the dead languages of Latin, Greek, and Hebrew, plus medieval Moorish, Calo, originally Zincalo, was the idiom of the Spanish Gypsies—one of the many minorities in Spain. The conquistadores brought Calo to the New World. Already identified by the upper classes as the argot of the criminal, the poor, and the uneducated, Calo and its variants became well known to the conquered Indian…

— Mauricio Mazon, *The Zoot-Suit Riots*, p. 3

To followers of scat and the spoken-word traditions of jazz and bebop, Calo probably sounds little different than the jive scat of Cab Calloway or the inverted *Vout* language of Slim Gaillard. In some ways today it operates much like early hepster phraseology—hip Calo terms like homeboy and loc have completely penetrated hiphop and gang culture. But for the *pachucos* of the forties and in the *varrios*, of today, Calo is also an important way to mark cultural difference/peripherality through language. Frequently referred to as "Spanglish" (half English, half Spanish) Calo is in fact a tongue all its own, a "living language" whose words and meanings change from location to location and person to person.

Muy Loco, Crazy

Ever since I come from Mexico

I don't want to do the Mambono

All I want to do is go go go

When the crazy band she starts to blow

All the senoritas say to me

Come on Pancho dance with me

Pancho Pancho don't go to the Rancho

Til you do the Pancho Rock with me

— Lalo Guerrero and His Orchestra, "Pancho Rock"

The great Latin bandleader Lalo Guerrero was one of the first to incorporate Calo into the Los Angeles club scene in the forties. *Pachuco* and zoot cultures gravitated towards the big band sound, which Guerrero fused with the structures of swing and rumba in songs like "Chuco Suave," "Marijuana Boogie," and "Vamos a bailar."[10] Another Calo favorite was the Don Tosti band's "Pachuco Boogie," characterized by Johnny Otis as Chicano Jump Blues, "which consisted of a jump type shuffle with either Raul [Diaz] or Don [Tosti] rapping in Calo about getting ready to go out on a date. Very funny stuff and another candidate for the title of the first rap record."[11]

Through the fifties and sixties East Los Angeles developed an active recording and club scene, which, as Steven Loza explains in *Barrio Rhythm*, "was integrally related to the black music experience, for musical as well as economic reasons."[12] The influence went both ways, and in 1952 African American saxophonist Chuck Higgins released the hit single "Pachuco Hop." Loza quotes Ruben Guevara's description of the east LA music scene in the late fifties and early sixties at El Monte Legion Stadium, which reads like an early description of Go-Go:

> A lot of Anglo kids copied not only the styles (hair, dress) but the dances, the most popular of which were the Pachuco Hop, Hully Gully, and the Corrido Rock...the Corrido was the wildest, sort of an early form of slam dancing. Two or three lines would form, people arm in arm, each line consisting of 150 to 250 people. With the band blasting away at breakneck rocking tempo, the lines took four steps forward and four steps back, eventually slamming into each other (but making sure that no one got hurt).... After the dance, it was out to the parking lot for the grand finale. Where's the party? *Quien tiene pisto? Mota?* Who's got the booze? Weed? Rumors would fly as to which gangs were going to throw *chingasos*—come to blows. The Jesters Car Club from Boyle Heights, which dominated the Eastside, would parade around the parking lot in their lavender, maroon or gray primered cars, wearing T-Timer shades (blue or green colored glasses in square wire frames).[13]

Latin and Afro-Cuban rhythms seem to have penetrated the early hiphop scene at least a decade before we hear any bilingual or Calo phraseology. In the early seventies, at the same time as lowriders in Califas were bumpin' the sounds of Tierra, Señor Soul, and Rulie Garcia and the East LA Congregation, Jimmy Castor was creating hiphop beats in New York using a fusion of "one-chord riffing, a Sly Stone pop bridge, fuzz guitar, timbales breaks, and an idealistic lyric applicable to any emergent movement."[14] David Toop credits Jimmy Castor with being a hiphop innovator, at the center of the Latin soul movement in the sixties and highly influenced by Latin masters like Cal Tjader, Chano Pozo, and Tito Puente.[15] Seven years later Afrika Bambaataa would redefine "influence," straight cutting Slim Gaillard's unique *Vout* lyrics into the mix.

In *Hip-Hop: The Illustrated History*, Steven Hager describes the early tagging and writing scene in 1970s New York as being racially integrated: the first tagger on record, Taki 183, was Greek; the second, Julio 204, was Chicano; and Tracy 168, a young white kid living in Black Spades territory, founded one of the scene's largest crews, "Wanted," in 1972.[16] The internationally known Lee Quinones and Lady Pink (stars of *Wild Style*)[17] were both Puerto Rican, as were the members of the all-time great breaking group, the Rock Steady Crew.

In the Bronx, funk and early hiphop entered the already hot Puerto Rican street and dance scene around 1977–78, with members of the Zulu Nation schooling Puerto Ricans in the ways of breakdancing and Puerto Rican DJs like Charlie Chase spinning funk and sporting early B-boy styles at their then disco-dominated block parties.[18] Rammelzee ('Ramm-elevation-Z—Z being a symbol of energy which flows in two directions)[19] and RubyD, recently dubbed the Puerto Rican Old School by West Coast Puerto Rican funkster Son Doobie of Funkdoobiest, rocked the mike all over NYC. The 1983 hit "Beat Bop" (Rammelzee vs. K-Rob) showcases what Rammelzee is known best for—what he dubbed "slanguage,"[20] an ingenious combination of freestyle metaphor and over-trie-top hiphop drops delivered in the Shake Up King's particular nasal drawl:

Just groovin' like a sage y'all

Break it up, yeah, yeah, stage y'all

Like a roller coaster ride that can make ya bump

Groovin with the rhythm as you shake yer rump—rock rock ya don't stop

You got it now baby—ya don't stop

Just hiphop the day, yeah doobie doo

Yeah scoobie doo, whatcha wanna do crew?

Just freak it, ya baby, just freak up, ya ya baby

Drink it up here, I know my dear

I can rock you out this atmosphere

Like a gangster prankster, number one bankster

Got much cash to make you thank ya

Rock on to the break a dawn—Keep it on now keep it on

I know Zee Zee that can rock quick

Like a high kind a class

Hand yer rhythm to the stick…

— "Beat Bop," Rammelzee vs. K-Rob

In 1980 a young Samoan dancer named Sugar Pop would move west from the streets of New York to bring breaking to the poplockers of south central, Venice and Hollywood in Los Angeles. One of the groups Sugar Pop encountered was the Blue City Crew, a group of Samoan poplockers coming out of Carson in south LA. In Topper Carew's movie *Breakin and Entering* about the early eighties breaking scene in LA, the crew talks about how the advent of street dancing correlated with a drop in gangbanging in the hoods and *varrios* of LA—homies were taking their battles to the dance floor. "In LA it ain't like that.... If you got the moves, you can hold down. That's all it is."

It was also around this time that hiphop started to penetrate the LA Chicano dance scene. In the mid- to late seventies Chicanos were throwing giant dance parties at Will Rogers State Beach, Devonshire Downs and in parks and roller rinks in the San Fernando Valley, complete with battling mobile DJs, hundreds of Curwen Vegas, MCs to keep the crowd hyped and, of course, circling helicopters. Precursors of today's massive rave scene (which are approximately 75 percent Chicano in Los Angeles), the music of choice at these parties was alternative/new wave, disco, and early techno-based hiphop (Egyptian Lover, Magic Mike, Melle Mel, Grandmaster Flash). Due to popular demand, in 1983–1984 Uncle Jam's Army set up special Valley-side gigs at the Sherman Square roller rink in Sherman Oaks. Young Chicano, Latino, and Samoan MCs, many of them former dancers, were working their way through the LA house party scene at this time, but one of the earliest to make it to wax was Arthur Molina, Jr. (aka Kid Frost) in 1984 with the single "Rough Cut." The music, written by David Storrs of Electrobeat Records (the same Storrs who wrote the music for Ice T's "Body Rock"),[21] has a decidedly early West Coast flavor, but lyrically the song bears a strong resemblance to Run DMC's "It's Like That," also released in 1984.

Sometimes you wait around
Rockin' cold hard streets
People strugglin' hard
Just tryin' to make ends meet
I just stand tough
hold down my feet
Never understand the meaning
of the word Defeat
So you see it's like that
And that's the way it is
But when I'm on the microphone, it goes something like this:
Body breakin' Booty shakin'
Good money for the makin'
You just put it in my pocket
Cause you know I got talent
It's Rough, it's Tough
Let me see if you can handle my stuff
It's Rough Rough Rough Rough Rough...

— Kid Frost, "Rough Cut"

The earliest bilingual hiphop song that I've heard on record is out of New York—Carlos T (aka Spanish Fly) and the Terrible Two's hit "Spanglish."[22] Rapping over a classic Grandmaster Flash beat the Terrible

Two dominate the song in English, with Carlos T coming in short and fast. "This is the way we harmonize, everybody, everybody, I said Danse funky danse, y que danse, todo mundo, todo mundo."

In 1989 the Cuban-born Mellow Man Ace kicked bilingual lyrics throughout his album *Escape from Havana*, generally alternating line for line between English and Spanish, as in "Mentirosa," or verse for verse, as he does in "Rap Guanco," over the Kool and the Gang bassline from Lightnin' Rod's[23] cut "Sport" on the *Hustlers' Convention* album of 1973:

> ...I'm the lyrical, miracle founder of the talk style
>
> Put together intelligently wild
>
> And what I came up with is called Rap Guanco
>
> Different than house, nothing like GoGo
>
> And if you're wonderin' damn how'd he start this
>
> Well, last year I opened my own market
>
> Cause it was time for somethin' new to come along and I thought
>
> A bilingual single, that can't go wrong...
>
> ...
>
> Ahora si que vengo [And now yes I'm coming]
>
> Sabroso si caliente...[Flavor very hot]...
>
> **— Mellow Man Ace, "Rap Guanco"**

A year later, Kid Frost hit the streets with his classic adaptation of the Gerald Wilson/El Chicano tune "Viva La Tirado," "La Raza," matching in syntax and lingo the Pachuco street slang (Calo) of East LA.

> Quevo
>
> Aqui'stoy MC Kid Frost
>
> Yo estoy jefe [I am in charge]
>
> My cabron is the big boss
>
> My cuete is loaded [pistol/rod]
>
> It's full of balas [bullets]
>
> I'll put it in your face
>
> And you won't say nada. [nothing]
>
> Vatos, cholos, call us what you will [Chicano homeboys, lowriders]
>
> You say we are assassins,
>
> Train ourselves to kill
>
> It's in our blood to be an Aztec warrior

Go to any extreme

And hold to no barriers

Chicano and I'm brown and proud

Want this chingaso? [smack, wack, as in "beat down"]

Si mon I said let's get down

The foreign tongue I'm speaking is known as Calo

Y sabes que, loco? [And you know what, loc?]

Yo estoy malo [I am mean/bad]

Tu no sabes que I think your brain is hollow? [Don't you know that...]

And so I look and I laugh and say Que pasa? [What's happening?]

Yeah, this is for La Raza.

— Kid Frost, "La Raza," *Hispanic Causing Panic*

"La Raza" is important for several reasons. It marks a radical change in Kid Frost's work—the distance between the non-committal "So rough, so tough" of "Rough Cut" and "It's in our blood to be an Aztec warrior / Go to any extreme" marks a change in consciousness, at least of his perception of hiphop as a language of consciousness. Frost's use of Calo is an appeal to the authenticity of the streets and the *pachuco* lifestyle, but within the context of the song it is also a nod to Chicano pride, as is the claim "Chicano and I'm brown and proud." The term Chicano, derived from *mechicano* and once considered derogatory and indicative of lower-class standing, applies to all people of Mexican descent/all people of indigenous descent. To call yourself Chicano is to claim La Raza, to locate your origin within the struggle of a people for land and for cultural, political and economic self-determination. Also, Frost's use of an El Chicano hit, as opposed to the less culturally specific beat of "Rough Cut," is a nod to the *veteranos* (who to this day remain partial to Oldies over hiphop).

The early nineties have been watershed years for Chicano hiphoppers—a peak moment being the 1991 release of Cypress Hill's first album. Showcasing the combined talents of Mellow Man Ace's brother Sen Dogg, B-Real, DJ Muggs, *Cypress Hill* integrates the best of Rammelzee's hiphop tricknology, the Calo rap of Don Tosti and Raul Diaz, bad-ass West Coast gangsta mythology, humor, and trademark beats.

Gangsta Rid, What's up Y'all?

"It's a tribe thing..."

...

"Hey where you from homies?"

It's on

He sees 'em reach for his gun

Buckshot to the dome

He jumps in the bomb

Homies in tha back but she just wants to go home

But he trips to the store

Homeboy needs a 40

White boy's at the counter

Thinkin' "O Lordy Lordy"

Pushin' on the button

Panickin' for nuttin'

Pigs on the way

Hey yo he smells bacon...

Scooby doo y'all, scooby doo y'all

A scooby doo y'all

A doobie doobie doo y'all...

— Cypress Hill, *Hole in the Head*, 1991

It's a Tribe Thing

I am a revolutionary...because creating life amid death is a revolutionary act. Just as building nationalism in an era of imperialism is a life-giving act...We are an awakening people, an emerging nation, a new breed.

— Carlos Muñoz, Jr., *Youth Identity, Power*, p. 76

Corky Gonzales's Crusade for Justice in 1969 brought people from every corner of the *varrio* together in the name of self-determination and La Raza. One of the concepts put forth during the course of the conference was that Chicano students, needing "revolutionary role models, would do well to emulate their brothers and sisters in the streets, the *vatos locos* of the *varrio, Carnelismo*, or the code of absolute love in Chicano gangs, was to be adopted by radical student nationalists as the locus of their developing ideology.[24]

The Chicano hiphop that has made it to wax in the last two years frequently assimilates some combination of street mentality and nationalist politics, whether it be as simple as giving the nod to brown pride, or as complex as the cultural nationalism of Aztlan Underground. The gangsta presently dominates brown hiphop, good examples being Proper Dos (west LA), RPM (Valley), Street Mentality (Pico/Union), The Mexicanz (Long Beach) and Brown Town (east LA), to name a few. The music: generally simple beats, frequently scary, down with ganga, *rucas* and *cuetes*, sometimes intentionally educational, and occasionally hilarious. Groups like Of Mexican Descent represent a new generation of lyrical wizards, working in two tongues, with breath control, and kicking knowledge of self.

Cypress Hill are at the center of one of LA's finer hiphop posses, the Soul Assassins. The more recent group Funkdoobiest (consisting of Puerto Rican and Sioux MCs and a Mexican DJ) are down, as well as the Irish American group House of Pain, and allied are the Samoan brothers of the Boo Yaa Tribe, Mellow Man Ace, and Kid Frost. For me, the Soul Assassins represent some of the most radical (and difficult) aspects of living in Los Angeles. On one hand they describe the celebration of difference through hiphop (and the fierce potential in collaboration and in the music), on the other, their lyrics frequently demarcate territorial and personal boundaries (BOOM-in-your-face). But at its most elemental, the beats of hiphop are about walking all over those boundaries with no apologies.

Out of the east we've heard from groups like the Puerto Rican Powerrule (New York), and Fat Joe the Gangsta (Bronx), there's a Brewley MC in Puerto Rico, and reggae español posses in Panama and Mexico, but brown hiphop seems to be coming to fruition on the West Coast. Although the Latin Alliance project didn't hold, hopefully the concept was not outmoded but a little ahead of its time. In a city where 10 per cent of the world's population of El Salvado-rans lives around MacArthur Park (downtown), the possibilities for cross-cultural collaboration and unity seem, well, massive. And with cats like Kid Frost, Cypress, AUG, Proper Dos, and OMD sharpening their skills in every corner of LA, hiphop is where to make it happen. After all, it still remains true that (referring back to the Samoan brother from Carson City) in LA hiphop if you are down, you can hold down.

Special Thanks to Bulldog and Tate.

NOTES

1. Martin Sanchez Jankowski, *Islands in the Street*, Berkeley, Los Angeles and Oxford, 1991, pp. 25–7.
2. Mauricio Mazon, *The Zoot-Suit Riots; The Psychology of Symbolic Annihilation*, Austin, 1984, p. 5.
3. Ibid, p. 9.
4. Ibid, p. 108.
5. Steven Loza, *Barrio Rhythm; Mexican American Music in Los Angeles*, Urbana and Chicago, 1993, p. 42.
6. Ibid.
7. Dick DeLoach, "Bill Hines: The King of Lead," *Lowrider Magazine*, April 1992, p. 52.
8. Ibid, p. 53.
9. Dick DeLoach, "Jesse Valdez and Gypsy Rose," *Lowrider Magazine*, October 1992, p. 56.
10. *Barrio Rhythm*, p. 71
11. Ibid, p. 81.
12. Ibid.
13. Ibid, p. 83.
14. David Toop, *Rap Attack 2: African Rap to Global Hip Hop*, London and New York, 1991, p. 22.
15. Ibid, p. 24
16. Steven Hager, *Hip-Hop: The Illustrated History*, p. 21.
17. *Wild Style*, Charlie Ahearn, 1981. A 35mm rap-umentary about the early integration of the different elements of hiphop culture in New York. Also starring Fred Braithwaite and Patty Astor.
18. *An Illustrated History of Hip Hop*, p. 81.

19. *RapAttack 2*, p. 122.

20. Ibid.

21. Billy Jam, liner notes on *West Coast Rap, The First Dynasty*, Vol. 2, 1992, Rhino Records.

22. On *Greatest Hits of the Zulu Nation*, circa 1982.

23. AKA Jalal of the Last Poets.

24. Carlos Muñoz, Jr., *Youth, Identity, Power: The Chicano*, Verso, 1989, p. 76.

FURTHER READING

Rodolfo F. Acuna, *A Community Under Siege: A Chronicle of Chicanos East of the Los Angeles River, 1945–1975*. Monograph no. 11/Chicano Studies Research Center Publications, Los Angeles: University of California 1984.

Rodolfo F. Acuna, *Occupied America; A History of Chicanos*, New York: HarperCollins 1988.

Dick DeLoach, "Bill Hines: The King of Lead," *Lowrider Magazine* 14, 1992, pp. 52–3.

Dick DeLoach, "Jesse Valdez and Gypsy Rose," *Lowrider Magazine* 14, 1992, pp. 56–8.

Willard Gingerich, "Aspects of Prose Style in Three Chicano Novels: *Pocho, Bless Me, Ultima* and *The Road to Tamazunchale* in ed. Jacob Ornstein-Galicia, *Form and Function in Chicano English*, Rowley, Massachusetts: Newbury House 1994.

Steven Hager, *Hip-Hop: The Illustrated History, Rap Music and Graffiti*, New York: St. Martin's Press, 1984.

Martin Sanchez Jankowski, *Islands in the Street*, Berkeley, Los Angeles and Oxford: University of California Press 1991.

George Lipsitz, *Time Passages; Collective Memory and American Popular Culture*, Minneapolis: University of Minnesota Press 1990.

Steven Loza, *Barrio Rhythm: Mexican American Music in Los Angeles*, Urbana and Chicago: University of Illinois Press 1993.

Mauricio Mazon, *The Zoot-Suit Riots; The Psychology of Symbolic Annihilation*, Austin: University of Texas Press 1984.

Carlos Muñoz Jr, *Youth, Identity, Power; The Chicano Movement*, London and New York: Verso 1989.

Harry Polkinhorn, Alfredo Velasco and Mal Lambert, *El Libra De Calo; Pachuco Slang Dictionary*, San Diego: Atticus Press 1983.

Stan Steiner, *La Raza: The Mexican Americans*, New York, Evanston, and London: Harper & Row 1970.

David Toop, *Rap Attack 2: African Rap to Global Hip Hop*, London and New York: Serpent's Tail 1991.

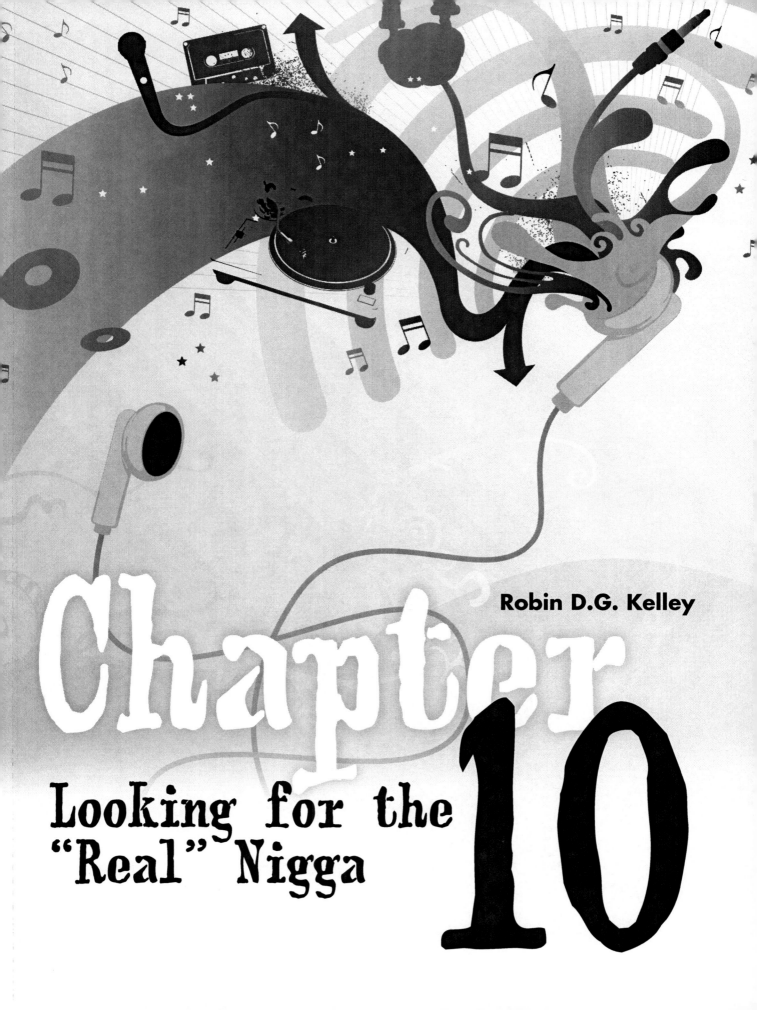

Robin D.G. Kelley

Chapter 10

Looking for the "Real" Nigga

Perhaps the supreme irony of black American existence is how broadly black people debate the question of cultural identity among themselves while getting branded as a cultural monolith by those who would deny us the complexity and complexion of a community, let alone a nation. If Afro-Americans have never settled for the racist reductions imposed upon them—from chattel slaves to cinematic stereotype to sociological myth—it's because the black collective conscious not only knew better but also knew more than enough ethnic diversity to subsume these fictions.

— Greg Tate, *Flyboy in the Buttermilk*

The biggest difference between us and white folks is that we know when we are playing.

— Alberta Roberts, quoted in John Langston Gwaltney, *Drylongso*

"I think this anthropology is just another way to call me a nigger." So observed Othman Sullivan, one of many informants in John Langston Gwaltney's classic study of black culture, *Drylongso*.[1] Perhaps a kinder, gentler way to put it is that anthropology, not unlike most urban social science, has played a key role in marking "blackness" and defining black culture to the "outside" world. Beginning with Robert Park and his proteges to the War on Poverty inspired ethnographers, a battery of social scientists have significantly shaped the current dialogue on black urban culture. Today sociologists, anthropologists, political scientists, and economists compete for huge grants from Ford, Rockefeller, Sage, and other foundations to measure everything measurable in order to get a handle on the newest internal threat to civilization. With the discovery of the so-called underclass, terms like *nihilistic, dysfunctional,* and *pathological* have become the most common adjectives to describe contemporary black urban culture. The question they often pose, to use Mr. Othman Sullivan's words, is what kind of "niggers" populate the inner cities?

Unfortunately, too much of this rapidly expanding literature on the underclass provides less an understanding of the complexity of people's lives and cultures than a bad blaxploitation film or an Ernie Barnes painting. Many social scientists are not only quick to generalize about the black urban poor on the basis of a few "representative" examples, but more often than not, they do not let the natives speak. A major part of the problem is the way in which many mainstream social scientists studying the underclass define *culture*. Relying on a narrowly conceived definition of culture, most of the underclass literature uses *behavior* and *culture* interchangeably.

My purpose, then, is to offer some reflections on how the culture concept employed by social scientists has severely impoverished contemporary debates over the plight of urban African Americans and contributed to the construction of the ghetto as a reservoir of pathologies and bad cultural values. Much of this literature not only conflates behavior with culture, but when social scientists explore "expressive" cultural forms or what has been called "popular culture" (such as language, music, and style), most reduce it to expressions of pathology, compensatory behavior, or creative "coping mechanisms" to deal with racism and poverty. While some aspects of black expressive cultures certainly help inner city residents deal with and even resist ghetto conditions, most of the literature ignores what these cultural forms mean for the practitioners. Few

---

Looking for the "Real" Nigga   173

scholars acknowledge that what might also be at stake here are aesthetics, style, and pleasure. Nor do they recognize black urban culture's hybridity and internal differences. Given the common belief that inner city communities are more isolated than ever before and have completely alien values, the notion that there is one discrete, identifiable black urban culture carries a great deal of weight. By conceiving black urban culture in the singular, interpreters unwittingly reduce their subjects to cardboard typologies who fit neatly into their own definition of the "underclass" and render invisible a wide array of complex cultural forms and practices.

"It's Just a Ghetto Thang": The Problem of Authenticity and the Ethnographic Imagination

A few years ago Mercer Sullivan decried the disappearance of "culture" from the study of urban poverty, attributing its demise to the fact that "overly vague notions of the culture of poverty brought disrepute to the culture concept as a tool for understanding the effects of the concentration of poverty among cultural minorities."[2] In some respects, Sullivan is right: the conservatives who maintain that persistent poverty in the inner city is the result of the behavior of the poor, the product of some cultural deficiency, have garnered so much opposition from many liberals and radicals that few scholars are willing even to discuss culture. Instead, opponents of the "culture of poverty" idea tend to focus on structural transformations in the U.S. economy, labor force composition, and resultant changes in marriage patterns to explain the underclass.[3]

However, when viewed from another perspective, culture never really disappeared from the underclass debate.[4] On the contrary, it has been as central to the work of liberal structuralists and radical Marxists as it has been to that of the conservative culturalists. While culturalists insist that the behavior of the urban poor explains their poverty, the structuralists argue that the economy explains their behavior as well as their poverty.[5] For all their differences, there is general agreement that a common, debased culture is what defines the "underclass," what makes it a threat to the future of America. Most interpreters of the "underclass" treat behavior as not only a synonym for culture but also as the determinant for class. In simple terms, what makes the "underclass" a class is members' common behavior—not their income, their poverty level, or the kind of work they do. It is a definition of class driven more by moral panic than by systematic analysis. A cursory look at the literature reveals that there is no consensus as to precisely what behaviors define the underclass. Some scholars, like William Julius Wilson, have offered a more spatial definition of the underclass by focusing on areas of "concentrated poverty," but obvious problems result when observers discover the wide range of behavior and attitudes in, say, a single city block. What happens to the concept when we find people with jobs engaging in illicit activities and some jobless people depending on church charity? Or married employed fathers who spend virtually no time with their kids and jobless unwed fathers participating and sharing in child care responsibilities? How does the concept of underclass behavior hold up to Kathryn Edin's findings that many so-called welfare-dependent women must also work for wages in order to make ends meet?[6] More importantly, how do we fit criminals (many first-time offenders), welfare recipients, single mothers, absent fathers, alcohol and drug abusers, and gun toting youth all into one "class"?

174   THE POLITICS OF GANGSTA RAP

When we try to apply the same principles to people with higher incomes, who are presumed to be "functional" and "normative," we ultimately expose the absurdity of it all. Political scientist Charles Henry offers the following description of pathological behavior for the very folks the underclass is supposed to emulate. This tangle of deviant behavior, which he calls the "culture of wealth," is characterized by a "rejection or denial of physical attributes" leading to "hazardous sessions in tanning parlors" and frequent trips to weight-loss salons; rootlessness; antisocial behavior; and "an inability to make practical decisions" evidenced by their tendency to own several homes, frequent private social and dining clubs, and by their vast amount of unnecessary and socially useless possessions. "Finally," Henry adds, "the culture of the rich is engulfed in a web of crime, sexism, and poor health. Drug use and white collar crime are rampant, according to every available index.... In sum, this group is engaged in a permanent cycle of divorce, forced child separations through boarding schools, and rampant materialism that leads to the dreaded Monte Carlo syndrome. Before they can be helped they must close tax loopholes, end subsidies, and stop buying influence."[7]

As absurd as Henry's satirical reformulation of the culture of poverty might appear, this very instrumentalist way of understanding culture is deeply rooted even in the more liberal social science approaches to urban poverty. In the mid- to late 1960s, a group of progressive social scientists, mostly ethnographers, challenged the more conservative culture-of-poverty arguments and insisted that black culture was itself a necessary adaptation to racism and poverty, a set of coping mechanisms that grew out of the struggle for material and psychic survival.[8] Ironically, while this work consciously sought to recast ghetto dwellers as active agents rather than passive victims, it has nonetheless reinforced monolithic interpretations of black urban culture and significantly shaped current articulations of the culture concept in social science approaches to poverty.

With the zeal of colonial missionaries, these liberal and often radical ethnographers (mostly white men) set out to explore the newly discovered concrete jungles. Inspired by the politics of the 1960s and mandated by Lyndon Johnson's War on Poverty, a veritable army of anthropologists, sociologists, linguists, and social psychologists set up camp in America's ghettos. In the Harlem and Washington Heights communities where I grew up in the mid- to late 1960s, even our liberal white teachers who were committed to making us into functional members of society turned out to be foot soldiers in the new ethnographic army. With the overnight success of published collections of inner city children's writings like *The Me Nobody Knows* and Caroline Mirthes's *Can't You Hear Me Talking to You?*, writing about the intimate details of our home life seemed like our most important assignment.[9] (And we made the most of it by enriching our mundane narratives with stories from *Mod Squad, Hawaii Five-O,* and *Speed Racer.*)

Of course, I do not believe for a minute that most of our teachers gave us these kinds of exercises hoping to one day appear on the *Merv Griffin Show.* But, in retrospect at least, the explosion of interest in the inner city cannot be easily divorced from the marketplace. Although these social scientists came to mine what they believed was the "authentic Negro culture," there was real gold in them thar ghettos since white America's fascination with the pathological urban poor translated into massive book sales.

Unfortunately, most social scientists believed they knew what "authentic Negro culture" was before they entered the field. The "real Negroes" were the young jobless men hanging out on the corner passing the bottle, the brothers with the nastiest verbal repertoire, the pimps and hustlers, and the single mothers who raised streetwise kids who began cursing before they could walk. Of course, there were other characters, like the men and women who went to work every day in foundries, hospitals, nursing homes, private homes, police stations, sanitation departments, banks, garment factories, assembly plants, pawn shops, construction sites, loading docks, storefront churches, telephone companies, grocery and department stores, public transit, restaurants, welfare offices, recreation centers; or the street vendors, the cab drivers, the bus drivers, the ice cream truck drivers, the seamstresses, the numerologists and fortune tellers, the folks who protected or cleaned downtown buildings all night long. These are the kinds of people who lived in my neighborhood in West Harlem during the early 1970s, but they rarely found their way into the ethnographic text. And when they did show up, social scientists tended to reduce them to typologies—"lames," "strivers," "mainstreamers," "achievers," or "revolutionaries."[10]

Perhaps these urban dwellers were not as interesting, as the hard-core ghetto poor, or more likely, they stood at the margins of a perceived or invented "authentic" Negro society. A note-worthy exception is John Langston Gwaltney's remarkable book, *Drylongso: A Self-Portrait of Black America* (1981). Based on interviews conducted during the 1970s with black working-class residents in several Northeastern cities, *Drylongso* is one of the few works on urban African Americans by an African American anthropologist that appeared during the height of ghetto ethnography. Because Gwaltney is blind, he could not rely on the traditional methods of observation and intereepretation. Instead—and this is the book's strength—he allowed his informants to speak for themselves about what *they* see and do. They interpret their own communities, African American culture, white society, racism, politics and the state, and the very discipline in which Gwaltney was trained—anthropology. What the book reveals is that the natives are aware that anthropologists are constructing them, and they saw in Gwaltney—who relied primarily on family and friends as informants—an opportunity to speak back. One, a woman he calls Elva Noble, said to him: "I'm not trying to tell you your job, but if you ever do write a book about us, then I hope you really do write about things the way they really are. I guess that depends on you to some extent but you know that there are more of us who are going to work every day than there are like the people who are git'n over."[11] While his definition of a "core black culture" may strike some as essentialist, it emphasizes diversity and tolerance for diversity. Gwaltney acknowledges the stylistic uniqueness of African American culture, yet he shows that the central facet of this core culture is the deep-rooted sense of community, common history, and collective recognition that there is indeed an African American culture and a "black" way of doing things. Regardless of the origins of a particular recipe, or the roots of a particular religion or Christian denomination, the cook and the congregation have no problem identifying these distinct practices and institutions as "black."

Few ghetto ethnographers have understood or developed Gwaltney's insights into African American urban culture. Whereas Gwaltney's notion of a core culture incorporates a diverse and contradictory range of practices, attitudes, and relationships that are dynamic, historically situated, and ethnically hybrid, social scientists of his generation and after—especially those at the forefront of poverty studies—treat culture as if it were a set of behaviors. They assume that there is one identifiable ghetto culture, and what they observed was it. These assumptions, which continue to shape much current social science and most mass media representations of the "inner city," can be partly attributed to the way ethnographers are trained in the West. As James Clifford observed, anthropologists studying non-Western societies are not only compelled to describe the communities under interrogation as completely foreign to their own society, but if a community is to be worthy of study as a group it must possess an identifiable, homogeneous culture. I think, in principle at least, the same holds true for interpretations of black urban America. Ethnographers can argue that inner city residents, as a "foreign" culture, do not share "mainstream" values. Social scientists do not treat behavior as situational, an individual response to a specific set of circumstances; rather, inner city residents act according to their own unique cultural "norms."[12]

For many of these ethnographers, the defining characteristic of African American urban culture was relations between men and women. Even Charles Keil, whose *Urban Blues* is one of the few ethnographic texts from that period to not only examine aesthetics and form in black culture but take "strong exception to the view that lower-class Negro life style and its characteristic rituals and expressive roles are the products of overcompensation for masculine self-doubt," nonetheless concludes that "the battle of the sexes" is precisely what characterizes African American urban culture.[13] Expressive cultures, then, were not only constructed as adaptive, functioning primarily to cope with the horrible conditions of ghetto life, but were conceived largely as expressions of masculinity. In fact, the linking of men with expressive cultures was so pervasive that the pioneering ethnographies focusing on African American women and girls—notably the work of Joyce Ladner and Carol Stack—do not explore this realm, whether in mixed-gender groupings or all-female groups. They concentrated more on sex roles, relationships, and family survival rather than expressive cultures.[14]

Two illuminating examples are the debate over the concept of "soul" and the verbal art form known to most academics as "the dozens." In the ethnographic imagination, "soul" and "the dozens" were both examples par excellence of authentic black urban culture as well as vehicles for expressing black masculinity. The bias toward expressive male culture must be understood within a particular historical and political context. In the midst of urban rebellions, the masculinist rhetoric of black nationalism, the controversy over the Moynihan report, and the uncritical linking of "agency" and resistance with men, black men took center stage in poverty research.[15]

Soul was so critical to the social science discourse on the adaptive culture of the black urban poor that Lee Rainwater edited an entire book about it, and Ulf Hannerz structured his study of Washington, D.C., on it.[16] According to these authors, *soul* is the expressive lifestyle of black men adapting to economic and political marginality. This one word supposedly embraces the entire range of "Negro lower class culture"; it constitutes "essential Negroness." Only authentic Negroes had soul. In defining *soul*, Hannerz reduces aesthetics, style, and the dynamic struggle over identity to a set of coping mechanisms. Among his many attempts to define *soul*, he insists that it is tied to the instability of black male-female relationships. He deduced evidence for this from his findings that "success with the opposite sex is a focal concern in lower-class Negro life," and the fact that a good deal of popular black music—soul music—was preoccupied with courting or losing a lover.[17]

Being "cool" is an indispensable component of soul; it is also regarded by these ethnographers as a peculiarly black expression of masculinity. Indeed, the entire discussion of cool centers entirely on black men. Cool as an aesthetic, as a style, as an art form expressed through language and the body, is simply not dealt with. Cool, not surprisingly, is merely another mechanism to cope with racism and poverty. According to Lee Rainwater and David Schulz, it is nothing more than a survival technique intended to "make yourself interesting and attractive to others so that you are better able to manipulate their behavior along lines that will provide some immediate gratification." To achieve cool simply entails learning to lie and putting up a front of competence and success. But like a lot of adaptive strategies, cool is self-limiting. While it helps young black males maintain an image of being "in control," according to David Schulz, it can also make "intimate relationships" more difficult to achieve.[18]

Looking for the "Real" Nigga

Hannerz reluctantly admits that no matter how hard he tried, none of the "authentic ghetto inhabitants" he had come across could define *soul*. He was certain that soul was "essentially J Negro," but concluded that it really could not be defined, for to do that would be to undermine its meaning: it is something one possesses, a ticket into the "in crowd." If you need a definition you do not know what it means. It's a black (male) thang; you'll never understand. But Hannerz obviously felt confident enough to venture his own definition, based on his understanding of African American culture, that *soul* was little more than a survival strategy to cope with the harsh realities of the ghetto. Moreover, he felt empowered to determine which black people had the right to claim the mantle of authenticity: when LeRoi Jones and Lerone Bennett offered their interpretation of soul, Hannerz rejected their definitions, in part because they were not, in his words, "authentic Negroes."[19]

By constructing the black urban world as a single culture whose function is merely to survive the ghetto, Rainwater, Hannerz, and most of their colleagues at the time ultimately collapsed a wide range of historically specific cultural practices and forms and searched for a (*the*) concept that could bring them all together. Such an interpretation of culture makes it impossible for Hannerz and others to see soul not as a thing but as a discourse through which African Americans, at a particular historical moment, claimed ownership of the symbols and practices of their own imagined community. This is why, even at the height of the Black Power movement, African American urban culture could be so fluid, hybrid, and multinational. In Harlem in the 1970s, Nehru suits were as popular and as "black" as dashikis, and martial arts films placed Bruce Lee among a pantheon of black heroes that included Walt Frazier and John Shaft. As debates over the black aesthetic raged, the concept of soul was an assertion that there are "black ways" of doing things, even if those ways are contested and the boundaries around what is "black" are fluid. How it manifests itself and how it shifts is less important than the fact that the boundaries exist in the first place. At the very least, *soul* was a euphemism or a creative way of identifying what many believed was a black aesthetic or black style, and it was a synonym for black itself or a way to talk about being black without reference to color, which is why people of other ethnic groups could have soul.

Soul in the 1960s and early 1970s was also about transformation. It was almost never conceived by African Americans as an innate, genetically derived feature of black life, for it represented a shedding of the old "Negro" ways and an embrace of "Black" power and pride. The most visible signifier of soul was undoubtedly the Afro. More than any other element of style, the Afro put the issue of hair squarely on the black political agenda, where it has been ever since. The current debates over hair and its relationship to political consciousness really have their roots in the Afro. Not surprisingly, social scientists at the time viewed the Afro through the limited lens of Black Power politics, urban uprising, and an overarching discourse of authenticity. And given their almost exclusive interest in young men, their perspective on the Afro was strongly influenced by the rhetoric and iconography of a movement that flouted black masculinity. Yet, once we look beyond the presumably male-occupied ghetto streets that dominated the ethnographic imagination at the time, the story of the Afro's origins and meaning complicated the link to soul culture.

First, the Afro powerfully demonstrates the degree to which soul was deeply implicated in the marketplace. What passed as "authentic" ghetto culture was as much a product of market forces and the commercial appropriation of urban styles as experience and individual creativity. And very few black urban residents/consumers viewed their own participation in the marketplace as undermining their own authenticity as bearers of black culture. Even before the Afro reached its height of popularity, the hair care industry stepped in and began producing a vast array of chemicals to make one's "natural" more natural. One could pick up Raveen Hair Sheen, Afro Sheen, Ultra Sheen, Head Start vitamin and mineral capsules, to name a few. The Clairol Corporation (whose CEO supported the Philadelphia Black Power Conference in 1967) did not hesitate to enter the "natural" business.[20] Listen to this Clairol ad published in *Essence Magazine* (November 1970):

> No matter what they say...Nature Can't Do It Alone! Nothing pretties up a face like a beautiful head of hair, but even hair that's born this beautiful needs a little help along the way.... A little brightening, a little heightening of color, a little extra sheen to liven up the look. And because that wonderful natural look is still the most wanted look...the most fashionable, the most satisfying look you can have at any age...anything you do must look natural, natural, natural. And this indeed is the art of Miss Clairol.

Depending on the particular style, the Afro could require almost as much maintenance as chemically straightened hair. And for those women (and some men) whose hair simply would not cooperate or who wanted the flexibility to shift from straight to nappy, there was always the Afro wig. For nine or ten dollars, one could purchase a variety of different wig styles, ranging from the "Soul-Light Freedom" wigs to the "Honey Bee Afro Shag," made from cleverly labeled synthetic materials such as "Afrylic" or "Afrilon."[21]

Second, the Afro's roots really go back to the bourgeois high fashion circles in the late 1950s. The Afro was seen by the black and white elite as a kind of new female exotica. Even though its intention, among some circles at least, was to achieve healthier hair and express solidarity with newly independent African nations, the Afro entered public consciousness as a mod fashion statement that was not only palatable to bourgeois whites but, in some circles, celebrated. There were people like Lois Liberty Jones, a consultant, beauty culturist, and lecturer, who claimed to have pioneered the natural as early as 1952! She originated "Coiffures Aframericana" concepts of hair styling which she practiced in Harlem for several years from the early 1960s.[22] More importantly, it was the early, not the late, 1960s, when performers like Odetta, Miriam Makeba, Abby Lincoln, Nina Simone, and the artist Margaret Burroughs began wearing the "au naturelle" style—medium to short Afros. Writer Andrea Benton Rushing has vivid memories of seeing Odetta at the Village Gate long before Black Power entered the national lexicon. "I was mesmerized by her stunning frame," she recalled, "in its short kinky halo. She had a regal poise and power that I had never seen in a 'Negro' (as we called ourselves back then) woman before—no matter how naturally 'good' or diligently straightened her hair was." Many other black women in New York, particularly those who ran in the interracial world of Manhattan sophisticates, were first introduced to the natural through high fashion models in au naturelle shows, which were the rage at the time.[23]

Helen Hayes King, associate editor of *Jet*, came in contact with the au naturelle style at an art show in New York, in the late 1950s. A couple of years later, she heard Abby Lincoln speak about her own decision to go natural at one of these shows and, with prompting from her husband, decided to go forth to adopt the 'fro. Ironically, one of the few salons in Chicago specializing in the au naturelle look was run by a white male hairdresser in the exclusive Northside community. He actually lectured King on the virtues of natural hair: "I don't know why Negro women with delicate hair like yours burn and process all the life out of it.... If you d just wash it, oil it and take care of it, it would be so much healthier.... I don't know how all this straightening foolishness started anyhow." When she returned home to the Southside, however, instead of compliments she received strange looks from her neighbors. Despite criticism and ridicule by her co-workers and friends, she stuck with her au naturelle, not because she was trying to make a political statement or demonstrate her solidarity with African independence movements. "I'm not so involved in the neo-African aspects of the 'au naturelle' look," she wrote, "nor in the get-back-to-your-heritage bit." Her explanation was simple; the style was chic and elegant and in the end she was pleased with the feel of her hair, It is fitting to note that most of the compliments came from whites.[24]

What is also interesting about King's narrative is that it appeared in the context of a debate with Nigerian writer Theresa Ogunbiyi over whether black women should straighten their hair or not, which appeared in a 1963 issue of *Negro Digest*. In particular, Ogunbiyi defended the right of a Lagos firm to forbid employees to plait their hair; women were required to wear straight hair. She rejected the idea that straightening hair destroys national custom and heritage: "I think we carry this national pride a bit too far at times, even to the detriment of our country's progress." Her point was that breaking with tradition is progress, especially since Western dress and hairstyles are more comfortable and easier to work in. "When I wear the Yoruba costume, I find that I spend more time than I can afford, re-tying the headtie and the bulky wrapper round my waist. And have you tried typing in an 'Agbada'? I am all for nationalisation but give it to me with some comfort and improvement."[25]

Andrea Benton Rushing's story is a slight variation on King's experience. She, too, was a premature natural hair advocate. When she stepped out of the house sporting her first Afro, perhaps inspired by Odetta or prompted by plain curiosity, her "relatives though I'd lost my mind and, of course, my teachers at Juilliard stole sideways looks at me and talked about the importance of appearance in auditions and concerts." Yet, while the white Juilliard faculty and her closest family members found the new style strange and inappropriate, brothers on the block in her New York City neighborhood greeted her with praise: " 'Looking good, sister,' 'Watch out, African queen!' " She, too, found it ironic that middle-class African woman on the continent chose to straighten their hair. During a trip to Ghana years later, she recalled the irony of having her Afro braided in an Accra beauty parlor while "three Ghanaians (two Akan-speaking government workers and one Ewe microbiologist)...were having their chemically-straightened hair washed, set, combed out, and sprayed in place."[26]

No matter what spurred on the style or who adopted it, however, the political implications of the au naturelle could not be avoided. After all, the biggest early proponents of the style tended to be women artists whose work identified with the black freedom movement and African liberation. In some respects, women such as Abby Lincoln, Odetta, and Nina Simone were part of what might be called black bohemia. They participated in a larger community—based mostly in New York—of poets, writers, musicians of the 1950s, for whom the emancipation of their own artistic form coincided with the African freedom movement. *Ebony, Jet,* and *Sepia* magazines were covering Africa, and African publications such as Drum were being read by those ex-Negroes in the States who could get their hands on it. The Civil Rights movement, the struggle against apartheid in South Africa, and the emergence of newly independent African nations found a voice in recordings by various jazz artists, including Randy Weston's *Uhuru Afrika*, Max Roach's *We Insist: Freedom Now Suite* (featuring Abby Lincoln, Roach's wife), Art Blakey's "Message from Kenya" and "Ritual," and John Coltrane's "Liberia," "Dahomey Dance," and "Africa." Revolutionary political movements, combined with revolutionary experiments in artistic creation—the simultaneous embrace and rejection of tradition—forged the strongest physical and imaginary links between Africa and the diaspora.[27] Thus, it is not surprising that Harold Cruse, in one of his seminal essays on the coming of the new black nationalism, anticipated the importance of the style revolution and the place of the au naturelle in it. As early as 1962, Cruse predicted that in the coming years "Afro-Americans...will undoubtedly make a lot of noise in militant demonstrations, cultivate beards and sport their hair in various degrees of la mode au natural, and tend to be cultish with African- and Arab-style dress."[28]

Of course, he was right. By the mid-1960s, however, the Afro was no longer associated with downtown chic but with uptown rebellion. It was sported by rock-throwing black males and black-leathered militants armed to the teeth. Thus, once associated with feminine chic, the Afro suddenly became the symbol of black manhood, the death of the "Negro" and birth of the militant, virulent Black man.[29] The new politics, combined with media representations of Afro-coifed black militants, profoundly shaped the ethnographic imagination. As new narratives were created to explain the symbolic significance of the natural style, women were rendered invisible. The erasure of women, I would argue, was not limited to histories of style politics but to ghetto ethnography in general.

The masculinism of soul in contemporary ghetto ethnography has survived to this day, despite the last quarter-century of incisive black feminist scholarship. The ethnographic and sociological search for soul has made a comeback recently under a new name: the "cool pose." In a recent book, Richard Majors and Janet Mancini Bilson have recycled the arguments of Lee Rainwater, Ulf Hannerz, Elliot Liebow, and David Schulz, and have suggested that the "cool pose" captures the essence of young black male expressive culture. Like earlier constructors of soul, they too believe that the "cool pose" is an adaptive strategy to cope with the particular forms of racism and oppression black males face in America. "Cool pose is a ritualized form of masculinity that entails behaviors, scripts, physical posturing, impression management, and carefully crafted performances that deliver a single, critical message: pride, strength, and control." Echoing earlier works, the cool pose is also a double-edged sword since it allegedly undermines potential intimacy with females.[30] By playing down the aesthetics of cool and reducing the cool pose to a response by heterosexual black males to racism, intraracial violence, and poverty, the authors not only reinforce the idea that there is an essential black urban culture created by the oppressive conditions of the ghetto but ignore manifestations of the cool pose in the public "performances" of black women, gay black men, and the African American middle class.

A more tangible example of black urban expressive culture that seemed to captivate social scientists in the 1960s is "the dozens." Yet, in spite of the amount of ink devoted to the subject, it has also been perhaps the most misinterpreted cultural form coming out of African American communities. Called at various times in various places "capping," "sounding," "ranking," "bagging," or "dissing," virtually all leading anthropologists, sociologists, and linguists agree that it is a black male form of "ritual insult," a verbal contest involving any number of young black men who compete by talking about each other's mama. There is less agreement, however, about how to interpret the sociological and psychological significance of the dozens. In keeping with the dominant social science interpretations of the culture concept, so-called ritual insults among urban black youth were either another adaptive strategy or an example of social pathology.

The amazing thing about the sociological and ethnographic scholarship on the dozens, from John Bollard's ruminations in 1939 to the more recent misreadings by Roger Lane and Carl Nightingale, is the consistency with which it repeats the same errors. For one, the almost universal assertion that the dozens is a "ritual" empowers the ethnographer to select what appears to be more formalized verbal exchanges (e.g., rhyming couplets) and ascribe to them greater "authenticity" than other forms of playful conversation. In fact, by framing the dozens as ritual, most scholars have come to believe that it is first and foremost a "contest" with rules, players, and mental scorecard rather than the daily banter of many (not all) young

African Americans. Anyone who has lived and survived the dozens (or whatever name you want to call it) cannot imagine turning to one's friends and announcing, "Hey, let's go outside and play the dozens." Furthermore, the very use of the term *ritual* to describe everyday speech reinforces the exoticization of black urban populations constructing them as Others whose investment in this cultural tradition is much deeper than trying to get a laugh.[31]

These problems, however, are tied to larger ones. For example, white ethnographers seemed oblivious to the fact that their very presence shaped what they observed. Asking their subjects to "play the dozens" while an interloper records the "session" with a tape recorder and notepad has the effect of creating a ritual performance for the sake of an audience, of turning spontaneous, improvised verbal exchanges into a formal practice. More significantly, ethnographers have tailor-made their own interpretation of the dozens by selecting what they believe were the most authentic sites for such verbal duels—street corners, pool halls, bars, and parks. In other words, they sought out male spaces rather than predominantly female and mixed-gender spaces to record the dozens. It is no wonder that practically all commentators on the dozens have concluded that it is a boy thing. The fact is, evidence suggests that young women engaged in these kinds of verbal exchanges as much as their male counterparts, both with men and between women. And they were no less profane. By not searching out other mixed-gender and female spaces such as school buses, cafeterias, kitchen tables, beauty salons, and house parties, ethnographers have overstated the extent to which the dozens were the sole property of men.[32]

Folklorist Roger Abrahams, who pioneered the study of the dozens in his book on black vernacular folklore "from the streets of Philadelphia," is one of the few scholars to appreciate the pleasure and aesthetics of such verbal play. Nevertheless, he argues that one of the primary functions of the dozens is to compensate for a lack of masculinity caused by too many absent fathers and domineering mothers, which is why the main target of insults is an "opponent's" mother. "By exhibiting his wit, by creating new and vital folkloric expression, [the dozens player] is able to effect a temporary release from anxiety for both himself and his audience. By creating playgrounds for playing out aggressions, he achieves a kind of masculine identity for himself and his group in a basically hostile environment."[33] David Schulz offers an even more specific interpretation of the dozens as a form of masculine expression in an environment dominated by dysfunctional families. He writes: "Playing the dozens occurs at the point when the boy is about to enter puberty and suffer his greatest rejection from his mother as a result of his becoming a man. The dozens enables him to develop a defense against this rejection and provides a vehicle for his transition into the manipulative world of the street dominated by masculine values expressed in gang life." It then serves as a "ritualized exorcism" that allows men to break from maternal dominance and "establish their own image of male superiority celebrated in street life."[34]

Allow me to propose an alternative reading of the dozens. The goal of the dozens and related verbal games is deceptively simple: to get a laugh. The pleasure of the dozens is not the viciousness of the insult but the humor, the creative pun, the outrageous metaphor. Contrary to popular belief, mothers are not the sole target; the subjects include fathers, grand-parents, brothers, sisters, cousins, friends, food, skin color, smell, and hairstyles. I am not suggesting that "your mama" is unimportant in the whole structure of these verbal exchanges. Nor am I suggesting that the emphasis on "your mama" has absolutely nothing to do with the ways in which patriarchy is discursively reproduced. However, we need to understand that "your mama" in this context is almost never living, literal, or even metaphoric. "Your mama" is a generic reference, a code signaling that the dozens have begun—it signifies a shift in speech. "Your mama" is also a mutable, nameless body of a shared imagination that can be constructed and reconstructed in a thousand different shapes, sizes, colors, and circumstances. The emphasis on "your mama" in most interpretations of the dozens has more to do with the peculiar preoccupation of social science with Negro family structure than anything else. Besides, in many cases the target is immaterial; your mama, your daddy, your greasy-headed granny are merely vehicles through which the speaker tries to elicit a laugh and display her skills. In retrospect, this seems obvious, but amid the complicated readings of masculine over-compensation and ritual performance, only a handful of writers of the period—most of whom were African Americans with no affiliation with the academy—recognized the centrality of humor. One was Howard Seals, who self-published a pamphlet on the dozens in 1969 titled *You Ain't Thuh Man Yuh Mamma Wuz.* In an effort to put to rest all the sociological overinterpretation, Seals explains: "The emotional tone to be maintained is that of hilariously, outrageously funny bantering."[35] Compare Seals's comment with linguist William Labov, who, while recognizing the humor, ultimately turns laughter into part of the ritual and thus reinforces the process of Othering:

> The primary mark of positive evaluation is laughter. We can rate the effectiveness of a sound in a group session by the number of members of the audience who laugh.
>
> A really successful sound will be evaluated by overt comments...the most common forms are: "Oh!," "Oh shit!" "God damn!" or "Oh lord!" By far the most common is "Oh shit!" The intonation is important; when approval is to be signalled the vowel of each word is quite long, with a high sustained initial pitch, and a slow-falling pitch contour.[36]

Without a concept of, or even an interest in, aesthetics, style, and the visceral pleasures of cultural forms, it should not be surprising that most social scientists explained black urban culture in terms of coping mechanisms, rituals, or oppositional responses to racism. And trapped by an essentialist interpretation of culture, they continue to look for that elusive "authentic" ghetto sensibility, the true, honest, unbridled, pure cultural practices that capture the raw, ruffneck "reality" of urban life. Today, that reality is rap. While studies of rap and Hip Hop culture have been useful in terms of nudging contemporary poverty studies to pay attention to expressive cultures, they have not done much to advance the culture concept in social science. Like its progenitor, the dozens, rap or Hip Hop has been subject to incredible misconception and overinterpretation. Despite the brilliant writing of cultural critics like Tricia Rose, Greg Tate, George Lipsitz, Brian Cross, James Spady, dream harnpton, Seth Fernando, Jonathan Scott, Juan Flors, Toure, and others, a number of scholars have returned to or revised the interpretive frameworks developed by the previous generation of ethnographers.[37]

For example, in a very recent book on poor black youth in postwar Philadelphia, Carl Nightingale suggests that the presumed loss of oral traditions like toasting (long, often profane vernacular narrative poetry performed orally) and the dozens, and the rise of rap music and similar commercialized expressive cultures partly explains the increase in violence among young black males. The former, he argues, has played a positive role in curbing violence while the latter is responsible for heightening aggression. He thus calls on young black men to return to these earlier, presumably precommercial cultural forms to vent emotions. Nightingale advocates resurrecting the ring shout, drumming, singing the blues, even toasting, to express black male pain and vulnerability.

The suggestion that rap music has undermined black cultural integrity is made even more forcefully in a recent article by Andre Craddock-Willis. He criticizes nearly all rap artists—especially hard-core gangsta rappers—for not knowing the "majesty" of the blues. The Left, he insists, "must work to gently push these artists to understand the tradition whose shoulders they stand on, and encourage them to comprehend struggle, sacrifice, vision and dedication—the cornerstones for the Black musical tradition."[38] (A tradition, by the way, that includes the great Jelly Roll Morton, whose 1938 recording of "Make Me a Pallet on the Floor" included lines like: "Come here you sweet bitch, give me that pussy, let me get in your drawers / I'm gonna make you think you fuckin' with Santa Claus.")[39]

On the flip side are authors who insist that rap music is fundamentally the authentic, unrnediated voice of ghetto youth. Tommy Lott's recent essay, "Marooned in America: Black Urban Youth Culture and Social Pathology," offers a powerful critique of neoconservative culture-of-poverty theories and challenges assumptions that the culture of the so-called underclass is pathological, but he nevertheless reduces expressive culture to a coping strategy to deal with the terror of street life. For Lott, the Hip Hop nation is the true voice of the black lumpen-proletariat whose descriptions of street life are the real thing. "As inhabitants of extreme-poverty neighborhoods," he writes, "many rap artists and their audiences are entrenched in a street life filled with crime, drugs, and violence. Being criminal-minded and having street values are much more suitable for living in their environment." Of course, most rap music is not about a nihilistic street life but about rocking the mike, and the vast majority a JS of rap artists (like most inner city youth) were not entrenched in the tangled web of crime and violence. Yet, he is convinced that Hip Hop narratives of ghetto life "can only come from one's experiences on the streets. Although, at its worst, this knowledge is manifested through egotistical sexual boasting, the core meaning of the rapper's use of the term 'knowledge' is to be *politically* astute, that is, to have a full understanding of the conditions under which black urban youth must survive."[40]

By not acknowledging the deep visceral pleasures black youth derive from making and consuming culture, the stylistic and aesthetic conventions that render the form and performance more attractive than the message, these authors reduce expressive culture to a political text to be read like a less sophisticated version of *The Nation* or *Radical America*. But what counts more than the story is the "storytelling"—an emcee's verbal facility on the mic, the creative and often hilarious use of puns, metaphors, similes, not to mention the ability to kick some serious slang (or what we might call linguistic inventiveness). As microphone fiend Rakim might put it, the function of Hip Hop is to "move the crowd." For all the implicit and explicit politics of rap lyrics, Hip Hop must be understood as a sonic force more than anything else.

Despite their good intentions, ignoring aesthetics enables these authors not only to dismiss "egotistical sexual boasting" as simply a weakness in political ideology but also to mistakenly interpret narratives of everyday life as descriptions of personal experience rather than a revision of older traditions of black vernacular poetry and/or appropriations from mainstream popular culture. To begin with rap music as a mirror image of daily life ignores the influences of urban toasts and published "pimp narratives," which became popular during the late 1960s and early 1970s. In many instances the characters are almost identical, and on occasion rap artists pay tribute to toasting by lyrically "sampling" these early pimp narratives.[41]

Moreover, the assumption that rappers are merely street journalists does not allow for the playfulness and storytelling that is so central to Hip Hop specifically, and black vernacular culture generally. For example, violent lyrics in rap music are rarely meant to be literal. Rather, they are more often than not metaphors to challenge competitors on the microphone. The mic becomes a Tech-9 or AK-47, imagined drive-bys occur from the stage, flowing lyrics become hollow-point shells. Classic examples are Ice Cube's "Jackin' for Beats," a humorous song that describes sampling other artists and producers as outright armed robbery, and Ice T's "Pulse of the Rhyme" or "Grand Larceny" (which brags about stealing a show).[42] Moreover, exaggerated and invented boasts of criminal acts should sometimes be regarded as part of a larger set of signifying practices. Growing out of a much older set of cultural practices, these masculinist narratives are essentially verbal duels over who is the "baddest." They are not meant as literal descriptions of violence and aggression, but connote the playful use of language itself.[43]

Of course, the line between rap music's gritty realism, storytelling, and straight-up signifying) is not always clear to listeners nor is it supposed to be. Hip Hop, particularly gangsta rap, also attracts listeners for whom the "ghetto" is a place of adventure, unbridled violence, erotic fantasy, and/or an imaginary alternative to suburban boredom. White music critic John Leland, who claimed that Ice Cube's turn toward social criticism "killed rap music," praised the group NWA because they "dealt in evil as fantasy: killing cops, smoking has, filling quiet nights with a flurry of senseless buckshot." This kind of voyeurism partly explains NWA's huge white following and why their album *Efil4zaggin* shot to the top of the charts as soon as it was released. As one critic put it, "In reality, NWA have more in common with a Charles Bronson movie than a PBS documentary on the plight of the inner-cities." NWA members have even admitted that some of their recent songs were not representations of reality "in the hood" but inspired by popular films like *Innocent Man* starring Tom Selleck, and *Tango and Cash*.[44]

Claims to have located the authentic voice of black ghetto youth are certainly not unique. Several scholars insist that Hip Hop is the pure, unadulterated voice of a ghetto that has grown increasingly isolated from "mainstream" society. Missing from this formulation is rap music's incredible hybridity. From the outset, rap music embraced a variety of styles and cultural forms, from reggae and salsa to heavy metal and jazz. Hip Hop's hybridity reflected, in part, the increasingly international character of America's inner cities resulting from immigration, demographic change, and new forms of information, as well as the inventive employment of technology in creating rap music. By using two turntables, and later digital samplers, deejays played different records, isolated the "break beats" or what they identified as the funkiest part of a song, and boldly mixed a wide range of different music and musical genres to create new music. And despite the fact that many of the pioneering deejays, rappers, and break dancers were African American, West Indian, and Puerto Rican and strongly identified with the African diaspora, rap artists wrecked all the boundaries between "black" and "white" music. Deejay Afrika Islam remembers vividly the time when Hip Hop and punk united for a moment and got busy at the New Wave clubs in New York during the early 1980s. Even before the punk rockers sought a relationship with uptown Hip Hop deejays, Afrika Islam recalls, in the Bronx they were already playing "everything from Aerosmith's 'Walk This Way' to Dunk and the Blazers." Grand Master Caz, whose lyrics were stolen by the Sugarhill Gang and ended up in *Rapper's Delight* (the first successful rap record in history), grew up in the Bronx listening to soft rock and mainstream pop music. As he explained in an interview, "Yo, I'd bug you out if I told you who I used to listen to. I used to listen to Barry Manilow, Neil Diamond, and Simon and Garfunkel. I grew up listening to that WABC. That's why a lot of the stuff that my group did, a lot of routines that we're famous for all come from all white boy songs."[45]

If you saw a picture of Caz, this statement would seem incongruous. He looks the part of an authentic black male, a real ruffneck, hoodie, "G," nigga, criminal, menace. And yet, he is a product of a hybrid existence, willing to openly talk about Simon and Garfunkel in a book that I could only purchase from a Nation of Islam booth on 125th Street in Harlem. He is also the first to call what he does "black music," structured noise for which the beat, no matter where it is taken from, is everything. Moreover, like the breakers who danced to his rhymes, the kids who built his speakers, the deejay who spun the records, Caz takes credit for his creativity, his artistry, his "work." This is the "black urban culture" which has remained so elusive to social science; it is the thing, or rather the process, that defies concepts like "coping strategy," "adaptive," "authentic," "nihilistic," and "pathological."

Revising the Culture Concept: Hybridity, Style, and Aesthetics in Black Urban Culture

Aside from the tendency to ignore expressive/popular cultural forms, and limit the category of culture to (so-called dysfunctional) behavior, the biggest problem with the way social scientists employ the culture concept in their studies of the black urban poor is their inability to see what it all means *to the participants and practitioners*. In other words, they do not consider what Clinton (George, that is) calls the "pleasure principle." If I may use a metaphor here, rather than hear the singer they analyze the lyrics; rather than hear the drum they study the song title. Black music, creativity and experimentation in language, that walk, that talk, that style, must also be understood as sources of visceral and psychic pleasure. Though they may also reflect and speak to the political and social world of inner city communities, expressive cultures are not simply mirrors of social life or expressions of conflicts, pathos, and anxieties.

Paul Willis's concept of "symbolic creativity" provides one way out of the impasse created by such a limited concept of culture. As Willis argues, constructing an identity, communicating with others, and achieving pleasure are all part of symbolic creativity—it is literally the labor of creating art in everyday life. Despite his distrust of and vehement opposition to "aesthetics," he realizes that, in most cases, the explicit meaning or intention of a particular cultural form is not the thing that makes it attractive. The appeal of popular music, for example, is more than lyrical: "Songs bear meaning and allow symbolic work not just as speech acts, but also as structures of sound with unique rhythms, textures and forms. Thus, it is not always what is sung, but the way it is sung, within particular conventions or musical genres which gives a piece of music its communicative power and meaning."[46] Indeed, words like soul and funk were efforts to come up with a language to talk about that visceral element in music, even if they did ultimately evolve into market categories. Over two decades ago, black novelist Cecil Brown brilliantly captured this "thing," this symbolic creativity, the pleasure principle, soul, or whatever you want to call it. Writing about the godfather of soul, James Brown, he argued that his lyrics are less important than how they are uttered, where they are placed rhythmically, and "how he makes it sound." "What, for instance, does 'Mother Popcorn' mean? But what difference does it make when you're dancing to it, when you are feeling it, when you are it and it you (possession). It's nothing and everything at once; it is what black (hoodoo) people who never studied art in school mean by art."[47]

Yet to say it is a "black" thing doesn't mean it is made up entirely of black things. As Greg Tate makes clear in his recent collection of essays, *Flyboy in the Buttermilk*, and in the epigraph to this chapter, interpreters of the African American experience—in our case social scientists—must bear a large share of the responsibility for turning ghetto residents into an undifferentiated mass. We can no longer ignore the fact that information technology, new forms of mass communication, and immigration have made the rest of the world more accessible to inner city residents than ever before.[48] Contemporary black urban culture is a hybrid that draws on Afrodiasporic traditions, popular culture, the vernacular of previous generations of Southern and Northern black folk, new and old technologies, and a whole lot of imagination. Once again, James Clifford's ruminations on the "predicament of culture" are useful for exposing the predicament of social science. He writes: "To tell…local histories of cultural survival and emergence, we need to resist deep-seated habits of mind and systems of authenticity. We need to be suspicious of an almost-automatic tendency to relegate non-Western (read: black) peoples and objects to the pasts of an increasingly homogeneous humanity."[49]

NOTES

1. John Langston Gwaltney, *Drylongso: A Self-Portrait of Black America* (New York: Random House, 1980), xix.

2. Mercer L. Sullivan, "Absent Fathers in the Inner City," *The Annals* 501 (January 1989): 49–50.

3. Recent proponents of a new "culture of poverty" thesis include Ken Auletta, *The Underclass* (New York: Random House, 1982); Nicholas Lemann, "The Origins of the Underclass: Part I," *Atlantic Monthly* 257 (June 1986): 31–61, and "The Origins of the Underclass: Part II," *Atlantic Monthly* 258 (July 1986): 54–68; Nicholas Lemann, *The Promised Land: The Great Black Migration and How It Changed America* (New York: Knopf, 1991); Charles Murray, *Losing Ground: American Social Policy, 1950–1980* (New York: Basic Books, 1984); and Lawrence Mead, *The New Dependency Politics: Non-Working Poverty in the U.S.* (New York: Basic Books, 1992). These works are quite distinct in scope, methods, and ideology from the pioneering studies of Oscar Lewis, who introduced the "culture of poverty" idea to American social science. Unlike the more recent works, he did not argue that poor people's behavior is the *cause* of their poverty. Rather, he insisted that capitalism impoverished segments of the working class, who were denied access to mainstream institutions. The culture they created to cope with poverty and disfranchisement was passed down through generations and thus led to passivity and undermined social organization. Lewis had no intention of using the culture-of-poverty thesis to distinguish the "deserving" from the "undeserving poor." See Oscar Lewis, *The Children of Sanchez* (New York: Random House, 1961) and *La Vida: A Puerto Rican Family in the Culture of Poverty, San Juan and New York* (New York: Random House, 1966).

   Critics of the culture-of-poverty thesis are many, and they do not all agree with each other as to the relative importance of culture or the causes of poverty. See especially Charles Valentine, *Culture and Poverty: Critique and Counter-Proposals* (Chicago: University of Chicago Press, 1968); Herbert J. Gans, "Culture and Class in the Study of Poverty: An Approach to Antipoverty Research," in *On Understanding Poverty: Perspectives from the Social Sciences*, ed. Daniel Patrick Moynihan (New York: Basic Books, 1968); Sheldon Danzinger and Peter Gottschalk, "The Poverty of *Losing Ground*," *Challenge* 28 (May–June 1985): 32–38; William Darity and Samuel L. Meyers, "Does Welfare Dependency Cause Female Headship? The Case of the Black Family," *Journal of Marriage and the Family* 46, no. 4 (1984): 765–79; and Mary Corcoran, Greg J. Duncan, Gerald Gurin, and Patricia Gurin, "Myth and Reality: The Causes and Persistence of Poverty" *Journal of Policy Analysis and Management* 4, no. 4 (1985): 516–36.

4. Michael Katz, "The Urban 'Underclass' as a Metaphor of Social Transformation," in *The Underclass Debate: Views from History*, ed. Michael Katz (Princeton, N.J.: Princeton University Press, 1993), 3–23.

5. The The most prominent of the structuralists adopt some cultural explanation for urban poverty, suggesting that bad behavior is the outcome of a bad environment. William Julius Wilson's most recent work argues that the lack of employment has eroded the work ethic and discipline of the underclass, leading to behaviors that allow employers to justify not hiring them. See especially William Julius Wilson, *When Work Disappears: The World of the New Urban Poor* (New York: Knopf, 1996); William J. Wilson, *The Truly Disadvantaged: The Inner City, the Underclass, and Public Policy* (Chicago: University of Chicago Press, 1987); David T. Ellwood, *Poor Support: Poverty in the American Family* (New York: Basic Books, 1988); Elijah Anderson, *Streetwise: Race, Class, and Change in an Urban Community* (Chicago: University of Chicago Press, 1990); Elijah Anderson, "Sex Codes and Family Life among Poor Inner City Youth," *The Annals* 501 (January 1989): 59–78; Troy Duster, "Social Implications of the 'New' Black Underclass," *Black Scholar* 19 (May–June 1988): 2–9; Christopher Jencks, *Rethinking Social Policy: Race, Poverty, and the Underclass* (Cambridge: Harvard University Press, 1992); Mark S. Littman, "Poverty Areas and the Underclass: Untangling the Web," *Monthly Labor Review* 114 (March 1991): 19–32; Jacqueline Jones, *The Dispossessed: America's Underclasses from the Civil War to the Present* (New York: Basic Books, 1992); Douglas G. Glasgow, *The Black Underclass: Unemployment and Entrapment of Ghetto Youth* (New York: Random House, 1981); William Julius Wilson and Loic J. D. Wacquant, "The Cost of Racial and Class Exclusion in the Inner City," *The Annals* 501 (January 1989): 8–25; John D. Kasarda, "Caught in a Web of Change," *Society* 21 (November/December 1983): 41–47; John D. Kasarda, "Urban Industrial Transition and the Underclass," *The Annals* 501 (January 1989): 26–47; Maxine Baca Zinn, "Family, Race, and Poverty in the Eighties," *Signs* 14, no. 4 (1989): 856–74; Mary Corcoran, Greg J. Duncan, and Martha S. Hill, "The Economic Fortunes of Women and Children: Lessons from the Panel Study of Income Dynamics," *Signs* 10, no. 2 (1984): 232–48; Mary Jo Bane, "Household Composition and Poverty," in *Fighting Poverty: What Works and What Doesn't*, eds. Sheldon Danzinger and Daniel Weinberg (Cambridge: Harvard University Press, 1986); David Ellwood, *Poor Support* (New York: Basic Books, 1988); Barry Bluestone and Bennett Harrison, *The Deindustriatization of America* (New York: Basic Books, 1982); Richard Child Hill and Cynthia Negrey, "Deindustrialization and Racial Minorities in the Great Lakes Region, USA," in *The Reshaping of America: Social Consequences of the Changing Economy*, eds. D. Stanley Eitzen and Maxine Baca Zinn (Englewood Cliffs, N.J.: Prentice-Hall, 1989); Elliot Currie and Jerome H. Skolnick, *America's Problems: Social Issues and Public Policy* (Boston: Little, Brown and Co., 1984); Carl Nightingale, *On the Edge: A History of Poor Black Children and Their American Dreams* (New York: Basic Books, 1993); and Staff of *Chicago Tribune*, *The American Millstone: An Examination of the Nation's Permanent Underclass* (Chicago: Contemporary Books, 1986). While most of these authors focus on deindustrialization and the effects of concentrated poverty, Douglas S. Massey and Nancy A. Denton have argued that racial segregation is the key to explaining the persistence of black urban poverty. See their *American Apartheid: Segregation and the Making of the Underclass* (Cambridge: Harvard University Press, 1993).

6. Kathryn Edin, "Surviving the Welfare System: How AFDC Recipients Make Ends Meet in Chicago," *Social Problems* 38 (November 1991): 462–74

7. Charles P. Henry, *Culture and African-American Politics* (Bloomington, Ind.: Indiana University Press, 1990), 12–13. Likewise, social philosopher Leonard Harris asks us to imagine what would happen if we used the same indices to study the "urban rich": "Suppose that their behavior was unduly helpful to themselves; say they rarely married, had more one-child families, were more likely than previous rich to be sexual libertines practicing safe sex, were health conscious, and were shrewd investors in corporate and ghetto property without moral reflection." Leonard Harris," Agency and the Concept of the Underclass," in *The Underclass Question*, ed. Bill E. Lawson (Philadelphia: Temple University Press, 1992), 37.

8. Lee Rainwater, *Behind Ghetto Walls: Black Families in a Federal Slum* (Chicago: Aldine Publishing Co., 1970); Elliot Liebow, *Tally's Corner. A Study of Negro Streetcorner Men* (Boston: Little, Brown and Co., 1967); Ulf Hannerz, *Soulside: Inquiries into Ghetto Culture and Community* (New York: Colum-

bia University Press, 1969); Carol B. Stack, *All Our Kin: Strategies for Survival in a Black Community* (New York: Harper and Row, 1974); Betty Lou Valentine, *Hustling and Other Hard Work: Life Styles in the Ghetto* (New York: Free Press, 1978); Joyce Ladner, *Tommorrow's Tommorrow: The Black Woman* (Garden City, N.Y.: Anchor, 1971); David Schulz, *Coming Up Black: Patterns of Ghetto Socialization* (Englewood Cliffs, N.J.: Prentice-Hall, 1969).

9. Stephen M. Joseph, ed., *The Me Nobody Knows: Children's Voices from the Ghetto* (New York: Avon Books, 1969); Caroline Mirthes and the Children of P.S. 15, *Can't You Hear Me Talking to You?* (New York: Bantam Books, 1971).

10. These typologies are drawn from Hannerz, *Soulside,* William McCord, John Howard, Bernard Friedberg, Edwin Harwood, *Life Styles in the Black Ghetto* (New York: W. W. Norton, 1969).

11. Gwaltney, *Drylongso,* xxiv, xxxii.

12. James Clifford,"On Collecting Art and Culture," in *The Predicament of Culture: Twentieth-Century Ethnography, Literature, and Art* (Cambridge: Harvard University Press, 1988), 246. Don't get me wrong. The vast and rich ethnographic documentation collected by these scholars is extremely valuable because it captures the responses and survival strategies hidden from economic indices and illuminates the human aspects of poverty. Of course, these materials must be used with caution since most ethnographies do not pay much attention to historical and structural transformations. Instead, they describe and interpret a particular community during a brief moment in time. The practice of giving many of these communities fictitious names only compounds the problem and presumes that region, political economy, and history have no bearing on opportunity structures, oppositional strategies, or culture. For an extended critique, see Andrew H. Maxwell, "The Anthropology of Poverty in Black Communities: A Critique and Systems Alternative," *Urban Anthropology* 17, nos. 2 and 3 (1988): 171–92.

13. Charles Keil, *Urban Blues* (Chicago: University of Chicago Press, 1966), 1–12, 23.

14. Stack, *All Our Kin;* Ladner, *Tommorrow's Tommorrow.* This dichotomy also prevails in Anderson's more recent Streetwise.

15. Lee Rainwater, ed, *Soul* (Trans-Action Books, 1970), 9.

16. Rainwater, *Soul* (especially essays by John Horton, Thomas Kochman, and David Wellman); Ulf Hannerz, "The Significance of Soul" in *ibid.,* 15–30; Hannerz, *Soulside,* 144–58. For other interpretations of soul, see Keil, *Urban Blues,* 164–90; William L. Van Deburg, *New Day in Babylon: The Black Power Movement and American Culture, 1965–1975* (Chicago: University of Chicago Press, 1992), 194–97; Claude Brown, "The Language of Soul," in *Mother Wit from the Laughing Barrel: Readings in the Interpretation of Afro-American Folklore,* ed. Alan Dundes (New York: Garland Publishing Co., 1981), 232–43; and Roger D. Abrahams, *Positively Black* (Englewood Cliffs, N.J.: Prentice-Hall, 1970), 136–50.

17. Hannerz, "The Significance of Soul," 21.

18. Schulz, *Coming Up Black,* 78, 103; Rainwater, *Behind Ghetto Walls,* 372. See also John Horton, "Time and Cool People," in Rainwater, *Soul,* 31–50.

19. Hannerz, "The Significance of Soul," 22–23.

20. Robert L. Allen, *Black Awakening in Capitalist America: An Analytic History* (Garden City, N.Y.: Doubleday, 1969), 163; Van Deburg, *New Day in Babylon,* 201–2.

21. Van Deburg, *New Day in Babylon,* 201–2.

22. Lois Liberty Jones and John Henry Jones, *All about the Natural* (New York: Clairol, 1971).

23. Andrea Benton Rushing, "Hair-Raising," *Feminist Studies* 14, no. 2 (1988): 334; Jones and Jones, *All about the Natural;* Helen Hayes King and Theresa Ogunbiyi, "Should Negro Women Straighten Their Hair?" *Negro Digest* (August 1963): 68.

24. King and Ogunbiyi, "Should Negro Women Straighten Their Hair?" 69–70, 71.

25. King and Ogunbiyi, "Should Negro Women Straighten Their Hair?" 67–68.

26. Rushing, "Hair-Raising," 334, 326.

27. Harold Cruse, *Rebellion or Revolution?* (New York: Morrow, 1968); Norman C. Weinstein, *A Night in Tunisia: Imaginings of Africa in Jazz* (New York: Limelight Editions, 1993); Penny von Eschen, *Democracy or Empire: African Americans, Anti-Colonialism, and the Cold War* (Ithaca, N.Y.: Cornell University Press, 1997); Immanuel Geiss, *The Pan-African Movement* (London: Methuen and Co., 1974); Robert Weisbord, *Ebony Kinship: Africa, Africans, and the Afro-American* (Westport, Conn.: Greenwood Press, 1973); P. Olisanwuch Esedebe, *Pan-Africanism: The Idea and Movement, 1776–1963* (Washington, D.C.: Howard University Press, 1982).

28. Cruse, *Rebellion or Revolution?*, 73.

29. As Linda Roemere Wright's research reveals, ads and other images of Afrocoifed women in *Ebony* magazine declined around 1970, just as the number of images of black men with Afros was steadily rising. See Linda Roemere Wright, "Changes in Black American Hairstyles from 1964 through 1977, As Related to Themes in Feature Articles and Advertisements" (M.A. thesis, Michigan State University, 1982), 24–25.

30. Richard Majors and Janet Mancini Billson, *Cool Pose: The Dilemmas of Manhood in America* (New York: Lexington Books, 1992), 4.

31. Historian Roger Lane treats the dozens as a manifestation of a larger pathological culture: "Afro-American culture was marked by an aggressively competitive strain compounded of bold display, semi-ritualistic insult, and an admiration of violence in verbal form at least. 'Playing the dozens,' a contest involving the exchange of often sexual insults directed not only at the participants but at their families, especially their mothers, was one example of this strain." Lane, *Roots of Violence in Black Philadelphia, 1860–1900* (Cambridge: Harvard University Press, 1986), 146–47. See also Roger D. Abrahams, *Deep Down in the Jungle: Negro Narrative Folklore from the Streets of Philadelphia*, new ed. (Chicago: Aldine, 1970), 52–56; Herbert Foster, *Ribin', Jivin', and Playin' the Dozens* (Cambridge, Mass.: Ballinger, 1986); Thomas Kochman, *Black and White Styles in Conflict* (Chicago: University of Chicago Press, 1981), 51–58; Majors and Billson, *Cool Pose*, 91–101; and Nightingale, *On the Edge*, 26–28. There are some remarkable exceptions, such as the work of linguists, historians, literary scholars, and first-person practitioners, who treat the dozens as a larger set of signifying practices found in black vernacular culture or focus on the art and pleasures of verbal play. For these authors, the dozens is not merely a mirror of social relations. See Claudia Mitchell-Kernan, "Signifying, Loud-talking, and Marking," in *Rappin and Stylin' Out: Communication in Urban Black America*, ed. Thomas Kochman (Urbana, Ill.: University of Illinois Press, 1972); H. Rap Brown, *Die, Nigger, Die* (New York: Dial, 1969); Geneva Smitherman, *Talkin' and Testifyin': The Language of Black America* (Boston: Houghton Mifflin Co., 1977), 128–33; Henry Louis Gates, Jr., *The Signifying Monkey: A Theory of African-American Literary Criticism* (New York: Oxford University Press, 1988), especially 64–88; and Houston Baker, *Long Black Song: Essays in Black American Literature and Culture* (Charlottesville, Va.: University Press of Virginia, 1972), 115. Despite disagreements between Baker and Gates, both try to make sense of black vernacular culture—including the dozens—as art rather than sociology. Although Lawrence Levine took issue with the functionalist approach to the dozens over fifteen years ago, he did not reject it altogether. He suggests that the dozens helped young black children develop verbal facility and learn self-discipline. See Lawrence Levine, *Black Culture and Black Consciousness: Afro-American Folk Thought from Slavery to Freedom* (New York: Oxford University Press, 1977), 345–58.

32. Levine, *Black Culture and Black Consciousness*, 357. A beginning is Marjorie Harness Goodwin, *He-Said-She-Said: Talk as Social Organization among Black Children* (Bloomington, Ind.: Indiana University Press, 1990), especially 222–23. However, Goodwin emphasizes "ritual insult" as a means of

dealing with disputes rather than as an art form and thus is still squarely situated within social scientists' emphasis on function over style and pleasure.

33. Roger D. Abrahams, *Deep Down in the Jungle*, 60, 88–96; see also Roger D. Abrahams, *Talking Black* (Rowley, Mass.: Newbury House Publishers, 1976).

34. Schulz, *Coming Up Black*, 68. In McCord, et al. *Life Styles in the Ghetto*, Edwin Harwood argues further that the lack of a father leads to violent uprisings and low self esteem among black male youth: "Negro males who are brought up primarily by mothers and other female relatives pick up from them their hostility toward the males who are not there, or if they are, are not doing worth-while work in society. In such an environment it must be difficult to develop a constructive masculine self-image and the ambivalent self-image that does emerge can only be resolved in ways destructive both to the self and the society, through bold and violent activities that are only superficially masculine. If this analysis is correct, then the Negro youth who hurls a brick or an insult at the white cop is not just reacting in anger to white society, but on another level is discharging aggression toward the father who 'let him down' and females whose hostility toward inadequate men raised doubts about his own sense of masculinity" (32–33).

35. Eugene Perkins, *Home Is a Dirty Street: The Social Oppression of Black Children* (Chicago: Third World Press, 1975), 32.

36. William Labov, *Language in the Inner City: Studies in the Black English Vernacular* (Philadelphia: University of Pennsylvania Press, 1972), 325. David Schulz, however, does not even trust the laughter of his subjects. He writes, "With careful listening one becomes suspicious of the laughter of the ghetto. So much apparent gaiety has a purpose all too often in the zero-sum contest system of interpersonal manipulation for personal satisfaction and gain" (Schulz, *Coming Up Black*, 5).

37. See, for example, Venise T. Berry, "Rap Music, Self-Concept and Low Income Black Adolescents," *Popular Music and Society* 14, no. 3 (Fall 1990); Nightingale, *On the Edge*, 132–33, 162–63, 182–84; Wheeler Winston Dixon, "Urban Black American Music in the Late 1980s: The 'Word' as Cultural Signifier," *Midwest Quarterly* 30 (Winter 1989): 229–41; Mark Costello and David Foster Wallace, *Signifying Rappers: Rap and Race in the Urban Present* (New York: Ecco, 1990); and Andre Craddock-Willis, "Rap Music and the Black Musical Tradition: A Critical Assessment," *Radical America* 23, no. 4 (June 1991): 29–38. The case of Hip Hop might be unusual since social scientists working on the black urban poor have been conspicuously silent, leaving most of the discussion to music critics and cultural studies scholars. The result has been a fairly sophisticated body of work that takes into account both aesthetics and social and political contexts. See, for example, Tricia Rose, *Black Noise: Rap Music and Black Culture in Contemporary America* (Hanover, N.H.: Wesleyan University Press, 1994); Tricia Rose, "Black Texts/Black Contexts," in *Black Popular Culture*, ed. Gina Dent (Seattle: Bay Press, 1992), 223–27; Tate, *Flyboy in the Buttermilk*; Juan Flores, "Puerto Rican and Proud, Boy-ee!: Rap, Roots, and Amnesia," in *Microphone Fiends: Youth Music and Youth Culture*, ed. Tricia Rose and Andrew Ross (New York: Routledge, 1994), 89–98; William Eric Perkins, ed., *Droppin' Science: Critical Essays on Rap Music and Hip Hop Culture* (Philadelphia: Temple University Press, 1996); Joseph G. Eure and James G. Spady, *Nation Conscious Rap* (Brooklyn: P. C. International Press, 1991); James G. Spady, Stefan Dupree, and Charles G. Lee, *Twisted Tales in the Hip Hop Streets of Philadelphia* (Philadelphia: UMUM LOH Publishers, 1995); Brian Cross, *It's Not About a Salary...Rap, Race and Resistance in Los Angeles* (London: Verso, 1993); Michael Eric Dyson, *Reflecting Black: African-American Cultural Criticism* (Minneapolis: University of Minnesota Press, 1993); George Lipsitz, *Dangerous Crossroads: Popular Music, Postmodernism, and the Poetics of Place* (London: Verso, 1994); Jeffrey Louis Decker, "The State of Rap: Time and Place in Hip Hop Nationalism," Social Text 34 (1989): 53–84; Jonathan Scott, " 'Act Like You Know': A Theory of Hip Hop Aesthetics" (unpublished paper in author's possession, 1994); and S. H. Fernando, *The New Beats: Exploring the Music, Culture and Attitudes of Hip Hop* (New York: Anchor Books, 1994). Two good general histories are Steve Hager, *Hip Hop: The Illustrated History of Breakdancing, Rap Music, and Graffiti* (New York: St. Martin's Press, 1984); and David Toop, Rap Attack 2 (London: Pluto Press, 1991).

38. Craddock-Willis, "Rap Music and the Black Musical Tradition," 37.

39. "Rockbeat," *Village Voice* 39, no. 4 (January 25, 1994): 76.

40. Tommy Lott, "Marooned in America: Black Urban Youth Culture and Social Pathology," in *The Underclass Question*, ed. Bill E. Lawson (Philadelphia: Temple University Press, 1992), 71, 72, 80–81.

41. Digital Underground's song "Good Thing We're Rappin'," *Sons of the P* (Tommy Boy Records, 1991) is nothing if not a tribute to the pimp narratives. One hears elements of classic toasts, including "The Pimp," "Dogass Pimp," "Pimping Sam," "Wicked Nell," "The Lame and the Whore," and perhaps others. Even the meter is very much in the toasting tradition. (For transcriptions of these toasts, see Bruce Jackson, *"Get Your Ass in the Water and Swim Like Me": Narrative Poetry from Black Oral Tradition* [Cambridge: Harvard University Press, 1974], 106–30.) Similar examples which resemble the more comical pimp narratives include Ice Cube, "I'm Only Out for One Thing," *AmeriKKKa's Most Wanted* (Priority Records, 1990) and Son of Bazerk, "Sex, Sex, and More Sex" *Son of Bazerk* (MCA Records, 1991).

42. Other examples include Capital Punishment Organization's aptly tided warning to other perpetrating rappers, "Homicide," *To Hell and Black* (Capitol Records, 1990); NWA's "Real Niggaz," *Efil4zaggin* (Priority Records, 1991); Dr. Dre's "Lyrical Gangbang," *The Chronic* (Deathrow/Interscope Records, 1992); Ice Cube's, "Now I Gotta Wet'cha," *The Predator* (Priority Records, 1992); Compton's Most Wanted's, "Wanted" and "Straight Check N' Em," *Straight Check N' Em* (Orpheus Records, 1991); as well as many of the songs on Ice Cube, *Kill at Will* (Priority Records, 1992); Ice T, *OG: Original Gangster* (Sire Records, 1991); Ice T, *Power* (Warner Bros., 1988); NWA, *100 Miles and Runnin'* (Ruthless Records, 1990). See also chapter 8 of my book *Race Rebels: Culture, Politics, and the Black Working Class* (New York: The Free Press, 1994).

43. Ice T [and the Rhyme Syndicate], "My Word Is Bond," *The Iceberg/Freedom of Speech...Just Watch What You Say* (Sire Records, 1989); Ice Cube, "J. D.'s Gafflin'," *AmeriKKKa's Most Wanted* (Priority Records, 1990). West Coast rappers also create humorous countercritiques of gangsterism, the most penetrating is perhaps Del tha Funkee Homosapien's hilarious, "Hoodz Come in Dozens," *I Wish My Brother George Was Here* (Priority Records, 1991).

44. See John Leland, "Rap: Can It Survive Self-importance?" *Details* (July 1991): 108; Frank Owen, "Hanging Tough," *Spin* 6, no. 1 (April 1990): 34; and James Bernard, "NWA [Interview]," *The Source* (December 1990): 34.

45. Quoted in Spady and Eure, *Nation Conscious Rap*, xiii, xxviii. On the early history of Hip Hop in New York, see Rose, *Black Noise*; Hager, *Hip Hop*; and Toop, *Rap Attack 2*.

46. Paul Willis, *Common Culture: Symbolic Work at Play in the Everyday Cultures of the Young* (Boulder, Colo.: Westview Press, 1990), 1–5, 65.

47. Cecil Brown, "James Brown, Hoodoo and Black Culture," *Black Review* 1 (1971): 184.

48. For insightful discussions of the way information technology in the late twentieth century opened up new spaces for building cultural links between black urban America and the African diaspora, see Lipsitz, *Dangerous Crossroads*; and Paul Gilroy, *The Black Atlantic: Modernity and Double-Consciousness* (Cambridge: Harvard University Press, 1993).

49. James Clifford, *The Predicament of Culture: Twentieth-Century Ethnography, Literature, and Art* (Cambridge: Harvard University Press, 1988), 246.

Todd Boyd

Chapter 11

Check Yo Self Before You Wreck Yo Self

Rap music is the most visible form of African American cultural expression in contemporary society. With its emergence we have also seen a change in African American popular culture specific to the late 1980s and early 1990s. The recent proliferation of African American film and televisual representation, with rap music serving as a primary means of influence, has led to new definitions of contemporary African American popular culture in both the academic and the public domain.[1]

One of the most interesting discussions has involved the thematic resurgence of a politically charged voice that these forms provide a perfect venue for expressing. The rise and eventual fall of this political discourse in popular culture is closely tied to the public presentation of popular forms. In its political dimensions, popular culture, having reached an apex with the release of Public Enemy's second album, *It Takes a Nation of Millions to Hold Us Back* (1988), seems to have functioned as a genre whose popularity had passed, instead of a sustained movement which connected both cultural artifacts and "real" political events, as did similar movements in the late 1960s and early 1970s.[2]

The emergence of gangsta rap has seen an open rejection of politics by those involved. Publicly echoed in Dr. Dre's ever-popular "Dre Day" we hear a complete disregard for "medallions, dreadlocks, and black fists," obvious markers for the more political aspirations of those interested in Black nationalism or what is now commonly called "Afrocentricity." This rejection of a political agenda is consistent with Spike Lee's mainstreaming of the most important figure of Black nationalism, Malcolm X, in the 1992 film by that title. These events mark the end of a political flirtation in rap music and, by extension, African American popular culture.

An interesting case study that examines the highs and lows of political discourse in rap music—similar to what Cornel West calls the "new cultural politics"—and the gradual displacement of this agenda by gangsta rap can be found in the meteoric rise of 1993's Grammy Award-winning best new act, Arrested Development. Using images of a critical spirituality, southern existence, stylized forms of dress, and an overall ideology of Afrocentrism, Arrested Development engaged an empowered critique of both external racism and the internal neglect that set them apart from other rap acts in the early 1990s. This political stance endeared them to many as the embodiment of a progressive discourse surrounding culture, society, and politics.

Rap and the "New Cultural Politics of Difference"

Rap can be used to analyze the mutually illuminating yet divergent categories of race, class, and gender in African American society. More often than not, questions of race dominate both popular and critical discussions about rap music. Though this discussion is undoubtedly important, contemporary society, especially in the post-Reagan/Bush era, forces us to deal with the influence of the class struggle on African American society.

At the same time, an empowered female voice that fuses the issues of race, class, and gender would also open up possibilities for understanding the nuances of contemporary African American culture. As Tricia Rose points out, "through their lyrics and video images,...black women rappers form a dialogue with working class black women and men, offering young black women a small but potent culturally-reflexive public space" (Rose, 1990, 114). Though this female voice in rap has gained significant momentum over the last few years, there remains much to be desired, both artistically and in terms of intellectual response.[3]

The cultural and economic base of this music emphasizes the African presence in American society, which makes the foregrounding of race and class struggle paramount in understanding this cultural practice. Certain elements of rap music seem to have the potential to exemplify what Cornel West has labeled the "new cultural politics of difference."

> The new cultural politics of difference are neither simply oppositional in contesting the mainstream for inclusion, nor transgressive in the avant-gardist sense of shocking conventional bourgeois audiences. Rather, they are distinct articulations of talented contributors to culture who desire to align themselves with demoralized, demobilized, depoliticized and disorganized people in order to empower and enable social action and, if possible, to enlist collective insurgency for the expansion of freedom, democracy, and individuality. (West, 1990, 19–20)

African American culture is replete with examples of this new cultural politics of difference, particularly in regard to the influence of lower-class politics in understanding race. In many respects, by the late 1980s and the early 1990s, the presentation of anything as an "authentic" reflection of African American culture had to revolve in some way around the exploits and endeavors of the lumpen proletariat. It was necessary in this construction for race and class to consistently inform one another.

The most overt demonstration of this desire for cultural "authenticity" was white rapper Vanilla Ice's claim that he grew up in the midst of African American poverty and was once a victim of gang violence. He was identifying with Blackness based not on his race but on the extent of his association with lower-class African American existence. In other words, his class status made him "Black."

Along the same lines, the all-white rap group Young Black Teenagers claim that Blackness is a "state of mind"—undoubtedly a ghetto mindset. The impetus for forming the rock band in the film *The Commitments* (1991) serves as another example. According to the film's main character, the group members can identify with African American music because of their multiple oppression as Northern Irish working-class Catholics. "The Irish are the Blacks of Europe, and the Dubliners are the Blacks of Ireland, and the Northsiders are the Blacks of Dublin. So say it loud, I'm Black and I'm proud." In this case, race, as expressed through a specific cultural artifact, the music of James Brown, is used to justify an argument rooted in the political economy of class articulation in European society.

Using the "ghetto" or the "'hood" as the dominant metaphor, rap music has vividly presented this emphasis on the lower class. Whereas the earlier days of the genre were dominated by macho posturing, "dick" grabbing, and braggadocio, recently the thematic core of rap music has tended toward a narrative of life in the "'hood." With the advent of West Coast (primarily Los Angeles) rap, the life of a young African American male and his struggle to survive have become a recurrent theme, demonstrating firm entrenchment in the jungle-like setting known as the ghetto.[4] Rappers who resisted this emphasis were regarded as impostors of the tradition. Thus, a concentration on class struggle has been central to defining the cutting edge of rap music during this phase.

The reliance on this now-clichéd narrative and the media's eager embrace of the ghetto lifestyle encouraged the eventual transformation of the "'hood" scenario from initially sublime to utterly ridiculous. Through an intense combination of media manipulation and artistic culpability, the issue of class struggle has been reduced to mere spectacle, as opposed to a sustained critical interrogation of domination and oppression. This genre of rap is becoming the modern-day equivalent of the 1970s "Blaxploitation" film, the earliest examples of which, works of African American grassroots financial struggle turned into valuable products of the culture, were duplicated, depoliticized, and ultimately rendered devoid of all cultural significance.

Rap represents the emotional range of urban, mostly male, existence. At the same time, the commodifying impulses of the music industry have opened a space for selling cultural products that in their very construction undermine the structure that distributes them. It is well known that rap's massive popular audience consists of dominant and marginal audiences. Nor is it a revelation that the capitalistic courting of this massive audience at some level solidifies the music's political message. However, there is a point at which radical political discourse meets the demands of the marketplace and the two merge. The space between the points where radical political discourse can critique dominant culture and dominant culture becomes financially viable through the selling of this contrary discourse is the only available space for a reasoned understanding of contemporary political culture.

West's notion of a "politics of difference" sees the current cultural situation as indicative of an "inescapable double bind." This bind involves the reality of financial dependence that defines the structural dimension of rap music as a metaphorical "escape" from oppressive conditions, much like society's regard for African American professional athletes. The rapper, in this sense, is "simultaneously progressive and co-opted" (West, 1990, 20).

Although a thin theoretical line separates radical political discourse in rap and the commodifying impulses of the dominant culture, our understanding of popular culture requires that we critique both sides. Thus, the contemporary spectacle of the "ghetto" operates primarily to reinforce the dominant society's view of African American culture as a deprived wasteland. "Gangsta" rap offers original commentary on the horrific nuances of ghetto life. In many cases, what was once thought of as a radical critique of repressive state apparatuses, as in NWA's *Fuck tha Police*, has been transformed into a series of unapologetic narratives that celebrate violence, humiliate women, and indulge marijuana use to excess. Race and class struggle have become a series of rhetorical catch phrases and visual signposts absent of any political or social relevance. This overt rejection of politics has now become a theme unto itself—one that is reflective of several larger issues.

Yet what many consider the redundant "nigga in the 'hood" scenario is actually much more complex. Instead of relying solely on this gangsta trend, a small core of rappers have continued to advance what was at one time thought of as a progressive political agenda which analyzes race, class, and in some cases gender through rigorous cultural critique. Foremost in this group of political rappers concerned with cultural politics are Public Enemy, Sister Souljah, KRS-One, and Arrested Development. A certain Afrocentric theme runs through each of the above, yet their individual positions cover a spectrum of topics related to living in late-twentieth-century American society. Nevertheless, none of these acts has had a record of any significance, financially or culturally, in quite some time.

As with the declining significance of Spike Lee as a political voice, though, and of the new Black aesthetic, these political rappers have not been able to link their progressive politics with the ever-changing demands of the music industry or the rap audience; thus their critiques have lately fallen on deaf ears, and their cultural significance has almost completely disappeared. Witness the breakup of the one-time leaders of this political trend, Public Enemy, in the summer of 1995. In contemporary culture it is not only important to bring the political noise, but one must remain significant from an audience perspective as well.

Progressive politics minus the ability to flow lyrically and pump out phat beats has no place in rap culture. This is not to diminish political rap, but to point out that we are analyzing music, as opposed to a rhetoric of pure politics. In addition, the definition of politics, or at least what is political, has changed as the various generational shifts and their class dispositions have occurred.

Arrested Development

The Atlanta-based rap group Arrested Development was the most interesting new act of 1992. The group's male and female members sing as well as rap, while their image is built around the wearing of dreadlocks and African-style clothing. This is in contrast to the image of both the "b-boy" of the East Coast and the West Coast gangsta. Arrested Development suggests a strong stylistic exception to conventions determined by the prevalence of the more popular East and West Coast images; they also can be easily linked with the politics of the new Black aesthetic.

Arrested Development shares its context with a segment of the contemporary African American collegiate audience who use African fashion and hairstyles to demonstrate their political connection to that continent. In this sense, fashion and style function as both icon and commodity. This emphasis on an Afrocentric style not only is a response to the monotonous fashions of other rappers, but also is a rejection of the conservative "preppie" image favored by a certain group of white collegiates, which took on added cultural currency during the Reagan/Bush era. On the other hand, this emphasis on Afrocentricity in fashion becomes easily devalued as it is transformed into a mass commodity. This is the strong contention of Kobena Mercer, who suggests that hairstyles such as the afro and dreadlocks

> counter-politicized the signifier of ethnic devalorization, redefining blackness as a positive attribute, but on the other hand, perhaps not, because within a relatively short period both styles became rapidly depoliticized and, with varying degrees of resistance, both were incorporated into mainstream fashions in the dominant culture. (Mercer, 1990, 251)

This situation demonstrates, once again, the seemingly contradictory nature of political culture in the age of commodity fetishism. Signifiers of leftist political culture are easily corrupted as they are co-opted by the fashion industry of dominant society.

Musically, Arrested Development challenges the traditions of rap, the most visible difference being the use of singing in conjunction with the traditional rapping over beats (this singing style has since become quite popular). The group's songs address topics ranging from homelessness to the search for spirituality and African Americans' connection with Africa. Their popular appeal is demonstrated by their appearance as opening act on the 1992–1993 En Vogue tour, the use of the song "Tennessee" as the theme for the short-lived NBC situation comedy *Here and Now*, their appearance as the only contemporary voice on the soundtrack for Lee's *Malcolm X* (1992), and their selection as both "Best New Artist" and "Best Rap Artist" at the 1993 Grammy Awards.

Arrested Development benefits from a series of other African American acts that have foregrounded a certain leftist bohemian political agenda. Arrested Development belongs to the musical tradition that includes the 1970s band Sly and the Family Stone—this group is sampled on "People Everyday"—the multicultural rhythm and blues group War, and most recently African American female folk singer Tracy Chapman. Yet, the combination of a derivative folk song content, politics associated with the peace movement, and rap is probably best exemplified by the rap organization Native Tongues, of which groups such as De La Soul and A Tribe Called Quest most easily demonstrate this pattern.[5]

A close analysis of Arrested Development's "People Everyday" song and video helps to reveal their political agenda. Using the sample from Sly Stone's track "Everyday People," Arrested Development argues for a kind of cultural innocence or purity. This notion of purity is exemplified through a juxtaposition of the harsh urban realities of the street prominent in contemporary rap and their embrace of the premodern "country" simplicity of a rural landscape. At one level the group attempts to be all-inclusive in its outlook, forwarding an Afrocentric version of political correctness that critiques race, class, and gender, as opposed to privileging the male-dominated discourse that rap has often been guilty of presenting. Yet in doing so the group offers a position that unintentionally erects a class hierarchy while simultaneously trying to destroy existing hierarchies.

The video's time frame spans one day, as marked by the rising of the sun at the beginning of the video and its setting at the conclusion. Thus we are alerted to the concern with time and the extent to which time and space function in defining African American politics. This concern with time is also evident in the title of the album, *3 Years, 5 Months, and 2 Days in the Life of Arrested Development*.

The video begins by calling on multiple aspects of the African oral tradition. Group member Headliner offers a verbal and visual address. After he announces who he is, we get an extreme close-up of his lips. In American society, lips have gone from a regressive stereotype that emphasized the excessive fullness of African American lips through numerous visual objects in American culture (Sambo pictures, lawn jockeys, etc.) to the current trend toward using this fullness as a visual demonstration of one's Africanness. White models and actresses appropriate these features through chemical or surgical treatment as a fashionable sign of what is considered beauty.[6] This modern-day example of exploitiveness is what bell hooks describes as "eating the other."

From this tight close-up, we move to a series of rapidly edited shots that alternate between Headliner's reggae-style call and visual images of the group's response. This visual dimension is edited to visually replicate the verbal call-and-response pattern that the group establishes. It also alternates between black and white and color images and privileges the oral as it motivates the visual direction of the iconography. Thus, oral culture is used in conjunction with the character's motivation of visuals to create a stimulating African American music video.

Through another series of rapidly edited shots, we witness the group's reliance on a strongly rural agrarian aesthetic. Riding on the back of a pickup truck, the equally mixed group of male and female participants are shown in their loosely fitting cast-off-style African clothing, either with their hair in knotty dreadlocks or bald. This emphasis on the rural is supplemented by various shots of the wide-open landscape, dirt roads, wooden porches, and an idyllic series of visual icons that foreground the technologically untainted and morally empowered version of African American life that Arrested Development argues for throughout this album, and especially in the song "People Everyday."

As we witness little children running, playing, and riding their bicycles, and older people enjoying life in a variety of rural settings, we are also clued in to the political agenda that informs Arrested Development. The rejection of modernity that this visual setting evokes harks back to the "pre-New Negro" ideas of Booker T. Washington. These ideas embraced the virtues of southern pastoral living in opposition to the supposed utopic images of the industrialized North. Washington's argument suggested that the independence that was made possible through this rural lifestyle and economy was superior to the technologically mechanized economy that was taking hold in northern society. Washington's now-redundant phrase "Lay your buckets down where you are" clearly emphasizes his desire to see the South, in all its simplicity, as the preferred landscape of his contemporaries and of future generations of African Americans as well.

The angst associated with the dilemma of migration as opposed to settling in the South has numerous other cultural manifestations, including blues singer Juke Boy Bonner's comically titled cut "I'm Going Back to the Country Where They Don't Burn the Buildings Down," soul singer Gladys Knight's hit "Midnight Train to Georgia," August Wilson's play *The Piano Lesson*, Julie Dash's film *Daughters of the Dust*, and Charles Burnett's *To Sleep with Anger*.

Arrested Development modernizes this argument in their first single, "Tennessee." In a video similar to "People Everyday," the group rhetorically engages in a quizzical and at times cynical exploration of African American existence in contemporary society. In a prayer-like address, they wonder aloud about their tenuous place in contemporary though problem-filled America: "Lord I've been really stressed / Down and out, losing ground / Although I am Black and proud / Problems got me pessimistic / Brothers and sisters keep messin' up / Why does it have to be so damn tough?"

The refrain of the song (and incidentally the portion used in the introduction to the short lived sitcom *Here and Now*) suggests the possibility of freedom and understanding that lies ahead. Speech asks the Lord to "Take me to another place / Take me to another land / Make me forget all the hurt / Let me understand your plan." This spiritually informed intellectual journey, using "Tennessee" as the metaphor of freedom, is not unlike the musical excursions undertaken by John Coltrane during the latter part of his life and career. On the popular *A Love Supreme* and all of his later albums, Coltrane uses spirituality to express his intellectual and creative explorations.

In the same sense, Arrested Development sees "Tennessee" as a site of struggle that informs both past and present: "Walk the streets my forefathers walked / Climb the trees my forefathers hung from / Ask those trees for all their wisdom." According to Arrested Development, a return to these humble roots is necessary for an understanding of contemporary society and the place of the African American therein. This is evident in the lines "Now I see the importance of history / Why my people be in the mess that they be / Many journeys to freedom made in vain / By brothers on the corner playing ghetto games." At one level, Arrested Development offers a political impossibility. Their nostalgia for a romanticized version of early African American culture emphasizes the southern roots of existence, the absence of the modern, and a better quality of life. This seems not only simplistic but untenable considering the difficulties of this style of life within contemporary society. On another level, though, they are able to critique members of their own culture for assisting in the slow destruction of the culture.

Their intellectual posture foregrounds a globally leftist notion of Afrocentric discourse, and some would suggest that this takes rap music in a new direction. Arrested Development criticizes the way that contemporary society has destroyed positive aspects of a supposed earlier communal nature of African American culture, as well as exposed the self-inflicted problems associated with "brothers on the corner," a reference to the urge to romanticize urban Black male ghetto culture in other rap circles. A religiously self-critical orientation is strengthened by the presence of the group's spiritual advisor, Baba Oje, who allows for the emergence of an intellectually empowered voice that points to the future by invoking the past, as opposed to becoming ensconced in the trappings of the present.

Arrested Development's song and video for "People Everyday" extend the practice of self-critique within the African American community, in particular the function of women. The group advocates progressive gender politics, especially given the traditional male rap agenda. The female rappers/singers in the group have equal voice in defining its political project. This collaborative effort, like the critical academic endeavor undertaken by bell hooks and Cornel West in *Breaking Bread* (1991), demonstrates the possibilities of empowered political discourse that avoids the retreading of misogyny in favor of collective articulation.

During the extended call-and-response segment of "People Everyday," female rapper Aerle Taree responds to Speech's call. She often repeats the last part of his dialogue in order to strengthen her point. At the point where Speech refers to his passivity, "but I ain't Ice Cube," Aerle Taree asserts an unequivocal "Who?" This demonstrates the group members' dialectical self-consciousness regarding Ice Cube's political struggles as well as their reluctance to identify themselves with the militant posture of African American masculinity associated with Ice Cube. The female voice again becomes significant during the video's conclusion, when Montesho Eshe states the "moral" of the story. She summarizes the events and has the "last word," further exemplifying the group's progressive gender politics.

The focal point of "People Everyday" is the issue of gender. The members of Arrested Development, particularly Speech, are contrasted to what they define as a "group of brothers." Throughout the video we see black-and-white shots of African American males who personify media stereotypes of macho working-class behavior. We see this "group of brothers" holding forty-ounce bottles of malt liquor, grabbing their crotches, and laughing among themselves. When an African-attired Black woman approaches, they encircle her. After one of the men grabs her buttock, the others give him "dap" for displaying his masculinity.

The lyrics emphasize this obvious act of sexual harassment. "My day was going great and my soul was at ease / Until a group of brothers started buggin' out / Drinkin' the 40 oz. / Going the nigga route / Disrespecting my Black Queen / Holding their crotches and being obscene." Speech's reference to his "Black Queen" affirms the group's valorization of women.

This segment also demarcates the intellectual politics of Arrested Development from those of their lower-class counterparts, who display their masculine hostility toward African American women and other African Americans who do not fit into their lower-class stereotypes. This is evident in the proclamation that they came to "test speech cuz of my hairdo / And the loud bright colors that I wear, boo / I was a target 'cause I'm a fashion misfit / And the outfit that I'm wearing brothers dissin' it." Speech's African-themed appearance, and by extension his politics, are rejected by the "brothers" as unwelcome in their small ghettoized world. Much like the overpublicized Los Angeles gang culture of identification by "colors," the "brothers" in the video identify not only on the basis of race but on the basis of distinctive class stereotypes, the most prominent of which is clothing and appearance. Thus, like the gangbangers, the "brothers" are presented as destroying their own African American community through debauchery and violence.

This distinction between the politically correct behavior of Arrested Development and the "group of brothers" is based on the difference, according to Speech, between a "nigga" and an "African." In numerous media interviews, Speech defines a "nigga" as someone who realizes that he/she is oppressed and wallows in it; an "African" realizes his/her oppression and through knowledge attempts to overcome it. "Nigga" is often used by rappers who consider themselves products and practitioners of the ghetto life. The "hardest" and often the most confrontational rappers have defined themselves as "niggas" in opposition to the dominant society. For instance, NWA, having called their 1991 album *EFIL4SAGGIN* ("Niggas 4 Life" spelled backward), proclaim that "Real Niggas Don't Die"; Ice T boldly alerts his listeners that "I'm a nigga in America and I don't care what you are" and rejects "African American and Black" as inconsistent with his ghetto identity. Ice Cube has described himself as both "the nigga you love to "ate" and "the wrong nigga to fuck wit." In each instance, "nigga" is politicized to indicate class as well as racial politics. This usage often involves a strong identification with the ghetto, but a regressive posture against women. "African" has recently been used to signify a spiritual connection with the continent and an Afrocentric political connection. Flavor Flav of Public Enemy has declared, "I don't wanna be called yo nigga" on the 1991 cut "Yo Nigga," which leads into Sister Souljah's assertion about "African people, too scared to call themselves African" on her 1992 cut "African Scaredy Cat in a One Exit Maze." Calling oneself African is supposed to demonstrate an advanced consciousness that eliminates any connection to America, and affirms one's links with an Afrocentric cultural, political, and spiritual base Souljah suggests that those who reject this idea are "scared" to reject the ideological opposition that forces them to see America as home.

Arrested Development continually identify themselves as African in "People Everyday." Speech states, "I told the niggas please / Let us past friend / I said please 'cause I don't like killing Africans / But they wouldn't stop / & I ain't Ice Cube / Who? / But I had to take the brothers out for being rude!" Speech shows sympathy in his opposition to "niggas" by implying that they are ultimately "Africans." He also sees their masculine lower-class behavior as part of their definition as "niggas." Speech suggests that if they reject this class-based behavior, they can then be seen as "Africans." Yet in the end, they can aspire no higher than their lower-class status permits, as Speech declares, "That's the story yaw'll / Of a Black man / Acting like a nigga / And get stomped by an African!" This final statement emphasizes the contrast between "nigga" as defined by offensive behavior and African as defined by intellectual and political sophistication.

Much as in the confrontation scene in Lee's *School Daze* (1988) between the "fellas" and the men from the neighborhood at Kentucky Fried Chicken, Arrested Development enunciates class difference within the African American community, but they offer no critical analysis. Representations of class positions are reproduced through the reliance on this stereotyped behavior. Foregrounding this incident increases the possibility for it to replicate the dominant view of lower-class African American males as menacing.

Arrested Development brings an important intellectual and critical dimension to rap music and culture. It breaks away from the redundant "boy 'n the 'hood" scenario, which has become almost counterproductive through the media's overwhelming emphasis of it and the rap community's willingness to participate in such exploitation. Arrested Development's female members are central to determining and articulating the group's political position. Their collaborative effort helps to provide an empowered position for female speakers without necessarily privileging the male voice. Unfortunately, in comparison to the rest of the rap community, the group's gender politics is uncommon.

Arrested Development's critical Afrocentricity involves an unconscious co-optation of regressive class politics. Through their sophisticated and at times self-righteous political position, they can critique modernity, capitalism, and gender. However, this position does not articulate an empowered position on class. Much like W.E.B. Du Bois's notion of the "talented tenth," (Du Bois, 1993) Arrested Development attempts to close the societal gap on race, but widen it on class, and fails to engage in a political dialogue that could strengthen both areas. While Arrested Development does not blame the victim, they intensify class divisions with their intellectually elitist argument on the ghetto and African American male culture. While they claim to be concerned with "everyday people," it is obvious that they locate the "group of brothers" that they critique somewhere else. Yet as I asserted earlier, my interest in Arrested Development relates to how they open up the dialogue on politics and rap culture through the invocation of their gendered Afrocentric position. Thus, multiple levels of political discourse can now be both demonstrated and juxtaposed within contemporary African American culture.

Arrested Development is clearly linked to a revisionist southern history, and they locate the problems of contemporary African American existence in the limits imposed by urbanization. This critical posture, in light of most other rap music, seems progressive and somewhat liberating. Yet when extrapolated to the larger themes just articulated, this position can be regarded as uncomplicated and ultimately mainstream. With conservative media manipulation of the popular term "political correctness" having all but cut this term off from its originally noble aspirations, Arrested Development can be easily viewed as aligned with this weakened position, as indicated by their public acceptability across race and gender lines. The group indicates in many ways the mainstreaming of Afrocentricity and the death of an earlier revolutionary agenda.

"But I Ain't Ice Cube!"

This limited political agenda, which is furthered by their inability to address the many class inequities in contemporary society, is best understood when comparing Arrested Development to their logical antithesis, Ice Cube, whose political agenda entails the iconic packaging of gangsta culture and the racialized urban American landscape—namely South Central L.A. In a sense, it is Ice Cube and what he represents that motivates much of Arrested Development's critical posture, as alluded to in the refrain "But I ain't Ice Cube" from "People Everyday." Ice Cube functions not only as an extension of the political argument in rap music, but also to expose the limitations of Arrested Development.

Ice Cube's strength lies in his ability to move easily between the general and the specific, simultaneously analyzing individual actions as well as societal oppression. Whereas Arrested Development can be seen in the same tradition as advocating an empowered version of religion, much like James Cone's idea of "Black Liberation Theology" or Albert Cleage's theory of the "Pan-African Orthodox," Ice Cube embraces the controversial tenets of Louis Farrakhan and the Nation of Islam. Unlike Arrested Development, who advocate a return to southern tradition as the solution to the problems of contemporary African American existence, Ice Cube's focus is the inner city in all its blighted glory.

Ice Cube's politics of location is clearly conversant with Burnett's To Sleep with Anger. Instead of focusing on the Deep South and the northward migration pattern of the early part of this century so often discussed in popular versions of African American history, Ice Cube, like Burnett, finds critical solace in a neglected segment of African American migration, the westward migration of southwestern (Arkansas, Louisiana, Texas) Blacks to Los Angeles primarily after World War II. Thus, Ice Cube's concerns with history are more contemporary, and in a sense better able to engage certain aspects of present-day culture. Whereas Arrested Development is interested in issues of modernity, Ice Cube is clearly associated with post-modernity.

This postmodern urban agenda is visually underscored through scenes in the "True to the Game" video of the burned-out remains of post-uprising Crenshaw Boulevard—a direct contrast to the rural landscapes that dominate Arrested Development's videos. Ice Cube sees African Americans' self-destruction and the propensity toward assimilating into mainstream society, thus losing one's identity, as the social hindrances to self-empowerment. Though these agenda items are not radically different from those advocated by Arrested Development, it is the urban setting, the embrace of the Nation of Islam, a postmodern criticism of societal institutions, and a rigorous critique of class politics that allow for a clear distinction between the two rap acts.

Ice Cube fuses these ideas into a coherent critical position on the album Death Certificate, which brings together the Nation of Islam's notion of race and a concern for the problems within African American society resulting from late commodity culture and the neoconservatism of the Reagan/Bush era. The album is equally divided between what Ice Cube describes as the "Death" and the "Life" sides. On the "Death" side, Ice Cube documents the violently destructive mentality of much of lower-class African American culture. Gangbanging, sexism, wanton violence, and other abusive behaviors are presented without the usual saccharine justification or uninformed rejection, but as harsh realities. This is what he wants to "kill." The "Life" side concerns revitalization and getting at the roots of these societal problems, dealing with them efficiently, and moving on to more concrete solutions.

The "Death" side begins with the funeral of another of Ice Cube's long line of "dead homiez." When Minister Khallid Muhammad of the Nation of Islam eulogizes the victim, he establishes the album's critical posture. Muhammad concludes by stating that the person being eulogized, who we know by this time is Ice Cube, was "the wrong nigga to fuck wit." It is at this point that Ice Cube begins his verbal assault on the racism, conformity, and overall lack of self-expression in contemporary society. Still seeing himself as the ultimate rebel who exists outside of both Black and white society, Ice Cube goes on a verbal rampage, attacking everything from contemporary African American popular music to police brutality. Much as in his opening declaration on Amerikkka's Most Wanted, "The Nigga You Love to Hate," Ice Cube revels in his utter disgust with American culture. African American complacency is as detrimental to progress as the most vile forms of white supremacy. Ice Cube's unrelenting attack on these cultural manifestations becomes the core of his identity: the angry Black man, the enraged lyricist.

At the conclusion of the "Death" side we are slowly transformed from sympathetic yet passive listeners into unconscious perpetrators of the very acts and attitudes that reinforce oppressive behavior. Once again, Ice Cube treats African Americans and the dominant society as equal culprits in the continual destruction of African American culture. Yet as the "Life" side begins with the cries of a newborn baby, we are given a glimpse of hope as to the future undoing of the shackles of oppression. Ice Cube implies through the metaphor of "life" that a strong critical, and at times self-critical, posture is necessary to fully understand the dynamics that restrict African American progress and ultimate empowerment in the larger society. The "Life" side proceeds with a critical analysis of sexual harassment, forced patriotism, assimilation, the self-destructive nature of gang violence, and the unwitting rejection of one's culture and soul for financial gain. The "Life" side takes Ice Cube's project to the next level, as he has successfully found a way to neither romanticize nor unequivocally reject the societal problems facing African Americans. Instead, he seems to have found a much-needed ground of critical scrutiny with useful extrapolation for the future. As underscored below by Khallid Muhammad's sermon, the implications of "life" for future directions become the source of potential empowerment.

> No longer dead, deaf, dumb, and blind
>
> Out of our mind
>
> Brainwashed with the white man's mind
>
> No more homicide!
>
> No more fratricide, genocide, or suicide!
>
> Look the goddamn white man in his cold blue eyes
>
> Devil don't even try
>
> We like Bebe's kids
>
> We don't die
>
> We multiply
>
> You've heard the death side
>
> So open your black eyes to the resurrection, rebirth, and rise.

In Ice Cube's use of Muhammad's oratorical qualities, Nation of Islam icons ("blue-eyed devil") are fused with icons of the gang subculture ("we don't die, we multiply") and popular African American media culture (Robin Harris's "Bebe's kids") to create an empowered rhetorical articulation that points toward the possibility of a future free of these restraints. Muhammad also relies on a liberatory notion of freedom as expressed through popular religious icons (resurrection, rebirth, and rise), giving new meaning to the at times constraining position that organized religion has always occupied for African Americans. Thus, the "Life" side places contemporary African American culture under a critical microscope, while refusing to relinquish the nature of dominant culture as it separates and ultimately destroys the fabric of African American society.

Central to Ice Cube's political agenda is a critique of the nihilism that exists throughout lower-class African American society. In conjunction with Cornel West's argument in *Race Matters*, where this nihilism is seen in the form of "psychological depression, personal worthlessness, and social despair" (West, 1993, 13), Ice Cube, in the provocative tune, "Us," vividly extents this argument by discussing the contradictory nature of African American culture as it often assumes a posture of victimized helplessness. "Sometimes I believe the hype, man / We mess it up ourselves and blame the white man."

In a society where conservative political criticism of African Americans is abundant and encourages a defensive posture that romanticizes societal problems, Ice Cube has rejected the idea of the "airing of one's dirty laundry in public"—or to use the more succinctly Black phrase, "putting one's business in the street"—in favor of exposing the problems of the community for public debate. This rejection of victimization for an empowered critical agenda goes against the grain of African American public etiquette. But unlike conservative African American critics such as Clarence Thomas, Stanley Crouch, and Shelby Steele, Ice Cube takes a position that cannot be easily co-opted. He uses this self-critical posture as an instance of cultural empowerment. His analysis of race and emphasis on class opens up the dialogue on the problems of contemporary culture, as opposed to closing off this debate through a needed, but often uninformed, cultural deconstruction.

This self-critical duality is exemplified through Ice Cube's commentary on drugs and the subculture within which drugs circulate.

> And all y'all dope dealers
> You as bad as the police
> 'Cause you kill us
> You got rich when you started slingin' dope
> But you ain't built us a supermarket
> So we can spend our money with the blacks
> Too busy buying gold and Cadillacs.

The nightly news is full of stories about the entrenchment of drugs in the African American community and the ghettoized culture that breeds this behavior. Conservatives argue that local dealers should be treated as felons and be given the death penalty. It is no surprise that many African Americans who live in the midst of what amounts to an open-air drug market corroborate elements of this conservative argument out of sheer necessity, as their lives are in constant danger.

On the other hand, in the gangsta rap community from which Ice Cube emerged, many glamorize the lifestyle and economic independence of the drug dealer. Rapper Scarface has even rejected the usual female sexual subservience by stating, "Fuck the bitches / I want money and the power" to demonstrate his complicity with the excesses of late commodity capitalism within the drug culture.

Ice Cube is careful not to fall into either ideological trap as he turns his critique of the drug culture into a positive vision for the community. The drug dealer's embrace of the fetishized commodity—gold and Cadillacs—is seen as hindering an economically informed Black nationalism that allows African Americans to spend their capital within their own self-sufficient communities. Drug dealing is not condemned in terms of "family values" but, as in the case of Gordon Parks Jr.'s *Super fly* (1972), is seen as an imposed necessity that can potentially be turned into an economic means of cultural empowerment.

Ice Cube goes on in "Us" to enunciate the contradictory nature of much within the African American community:

Us gonna always sing the blues

'Cause all we care about is hair styles and tennis shoes

If you mess with mine

I ain't frontin'

'Cause I'll beat you down like it ain't nothin'

Just like a beast

But I'm the first nigga to holler out, peace

beat my wife and children to a pulp

hen I get drunk and smoke dope

Got a bad heart condition

Still eat hog mauls and chitlins

Bet my money on the dice or the horses

Jobless

So I'm a hoe for the armed forces

Go to church but they tease us

With a picture of a blue-eyed Jesus

Used to call me Negro

After all this time I'm still bustin' up the chiferow.

His claim that African Americans engage with oppressive economic and cultural forces by an overemphasis on style and commodity culture reflects how corporations target African Americans as the prime market for their products. The Nike/Michael Jordan advertisements are probably the most popular, with the Gatorade slogan "I want to be like Mike" furthering the link between stylish commodity and African American culture. With other shoe companies having entered the fray, ads for athletic shoes are located in an urban environment dominated by African Americans. The proliferation of such products in music videos makes increasingly apparent how mediated slices of African American life have become oversaturated with stylish commodities.

Ice Cube argues that the suturing effects of commodity culture cause those who are oppressed to lose sight of their oppression as a result of this willing yet uncritical relationship with the dominant society. The "singing of the blues" is a direct result of this uneasy identity with popular elements of the dominant culture. African American identity is depoliticized as possessing commodities becomes superior to knowing the political dynamics that fuel consumption.

Witness the recent fashion for the letter X on baseball caps and clothing. Originally created as an endorsement for Spike Lee's film about Malcolm X, the letter has become a vulgar postmodern reification of what Jean Baudrillard described as simulation, where signs are detached from all referents and exist simply as signs. A knowledge of Malcolm X, his life, and his philosophies is no longer required. The X stands for all of the above and simultaneously allows those wearing it to demonstrate their culture hipness and their stylish political agenda. Ultimately, the X loses all association with Malcolm and simply becomes the sign of popular commodity culture. Regardless of a wearer's politics, it becomes the moment's most fashionable statement.

In addition to pointing out the many contradictions of African American life, Ice Cube offers several examples of gaps in relation to the dominant society. His political agenda stresses public self-criticism to force African Americans to deal with internal problems and not use racism as an answer to all questions of oppression. While he acknowledges that racism exists and should not be ignored, he suggests that it often is exacerbated through an uncritical relationship with commodity culture and other self-destructive activities. Ice Cube moves between conservative and liberal positions in making this assertion. The fact that an African American popular figure, albeit a self-proclaimed nationalist, has taken this stance through a strong cultural product opens up a dialogue that allows for solutions to the difficulties imposed by late white supremacist capitalist culture.

Ice Cube also sees another problem facing African American empowerment: attempts to assimilate into mainstream society, especially when it involves compromising one's cultural identity. In a sophisticated class critique, assimilation into middle-class existence is portrayed as consistent with oppression. This argument is clearly articulated through the song and video "True to the Game."

The most informative of Ice Cube's arguments about compromising one's identity appears in the metaphor of musical assimilation—the tendency of many rappers to reject the genre's hard political edge for success in mainstream culture. In Ice Cube's video we see a rapper dressed in what is coded as hard-core clothing—a skullcap, sweatshirt, and work khakis—slowly dissolve into an entertainer attired in red sequins who smiles repeatedly and performs elaborate dance moves. While the immediate reference is pop star Hammer—who in his recent comeback has contradicted his earlier self by embracing gangsta culture—the video implicates all who use the ghettoized trappings of hardcore rap to facilitate their transition into the more lucrative musical mainstream.

The transition from hard-core rapper to pop star is at the expense of one's cultural and class identity. The rapper attempts to change his style for the sake of mainstream culture, only to be exploited and ultimately rejected.

> On MTV
> But they don't care
> They'll have a new nigga next year
> Out in the cold
> No more white fans and no more soul
> And you might have a heart attack
> When you find out black folks don't want you back
> And you know what's worst?
> You was just like the nigga in the first verse

Stop sellin' out your race

And wipe that stupid ass smile off your face

Niggas always gotta show they teeth

Now I'm gonna be brief

Be true to the game.

While Black Entertainment Television (BET) and the Miami-based video jukebox THE BOX have long featured African American music videos, receiving play on cable network MTV is now seen as the ultimate mark of crossover success. Ironically, it was only recently, after much initial reservation, that MTV began playing African American music on a regular basis. Though programs such as *Yo MTV Raps* and *MTV Jams* are popular, it is the cable station's association with rock and roll and heavy metal that has made it a symbol of mainstream white culture in the music industry.

Ice Cube's assertion that "they don't care" directly comments on the long-standing exploitive nature of the music industry, as recently exemplified by MTV, and how it has historically used African American culture as trendy and disposable material: "they'll have a new nigga next year." Ice Cube also suggested that once the assimilative rapper, characterized by an excessive smile, has been rejected by mainstream culture, the African American cultural community will have no further need for him. In this sense these rappers, and by extension the desire to assimilate in any form, function as complicit in their own oppression.

Ice Cube has demonstrated through both "Us" and "True to the Game" an empowered class critique of nihilistic individuals as well as societal institutions. This critique is furthered by his continual use of Nation of Islam ideology. Historically the Nation of Islam has been a solid avenue of empowerment for individuals who exist outside mainstream society, in African American society as well as in society as a whole. Their focus on convicts, ex-convicts, and reformed drug abusers, especially African American males, is without equal. Nation of Islam patriarch Elijah Muhammed clearly foregrounds this in the title of his popular book, *Message to the Black Man*. It is no coincidence that Ice Cube's manipulation of this ideology, with the trappings of L.A. gang culture, can forward an empowered critique of those things that entrap the lower-class Black male. The gaps in Arrested Development's elitist critical agenda are here fully exposed.

Yet the limitations to Ice Cube's project lie in the same arena as does his strength. Though the Nation of Islam can critique bourgeois Black society, it cannot empower those who exist outside of the underclass that it so effectively targets. The xenophobic anti-intellectualism and the passive approach to critically engaging mainstream society while existing in it are the point at which this form of critique loses its usefulness. These are the limitations that forced Malcolm X, a true intellectual, to leave the Nation of Islam in search of wisdom elsewhere. And while Ice Cube's clever fusion of Nation of Islam ideology with gangsta iconography is an important form of class critique, it cannot take the questions of race and class to the next level of understanding.

The strength of the Nation of Islam has always been its ability to erect a solid image of defiance. While this is a useful tool in a people's rise to consciousness, defiance should not be the embodiment of all political understanding. If in contemporary society an embrace of the Nation of Islam, which has always been misunderstood as an empowered expression of Black nationalism, is the extent of our historical knowledge, then we are truly at an intellectual impasse. Ice Cube's, and the Nation's, refusal to properly engage a gender critique notwithstanding, it is the limitation of their class critique that ultimately leaves much to be desired.

Much of the political dimension that for a brief period defined rap music, and by extension African American popular culture, has been effectively killed off. Discussions of the resurgence of Black nationalism or attempts to define the elusive term "Afrocentricity" have subsided; in their place we began to hear discussions about the rights to linguistic property: "niggas," "bitches," "hoes," etc. We also began to hear denouncements of the hyperviolent atmosphere surrounding gangsta culture, which eventually led to congressional hearings on the impact that this nihilism is having at a societal level.

The fact that these issues would move outside the rap world into the United States Congress attests to the magnitude of this culture in the larger society. Yet it also wrongly reasserts the "moral imperative" of African American criticism, which has often been the rallying cry for a problematic censorship under the guise of "what's good for our children," as in the critical rejection of a film such as Melvin Van Peebles's *Sweetsweetback's Badass Song* (1971) on these grounds. While these moralistic cries shed no light on the real issues that underlie a systematic suturing of self-hatred with which African Americans have been forced to identify, rap music, in this sense of a new cultural politics, has been a vehicle for the expression of multiple voices—such as Arrested Development and Ice Cube—that have always had difficulty being heard. The real question becomes, when will there be a sustained movement that examines this historical self-hatred, while linking both politics and culture in a way that truly empowers all who subscribe to a liberated notion of existence in an otherwise oppressive society? These concerns clearly prompt Ice Cube's self-critical imperative to "check yo self, before you wreck yo self."

NOTES

1. Texts devoted to analyzing rap music and contemporary culture have been appearing with increasing regularity, especially in light of past omissions. For instance, academic texts such as Houston Baker Jr.'s *Rap Music, Black Studies, and the Academy*, Tricia Rose's book *Black Noise: Rap Music and Black Culture in Contemporary America*, and a large segment of Gina Dent's edited volume *Black Popular Culture* are devoted to the subject. In addition, Nelson George, whose work on rap is largely chronicled in *Buppies, B-Boys, BAPS, and Bohos*, and Greg Tate, author of *Flyboy in the Buttermilk*, both former *Village Voice* writers, have gained increased attention as authorities in this regard. The popularity of magazines such as *The Source* and *Vibe* adds to this recent phenomenon.

2. For an extended explanation of the "death of politics" relative to popular culture, see my analysis of Spike Lee's *Malcolm X*, "Popular Culture and Political Empowerment," in the *Cineaste* critical symposium on the same subject.

3. In addition to female rappers such as Salt n Pepa, Queen Latifah, and MC Lyte, whom Rose discusses extensively in her book *Black Noise*, the emergence of West Coast gangsta rap, which is absent from Rose's analysis, does not directly address women rappers such as Yo Yo and Boss, who offer interesting possibilities for the continued exploration of gender issues in rap music.

4. The following West Coast rappers exemplify thematically my argument for Black male angst: Snoop Doggy Dog, Ice-T, the late Easy E, Niggas Wit Attitude (NWA), Compton's Most Wanted (CMW), Tha Dogg Pound, Dr. Dre, King Tee, 2 Pac, Paris, Too Short, Warren G, Coolio, Mack 10, and most notably Ice Cube.

5. As an example, De La's first single, "Me, Myself, and I," critiqued how many rappers assume a monolithic posture instead of being themselves. Thus, they rejected the b-boy style of wearing gold chains,

Kangol caps, and lambskin coats for their own stylized attire of uncombed hair and nondescript baggy clothes. As the title, "Me, Myself, and I," states, they were concerned with asserting their own identity, while simultaneously offering a plural definition of "self" and affirming that "Blackness" contained multiple subject positions. This reaffirms the fact that Blackness can be defined from multiple perspectives. De La Soul assumed this posture for their first album, *3 Feet High and Rising*. On their second album they boldly declared that "De La Is Dead," short-circuiting the continuation of this style of rap.

6. The definition of function regarding African American lips in the larger culture can be seen in two recent cinematic examples. Use of the close-up and emphasis on the lips as derogatory stereotype occur in the repeated shots of the African American female radio announcer in the Walter Hill film *The Warriors* (1979). Though the character offers exterior commentary on the plight of the main characters, the street gang the Warriors, as they proceed along the narrative's mysterious path, this character has no identity; she is reduced to her function without recourse to any sustained narrative or visual involvement other than these repeated tight shots that emphasize her "nigger lips."

More recently, and in contrast to the earlier example, this tight shot of the lips was utilized in Spike Lee's *Do the Right Thing* (1989) with the character of Mr. Señor Love Daddy. In this case, the emphasis on lips becomes an example of the bodily vehicle for the oral tradition. While also functioning as the voice of exterior commentary, Love Daddy is able to articulate the film's rational direction from his empowered position and is also used as a voice of reason in relation to the societal conflicts presented in this film. In addition, Love Daddy connects the film to its oral roots when he engages in a roll call of prominent African American musical figures, both past and present. This use of the lips as vehicle for the oral tradition is also referenced repeatedly throughout *Mo Better Blues* (1990). The film's main character, Bleek Gillam, is shown as being obsessed with his lips as they determine his professional and emotional stability, especially when connected with the jazz that emerges from his trumpet.

Arrested Development's use of this racial trope can be seen as an extension of Mr. Señor Love Daddy and Bleek's function as oral facilitators within the Spike Lee films. This racial trope is also an embrace of the Africanness of their bodily features, and in turn a rejection of the traditionally Eurocentric standards of beauty in American society. Much like the often-mentioned griot of African society, the lips as visual metaphor, emphasized through extreme close-up in this case, become very useful in exemplifying the oral nature of African American culture. Also, the critique of dominant standards of beauty, at both white and African American levels, can be seen in the group's most prominent female character, who sports a bald head. While Irish female singer Sinead O'Connor is the most visible example of this style in popular white culture, the female participant in Arrested Development uses this stylistic device to affirm the group's Afrocentric cultural project.

REFERENCES

Baker, Houston, Jr. *Rap Music, Black Studies, and the Academy*. Chicago: University of Chicago Press, 1993.

Baudrillard, Jean. *Simulations*. New York: Columbia University Press, 1983.

Boyd, Todd. Popular Culture and Political Empowerment. *Cineaste* XIX, no. 4 (1993): 12–13.

Cleage, Albert. *The Black Messiah*. New York: Sheed and Ward, 1968.

Cone, James. *Black Theology: A Documentary History*. New York: Orbis Books, 1993.

Dent, Gina, ed. *Black Popular Culture*. Seattle: Bay Press, 1993.

Du Bois, W.E.B. *The Souls of Black Folk*. New York: Knopf, 1993.

George, Nelson. *Buppies, B-Boys, BAPS, and Bohos*. New York: Harper Collins Publishers, 1992.

hooks, bell. *Black Looks: Race and Representation*. Boston: South End Press, 1992.

hooks, bell, and Cornel West. *Breaking Bread: Insurgent Black Intellectual Life.* Boston: South End Press, 1991

Mercer, Kobena. Black Hair/Style Politics. In *Out There: Marginalization and Contemporary Cultures,* ed. Russell Ferguson, Martha Gever, Trinh T. Minhha, and Cornel West. New York and Cambridge: The New Museum of Contemporary Art and MIT Press, 1990.

Muhammed, Elijah. *Message to the Black Man.*

Rose, Tricia. *Black Noise: Rap Music and Black Culture in Contemporary America.* Boston: University Press of New England, 1994.

Rose, Tricia. Never Trust a Big Butt and a Smile. *Camera Obscura* 23 (1990).

Tate, Greg. *Flyboy in the Buttermilk,* New York: Fireside Press, 1992.

Washington, Booker T. *Up From Slavery.* New York: Dell Publishing, 1965.

West, Cornel. The New Politics of Difference. In *Out There: Marginalization and Contemporary Cultures,* ed. Russell Ferguson, Martha Gever, Trinh T. Minh-ha, and Cornel West. New York and Cambridge: The New Museum of Contemporary Art and MIT Press, 1990.

_____. *Race Matters.* Boston: Beacon Press, 1993.

Davarian L. Baldwin

Chapter 12

Black Empires, White Desires

We have reached the point where our popular culture threatens to undermine our character as a nation.

— Bob Dole

People are outraged, man, you get to the point where you're constantly hearing over and over talk about mugging people, killing women, beating women, sexual behavior. When young people see this—14, 15, 16 years of age—they think this is acceptable behavior.

— Rev. Calvin O. Butts

I have seen a rise lately in the disrespect of black women…. Are we the ones influencing the world? If that was the case, what music was Bill Clinton listening to when he whirlpooled Lani Guinier?

— Joseph Simmons (of Run DMC)

1997 was a pivotal year for black popular culture in general and hip hop in particular. Caught in the crossfire of the William Bennett/C. Delores Tucker censorship movement, the deaths of Tupac Shakur and the Notorious BIG (in a so-called East/West Coast battle), and an increase in its consumption (especially of "gangsta rap") among suburban white youth, hip hop has been placed under the "microscope and found…to be the source of all that is wrong with American society" (Diawara, 1993, 2). From the right, hip hop is attacked as a practice that started in urban America but is infecting the morals and family values of suburban teens. At the same time, sectors of the left and the black middle-class distance themselves from hip hop because of its misogyny and homophobia. The critique of hip hop as a black popular culture form that exists as an outside threat or infection, ravaging "American" (and black middle-class) culture and values, must be understood within a history of identification located squarely in the ideological and material spaces of colonialism, racism, and national identity. The ability to fix hip hop as pure difference from the norm or as the source of wrongdoing must be interrogated. It suggests that there is an already-agreed-upon national character threatened by a deviant popular culture (Dole) and leaves unquestioned the border where national character ends and popular culture begins.[1]

Hip hop itself is not purely a U.S., let alone black, cultural form. However, it is not an understatement to say that the deviancy or threat in popular culture is racialized, particularly through old narratives of the dysfunction of the black family (Kelley, 1997). These stories are now being deployed to identify the source of the problem within hip hop culture. After the death of the Notorious BIG, *Village Voice* writer Toure suggests this vision: "I can see now that the murder and killings are coming from the same hands that make the beats and rhymes; how is living in hip hop any different than living in the dysfunctional black family writ large?" (1997, 30).

For many, it appears that the hip hop nation and the nation at large are no longer safe from the deviancy that the black family produces. Discourse on the black family with its female-headed home becomes shorthand to make sense of the supposedly unique violence and sexuality in certain genres of hip hop. The lazy

---

Black Empires, White Desires   219

connections made between mythologies of dysfunctional black families and hip hop ignore the performative aspects of black popular culture. These narratives understand the deviancy in hip hop to be an uncomplicated (re)presentation of black culture (Fanon, 1967). The performance of hip hop as a black cultural form, for better or worse, becomes a reference for "authentic" blackness. As an action and reaction against conservative and liberal backlash,[2] at times hip hop attempts to counter negative notions of blackness with its own "racial authenticity," where the position of absolute difference is self-induced. Racial authenticity is best articulated in these instances through the stance that the artistic production is pure and untouched by any means of dilution.[3]

Within black communities, this process of black authenticity has historically oscillated between the binaries of excess and austerity. As Greg Tate contends, "the controversies surrounding hip hop in the black community have revived an ongoing debate over who best tells black stories: our blues people or our bourgeoisie" (1997, 70). In order to combat the "negative" idealizations of blackness, middle-class moral purists (even draped in kente cloth) attack the sexual frankness of hip hop as "excessive" and tend to support what is understood as "positive rap" because of its Afrocentric rhetoric and/or political awareness,[4] where as some "Ghettocentric" advocates defend the explicit lyrics as reality-based and resent the possibilities of censorship as dilutions of the authentic "realness" of black experiences. This position in hip hop is exemplified by the characterization of the "keepin-it-real nigga."

It must be noted that these positions are not set in stone and often overlap and intersect. For example, a third position might be the one articulated by KRS-One, which contains a nationalist hip hop edge but is rooted in nostalgia, not for Africa's golden era, but for a hip hop golden age. In the midst of hip hop's international growth and change, this "reaching back" for better times attempts to figure out "what went wrong, and why did hip hop become the revolution that failed?" Instead of attempting to "keep it real," this position is set on correcting rap music's ills, so that, as a culture, the hip hop nation can "keep it right." In what way are the articulations of the "keepin'-it-real nigga" or the "African" complicit with a white patriarchal order by designating what behaviors, sexualities, and representations will be accepted into the space of black popular culture? In what way is the masking of these performances as "natural," "accurate," or "real" complicit with the traditional order, and in what way are they disruptive?

Ironically, both extreme critiques and defenses of hip hop as an authentic representation of black life converge upon a certain refashioning of the infamous Moynihan (1965) report. When black families and women are the point of focus, representations of black women stand in for authentic blackness. In turn, the visibility of black female purity or contamination signifies the success or failure of black culture; women's bodies become the terrain on which battles over black authenticity are waged. In this context, C. Delores Tucker is able to attend a Time Warner board meeting and exclaim that Lil' Kim's songs must be banned. As an example of what she calls "pornographic," Tucker quotes "No Time": "No money, money / No licky, licky / Fuck the dicky, dicky and the quickie" (1996). Kim's lyrics could be (and have been) read as part of a long musical history of black women taking a stance for sexual and economic self-satisfaction (Rose, 1994; Davis, 1998). However, alternative voices are now silenced as deviant, as false articulations of blackness, and therefore irrelevant. The primacy of familial and traditional values nearly overrides any focus on social/ sexual inequalities. But the insistence on making an artist like Kim irrelevant also shows the centrality of her work. Despite the attempts to repress and regulate personal and interpersonal black conduct, artists like Kim have emerged as part of a hip hop-inspired black bourgeois aesthetic.

This aesthetic rejects both black petit-bourgeois respectability and ghetto authenticity. Its practitioners accept the black bourgeois notion of upward mobility without rejecting the desires and consumption habits of the black working class. This new black aesthetic offers a new identity outside the workplace by endorsing the consumption of luxury goods. As a form of "dressing up," it also offers a status for subordinate groups that blurs distinctions between themselves and their oppressors (Kelley, 1994, 167–69). They are changing what it means to be black and middle class in ways that make our proponents of traditional values cringe because they refuse to be disciplined into puritan characterizations of normative middle-class behavior. They have all the trappings of the middle and elite classes but wear Versace and Armani in a different way, drive their Bentleys to different places, and play out private inequalities in public arenas.

This black aesthetic potentially de-naturalizes the divides of black/white, male/female, authentic/commodified, and challenges normative notions of hip hop as a space that can purify the impure. It debunks the contention that if hip hop were practiced in its truest form, it could bring in the straying brothers and sisters who lack "knowledge of self" or who "ain't keepin it real," as if such pronouncements of identity were ever stable. The artists remind us that "in concept, hip hop was never anti-capitalist, pro-black or intentionally avant-garde. Up until Public Enemy, hip hop's intent was never to shock the world but to sell the market on its novelty and profitability" (Tate, 1997, 70). Hip hop as a musical form could never follow the traditional association of commodification with cooptation, because the revolution of hip hop was fought out within the circuits of the market. These artists have begun to discover that a black politics can also be organized within the processes of consumption.

In the same way as we consume these artists, they consume other American cultural icons. Through their performance of gangsters, rich women, and corporate culture icons, the new gangsta rappers like Biggie, Lil' Kim and Jay-Z are living the American dream of commodity obsession and appropriation. However, the appropriation of cultural icons is not a new formulation. Throughout the 20th century, Americans of all hues who have been marginalized as ethnic or "other" have utilized the "gangsta" as a site of socio-economic mobility. In this particular moment, the grammar of the gangsta's "hustle" or "game" has become the language of the culture industry. Hip hop artists and other culture workers have become "playas," and those who attempt to stop black progress in the game have become dubbed "playa haters." These workers have aesthetically, and begun to materially, appropriate the culture industry as a site for black institution-building and contestation.

Their music describes the American entrepreneur, for whom competitiveness is a way of life. While they don't like government restrictions any more than the Republicans and endorse rampant individualism within the markets, they also expose how the fervor for deregulation extends to everything except certain genres of the American music industry, genres which dominate the world market. In addition to money makers, these lyricists speak to the inequalities, restrictions, and uneven developments that have been aimed at African-Americans and women in their quest for the "American dream."

In the current backlash against gangsta rap, however, may be heard a decline-and-fall narrative that understands hip hop to be over-commodified and calls for a return to the roots of street parties and the "yes yes y'all" freestyle rhyme, which exemplifies a pre-commodified, undiluted era. This can be heard in KRS-One's 1997 hit, "Rapture," where the hook to the song says, "step into a world where hip hop is real." In the video, we see the re-invocation of a bygone era in the historic Boogie Down South Bronx, where breakdancers and graffiti artists don the early 80s fashions of warm-up suits and Puma sneakers while performing a corrective memory of the old-school concert as a utopic space.

But this utopic space has been (re)constructed in 1997, where people no longer perform or consume hip hop in the same ways. This video intentionally decontextualizes hip hop's transformations in the pursuit of a fictive realness. Such an excavation of a hip hop past doesn't question whether hip hop was ever purely outside the circuits of commodification or consistently and totally oppositional. Rather, it assumes the location of the South Bronx and the rhyming of KRS-One as correctives to contemporary hip hop. Through performances like the one above, hip hop becomes visually fixed through the designation of which images and behaviors will exemplify an "authentic" black cultural practice. However, the new gangsta/playa aesthetic is not a full embrace of marketplace ideology and commodified cultural production. The identities produced therein are important sites for a black politics at the end of the 20th century.

The general critiques circulating around gangsta rap highlight the patriarchal masculinity, drugs, sex, gunplay, and consumption habits without either remembering the Dapper Dan and Gucci days of hip hop's "golden age" or noting the earlier progressive move that gangsta rap was making against the evolution of nation-conscious hip hop in the early 90's. What many now term "positive" or conscious rap had begun to evoke a sense of gatekeeping that designated who was and was not authentically black.

"Moving on Up": Black Respectability in the Era of Nation-Conscious Hip Hop

The massive economic and cultural reorganization of life in the 1980s pulled black people in all directions. At the same time that a black middle-class was growing (in part due to affirmative action), a larger critical mass of African-Americans were left behind in the urban enclaves of all the major U.S. cities and rural locations. The Brooklyn Heights location of the *Cosby Show* and hip hop's "Boogie Down" South Bronx were talking to each other in previously unthinkable ways. The desire for upward class mobility through the market was confronting the black cultural form of hip hop, which in some ways was marketable because of its origins in urban poverty. The urban origins of hip hop and its artists' desire to become, as Eric B. and Rakim stated, "Paid in Full" (1987), were met by black audiences, who were grappling with what it meant to be paid and black. Up to this point, authentic blackness in hip hop was associated with the inner city. When African-Americans became more upwardly mobile in the 1980s, with (for example) many black youths entering the nation's elite universities, anxieties grew within the black middle class over its relationship to blackness. Black people's "moving on up" was accompanied by a sense of alienation from authentic spaces.

The icons of Afrocentricity and Africa itself served as bridges between upward mobility and historically black experiences. The notion that success and academic achievement were necessarily white experiences was met with a wave of Afrocentricity, where the study and consumption of Afrocentric goods and literature could justify a class distinction without raising issues of black authenticity. Designer wear and bourgeois habits were legitimized with, respectively, kente cloth and reconstructed Yoruba origins.

Concurrently, as hip hop became more mainstream, the nation-conscious Afrocentric genre grew. It does not seem a coincidence that in 1988, the formerly "criminally-minded" (1986) KRS-One took on the role of Malcolm X in "By All Means Necessary" (1988) and Long Island-based Public Enemy, who in 1986 were "rollin in their 98 Olds-mobile" began to state that "It Takes a Nation of Millions to Hold [Them] Back" (1988). In part, nation-conscious rap became a cipher to understand blackness in arenas of upward mobility and hip hop's national growth. As well, this music shared its terrain with an African-American and white college-age audience who used African and Black Power fashions, hairstyles, and rhetoric to demonstrate political acts of rebellion and resistance. The academic Afrocentricity of Molefi Asante countered dominant academic politics by positioning "Africa" at the center of study and analysis (1987, 187).

Afrocentricity served as a powerful tool for African-American students as their professors and administrators questioned the validity of integrating multicultural education into the canon and strengthening African-American Studies programs. The aesthetic of the "African" became a stance where students could mount a counterattack against the academic claims that African-Americans had no culture worthy of the canon. Afrocentricity served as a safe space in threatening academic waters, a complement to nationhood rhetoric within the Reagan/Bush regime, and a language to maintain borders around the definition of hip hop during its national expansion.

The move toward empowering black populations outside urban spaces through a kind of Afrocentric/nation-conscious hip hop form was not entirely new. Its roots are visible in the collective known as the "Native Tongues," which was roughly comprised of the Jungle Brothers, A Tribe Called Quest, Queen Latifah, Monie Love, and De La Soul (Boyd, 1995, 299). Their origins point even further back toward the Universal Zulu Nation of the Bronx-based Afrika Bambaataa, who in the late 70s was hell-bent on not just transmitting his Kraftwerk-inspired "techno funk" to the nation, but on making the "Planet Rock."

Native Tongues followed in Bambaataa's footsteps by not letting their musical influences or artistic vision be impeded by fictive standards of how hip hop should sound. For example, De La Soul's first single "Me, Myself and I" ironized earlier rap posturings by counterpoising the popular b-boy stance to "being one's self." De La Soul is known for initiating hip hop's breakaway from the recycling of the same James Brown beats by introducing the samples of everything from Steely Dan to Disney. Introducing a class consciousness, De La Soul was also clear about being from a relatively affluent Long Island background, stating that this heavily influenced their sound and aesthetics, which ran contrary to the stereotypical urban style. Within this distinction, they rejected what had become the authentic style of sweatsuits, gold chains, and Kangol hats by presenting their bohemian style of flowered shirts, dreaded hair, and African medallions.

Released in 1988, "Me, Myself and I" attempted to open a space where blackness could be understood through parody and the interrogation of multiple identities within hip hop, while simultaneously making subtle political statements to the nation at large:

> *Glory, glory hallelu*
>
> *glory for plug one and two*
>
> *But that glory's been denied by*
>
> *kudzids and gookie eyes*
>
> *people think they dis my person by*
>
> *stating I'm darkly packed*
>
> *I know this so I point at Q-Tip and he*

states "Black is Black"

mirror, mirror on the wall

shovel chestnuts in my path

please keep all nuts with the nuts

so I don't get an aftermath

but if I do I'll calmly punch them in

the 4th day of July

cause they tried to mess with 3rd

degree

that's Me, Myself and I

In this song, De La Soul is exploring issues of cultural individualism within blackness through an ironic reference to American patriotism. They are asking that the rhetoric of cultural freedom be applied both inside and outside of "the race." But the political impetus of this Afrocentric style became statically and dangerously interpreted as the only option within blackness, a turn that may have prompted De La Soul to title their second album *De La Soul Is Dead*. The "Soul" in Afrocentric rap began to articulate an essentialist position that equated musical "soul" with a particular black nationalist, Afrocentric identity, instead of allowing for a multiplicity of black experiences to be heard. Afrocentric versions of nation-conscious rap deployed the sunny disposition of Egypt and a re-imagined Egyptian/African culture as sources of racial legitimacy in the face of racial oppression. But in its attempts to create a powerful picture of black life, Afrocentrism expected blacks to live up to an imagined identity based on a particular version of African-American history and painted over issues of gender with broad strokes. Black life was articulated primarily in the voice of black men, and if not from men, then from the position of patriarchy.[5]

The "fertile" soil of Egypt and "Mother Africa' were fetishized as female objects, primarily valuable for their production of melanin babies, otherwise known as the "original black man." Taking material from Asante, psychologist Frances Cress Welsing, and even 18th century white scholars (like the biologist Gregor Mendel), the melanin in black skin or the culture of African people is understood as making the black man naturally good, artistic, and superior.

As Jeffrey Decker has stated, work by the artist Isis was emblematic of this phenomena. In her music video "The Power of Myself Is Moving," she plays the part of a fertility goddess along the Nile: "I'm a self coming forth a creature bearing life / a renaissance, a rebirth" (1990). Even through a female voice, the message evokes the patriarchal order where women are revered solely for their inherent nurturing and reproductive skills. Because the black woman bears the seed of the black nation, she is viewed as an "object" that must be protected from both interracial and intraracial contamination.

As stated earlier, the absence of any discussion of intraracial class conflict is a crucial oversight in Afrocentric work. However, anxieties over class-based behaviors emerge through a rigid representation of regional differences and gendered behavior. One of the key groups to articulate this phenomenon was Arrested Development, which Todd Boyd rightly lauds for relocating hip hop outside urban spaces into the landscapes of the rural South, while also criticizing the group for its romanticization of this locale: "Arrested

Development argues for a kind of cultural innocence or purity. This notion of purity is exemplified through a juxtaposition of the harsh urban realities of the street prominent in contemporary rap and their embrace of the premodern "country," the simplicity of a rural landscape" (1995, 300). Arrested Development promotes the romantic rural by defining and denigrating its other: the urban subject.

This rural-urban dichotomy creates a class hierarchy between the positive images of pastoral Afrocentric rap and the depressing dangers of urban experiences. A binary, expressed this time in terms of the "true black self," is established between the haves and have-nots: "Now I see the importance of history / why my people be in the mess that they be / many journeys to freedom made in vain / by brothers on the corner playing ghetto games" (1992). This trope of "knowledge to be acquired" through mastering designated Afrocentric texts and behaviors is understood as the entryway to authentic blackness. The revisionist Southern history of Arrested Development (AD) can easily be mapped onto the "return to family values" narrative, best depicted in idealization of rural New England communities by white conservatives like Newt Gingrich. In both narratives, place and family space became the loci for the creation of "proper values." As well, both rhetorics claim to speak from the position of the popular or "everyday people," while masking their privileged class positions.

Scholars like Boyd have prized AD for their positive and progressive gender politics. However, I am skeptical of such a position, because the voices of their women rappers are constrained by their role as a prize. In AD's work, the "black queen" serves as an object that must not be contaminated by "niggas." In the video "People Everyday," black men are performing the stance of the "urban nigga"—drinking 40's and grabbing their crotches—when an, "African queen" approaches and one of the men grabs her butt. Simultaneously, Speech[6] can be heard in a voiceover criticizing their behavior: "My day was going great and my soul was at ease / until a group of brothers / started buggin out / drinking the 40 ounce / going the nigga route / disrespecting my black queen / holding their crotches and being obscene" (1992). The woman is given no agency and the nigga performs the stereotypical deviant role that gives the African the opportunity to do his duty and step in to protect his queen. An analogy is made between the ability of the African man to protect his woman and the intrinsic strength of the African identity: "That's the story y'all / of a black man / acting like a nigga / and get stomped by an African" (1992). Even in the midst of gender inclusion, masculine aggression rears its ugly head. The radical right's vision of the patriarchal family is upheld, but now in blackface and kente cloth. But what happens when the nigga speaks back?

"The Nigga You Love to Hate": Class Conflicts in the "G-Funk" Era

Rather than evading the nigga, gangsta rap actually engaged and mimicked the position of nigga as other, as performance. In the next section I, along with Robin Kelley and other scholars, postulate that the earliest manifestations of gangsta rap attempted to speak back to the middle-class-oriented position of nation-conscious rap. Kelley argues that, "L.A. gangsta rappers are frequent critics of black nationalists [as well]. They contend that the nationalist focus on Africa—both past and present—obscures the daily battles poor black folk have to wage in contemporary America" (1994, 212). In some regards, nation-conscious rap assumed that everyone agreed on the definition of "knowledge of self" and, in turn, blackness. Gangsta rap, however, provides another perspective on black life.

As well, gangsta rappers saw no inherent negativity in the term "nigga," defining themselves as niggas in defiance of the dominant society, both black and white. As hip hop was continuing to expand, more tensions arose around the definition of hip hop as a representation of blackness. Although hip hop originated and was most successful in urban New York and on the East Coast, the emergence of gangsta rap shifted the focus in hip hop to the lived experience of the post-industrial city on the West Coast, particularly Los Angeles.

The highly popular N.W.A. (Niggas With Attitude) album, *Straight Outta Compton* was released in 1988 at the same time that nation-conscious rap was becoming popular. However, it wasn't until the early 90s— when N.W.A.'s *efil4zaggiN* (Niggaz 4 life) reached number one on the *Billboard* charts before it was even released, Snoop Doggy Dogg was introduced on the *Deep Cover* soundtrack, and Dr. Dre's multi-platinum album *The Chronic* was heard on every street corner and video station—that everyone was forced to realize that gangsta rap was a force to be reckoned with. The West Coast began to dismantle New York's monopoly of hip hop and critiqued nation-conscious rap's politically correct disciplining of black bodies. Unlike the critiques of black nihilism that wax nostalgic for a bygone black community (West, 1993), gangsta rappers aren't anti-nationalist or apolitical, but they do oppose a political correctness which obscures the historical realities of class, gender, and locational difference within the representation of black communities.

On "Dre Day," Dr. Dre retorts: "no medallions / dreadlocks / or Black fist it's just that gangsta glare / with gangsta rap that gangsta shit, / brings a gang of snaps" (1992). Instead of seeing this position as exemplifying a movement of anti-politics, I see it as a shift in the way in which politics is articulated. In hindsight, it is an attempt to break the stranglehold of nation-conscious rap on hip hop expression. The political language of nation-conscious rap, in its most general sense, was traded in for the grammar of the hood and the particular day-to-day struggles of black people.

In gangsta rap, the nigga acquired a locational and economic specificity. Kelley argues that the experiences of young black men in the inner city were not universal to all black people, and furthermore, that "nigga does not mean black as much as it means being a product of the post-industrial ghetto" (1994, 210). This process exposes the limitations of politics based on skin color. Gangsta rap can be understood as resistance, where the nigga is seen as a performative identity that is not solely accessed by a black constituency.

Thus, we are encouraged to analyze the nigga within the American mainstream, especially since so much of the work in gangsta rap is inspired by popular action-adventure and gangster films and its biggest registered consumers are suburban white teens. Because of this phenomenon, we must think critically about white youth's influence over creating and maintaining the gangsta subject by purchasing the music. The gangsta subject would not continue to exist in commodified form if there were not buyers waiting for the product. Gangsta rap deals in fantasy and evil, constructing marketable stories that tell as much about its white teen listeners' desires as about its practitioners. In what ways do the consumption of and desire for a genre help to continue its existence?

The problematics that supposedly originate in the nigga subject are turned back onto America and its political/economic/racial regime. In Kelley's essay, a Chicano gang member makes visible his relation to the economic order in regard to his "deviant" behavior: "I act like they do in the big time, no different. There ain't no corporation that acts with morals and that ethics shit and I ain't about to either. As they say, if it's good for General Motors, it's good enough for me" (1994, 196). The desires of the "gangsta" are exposed equally as the desires of its consumers and creators, problematizing the belief in a pure pathological difference based on race. In other words, the behaviors of the nigga are found in all segments of American life.

Through the performance of the nigga, the gangsta rapper fights against fixity and attempts to make visible the multiple registers through which the hood, racial pathologies, and the nigga are actualized. In gangsta rap, individualism and criminality are continually tied to America culture. As Ice-T states: "America stole from the Indians sure and prove / what's that? / a straight up nigga move!" (1991). But in this position of rebelliousness, gangsta rap and the nigga became idealized as Ghettocentric, a counter move to the Afro-centricity and white supremacy of the day.

The nigga became the embodiment of black defiance against all comers through a highly masculinist imaginary, where the nigga was strong when he wasn't a "punk," "bitch," or "pussy." The project of uncovering the racially hybrid subjectivity of the nigga is halted when the nigga is flaunted as the only "real" black identity. The tropes of masculinity, promiscuity, and violence become naturalized as inherently black. However, this form of identification is no different from most young men in patriarchal societies who come to associate masculinity with aggression and violence. Blackness as hypermasculine becomes a romanticized position of strength and opposition that hopes to create "safe spaces" of uncontested male power. Furthermore, the belief that black family structures are deviant because of the instability of its women is a narrative that may also be found in gangsta rap.

The male rapper begins to call for the restoration of the patriarchal order, because for him, the female is fixed as a threat to the progress of his success or hustle. In the same way that gangsta rap performs the violence of an idealized America, it also calls upon traditional tales of black women as scapegoats for problems within the nation(hood). "African-American women are often portrayed as welfare queens making babies merely to stay on public assistance or 'gold-diggers' who use their sexuality to take black men's meager earnings" (Kelley, 1994, 217). This narrative can be found in Dr. Dre's song "Bitches Ain't Shit But Hoes and Tricks," or E-40's "Captain Save a Ho," in which men are chastised for taking care of a woman and her children, especially if they aren't his own. During this song's popularity, a man who listened to his girlfriend or spent too much time with a woman was accused of "having an S on his chest" because he was "savin" em" (his woman was in control). The woman is seen as putting the man's freedom in jeopardy by hustling him for his money and time.

At its most progressive, gangsta rap analyzes the contingent relationship between poverty and a racialized political economy but at the same time can explain women in poverty in terms of a behavioral problem, claiming that all a woman wants is to take you for your goods. Tricia Rose explains how black males fear the assertion of a strong woman's sexuality: within gangsta spaces, there is no guarantee that heterosexual male desires will be met because of women's capacity to reject or manipulate men's advances (1991). This is not a new narrative and indeed is based on longstanding fears of women's ability to trap men (e.g., through pregnancy), when sexual exchange is able to produce money and goods (Kelley, 1994, 219).

Just as the purified space of the black nationalist is insecure, so also is the stability of the gangsta. The terrain where black men attempt to assert their masculinity or evade the issues of class is always highly contested. Male gangsta rappers expose the vulnerability of heterosexual male desire in their exaggerated stories of dominance over female representations of black life.

The degree of anxiety expressed in these heavy-handed fantasies explains both an intense desire and distrust of women and the way in which their (in)subordination disrupts racial authenticity. However, gangsta rap is not vying for a sanitized vision of Africa, complete with corrective gender and class relationships. It forces us to deal with the everyday in a way that can't justify the harsh denigration of female and working-class desires, particularly in the marketplace. Gangsta rap seems suited for engaging the social contradictions and ambiguities of urban life.

In the context of racial distinctions, while gangsta rap's white consumers and critics are identifying the gangsta as something "other" than themselves or the white middle-class values they purport to inherit, these artists are parodying "normative" behavior. Peter Stallybrass and Allon White argue that:

> The "top" attempts to reject and eliminate the "bottom" for reasons of prestige and status, only to discover, not only that it is in some way frequently dependent upon the low-Other, but also that the top *includes* the low symbolically, as a primary eroticized constituent of its own fantasy life. The result is...a psychological dependence upon precisely those others which are being rigorously opposed and excluded at the social level. It is for this reason that what is socially peripheral is so frequently *symbolically* central. (5, 1986)

Although gangsta rap has been constructed as deviant from middle-class normativity, examining the social texts of desire and consumption shows its relationship to those very norms. For example, the "vulgar" black female deviance performed or commented on in gangsta rap is not nor can be discretely separated from the sense of entitlement clothed in middle-class normative respectability. The gangsta performance forces those who embrace white middle-class patriarchy to stare the black gangsta in the face and see him- or herself. This shift to gangsta music has allowed black men and women trapped by oppressive systems to reinvent themselves through new performative acts, a reinvention defined by Manthia Diawara as the "defiant tradition in black culture that challenges every attempt to police the black body or mind" (1993, 4).

The Wretched of the Earth: Pleasure, Power, and the Hip Hop Bourgeoisie

Earlier conservative idealizations of black life evaded an engagement with the black body through policing it, whereas Diawara's notion of the "black good life society" "emphasizes the necessity for a productive space which is accompanied by consumption, leisure, and pleasure in black people's relation to modernity" (1993, 7). This engagement with pleasure and commodity consumption addresses realities that black middle-class and black church aesthetic forms often shun.

These traditional forms have historically functioned within ideologies that separate intellect and pleasure, mind and body, and have been articulated within the binary of a harsh middle class/working class divide. Historically, it has been black people's responsibility to link pleasure or freedom with the non-material. L.A.-based gangsta rap reopened a space where it is not sinful to link black pleasure with materialism. Rather than finding a politics through positive imaging, the "black good life" seeks a politics through performance and refashions identity through irony and play. If moral and cultural correctness is seen as denial, then open representations of sexuality and grotesque and carnivalesque characterizations/eroticizations of violence can be understood as potentially liberating.

The performance of so-called deviant acts and direct confrontations with black stereotypes create black industries, as well as make visible the social construction of what appear as natural black characteristics. These performances expose the interracial and intraracial formation of the nigga identity and "take ethical decisions away from the church, out of the moral and religious arena, and place them squarely at the feet of material well being and pleasure" (Diawara, 1993, 7). I argue that the backlash against the new cadre of male and female gangsta rappers, whether it be voiced by C. Delores Tucker, William Bennett, Rev. Calvin Butts, or hip hop purists, is mobilizing around an ethic that purports to speak "for the people" but in actuality does not. The gatekeepers of "authentic blackness" are anxiety-ridden over public displays of the black good life society, exemplified in the emergence of a new hip hop identity; a black middle-class aesthetic that will not be policed by traditional notions of morality and class status.

Confident in the freedom offered by the pleasures and profits of performing gangsta, New York-based Lil' Kim, Foxy Brown, Jay-Z, and The Notorious BIG are exemplars of this hip hop shift. Consequently, these artists are specifically attacked for their lines of commodity endorsements from Versace to Lexus and for their obsession with Italian-American mobsters. Yet, in the same way that white supremacy has created the nigga as a repository for its own not-so-laudable activities, "gangsta/playa" rappers have taken white American commodities as signs of achieving "the dream." By performing the roles of Italian-American mobsters and movie characters, they continue to question the idea that gangsta behaviors in hip hop are inherently an extension of deviant, let alone black, culture. At the same time, their gangsta performance critiques the notions of blackness expressed through ghetto authenticity or black bourgeois respectability. This version of gangsta rap questions the fictive boundaries placed around class status as a means of social exclusion.

One way in which upward mobility has historically been policed is by the coupling of class status with behavioral dictates. As working-class blacks advance financially through the entertainment arena, they are expected to change their behaviors in a way that "properly" suits their new economic status. However, the privacy traditionally afforded middle-class citizens is not given to these black cultural workers, who are placed under strict scrutiny as if their social advancement warranted a special kind of public attention. So many perceptions are shaped by the "you can take a nigga out of the hood, but you can't take the hood out of the nigga" narrative, that entertainment and sports pages begin to look like the Metro section. But I wonder if these entertainers are becoming more of an embarrassing spectacle, or whether there are larger anxieties about the changing composition of the American middle and upper class? This belief that particular behaviors can be linked to a specific class standing hardly ever makes visible that entree into the normative middle-class space has historically been acquired and maintained through not-so-middle-class behaviors.

Instead of reacting to "culture of poverty" rhetorics by disassociating blackness from American culture, these gangsta collectives have crowned themselves Junior M.A.F.I.A., The Firm, and Roc-A-Fella (Rockefeller) Records. They problematize the lines drawn between legality and illegality, morality and immorality, by articulating not the culture of poverty but mainstream American culture. This American tale potentially tears the racial and economic structure of U.S. life away from the current trends in neo-Social Darwinist ideology (i.e., that there is something particular to black culture that is intrinsically deviant). Critics of gangsta rap hold to the claim that inherent to the middle-class identity are distinguishably different values. The lyrics of the new gangstas make it clear that the rhetoric of individualism pays homage to traditional mainstream values that are being used "to redistribute more income, wealth and power to classes that are already most affluent in those aspects" (Gans, 1995, 7).

Born amidst the same media that chain black identity to cultural pathology, this new black-entertainment middle class has viewed the slippery slope of ethical behavior in American life. They were children of the 1980s Yuppie and Buppie culture, when conspicuous consumption was a normative, elite class behavior.

These artists have witnessed on television and movie screens the prominence of John Gotti, Manuel Noriega, and Saddam Hussein, all as a result of U.S. state intervention. For them, corporate culture is gangsta culture. Could witnessing and experiencing life within the American context have possibly encouraged and nurtured the violation of so-called family values within marginal communities? Jay-Z, owner of Roc-A-Fella Records, seems to think so:

> Your worst fear confirmed
>
> me and my fam' (ily) roll tight like the firm
>
> gettin' down for life, that's right, you betta learn
>
> why play with fire, burn
>
> we get together like a choir, to acquire what we desire
>
> we do dirt like worms, produce g's [thousands of dollars] like sperm
>
> Til legs spread like germs...
>
> I sip fine wines and spit vintage flows—what y'all don't know?
>
> 'Cuz you can' knock the hustle
>
> Y'all niggas lunchin' punchin' a clock
>
> function is to make and lay back munchin'
>
> sippin' Remy on the rocks
>
> my crew, something to watch
>
> notin' to stop
>
> un-stoppable...
>
> you ain't havin' it? Good me either
>
> Let's get together and make this whole world believe us, son
>
> at my arraignment screamin'
>
> All us blacks got is sports and entertainment—until we're even
>
> thievin' as long as I'm breathin'
>
> can't knock the way a nigga eatin' fuck you even
>
> (1996)

These lyrics might easily seem to promote illegality, self-indulgence, misogyny, and crudely hedonistic tendencies; however, they also provide a critique of the socio-economic structure that prevents many African-Americans access to decent wage labor. Jay-Z makes clear that large populations of African-Americans are still excluded from middle-class consumption except through sports and entertainment. On Jay-Z's latest album, he is inspired by the hook in the theme song from the musical *Annie*. While the song refers to a little white orphan, Jay-Z argues that "instead of treated we get tricked / instead of kisses we get kicked / it's a hard knock life" is an archetypal "ghetto anthem" (1998). Both sets of lyrics endorse a hustler's mentality, a strategic manipulation of the opportunities made available in light of socio-economic inequalities. This perspective suggests that consumption and pleasure could serve as working-class critiques of middle-class ideals and also utilizes the trope of the gangsta/playa to appropriate the terrain of the "free" market for black institution-building.

Another example of this manipulation of black identity is the platinum-selling artist, The Notorious BIG (aka Biggie Smalls). Before his untimely death, Biggie was one of the artists who freed hip hop from the tight grip of the "keepin it real" persona. After the Ghettocentric turn, rappers were forced to write their rhymes as if they reflected authentic lived experience. So as "keepin it real" in gangsta rap became prevalent, artists competed with one another to see who could depict the most devastatingly grim "personal" narratives. Biggie, however, was unabashed about his goal of upward mobility within the narratives of his ghetto background. He did not feel that he had to stay in the ghetto or necessarily back up his lyrics with authentic acts. In his first single, "Juicy," Biggie remarks, "fifty-inch screen / money green leather sofa / got two cars / a limousine / with a chauffeur / phone bill about two g's fat / no need to worry / my accountant handles that / and my whole crew is lounging / celebratin' everyday / no more public housing" (1994).

In his short career, Biggie took advantage of what was marketable and was never bound by the New York-centric formalism about how real hip hop should sound. In fact, he worked with Luke Skyywalker, Bone Thugs-n-Harmony, and even Michael Jackson, collaborations that would suffice to bar most from the "authentic" hip hop nation. He didn't totally leave the hood behind, but he was more self-conscious in his "performance" of the gangsta lifestyle.

On a number of occasions, Biggie stated that The Notorious BIG was nothing but a character or role that he performed; he was Christopher Wallace. In fact, the name "Biggie Smalls" comes from the 70s film Let's Do It Again, starring Sidney Poitier and Bill Cosby. Biggie even goes as far as to assume the role of a white movie figure, Frank White, from the film King of New York, and concluded his rhymes by exclaiming "MAFIOSO!"

This performance of Mafia culture begs the questions: whose culture is deviant? Isn't the acceptance of certain gangsta ethics in mainstream entertainment deviant? The rise of Roc-A-Fella, Death Row, and Bad Boy, with their commodification of illegality, cannot be divorced from the actual rise during Prohibition of the Irish-American Kennedy family or the Italian-American Gambino family. Likewise, these artists' conspicuous consumption habits cannot be seen as distinct from the mansion-and-yacht stories of Larry Ellison at Oracle, Jim Clark at Netscape, and Bill Gates at Microsoft, complete with feuds over who has the biggest "Cyber Boy Toy" (Kaplan, 1998), whose Horatio Alger narratives have served as models for this country's "formal" economy.

The posthumous indictment of Biggie at his 1997 memorial by Khallid Muhammad couldn't be more correct: "wearing the white man's clothes, showing up on TV dressed like you're Al Capone Baby Face Nelson, ugly as you are" (Marriott, 1997). Indeed, Biggie's is an ugly and messy performance that illuminates the muddled realities of racial and national identity and concurrently unfolds along the axis of gender. Even in his misogynist lyrics, Biggie wasn't shy about passing the mic. He gives props to "the honeys getting money, playing niggas like dummies" (1994). From this gangsta genre emerged a cadre of women artists headed by Lil' Kim of Junior M.A.F.I.A. and Foxy Brown of "The Firm."

These women questioned normative notions of male-female relations; in their stories, they acquire capital, express dissatisfaction with sexual partners, and reverse stereotypical gender roles. Foxy Brown declares:

No more sex me all night

thinking it's alright

while I'm looking over your shoulder

watching your whole life

you hate when it's a ball right ladies this ain't hand ball

nigga hit these walls right

before I call Mike

in the morning when it's all bright

eggs over easy

hope you have my shit tight

when I open my eyes

while I'm eating getting dressed up

this ain't your pad

I left money on the dresser

find you a cab

(1996)

In most scenarios, black males monopolize blackness through a relegation of the black female to the role of fetish, but here men have become the objects of desire. When patriarchal desires suddenly become articulated in a female voice, these desires are deemed "unnatural." Questions emerge as to what is ladylike and why a woman can't get hers like any man?[7]

Female identity in these musical texts becomes performance by coupling highly materialistic and aesthetically violent and excessive personas with infectious beats and rhymes.

The rhymes make it obvious that the relentless pursuit of status, power, and sexual satisfaction is not gender-specific, and thus reverse the objectification of women as sexual objects by viewing men as accesses to pleasure and capital accumulation, if necessary, through sexual exchange. Lil' Kim debunks the old myth that women only give sex for love and men only give love for sex; she makes it clear that the terms on which masculinity will be recognized will be her economic and sexual self-satisfaction:

I knew a dude named Jimmy

he used to run up in me

night time pissy drunk

off the Henne and Remy

I didn't mind it

when he fucked me from behind

It felt fine

especially when he used to grind it

he was a trip

when I sucked his dick

he used to pass me bricks

credit cards and shit

I'd suck 'im to sleep

I took the keys to the jeep

tell him I'd be back

go fool with some other cat...

it was something about this dude I couldn't stand

something that coulda made his ass a real man

something I wanted

But I never was pushy

the motherfucker never ate my pussy

(1996)

In a *Vibe* interview, Lil' Kim describes this sexual commerce as the American way: "Sex...Money is power to me. It's not power alone, but you wanna have money to get the girls. To me, men like what women like, or they learn to like it" (Good, 1997, 176). She and her fellow female artists have understood that "sex sells" and have indirectly initiated a transformation of the color-coded and gender-laden rules by which social relations are scrutinized. This is in no way a proto-feminist position; neither Kim nor Foxy increases the value of women's sexuality. Nonetheless, their performances in the cultural marketplace open up a dialogue about "natural" gender roles and explore issues of female pleasure.

However, the power in articulating bodily pleasure is not purely narcissistic; indeed, it is not just about individual freedom but also concerns the transformation of institutions. Transgressions of black/white, male/female binaries have led artists to challenge the "old-school" belief that "real" hip hop must reside only outside the market. We then begin to remember that hip hop nationalism or nation-conscious rap was created through commodification and market growth. Even the idea of a hip hop national consciousness was raised through the market and utilized market tools, including records, tapes, and stage shows. For example, the "Fresh Fests" of the mid-80s did more than make money; they became a medium to circulate and exchange dance steps, clothing styles, lyrics, and ideas. The commodification of hip hop fashions and aesthetics became a common point of reference for its fans nationwide. The concept of a national consciousness or hip hop nation was not diluted but was in many ways strengthened through the circuits of mass media.

Technological advances within the market such as the music video have revealed the regional and aesthetic diversity of hip hop. Music videos allowed regional artists the space to craft personal and social narratives and "represent" their home not only with visuals but by contextualizing the style and delivery of their rhymes to a national audience without fear of retribution. An example of the power of musical/visual context

Black Empires, White Desires   233

is the artist Tongue Twista from the group Do or Die. Before Do or Die's breakthrough single "Po Pimps" (Emotions), Tongue Twista had been considered a one-hit wonder in the late 80s, when he was performing Afrocentric styles, wearing African beads and Cross-Colors gear. His claim to fame was recognition by the *Guinness Book of World Records* as "the world's fastest rapper." But thanks, to the space opened up by music videos and other alternative outlets, we may now learn that his rapid rhyme style can be located within a Midwest/Southern-influenced hip hop aesthetic identifiable by its staccato delivery blended with doo-wop harmonies and laid over rich Stax-style horns and bass lines. In addition, music video production has enabled the formation of black directors, camera operators, and production crews. Due to video training, these positions have bypassed the white male unions that control apprenticeship systems and employment networks. A perfect example of this breakthrough is F. Gary Gray, who started out directing hip hop/R&B videos and who in 1995 parlayed these skills into a highly successful feature film, *Friday.*

For the regional developments in gangsta/playa hip hop, technological innovations have made it easier and cheaper to own recording studios and gain access to other professional recording resources. Ironically, when conservatives like C. Delores Tucker led the backlash against "gangsta rap," its listeners were drawn closer together. The major labels that produced gangsta rap decided to stop manufacturing it at the same pace. However, while the production side submitted to "public opinion," consumers utilized music technologies to rework the genre based on regional tastes. The consumers of gangsta rap realized that they had more in common musically with the South, West, and Midwest than with the Northeast. For so long, New York had dictated what "real hip hop" is and how it should sound and look.[8] In the face of resistance from both conservative movements and "old school" purists, independent compilations were circulated locally that included artists from emerging Southern and Midwestern versions of California-based gangsta rap. Due to the regional desire for the music, car-trunk distribution turned into independent label empires.

This process has encouraged the formation of semi-independent hip hop labels nation-wide, including Death Row and Ruthless Records in Los Angeles; Sick Wit It Records in Vallejo, California; Rap-A-Lot and Suave House Records in Houston; Fully Loaded Records in Decatur, Georgia; So So Def Records in Atlanta; Blackground Records in Virginia; and the Cash Money Clique in New Orleans. While these developments are laudable, it has not been easy for female artists to take advantage of this phenomenon. With the notable exceptions of Queen Latifah, Missy Elliott, and Lil' Kim, women artists/entrepreneurs have not been able to utilize this gangsta grammar to build independent labels. However, artists have been encouraged to look at the relationship between work and culture and to understand the business side of music. The No Limit Empire, headed by Master P, is something to take special note of. P inaugurated the two-pronged strategy of high production (between April 1996 and March 1997, his label released seven albums) and business autonomy that is more reminiscent of West Indian dance-hall culture: "You have a product, a rap product. It belongs to you. And you're just going to give somebody 85% of what you make on the product? To do what? Organize your life, basically call you in the morning and tell you to be across town at such and such a time...shit, I can wake my own damn self up" (Green, 1997, 100). The only aspect of P's business that is not self-contained is a distribution deal with Priority Records.[9]

Probably the most important aspect of P's business is his engagement with multiple media. Unlike conventional black media entrepreneurs, he feels that nothing is beyond his grasp. Instead of trying to pitch a film deal to a movie conglomerate, P conceived, marketed, and created his own visual autobiography, *I'm 'Bout It.* He released it himself, taking it straight to video and distributing it through record stores and the Blockbuster Video chain. In 1997, the film had sold over 250,000 units and has surpassed video giants like *Jurassic Park* in weekly sales.

The strategic marketing of P's film projects used the subversive strategies of the new independent labels. Each No Limit CD is packaged with ads about upcoming work. His projects are a success because he eliminates intermediaries and up-front advances from other sources. P states: "Of course they gonna pop some money at you...but how much money can they pop at me that I ain't already seen? That's how white boys do ya. That's how they get our ideas, our inventions" (Jackson, 1998, 74). Master P's aim is to maintain ownership over the means of production by being clear about the consumption habits and tastes of his consumer base.

Whether an artistic flop or a stroke of marketing genius, *I'm Bout* It has been hailed as paving the way for a new wave of independent hip hop films from cities outside New York or L.A. While Master P was working on his second film, a comedy called *I Got the Hookup*, other black entrepreneurs and aspiring film-makers had been given an example of how to be "playas in the game." From Bruce Brown's D.C.-based 24–7 (1997), which is driven by a hip hop and go-go soundtrack, to Robert Hayes's urban crime drama *Winner Takes All* (1998), which depicts the post-industrial landscape of Louisville, Kentucky, a wide range of black filmic expressions abound. The strength of this new wave of filmmaking lies in its manipulation of technologies as a means of autonomy. The first wave of hood films in the early 90s (*Boyz in the Hood, Menace II Society*) were largely dependent on multimedia conglomerates for distribution and heavily targeted by the gatekeepers of "official" depictions of black life. But the new movie-makers no longer have to bow down to revenue sources or critics. They can go straight to TV or DVD or sell films in record stores. These filmmakers are breaking the rules of conventional budgets, subject matter, marketing, and distribution (Shaw, 1998, 102).

Conclusion

I don't want to suggest that these transgressions of the black/white, male/female authentic/ commodified binaries contain any overtly political agenda, because, as we've seen, two artists have died over these attempts to build black empires. Biggie, who labeled himself the "Teflon Don" (aka Mafia boss John Gotti), was not invincible. Concurrently, young children are performing these identities to death, which only fuels the debate for hip hop's critics. Nonetheless, hip hop cannot be singled out without scrutinizing George Bush's endorsement of the violent and misogynist Arnold Schwarzenegger film *True Lies* as "friendly to families" (Pareles, 1995).

Moreover, hip hop can't be seen as all that is wrong with American life. The cultural oscillations of hip hop and the current gangsta trends bear witness to our national history. This music cannot be divorced from the numerous American-dream stories of this nation. Like early gangsta and Afrocentric rappers, the new rappers are not trying to hold black identity to some place of total opposition to consumption, commodification, or social mobility. They are claiming their U.S. citizenship by partaking of conspicuous consumption and performing the identities of a U.S. gangsta government and elite-class capitalists.

The gangsta/playa and the subject matter associated with this icon can now be understood as a strategy, a work in progress. This is a position of maneuverability, which in its present form doesn't endorse the cult of authenticity that must explicitly be a "pure" counter to the mainstream. Womanhood is not purely fetishized as the African Queen or the Streetcorner Ho. While one can still see black women being singled out as locations of deviance, so-called deviant tropes are seen as central to constructing not only successful black women but also, as Lil' Kim charges, "Miss Ivana...Zsa Zsa Gabor, Demi Moore, Princess Diana and all them rich bitches" (1996). For so long, space had been the chief signifier of racial difference, and freedom and movement had become white prerogatives. Yet these artists are now turning static space into sites of creative play and parody. They are appropriating and rearticulating each and every identity like music samples, cutting and scratching the rigid binaries until they are no longer comprehensible. Democracy, nationhood, and struggles over identity are being theorized through the circuits of desire and spectacle and are best summed up by Jay-Z, who doesn't ask to "Rock the Vote" or "Just Say No," but "Can I live?"

NOTES

1. Jon Pareles, "Rapping and Politicking: Showtime on the Stump," *New York Times*, June 11, 1995.

2. Michel Marriott, "Hard Core Rap Lyrics Stir Backlash," *New York Times*, August 15, 1995.

3. Marriott, "Hard Core Rap Lyrics Stir Backlash."

4. This class-based form of policing black bodies can be found in all aspects of black life. One important example was covered by *Village Voice* writer Lisa Jones in a review of a book entitled *Basic Black: Home Training for Modern Times* (ed., Elyse Hudson and Karen Grisby Bates; 1997). These women attempt to map "down-home training" onto the typical etiquette book: teaching black people how to receive first-class service in a first-class restaurant, telling black folk to avoid talking to characters on movie screens, etc. In music, this backlash can be found in the black media's embrace of the hip hop/soul artists Erykah Badu in 1997 and Lauryn Hill in 1998. Without minimizing these artists' talent, they were both praised for their mixture of Afrocentric/Rastafarian/Five-Percenter ideology and "old-school" credibility. Badu and Hill became exemplars of the "purist" revival against "negative" female artists like Lil' Kim, and have been particularly lauded for dressing and acting with self-respect and dignity.

5. Within the nation-conscious genre, not all groups or artists ignored issues of class or gender, e.g., Queen Latifah or the L.A.-based group The Coup. However, this essay is attempting to take note of a general "common sense" that located black authenticity within the simultaneous reverence for and restriction of the black woman. For example, see Decker's analysis of Public Enemy's song "She Watched Channel Zero." True, as Queen Latifah has commented, the women of the nation-conscious genre were not called bitches or hoes, but "queen" status also restricts the ways in which black femininity can be displayed. The weight of the queen's crown was sometimes too heavy a burden to bear.

6. Speech, the lead rapper of Arrested Development, belongs to a prominent black family in Milwaukee, Wisconsin, that runs a black-owned newspaper, *The Community Journal*, where his op-ed "racial uplift" pieces ran in his series, "20th-century African." This series was known for its catchy and suggestive byline, "Here's the run-down, so you don't get gunned down." This phrase and column foreshadow the urban/African divide that becomes so prominent in his musical ideology.

7. While Foxy's disruption of gender roles within black communities is encouraging, it appears that her exploration of sexuality also reinforces the same patriarchal order. On her new album, *China Doll*, Foxy locates her sexual freedom within the stereotypical image of the exotic Asian woman.

8. In the 1980s, Miami Bass had been marginalized from hip hop as not "real" because it focused more on beats than lyrics. But as other regional versions of hip hop have gained economic and technological resources, this idea of "realness" was exposed as particular to the Northeast. Although conversation in this area is just beginning to emerge, New Yorkers have tended to see hip hop in other regions as "country," "bama," and unsophisticated. However, newer groups like Outkast and Goodie Mob from

Atlanta and Timbaland and Missy Elliott from Portsmouth, Virginia, have gone on to parody and play with stereotypes aimed at the "Dirty South."

9. While it is encouraging that black artists/entrepreneurs are breaking into the production side of the music industry, they have yet to shatter the final frontier of the business: distribution. For example, two of gangsta/playa rap's powerhouse semi-independent labels, No Limit and Death Row, are both distributed by Priority Records. Until these labels develop distribution autonomy, they will be forever bound to the structural dictates of the music industry's multinationals.

REFERENCES

Asante, Molefi Kete. *The Afrocentric Idea*. Philadelphia: Temple UP, 1987.

Barnekov, Timothy, Robin Boyle, and Daniel Rich. *Privatism and Urban Policy in Britain and the U.S.* New York: Oxford UP, 1996.

Boyd, Todd. "Check Yo'Self. Before You Wreck Yo'Self: Variations on a Political Theme in Rap Music and Popular Culture." Black Public Sphere Collective (ed.). *The Black Public Sphere*. Chicago: U. of Chicago P., 1995.

Brown, Elaine. *A Taste of Power*. New York: Pantheon, 1992.

Davis, Angela. *Blues Legacies and Black Feminism: Gertrude "Ma" Rainey, Bessie Smith, and Billie Holiday*. New York: Pantheon Books, 1998.

Decker, Jeffrey Louis. "The State of Rap: Time and Place in Hip Hop Nationalism." Andrew Ross and Tricia Rose (eds.), *Microphone Fiends: Youth Music and Youth Culture*. New York: Routledge, 1994.

Diawara, Manthia. "A Symposium on Popular Culture and Political Correctness." *Social Text*, 1993.

Fanon, Frantz. *Black Skin. White Masks*. Trans. Charles Lam Markmann. New York: Grove, 1967.

Gans, Herbert J. *The War Against the Poor: The Underclass and Anti-Poverty Policy*. New York: Basic Books, 1995.

Gilroy, Paul. "Revolutionary Conservatism and the Tyrannies of Unanimism." *New Formations* 28. Spring 1996.

_____. "After the Love Has Gone: Bio-Politics and Etho-Poetics in the Black Public Sphere." Black Public Sphere Collective (ed.), *The Black Public Sphere*. Chicago: U. of Chicago P., 1995.

Good, Karen R. "More Than a Lil' Bit." *Vibe*. September 1997.

Green, Tony. "Stairway to Heaven." *Vibe*. June-July 1997.

Hall, Stuart. "The After-life of Frantz Fanon: Why Fanon? Why Now? Why "Black Skin, Where Masks?" Alan Read (ed.), *The Fact of Blackness*. Seattle: Bay Press, 1996.

_____. "What Is This 'Black' in Black Popular Culture?" Gina Dent (ed.), *Black Popular Culture*. Seattle: Bay Press, 1992.

Jackson, Scoop. "Soldiers on the Set." *Vibe*. May 1998.

Jones, Lisa. "Home(girl) Training." *Village Voice*. March 19, 1997.

Kaplan, Tony. "Cyber Boy Toys." *Time*. July 1998.

Kelley, Robin D. G. *Race Rebels*. New York: Free Press, 1994.

Marriott, Michel. "At a Ceremony for Shakur. Appeals for Peace." *New York Times*. September 23, 1996.

_____. "Hard Core Rap Lyrics Stir Backlash." *New York Times*. August 15, 1993.

Moynihan, Daniel Patrick. *The Negro Family: The Case for National Action.* Washington, D.C.: Office of Policy Planning and Research, U.S. Department of Labor, 1965.

Pareles, Jon. "Rapping and Politicking: Showtime on the Stump." *New York Times.* June 11, 1995.

_____. "A Symposium on Popular Culture and Political Correctness. *Social Text.* 1993.

_____. "Never Trust a Big Butt and a Smile." *Camera Obscura.* #23, 1991.

Rose, Tricia. *Black Noise: Rap Music and Black Culture in Contemporary America.* Hanover, NH: Wesleyan UP/UP of New England, 1994.

Shaw, William. "Bustin" a Movie." *Details.* March 1998.

Smith, R. J. "Bigger Than Life." *Village Voice.* March 19, 1997.

Stallybrass, Peter, and Allon White. *The Politics and Poetics of Trangression.* Ithaca: Cornell UP, 1986.

Tate, Greg, "Funking Intellect." *Vibe.* June/July 1997.

Toure. "Bigger Than Life." *Village Voice.* March 19, 1997.

Weinraub, Bernard. "National Desk." *New York Times.* June 1, 1995.

West, Cornel. *Race Matters.* Boston: Beacon, 1993.

DISCOGRAPHY

Arrested Development. "People Everyday." *3 Years, 5 Months and 2 Days in the Life Of.* Chrysalis, 1992.

De La Soul. "Me, Myself and I." *3 Feet High and Rising.* Tommy Boy, 1988.

Dr. Dre. "Dre Day." *The Chronic.* Death Row Interscope, 1992.

Eric B. and Rakim. *Paid in Fall.* Island, 1987.

Foxy Brown. "Ill Nana." *ILL NANA.* Rush Recordings, 1996.

Ice Cube. "Species (Tales from the Darkside)." *AmeriKKKa Most Wanted.* Priority, 1990.

Ice T. "New Jack Hustler." *OG: Original Gangster.* Sire, 1991.

Isis. "The Power of Myself Is Moving." *Rebel Soul.* 4th and Broadway, 1990.

Jay-Z. "Can't Knock the Hustle." *Reasonable Doubt.* Roc-A-Fella/Priority, 1996.

_____. "Hard Knock Life." *Hard Knock Life* Vol. II. Roc-A-Fella/Def Jam, 1998.

KRS-One. *Criminal Minded.* Sugar Hill, 1986, Reprint, 1991.

_____. *By All Means Necessary.* Jive, 1988.

Lil' Kim. *Hard Core.* Big Beat, 1996.

The Notorious BIG *Ready to Die.* Arista, 1994.

N.W.A. *Straight Outta Compton.* Ruthless, 1988.

Public Enemy. "My 98 Oldsmobile." *Yo! Bum the Rush Show.* Def Jam, 1987.

_____. "She Watched Channel Zero." *It Takes a Nation of Millions to Hold Us Back.* Def Jam, 1988.

_____. "Welcome to the Terrordome." *Fear of a Black Planet.* Def Jam, 1990.

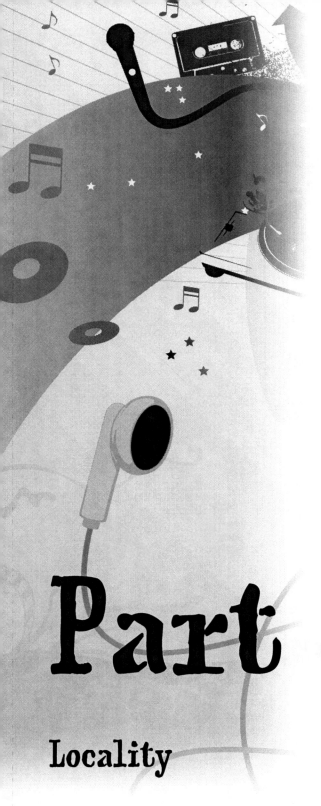

As we have observed, hip hop draws on musical styles and aesthetics from beyond the United States. Strands from the Caribbean, South America, Africa, the U.S., and Europe came together in the South Bronx in the 1970s, producing the breaking, writing, DJing, and rapping elements that comprise hip hop. Almost immediately after this convergence, however, hop hop itself spread beyond New York City, first to nearby cities on the East Coast, then throughout the United States and the world. Afrika Bambaataa's landmark European tour in the early 1980s was a key event in this regard. Notable rap artists now hail from, among other places, Great Britain, France, Algeria, Japan, and Brazil.

The propagation of rap music and hip hop culture on a global scale raises questions about locality and its relation to musical style. How are regional and local styles defined? How do these newer styles relate to established ones in the U.S. and elsewhere? Are there common themes that unite hip hop localities as a "movement" or "generation," such as opposition to social and economic oppression? The first two articles in this section take up these questions.

The view of hip hop as a unified movement with clearly identified "roots" in African–American aesthetics and culture has profound implications for some of the debates surrounding rap music in today's society, and for the legal status of the music itself. The third article in this section takes up the issue of sampling, its essential artistic function in rap music, and its difficult position in today's legal system. Keep these questions in mind as you complete study these readings:

How has hip hop responded to globalization?

If hip hop emphasizes "locality" so much, can we view it as a unified "culture" or "movement?"

How do these accounts of hip hop in a global context compare with those from other materials in this course?

Part 4

Locality

Murray Forman

Chapter 13

"Represent"

Say somethin' positive, well positive ain't where I live

I live around the corner from West Hell

Two blocks from South Shit and once in a jail cell

The sun never shined on my side of the street, see?

**— Naughty By Nature, "Ghetto Bastard
(Everything's Gonna Be Alright)," 1991,
Isba/Tommy Boy Records**

If you're from Compton you know it's the 'hood where it's good

**— Compton's Most Wanted, "Raised in Compton,"
1991, Epic/Sony**

Introduction

Hip hop's[1] capacity to circumvent the constraints and limiting social conditions of young Afro-American and Latino youths has been examined and celebrated by cultural critics and scholars in various contexts since its inception in the mid-1970s. For instance, the 8 February 1999 issue of the U.S. magazine *Time* featured a cover photo of ex-Fugees and five-time Grammy award winner Lauryn Hill with the accompanying headline "Hip-Hop Nation: After 20 Years—how it's changed America." Over the years, however, there has been little attention granted to the implications of hip hop's spatial logics. *Time*'s coverage is relatively standard in perceiving the hip hop nation as a historical construct rather than a geo-cultural amalgamation of personages and practices that are spatially dispersed.

Tricia Rose (1994) arguably goes the furthest in introducing a spatial analysis when she details the ways that hip hop continually displays a clever transformative creativity that is endlessly capable of altering the uses of technologies and space. Her specific references to hip hop culture and space stress the importance of the "postindustrial city" as the central urban influence, "which provided the context for creative development among hip hop's earliest innovators, shaped their cultural terrain, access to space, materials, and education" (1994, p. 34). As this suggests, the particularities of urban space themselves are subjected to the deconstructive and reconstructive practices of rap artists. Thus, when, in another context, Iain Chambers refers to rap as "New York's 'sound system'...sonorial graffiti" with "the black youth culture of Harlem and the Bronx twisting technology into new cultural shape" (1985, p. 190), he opens the conceptual door onto corresponding strategies that give rise to the radical transformation of the sites where these cultures cohere and converge or the spaces that are reimagined and, importantly, remapped. Rap artists therefore emerge not only as aberrant users of electronic and digital technologies but also as alternative cartographers for what the Samoan-American group Boo Yaa Tribe has referred to in an album title as "a new funky nation."

Indeed, there is very little about today's society that is not, at some point, imbued with a spatial character and this is no less true for the emergence and production of spatial categories and identities in rap music and the hip hop cultures of which it is a central component. Rap music presents a case worthy of examination and provides a unique set of contexts for the analyses of public discourses pertaining to youth, race, and space. Rap music is one of the main sources within popular culture of a sustained and in-depth examination and analysis of the spatial partitioning of race and the diverse experiences of being young and black in America. It can be observed that space and race figure prominently as organizing concepts implicated in the delineation of a vast range of fictional or actually existing social practices that are represented in narrative and lyrical form. In this chapter, I seek to illuminate the central importance of spatiality in the organizing principles of value, meaning, and practice within hip hop culture. My further intent is to explore the question of how the dynamics of space, place, and race get taken up by rap artists as themes and topics and how they are located within a wider range of circulating social discourses. The prioritization of spatial practices and spatial discourses that form a basis of hip hop culture offers a means through which to view both the *ways* that spaces and places are constructed and the *kinds* of spaces or places that are constructed.

The chapter traces the way in which hip hop's popularity spread from New York to other U.S. cities, most notably Philadelphia and Los Angeles but eventually more geographically marginal cities such as Seattle, and it discusses changes that have taken place in rap production, particularly the rise of artist-owned labels. Such developments encouraged the emergence of distinctive regional rap sounds and styles, as well as strong local allegiances and territorial rivalries, as the identities and careers of rap acts became more closely tied to the city and to its specific neighborhoods ('hoods) and communities. The chapter examines the effects of all this on the spatial discourse of rap. It points to a gradual shift within rap from a concern with broad, generalized spaces, to the representation of specific named cities and 'hoods (as illustrated by Gansta Rap from the Californian city of Compton which celebrates and glorifies Compton as well as the street warrior and gang rivalry) and the representation of smaller-scale, more narrowly defined and highly detailed places (as illustrated by rap from the North West city of Seattle which has a distinctively local flavor).

Locating Hip Hop

Describing the early stages of rap music's emergence within the hip hop culture for an MTV "Rap-umentary," Grandmaster Flash, one of the core DJs of the early scene, recalls the spatial distribution of sound systems and crews in metropolitan New York:

> We had territories. It was like, Kool Herc had the west side. Bam had Bronx River. DJ Breakout had way uptown past Gun Hill. Myself, my area was like 138th Street, Cypress Avenue, up to Gun Hill, so that we all had our territories and we all had to respect each other.

The documentary's images embellish Flash's commentary, displaying a computer generated map of the Bronx with colored sections demarcating each DJ's territory as it is mentioned, graphically separating the enclaves that comprise the main area of operations for the competing sound systems.

This emphasis on territoriality involves more than just a geographical arrangement of cultural workers and the regionalism of cultural practices. It illuminates a particular relationship to space or, more accurately, a relationship to particular places. As Flash conveys it, the sound systems that formed the backbone of the burgeoning hip hop scene were identified by their audiences and followers according to the overlapping influences of personae and turf. The territories were tentatively claimed through the ongoing cultural practices that occurred within their bounds and were reinforced by the circulation of those who recognized and accepted their perimeters. It is not at all insignificant that most of the dominant historical narratives pertaining to the emergence of hip hop (i.e., Hager 1984; Toop 1984) identify a transition from gang-oriented affiliations (formed around protection of turf) to music and break dance affiliations that maintained and, in some cases, intensified the important structuring systems of territoriality.

Flash's reference to the importance of "respect" is not primarily addressing a respect for the skills or character of his competitors (although, elsewhere [George 1993] he acknowledges this as well). Rather, his notion of respect is related to the geographies that he maps; it is based on the existence of circumscribed domains of authority and dominance that have been established among the various DJs. These geographies are inhabited and bestowed with value, they are understood as lived places and localized sites of significance, as well as being understood within the market logic that includes a product (the music in its various live or recorded forms) and a consumer base (various audience formations). The proprietary discourse also implies, therefore, that even in its infancy hip hop cartography was to some extent shaped by a refined capitalist logic and the existence of distinct market regions. Without sacrificing the basic geographic components of territory, possession and group identity that play such an important role among gang-oriented activities, the representation of New York's urban spaces was substantially revised as hip hop developed.

Clearly, however, the geographical boundaries that Flash describes and which are visually mapped in the documentary were never firm or immovable. They were cultural boundaries that were continually open to negotiation and renegotiation by those who inhabited their terrains and who circulated throughout the city's boroughs. As the main form of musical expression within the hip hop culture, the early DJ sound systems featured a series of practices that linked the music to other mobile practices, such as graffiti art and "tagging." Together, these overlapping practices and methods of constructing place-based identities, and of inscribing and enunciating individual and collective presence, created the bonds upon which affiliations were forged within specific social geographies. Hip hop's distinct practices introduced new forms of expression that were contextually linked to conditions in a city comprised of an amalgamation of neighborhoods and boroughs with their own highly particularized social norms and cultural nuances.

Hip Hop, Space, and Place

Rap music takes the city and its multiple spaces as the foundation of its cultural production. In the music and lyrics, the city is an audible presence, explicitly cited and digitally sampled in the reproduction of the aural textures of the urban environment. Since its inception in the mid- to late 1970s, hip hop culture has always maintained fiercely defended local ties and an in-built element of competition waged through hip hop's cultural forms of rap, breakdancing and graffiti. This competition has traditionally been staged within geographical boundaries that demarcate turf and territory among various crews, cliques, and posses, extending and altering the spatial alliances that had previously cohered under other organizational structures, including but not exclusive to gangs. Today, a more pronounced level of spatial awareness is one of the key factors distinguishing rap and hip hop culture from the many other cultural and subcultural youth formations currently vying for attention.

Throughout its historical evolution, it is evident that there has been a gradually escalating urgency with which minority youth use rap in the deployment of discourses of urban locality or "place," with the trend accelerating noticeably since 1987–1988. With the discursive shift from the spatial abstractions framed by the notion of "the ghetto" to the more localized and specific discursive construct of "the 'hood" occurring in 1987–1988 (roughly corresponding with the rise and impact of rappers on the U.S. West Coast), there has been an enhanced emphasis on the powerful ties to place that both anchor rap acts to their immediate environments and set them apart from other environments and other 'hoods as well as from other rap acts and their crews which inhabit similarly demarcated spaces.

Commenting in 1988 on rap's "nationwide" expansions beyond New York's boroughs, Nelson George writes, "Rap and its Hip Hop musical underpinning is now the national youth music of black America…rap's gone national and is in the process of going regional" (George 1992, p. 80). George was right, as rap was rising out of the regions and acts were emerging from the South (Miami-based 2 Live Crew or Houston's The Geto Boys), the North-west (Seattle's Sir Mix-A-Lot and Kid Sensation), the San Francisco Bay area (Digital Underground, Tupac, Too Short), Los Angeles (Ice T, N.W.A.) and elsewhere. Indeed, the significance of the east-west split within U.S. rap cannot be overstated since it has led to several intense confrontations between artists representing each region and is arguably the single most divisive factor within U.S. hip hop to date. Until the mid-1990s, artists associated with cities in the Midwest or southern states often felt obligated to align themselves with either East or West, or else they attempted to sidestep the issue deftly without alienating audiences and deriding either coast. In the past several years, however, Houston, Atlanta, and New Orleans have risen as important rap production centers and have consequently emerged as powerful forces in their own right.

Today, the emphasis is on place, and groups explicitly advertise their home environments with names such as Compton's Most Wanted, Detroit's Most Wanted, the Fifth Ward Boyz, and South Central Cartel, or else they structure their home territory into titles and lyrics, constructing a new internally meaningful hip hop cartography. The explosion of localized production centers and regionally influential producers and artists has drastically altered the hip hop map and production crews have sprung up throughout North America. These producers have also demonstrated a growing tendency to incorporate themselves as localized businesses (often buying or starting companies unrelated to the music industry in their local neighborhoods, such as auto customizing and repair shops) and to employ friends, family members and members of their wider neighborhoods. Extending Nelson George's observation, it now seems possible to say that rap, having gone regional, is in the process of going local.

The Regional Proliferation of Artist-Owned Record Labels

Reflecting on the intensification of regional rap activity within the U.S. during what might be defined as the genre's "middle-school" historical period,[2] Nelson George writes that 1987 was "a harbinger of the increasing quality of non-New York hip hop," citing as evidence the fact that three of the four finalists in the New Music Seminar's DJ Competition were from "outside the Apple—Philadelphia's Cash Money, Los Angeles's Joe Cooley, and Mr. Mix of Miami's 2 Live Crew" (George 1992, p. 30). In the pages of *Billboard*, he observed that despite New York's indisputable designation as the "home" of rap, Philadelphia rappers in particular (most notably, DJ Jazzy Jeff and the Fresh Prince) were making inroads on the scene and on the charts, making it "rap's second city" (George, ibid.). This expansion was facilitated by the emergent trend in the development of artist-owned independent labels and management companies which entered into direct competition with non-artist-owned companies.

After years of bogus contracts, management conflicts, and poor representation, a growing number of artists began dividing their duties between recording or performing, locating and producing new talent, and managing their respective record companies. By forming self-owned labels and publishing companies and establishing themselves as autonomous corporate entities, forward-thinking rap artists were also able to maintain greater creative control over their production while ensuring increased returns on their sales. In a rather excessive discourse, artists spoke of throwing off the corporate shackles of the recording industry as well as invoking the quite separate issues of building something of which one can be proud or being remunerated in a more lucrative manner.

Once several key labels such as Luther Campbell's Skyywalker Records and Eazy-E's Ruthless Records had been established and had proven the viability of the venture, their initiatives were rapidly reproduced as numerous artists followed suit. For many recording artists, to gain wealth and material renumeration for their work suddenly meant learning the production and management side of the industry and exercising entrepreneurial skills as well. As the trend expanded, small artist-owned and operated labels burgeoned and another tier was added to the industry. With the rise of artist-owned labels there was also an increased emphasis on regional and local affiliations and an articulation of pride and loyalty in each label, its artist roster, and the central locale of operation.

Rap is characteristically produced within a system of extremely close-knit local affiliations, forged within particular cultural settings and urban minority youth practices. Yet the developments in the rap industry, whereby production houses or record labels might be identified on the basis of their regional and local zones of operation, are not unique to this current period. For instance, independent "race record" labels, which targeted blacks in the South and in larger northern urban centers throughout the 1920s and 1930s, flourished in part due to the enhanced mobility of black populations which maintained their affinities for the various regional blues styles. Nelson George's consistent attention to black musical tradition, the music industry's gradual permutations, and rap's growing national influence led him to note in *Billboard* that "regional music used to be the backbone of black music and—maybe—it will be again" (31 May 1986, p. 23). He recalls black American musical production in the immediate post-World War II period when independent labels were dispersed across the nation, recording locally and regionally based artists while servicing the needs of black music consumers within these regional markets.

Examining the history of black popular music in the 1960s and 1970s, the names Motown, Stax, or Philadelphia International Records (PIR) evoke images of composers, producers and musical talent working within very specific studio contexts in Detroit, Memphis, and Philadelphia. The dispersed independent labels and production sites that operated from the 1950s through the 1970s are therefore culturally meaningful and relevant to descriptions of black music of the period as they convey an idea of consistency and identifiable signature sounds or styles.[3] This trend has continued with rap, with more pronounced and explicit connection to specific locales and the articulations of geography, place and identity that sets the genre apart from many of its musical predecessors.

Of the smaller labels that had thrived in the 1950s, 1960s, and 1970s, most disappeared as musical tastes shifted, as economic transitions evolved, or as the industry majors swallowed them or bumped them out of the market by introducing their own specialty labels. Towards the end of the 1980s, the U.S. music industry was no longer even primarily American, with the major parent companies being massive transnational entities with corporate offices based in several countries. Yet, in both rock and rap there was a resurgence of regional production in the mid-to late 1980s and, with it, the resurgence of regionally distinct styles. In the black music sector these were exemplified by the Minneapolis funk that was a trademark of artists like Prince, The Time, Jimmy Jam and Terry Lewis, or Jesse Johnson; the Washington, D.C. go-go sound of Chuck Brown, Redd and the Boys, and especially Trouble Funk; and from Chicago, house music exemplified by DJ Frankie Knuckles. Rap production in New York, Los Angeles, and Miami also began to display regionally distinct "flavors" to a greater extent as individual producers emerged with their own trademark styles and influences. Individual studios such as Chung King in New York also became associated with specific production styles and sounds in rap.

As evidence of the arrival of artist-owned labels in the rap business, in December, 1989, *Billboard* featured advertisements in a special section on rap that illustrated the trend. Among these were ads for Eazy-E's Ruthless Records (Compton, CA), Luther Campbell's Skyywalker Records (Miami, FL), and Ice T's Rhyme Syndicate (South Central LA). Appearing alongside these were advertisements for the established independent rap labels Def Jam, Tommy Boy and Jive as well as ads for the newer "street" divisions of major labels including Atlantic ("The Strength of the Street"), MCA ("Wanna Rap? MCA Raps. Word!") and Epic ("Epic in Total Control. No Loungin', Just Lampin"). The phenomenon has since evolved to the extent that artist-owned operations have become relatively standard in the industry, existing as influential players alongside the major labels.

As a later entrant, Death Row Records (initiated in 1992 by principal investors Suge Knight and former member of the rap group Niggaz with Attitude [N.W.A.] Dr. Dre) flourished through a lucrative co-ownership and distribution alliance with upstart Interscope Records, which was itself half-owned by Time Warner's Atlantic Group. Although a series of misfortunes in 1996–97 decimated the label,[4] it rose to virtual dominance in the rap field between 1992 and 1997 with top-charting releases by Dr. Dre, Snoop Doggy Dogg, and Tupac Shakur as well as the soundtrack albums *Deep Cover* (1992) and *Murder Was the Case* (1994). One of the factors that characterized Death Row Records from its inception and which is common to the dozens of artist-owned and operated rap labels to emerge in the late 1980s and early 1990s, however, is an organized structure rooted in localized "posse" affiliations.

Homeboys and Production Posses

Greg Tate suggests that, "every successful rap group is a black fraternal organization, a posse" (1992, p. 134). On the same theme, Tricia Rose writes that "rappers' emphasis on posses and neighborhoods has brought the ghetto back into the public consciousness" (1994, p. 11). For Public Enemy's Chuck D, posse formations are a necessary response to the fragmentive effects of capitalism: "the only way that you exist within that mould is that you have to put together a 'posse', or a team to be able to penetrate that structure, that block, that strong as steel structure that no individual can break" (Eure and Spady 1991, p. 330). As each of these commentators suggests, the posse is the fundamental social unit binding a rap act and its production crew together, creating a collective identity that is rooted in place and within which the creative process unfolds. It is not rare for an entire label to be defined along posse lines with the musical talent, the producers and various peripheral associates bonding under the label's banner.

With collective identities being evident as a nascent reference throughout rap's history in group names like The Sugarhill Gang, Doug E. Fresh and the Get Fresh Crew, X-Clan, or the 2 Live Crew, the term "posse" was later unambiguously adopted by rap artists such as California's South Central Posse or Orlando's DJ Magic Mike, whose crew records under the name "the Royal Posse." In virtually all cases, recording acts align themselves within a relatively coherent posse structure, sharing labels and producers, appearing on each other's recordings and touring together.

The term posse is defined as a "strong force or company" (*Concise Oxford Dictionary*, 1985) and for many North Americans it summons notions of lawlessness and frontier justice that were standard thematic elements of Hollywood westerns in the 1940s and 1950s. This is, in fact, the basis of the term as it is applied within rap circles, although its current significance is related more precisely to the ways in which the Jamaican posse culture has over the years adapted the expressive terminology and gangster imagery of the cinema to its own cultural systems. In her illuminating research on the sinister complexities of the Jamaican posse underworld, Laurie Gunst (1995) explains how the posse system grew under the specific economic, political, and cultural conditions of mid-1970s Jamaica, evolving into a stratified and violent gang culture that gained strength through the marijuana, cocaine, and crack trade. As she explains, the Jamaican posse system has, since 1980, been transplanted to virtually every major North American city.

The Jamaican posse expansion is important in this context as it coincides almost precisely with the emergence of rap and hip hop in New York's devastated uptown ghetto environments. This connection is strengthened when rap's hybrid origins that were forged in the convergence of Jamaican sound systems and South Bronx funk are considered. The concept of the posse has, through various social mechanisms and discursive overlays, been traced upon many of rap's themes, images, and postures that take the forms of the pimp, hustler, gambler and gangster in the music's various sub-genres that evolved after 1987. Rap has also been influenced by the gangland models provided by the New York mafia and Asian Triad gangs.

Since roughly 1987 hip hop culture has also been influenced by alliances associated with West Coast gang systems. Numerous rap album covers and videos feature artists and their posses representing their gang, their regional affiliations or their local 'hood with elaborate hand gestures. The practice escalated to such an extent that, in an effort to dilute the surging territorial aggression, Black Entertainment Television (BET) passed a rule forbidding explicitly gang-related hand signs on its popular video programs.

"The 'Hood Took Me Under": Home, Turf and Identity

It is necessary to recognize that the home territory of a rapper or rap group is a testing ground, a place to hone skills and to gain a local reputation. This is accurately portrayed in the 1992 Ernest Dickerson film *Juice* where the expression "local" is attributed to the young DJ Q, in one instance suggesting community ties and home alliances whereas, in another context, it is summoned as a pejorative term that reflects a lack of success and an inability to mobilize his career beyond the homefront. In interviews and on recordings most rappers refer to their early days, citing the time spent with their "home boys," writing raps, perfecting their turntable skills, and taking the stage at parties and local clubs or dances (Cross 1993). Their perspective emerges from within the highly localized conditions that they know and the places they inhabit.

As a site of affiliation and circulation, the 'hood provides a setting for particular group interactions which are influential in rap music's evolution. In rap, there is a widespread sense that an act cannot succeed without first gaining approval and support from the crew and the 'hood. Successful acts are expected to maintain connections to the 'hood and to "keep it real" thematically, rapping about situations, scenes and sites that comprise the lived experience of the 'hood. At issue is the complex question of authenticity as rap posses continually strive to reaffirm their connections to the 'hood in an attempt to mitigate the negative accusations that they have sold out in the event of commercial or crossover success. Charisse Jones has noted a dilemma confronting successful rap artists who suddenly have the economic means to "get over" and leave the 'hood. As she writes in the *New York Times* (24 September 1995, p. 43), contemporary artists such as Snoop Dogg or Ice T are often criticized for rapping about ghetto Poverty and gang aggression while living in posh suburban mansions.

Those who stay in the 'hood generally do so to be closer to friends and family, closer to the posse. while a common rationale for staying in the 'hood is familiarity and family bonds, in numerous cases artists also justify their decisions to stay along a creative rationale, suggesting that the 'hood provides the social contexts and raw resources for their lyrics. Others leave with some regret, suggesting that the 'hood may constitute "home" but its various tensions and stresses make it an entirely undesirable place to live (this is even more frequent among rappers with children to support and nurture); there is no romanticizing real poverty or real danger.

The 'hood is, however, regularly constructed within the discursive frame of the "home," and the dual process of "turning the 'hood out" or "representing" (which involves creating a broader profile for the home territory and its inhabitants while showing respect for the nurture it provides) is now a required practice among hardcore rap acts. The posse is always explicitly acknowledged and individual members are greeted on disk and in live concerts with standard "shout outs" that frequently cite the streets and localities from which they hail. This continual reference to the important value of social relations based in the 'hood refutes the damning images of an oppressed and joyless underclass that are so prevalent in the media and contemporary social analyses. Rap may frequently portray the nation's gritty urban underside, but its creators also communicate the importance of places and the people that build community within them. In this interpretation, there is an insistent emphasis on support, nurture and community that coexists with the grim representations that generally cohere in the images and discourses of ghetto life.

As in all other popular music forms, "paying dues" is also part of the process of embarking on a rap music career, and the local networks of support and encouragement, from in-group affiliations to local club and music scenes, are exceedingly important factors in an act's professional development. One way that this is facilitated is through the posse alliances and local connections that form around studios and producers. For example, in describing the production house once headed by DJ Mark, The 45 King, the rap artist Fab 5 Freddy recalls that "he had this posse called the Flavor Unit out there in New Jersey.... He has like a Hip Hop training room out there, an incredible environment where even if you weren't good when you came in, you'd get good just being around there" (Nelson and Gonzales 1991, p. xiii).[5] This pattern is replicated in numerous instances and is also exemplified by the production/posse structure of Rap-A-Lot Records in Houston (home to acts such as the Geto Boys, Scarface, Big Mike, Caine, and The Fifth Ward Boyz) where the company was forced to relocate its offices because "artists were always kicking it there with their posses like it was a club" (*Rap Sheet*, October 1992, p. 18). By coming up through the crew, young promising artists learn the ropes, acquire lessons in craft and showmanship, attain stage or studio experience and exposure and, quite frequently, win record deals based on their apprenticeships and posse connections.

Few rap scholars (Tricia Rose and Brian Cross being notable exceptions) have paid attention to these formative stages and the slow processes of developing MC and DJ skills. There is, in fact, a trajectory to an artist's development that is seldom accounted for. In practice, artists' lyrics and rhythms must achieve success on the home front first, where the flow, subject matter, style and image must resonate meaningfully among those who share common bonds to place, to the posse and to the 'hood. In this sense, when rappers refer to the "local flavor," they are identifying the detailed inflections that respond to and reinforce the significance of the music's particular sites of origin and which might be recognized by others elsewhere as being unique, interesting and, ultimately, marketable.

The Spatialization of Production Styles

The posse structures that privilege place and the 'hood can be seen as influential elements in the evolution of new rap artists as well as relevant forces in the emergence of new, regionally definable sounds and discourses about space and place. For example, critics and rappers alike acknowledge the unique qualities of the West Coast G-funk sound which defined a production style that emerged with Dr. Dre's work on the Deep Cover soundtrack and the release of his 1992 classic *The Chronic* (Death Row/Interscope), and arguably reached its apex with the 1994 release of Warren G's Regulate...G Funk Era (Violator/Rush Associated Labels). Other local artists in this period, such as the Boo Yaa Tribe, Above the Law, Compton's Most Wanted, and DJ Quik, also prominently featured variations on the G-funk sound and reinforced its influence in the industry as an identifiable West Coast subgenre. G-funk makes ample use of standard funk grooves by artists including George Clinton, Bootsy Collins, Gap Band, or the late Roger Troutman, and is characterized as being "laid-back" and sparse, featuring slow beats and longer sample loops. While it was regarded as a regionally distinct sound, it was also often related specifically to Dr. Dre's production style and was comparatively categorized by its difference from the more cacophonous East Coast jams (recognizable in the early work of the Bomb Squad, the production crew of the rap act Public Enemy). As Brian Cross (1993) notes, however, the impact of the G-funk style among California rap acts is also related to the extended influence of late 1970s funk music in the Southwest that was a consequence of limited access to independently produced and distributed rap product in the early 1980s, delaying rap's geographic expansion from New York to the Los Angeles area.

Explaining the Bomb Squad's production processes following the release of Public Enemy's *Fear of a Black Planet* (1990, Def Jam), Chuck D describes his production posse's familiarity with various regional styles and tastes and their attempts to integrate the differences into the album's tracks. As he states:

> Rap has different feels and different vibes in different parts of the country. For example, people in New York City don't drive very often, so New York used to be about walking around with your radio. But that doesn't

really exist anymore. It became unfashionable because some people were losing their *lives* over them, and also people don't want to carry them, so now it's more like "Hey, I've got my Walkman." For that reason, there's a treble type of thing going on; they're not getting much of the bass. So rap music in New York City is a headphone type of thing, whereas in Long Island or Philadelphia...it's more of a bass type thing. (Dery 1990, p. 90)

These regional distinctions between the "beats" are borne out in the example of the Miami production houses of Luther Campbell or Orlando's Magic Mike. In Florida (and to some extent, Georgia) the focus is on the bass—Florida "booty bass" or "booty boom" as it has been termed—which offers a deeper, "phatter," and almost subsonic vibration that stands out as a regionally distinct and authored style.[6] Within U.S. rap culture, artists and fans alike reflect an acute awareness that people in different parts of the country produce and enjoy regional variations on the genre; they experience rap differently, structuring it into their social patterns according to the norms that prevail in a given urban environment. Thus, the regional taste patterns in South Florida are partially influenced by the central phenomenon of car mobility and the practice of stacking multiple 10- or 15-inch bass speakers and powerful sub-woofers into car trunks and truck beds.

Add to these stylistic distinctions the discursive differences within rap from the various regions (i.e., the aforementioned Gangsta Rap from the West Coast crews, the chilling, cold-blooded imagery from Houston's "Bloody Nickle" crews on Rap-A-Lot Records, or the "pimp, playa and hustla" themes that are standard among Oakland and San Francisco cliques), the localized posse variations in vocal style and slang, or the site-specific references in rap lyrics to cities, 'hoods, and crews, and a general catalogue of differences in form and content becomes clearly audible. What these elements indicate is that, while the rap posse provides a structured identity for its members, it can also provide a referential value to the production qualities and the sound of the musical product with which it is associated.

Rap's Spatial Discourse

In his enquiry into the cultural resonance and meanings of the term "the 'hood," Paul Gilroy poses the question, "how is black life in one 'hood connected to life in others? Can there be a blackness that connects, articulates, synchronizes experiences and histories across the diaspora space?" (1992, p. 308). He criticizes the idea of "nation" that has emerged as an important structuring concept in American hip hop culture (mainly after 1987) and remains skeptical of the value invested in the discourses of "family" unity (communicated in the rhetoric of black brotherhood and sisterhood) when there is so much territorial antagonism evident in the strands of rap that privilege the spatialities of gang culture and turf affiliation. Gilroy expresses his perplexity with the closed contours that the 'hood represents, suggesting that its inward-turning spatial perspectives inhibit dialogue across divided social territories and cultural zones. He further argues that redemptive attempts to appeal to either the black "nation," or to the "family" of internationally dispersed blacks in the rap subgenre known as "message rap" are ill-conceived and based in a particularly North Americanist viewpoint that harbors its own exclusive and hierarchically stratified biases.

Perhaps more in line with Gilroy's expansive, trans-Atlantic visions of rap's diasporic potential is the track "Ludi" (1991, Island Records) by the Canadian act the Dream Warriors. Based in Toronto, the group is part of one of the world's largest expatriate Caribbean communities. Like Gilroy's London, Toronto could be seen as an

> important junction point or crossroads on the webbed pathways of black Atlantic political culture. It is revealed to be a place where, by virtue of factors like the informality of racial segregation, the configuration of class relations, the contingency of linguistic convergences, global phenomena such as anti-colonial and emancipationist political formations are still being sustained, reproduced, and amplified. (Gilroy 1992, p. 95)

In mapping a cultural "crossroads," the song "Ludi" utilizes an early reggae rhythm and a lightly swinging melody (based on a sample of the Jamaican classic "My Conversation," released in 1968 by The Uniques) that taps into a particularly rich moment in the evolution of the reggae style and revives a well-known Jamaican track while relocating it within the performative contexts of hip hop.

"Ludi" (which refers to a board game) begins with rapper King Lou stating that the song is for his mother—who wants something to dance to—and his extended family to whom he offers the musical sounds of their original home environment. The family to which he refers is not, in the immediate sense, the family of black-identified brothers and sisters that cohere within nationalistic and essentialist discourse but literally his siblings. He then expands his dedication to the wider "family" of blacks with a comprehensive roll-call of the English and Spanish-speaking Caribbean islands and Africa which inform (but by no means determine) his cultural identity. There is no attempt to privilege an originary African heritage nor is there a nostalgic appeal to the Caribbean heritage. This extensive list recognizes Toronto's hybrid Afro-Caribbean community and refers directly to a locally manifested culture of international black traditions (rather than a single tradition of essentialist blackness) within which the Dream Warriors developed as young artists. The song's bridge also reinforces the Caribbean connection by making several references to the turntable practices of Jamaican sound systems that are mainstays throughout internationally dispersed Caribbean communities.

Later in the track, King Lou's cohort, Capital Q, reminds him that "there are other places than the islands that play Ludi. Why don't you run it down for the people?" Here, employing a distinctly Jamaican DJ "toaster" dialect, King Lou provides a wider expression of black diasporic identification as he expands his list to include Canada, the UK, and the United States, countries where the Afro-Caribbean presence is the largest and most influential. He concludes by mentioning his international record labels 4th and Broadway and Island Records and, finally, names the influential Toronto-based independent production house, Beat Factory, that first recorded the group. In this last reference to Beat Factory he effectively returns the scale to the local, closing the circle that positions the Dream Warriors within a global/local system of circulation.

There is no simple means of assessing the impact of this expansive global/local perspective but, within Gilroy's innovative theoretical *oeuvre*, the track can be celebrated for the ways in which its musical and lyrical forms reinforce the dispersed geographies of contemporary black cultures without falling victim to the conservative reductions of black essentialism. Without cleaving towards either the rhetorical rigidity of black nationalist Rap or the nihilistic vitriol of gangster rappers ("niggaz with (bad) attitude"), the Dream Warriors present an alternative path. As "Ludi" illustrates, the group unselfconsciously articulates an evolving hybrid identity informed by transnational migrations that are actively manifested on local grounds.

On the other end of the rap spectrum is the example of artists who mainly operate within a discursive field featuring spatialized themes of intense locality. Whereas the proponents of Message Rap evoke an expanded vision of black America, it is in contrast to the ghettocentric visions of urban black experience that also emerge in the genre, mainly within the lyrics of Gangsta Rap. Despite many shared perspectives on black oppression and systemic injustices, there exists a tension in the interstices between the expansive nationalisms of Message Rap and the more narrowly defined localisms of Gangsta Rap with its core emphasis on "the 'hood." This distance is widened in view of the unapologetic claim among numerous studio gangstas who, like the rap artist Ice Cube on the N.W.A. track "Gangsta, Gangsta" (1988, Ruthless/Priority), claim that "life ain't nothin' but bitches and money." The two subgenres are addressing generally common phenomena in their focus on black struggles for empowerment, yet they are deploying spatial discourses and programs of action that do not fit easily together.

The emergence of an intensified spatial terminology was not a sudden occurrence, but by 1987 when New York's Boogie Down Productions (also known as BDP), featuring rap acts such as KRS-1, Eazy-E, and Ice T broke onto the scene, the privileging of localized experience rapidly acquired an audible resonance. From New York, BDP released "South Bronx" (1987, B-Boy), a track that aggressively disputes the allegations of various rappers from Queens who, in the aftermath of Run-DMC's commercial successes, claimed that they were rap's true innovators. KRS-1's lyrics reaffirm his home turf in the South Bronx borough as the birthplace of hip hop, reinforcing the message in the now-classic chorus with its chant "South Bronx, the South, South Bronx."

Giving name to South Bronx locales and to the artists who inhabited them, anchors his testimony. He attempts to prove its dominance by recounting the genre's formative stages with close attention to locally specific and highly particularized details:

> Remember Bronx River, rolling thick
>
> With Cool DJ Red Alert and Chuck Chillout on the mix
>
> While Afrika Islam was rocking the jams
>
> And on the other side of town was a kid named Flash
>
> Patterson and Millbrook projects
>
> Casanova all over, ya couldn't stop it
>
> The Nine Lives crew, the Cypress Boys
>
> The Real Rock Steady taking out these toys
>
> As hard as it looked, as wild as it seemed
>
> I didn't hear a peep from Queen's...
>
> South Bronx, the South South Bronx...

The references to people and places provide a specificity that is comparatively absent in Eazy-E's important (but often overlooked) single release "Boyz-n-The Hood" (1988, Ruthless/Priority) from the same general period. Musically, "Boyz-n-The-Hood" is considered to have done little to advance the genre aesthetically. Yet, in its uncompromising linguistic turns and startling descriptions of homeboy leisure (involving beer, "bitches," and violence), it was riveting and offered a new hardcore funky model for masculine identification in hip hop:

> *'Cause the boyz in the hood are always hard*
>
> *Come talkin' that trash and we'll pull your card*
>
> *Knowin' nothin' in life but to be legit*
>
> *Don't quote me boy, 'cause I ain't savin' shit*

Describing the LP *Eazy-Duz-It* on which the single first appeared, Havelock Nelson and Michael Gonzales explain that it "overflows with debris from homophobia to misogyny to excessive violence. And yet, anyone who grew up in the project or any Black ghetto knows these extreme attitudes are right on target" (1991, p. 81). Despite such claims to authenticity, however, it is important to acknowledge that the rugged discourses and sensational imagery of violence and poverty are highly selective and are drawn from a range of mundane, less controversial and less marketable urban experiences.

Eazy-E's "Boyz-n-The Hood" reflects many of rap's earlier modes of spatial representation that conceive of the ghetto landscape as a generalized abstract construct, as *space.* The introduction of the terminology of the 'hood, however, also adds a localized nuance to the notion of space that conveys a certain proximity, effectively capturing a narrowed sense of *place* through which young thugs and their potential victims move in tandem. Claims to the representation of authentic street life or 'hood reality emerged with sudden frequency following the rise of Eazy-E and N.W.A., who were among the first to communicate detailed images of closely demarcated space in this manner. This suggests that "reality," authenticity and reduced spatial scales are conceptually linked among those who developed "Boyz-n-The Hood" is ultimately its influence on the popularization of a new spatial vocabulary that spread throughout hip hop from all regions as artists from the West Coast gained prominence in the field.

By most accounts, the spatial discourse that coheres around the concept of the 'hood emerges in rap by California-based artists with the greatest frequency and force. But in the popular media as well as in academic treatises, the focus on West Coast rap in this period tends to be on the expressions of "gangsta" violence and masculine aggression to the exclusion or minimization of prevalent spatial elements. For example, as David Toop writes, "the first release on Ruthless Records, launched by rapper Eazy-E and producer Dr. Dre in 1986, was like a tabloid report from the crime beat fed through a paper shredder" (1991, p. 180). The very term "gangsta rap" is more concretely concerned with the articulation of criminality than any other attributes that may emerge from its lyrical and visual texts. Having become sedimented in the popular lexicon as the key or trademark term for the subgenre, it is difficult to challenge critically the primacy of criminality and to replace it with a spatiality that precedes the "gangsta-ism" that saturates the lyrical texts. The criminal activities that are described in gangsta rap's intense lyrical forms are almost always subordinate to the definitions of space and place within which they are set. It is, therefore, the spatialities of the 'hood that constitute the ascendant concept and are ultimately deserving of discursive pre-eminence.

Since rap's invention, it has become somewhat of a convention for the rapper to be placed at the center of the world, as the subject around which events unfold and who translates topophilia (love of place) or topophobia (fear of place) into lyrics for wider dissemination. This is illustrated in Ice T's "Intro" track on his debut album *Rhyme Pays* (1987, Rhyme Syndicate/Sire). As an introduction, the track allows Ice T to present his hip hop curriculum vitae which is explicitly defined in spatial terms:

A child was born in the East one day

Moved to the West Coast after his parents passed away

Never understood his fascination with rhymes or beats

In poetry he was considered elite

Became a young gangster in the streets of LA

Lost connections with his true roots far away...

The description of a personal exodus embarked upon by the young rapper under conditions of extreme adversity is crucial to the construction of mystique and legend. Describing his entry into LA gang culture and the rap scene in the magazine *Rap Pages*, Ice T identifies cities, neighborhoods, high schools and housing projects that have meaning to him and to those familiar with these areas:

I went to a white school in Culver City, and that was chill, but I was livin' in Windsor Hills near Monterey Triangle Park.... When I got to high school all the kids from my area were gettin' bussed to white schools and I didn't want to go to them schools. So me and a few kids from the hills went to Crenshaw. That's where the gangs were. (Rap Pages, October 1991, p. 55)

Here, place is a lens of sorts that mediates one's perspective on social relations. It offers familiarity and it provides the perspectival point from which one gazes upon and evaluates other places, places that are "other" or foreign to one's own distinctly personal sites of security and stability (no matter how limited these may be). Ice T may be from the East, but he is shaped by Los Angeles and it is the spaces and places of LA that provide the coordinates for his movement and activities.

Ice T (ibid.) goes on to make the distinction between East Coast rap and the emerging LA "gangsta" style, noting that the latter developed out of a desire to relate incidents and experiences with a more specific sense of place and, subsequently, greater significance to local youths who could recognize the sites and activities described in the lyrics. In this regard, rap offers a means of describing the view from a preferred "here," of explaining how things appear in the immediate foreground (the 'hood) and how things seem on the receding horizon (other places).

Adopting a boastful tone and attitude, Ice T also locates his origins in the New Jersey–New York nexus, essentially fixing his own "roots" in hip hop's cultural motherland. Ice T is in this mode clearly centering himself, building his own profile. In the process, he relates a history that invests supreme value in New York as the first home of hip hop, naturalizing his connections to the art form and validating his identity as a tough, adaptive and street-smart LA hustler, the self-proclaimed "West Coast M.C. king." Ice T's references to New York illuminate the spatial hierarchy that existed at the time; the Northeast was still virtually unchallenged as the dominant zone of hip hop cultural activity. Battles among rap's pioneers and upstarts were still being waged on the local, interborough scale in New York although, gradually, New York's monopoly on rap production and innovation was lost as various other sites of production emerged. The rise of the LA rap sound and the massive impact of the gangster themes after 1987 resulted in the first real incursion on New York's dominance. This development had the additional effect of polarizing the two regions as the aesthetic distinctions based on lyrical content and rhythmic styles became more defined and audiences began spending their consumer dollars on rap from the nation's "West side."

"The West Side Is the Best Side": Representing Compton

The West's arrival was heralded by a deluge of recordings that celebrated and glorified the street warrior scenarios of the California cities of South Central Los Angeles (with help from the 1988 Dennis Hopper film *Colors* and Ice T's galvanizing title song on the soundtrack), Oakland and, especially, Compton. Starting with NWA's "Straight Outta Compton" (1988, Ruthless/Priority), numerous recordings circulated the narrative imagery of vicious gang-oriented activities in Compton, including the tracks "Raised in Compton" (1991, Epic) and "Compton 4 Life" (1992, Epic) by the group Compton's Most Wanted, and DJ Quik's "Born and Raised in Compton" (1991, Profile) or "Just Lyke Compton" (1992, Profile). Appearing on the cover of his album *Way 2 Fonky* (1992, Profile), DJ Quik poses alongside a chain-link fence topped with razor wire, sporting a jacket emblazoned with the Compton logo, proudly advertising his home territory. Through these multiple means of signification the city of Compton rapidly gained a notoriety informed by the image of tough and well-armed homeboys and the ongoing deadly conflict between rival gangs operating with a near-total lack of ethics or moral conscience. This last point can be most clearly discerned in the ubiquitous refrain that "Compton niggaz just don't give a fuck."

Tricia Rose and Brian Cross situate the rise of Compton-based rap in two quite different frames of understanding. Rose writes that

> during the late 1980s Los Angeles rappers from Compton and Watts, two areas severely paralyzed by the postindustrial economic redistribution, developed a West coast style of rap that narrates experiences and fantasies specific to life as a poor young, black, male subject in Los Angeles. (1994, p. 59)

Her assessment situates the phenomenon of West Coast styles and lyrical forms in an internally based set of socio-economic conditions that are responsive to transitions within a complex convergence of global and local forces, or what Kevin Robins (1991) refers to as "the global/local nexus."

Brian Cross locates the rise of Compton's rap scene within a wider and more appropriate cartographic relation to New York and other California locales:

> Hiphop Compton, according to Eazy, was created as a reply to the construction of the South Bronx/Queensbridge nexus in New York. If locally it served notice in the community in which Eazy and Dre sold their Macola-pressed records (not to mention the potential play action on KDAY), nationally, or at least on the East Coast, it was an attempt to figure Los Angeles on the map of hiphop. After the album had gone double platinum Compton would be as well known a city in hiphop as either Queens or the Bronx. (Cross 1993, p. 37)

Refuting Rose's interpretation, the general narrative content of "Straight Outta Compton" sheds little light on the city or its social byways and does not demonstrate any particular concern with the locality's economics. Its basic function as a geographical backdrop actually follows the same standard constructions of abstract space heard in Grandmaster Flash and the Furious Five's "New York, New York," recorded five years earlier, or in Eazy-E's solo effort, "Boyz-n-The-Hood."

Without detailed spatial descriptions of landmarks and environment, Compton does not emerge as a clearly realized urban space on the N.W.A. track even though it is the group's home town. The California city is instead treated as a bounded civic space that provides both specificity and scale for the communication of a West Coast Rap presence. The group is "representing" their home territory and the song's release was their bold announcement that the "boyz" from the 'hoods of Compton were "stompin'" onto the scene and could not be avoided by anyone who paid attention to developments in the business. The Compton and South Central LA crews were not only serving notice to their neighboring communities that they were in charge, but they were also serving notice to New York and the entire hip hop nation that the new sound had arrived and the balance of power (forged in a mix of arrogance and inventiveness) had tipped towards the West. This was the beginning of a decade-long antagonism between East and West Coast rap that has too frequently proven that the gangster themes comprising the lyrical content are based in more than mere lip service or masculine posturing.

On the track "Raised in Compton" (1991, Epic/Sony), MC Eiht of the rap group Compton's Most Wanted explicitly racializes the urban spaces of the city, more fully addressing the specificities of its cultural character and providing a further sense of the place that he recognizes as his formative home. He reproduces several of the general elements that N.W.A. had already imposed on Compton's representational repertoire, but for him the city also has a personally meaningful history that is manifested in his identity as a gangster turned rapper:

> Compton is the place that I touched down
> I opened my eyes to realize that I was dark brown
> And right there in the ghetto that color costs
> Brothers smothered by the streets meaning we're lost
> I grew up in a place where it was go for your own
> Don't get caught after dark roaming the danger zone
> But it was hell at the age of twelve
> As my Compton black brothers were in and out of jail

The attempt to historicize his relations to the city and the 'hood makes this track slightly more complex than "Straight Outta Compton," as MC Eiht's bonds to the localized Compton environment are defined as the product of an evolving growth process, as a child becomes a man. Subjective history, conveyed here in an almost testimonial form, and the experiences of space, together offer relevant insights on the social construction of a gangster attitude or a gang member's *raison d'être*.

George Lipsitz isolates similar tendencies with his focus on the socio-political importance of merging musical and non-musical sources of inspiration and experience among California chicano rock musicians since the 1960s.

Like the California chicano music Lipsitz describes, "Raised in Compton" explicitly high-lights customized car culture, urban mobility and the sartorial codes of the Compton streets ("T-shirt and khakis"). In its inclusiveness of the minor details that are, in practice, part of the daily norm for many urban black youth in the cities surrounding Los Angeles, the song accesses the spatial and racial characteristics of the city of Compton that have influenced and shaped the man that MC Eiht has become. The closely detailed articulation of spatial specifics (place names and site references, etc.) is still lacking but there is also a rich description of some of the social formations that are spatially distributed and which reproduce the forces underlying the black teen gangster ethos with which MC Eiht, and many others, so clearly identify.

Maintaining the gang member's pledge to defend the gang (or the "set") and the 'hood forever is the theme of MC Eiht's "Compton 4 Life" (1992, Epic/Sony). This track also offers a personal profile that ties MC Eiht into the neighborhood environment and inextricably links him with the deeper gang structures that prevail. Mid-point in the track he challenges outsiders to "throw up your 'hood 'cause it's Compton we're yellin," in a calculated "turf" statement that is entirely consistent with the structures of spatial otherness that are fundamental to LA gang culture. Eiht and other gangsta rappers enter into the discourses of alienation and social disenfranchisement as a negative factor compelling them towards a criminal lifestyle. Yet they also expound their own versions of alienating power, drawing on the imagery and codes of the street and entering into a discourse of domination that subjugates women, opposing gang members or those who are perceived as being weaker and thus less than them. Framed in terms of gun violence and human decimation, these expressions are intended to diminish the presence of others who represent other cities and other 'hoods. This is the articulation of control through domination, ghetto style.

Spatial domination and geo-social containment are conceived in the threatening form of "one time" or "five-o" (the police) and other gang members, each of whom constitute unavoidable negatives of life in the 'hood. Defeating the enemy forces is the ultimate goal, but in establishing the competitive dynamic, MC Eiht acknowledges that, even in victory, the local streets and the 'hood impose their own kind of incarcerating authority:

Compton 4 Life

Compton 4 Life

It's the city where everybody's in prison

Niggers keep taking shit 'cause ain't nobody givin'

So another punk fool I must be

Learn the tricks of the trade from the street

Exist to put the jack down, ready and willin'

One more Compton driveby killin'

There is a brief pause in the rhythm that could be heard as hanging like doom, stilling the song's pace and flow and creating a discomforting gap in the track. When the chorus "Compton 4 Life" suddenly breaks in with the final echoing syllable, it becomes clear that the title is formed around a double entendre: it is an expression of spatial solidarity and loyalty to the 'hood, yet it also refers to the pronouncement of a life sentence and the apparent hopelessness of eternal imprisonment in the city's streets and alleys.

As "Straight Outta Compton," "Raised in Compton" and "Compton 4 Life" suggest, "our sensibilities are spatialized" (Keith and Pile, 1993 p. 26). This point is made resonant when considering Compton artist DJ Quik's mobile narrative on the track "Jus Lyke Compton" (1992, Priority), in which he witnesses and describes the nation-wide impact of the Compton mythology, and Bronx-based rapper Tim Dog's defensive articulation of Bronx pride in the lyrical assassinations of N.W.A. and all Compton artists on the track "Fuck Compton" (1991, Ruff-house/Columbia). Compton's central significance is maintained through the lyrical representation of activities that are space-bound and which are then discursively traced onto the identities of the rappers who "claim" Compton as their own. The issue of whether or not the tracks refer back to a consistently verifiable reality is rendered moot by the possibilities they present as textual spaces of representation. Artists discursively locate themselves in an array of images and practices within the texts, constructing a relatively coherent identity out of the urban debris that is evidently a crucial aspect of the Compton they experience.

Despite claims by critics of gangsta rap, such as David Samuels (*New Republic*, 11 November, 1991), or folk musician Michelle Shocked, who suggests that "Los Angeles as a whole and South Central specifically bear little resemblance to the cartoon landscape—the Zip Coon Toon Town—of gangsta rap" (*Billboard*, 20 June, 1992, p. 6), the subgenre's narrative depictions of spaces and places are absolutely essential to an understanding of the ways that a great number of urban black youths imagine their environments and the ways that they relate those images to their own individual sense of self. The spaces of Compton and other similar black communities that emerge through their work are simultaneously real, imaginary, symbolic and mythical. With this in mind, the question that should be asked is not "is this real and true," but "why do so many young black men choose these dystopic images of spatial representation to orient their own places in the world?" By framing the question thus, the undeniable fascination with the grisly mayhem of the lyrical narratives is displaced and one can then embark on a more illuminating interrogation of the socio-spatial sensibilities at work.

Representing the Extreme Local: The Case of Seattle

By the end of the 1980s, Rap artists had provided an assortment of spatial representations of New York and Los Angeles that were both consistent with and divergent from the prevailing image-ideas of those urban centers. Rap artists worked within the dominant representational discourses of "the city" while agitating against a history of urban representations as they attempted to extend the expressive repertoire and to re-construct the image-idea of the city as they understood it. This proved to be a formidable challenge since New York and LA exist as urban icons, resonant signs of the modern (New York) and postmodern (LA) city. They are already well defined, the products of a deluge of representational images, narrative constructions and social interactions.

Rap's emergence from city spaces that are comparatively unencumbered by a deep history of representational images, which carry less representational baggage, presents a unique opportunity for lyrical innovators to re-imagine and re-present their cities. As a traditional frontier city and a prominent contemporary regional center, Seattle might, in this light, be conceived as an *underrepresented* city that lacks the wealth of representational history common to the larger centers to the South and the East.

In the mid-1980s the Pacific Northwest was, for much of the U.S., a veritable hinterland known best for its mountains, rivers and forests and as the home of Boeing's corporate and manufacturing headquarters. In the music industry, Jimi Hendrix was perhaps Seattle's most renowned native son, but the city was otherwise not regarded as an important or influential center for musical production or innovation. The city's profile changed considerably with the rise of Bill Gates's Microsoft corporation in the outlying area and the emergence of the Star-buck's coffee empire and, by 1990, it was also garnering considerable attention as the source of the massively influential (and commercially successful) "Grunge/Alternative" music scene that spawned bands such as Hole, Nirvana, Pearl Jam, Soundgarden, and the SubPop label. Music has subsequently emerged as an essential element in the construction of Seattle's contemporary image although the industry's rock predilections have not been as favorable to the city's rap and R&B artists.[7]

In the spring of 1986, Seattle rapper Sir Mix-A-Lot's obscure track "Square Dance Rap" (NastyMix Records) made an entry onto *Billboard* magazine's Hot Black Singles chart. The release failed to advance any radical new aesthetic nor did it make a lasting contribution to the rap form. Its relevance, however, is in its capacity to reflect the diverse regional activity in rap production at that time as artists and labels attempted to establish themselves within the rapidly changing conditions fostering regional and local expansion. Mix-A-Lot's emergence illustrates the fact that rap was being produced in isolated regions and, as the track's chart status suggests, that it was selling in significant volume within regional "home" markets.

Despite this, an advertisement for Profile Records appearing six years later in *Billboard*'s "Rap '92 Spotlight on Rap" (28 November 1992), portrays the proliferation of industry activity with a cartographic cartoon entitled "Rap All Over the Map: The Profile States of America." New York, Chicago, Dallas, St Louis, Vallejo and Los Angeles are all represented with the names of acts and their respective regions and cities of origin. The Pacific Northwest is conspicuously labelled "uncharted territory," which refers to Profile's inactivity there but which also reproduces the dominant image of the region as a distant and unknown frontier in the view of those from the nation's larger or more centralized rap production sites.

Regardless of the advertisement's centrist biases, the fact that Seattle was at this stage on the charts (and, in hip hop parlance, "in the house") indicates that rap's consumer base had extended geographically and, moreover, that new and unforeseen sites of production such as Seattle were also being established. In an interesting spatial inversion, Bruce Pavitt, co-founder of the Alternative-oriented SubPop label, actually regarded Seattle's spatial marginality as a positive factor for local musicians, stating that, "one advantage Seattle has is our geographical isolation. It gave a group of artists a chance to create their own sound, instead of feeling pressured to copy others" (*Billboard*, 18 August 1990, p. 30). Sir Mix-A-Lot slowly solidified his Northwest regional base. His single "Baby Got Back" reached the number one position on the *Billboard* pop charts, eventually selling double platinum.

Displaying pride in his Northwestern roots, Sir-Mix-A-Lot provides an excellent example of the organization of spatial images and the deployment of a spatial discourse. In general terms, details that might be overlooked speak volumes about space and place, presenting additional information about the ways that an individual's daily life is influenced by their local environments and conditions. For instance, the standard group photo in the inner sleeve of *Mack Daddy* depicts Mix-A-Lot's Rhyme Cartel posse wearing wet-weather gear consisting of name-brand Gore Tex hats and jackets. This is a totally pragmatic sartorial statement from the moist climate of the Pacific Northwest that remains true to hip hop's style-conscious trends. It displays a geographically particular system of codes conveying regionally significant information that, once again, demonstrates hip hop's capacity to appropriate raw materials or images and to invest them with new values and meanings.

Of all the CD's tracks, "Seattle Ain't Bullshittin'" is exceptional for the manner in which it communicates a sense of space and place with clarity, sophistication and cartographic detail. Establishing himself on the track as a genuine Seattle "player," as the original Northwestern "Mack Daddy" (a term for a top level pimp), Mix-A-Lot bases his claim to local prestige in his persona as a former Seattle hustler who successfully shifted to legitimate enterprises as a musician and businessman. He adopts a purely capitalist discourse of monetary and material accumulation, reproducing the prevailing terms of success and prosperity that conform to both the dominant social values and the value system inherent within the rap industry.

As the title suggests, Seattle is the centerpiece to the track. This is clear from the beginning as Mix-A-Lot and posse member the Attitude Adjuster ad lib over a sparse guitar riff:

> Boy, this is S.E.A.T.O.W.N., clown (forever)
>
> Sea Town, Yeah, and that's from the motherfuckin' heart
>
> So if you ain't down with your hometown
>
> Step off, punk
>
> Mix, tell these fakes what the deal is...

As the bass and drums are dropped into the track, Mix-A-Lot lyrically locates himself as a product of Seattle's inner-city core known as the CD (or Central District):

> I was raised in the S.E.A. double T.L.E.
>
> Seattle, home of the CD, nigga
>
> 19th and, yes, Laborda,
>
> pimpin' was hard...
>
> It wasn't easy trying to compete with my homies in the CD

Seattle's Central District is home to a sizeable concentration of black constituents who comprise roughly 10 per cent of Seattle's total population. Mix-A-Lot's portrayal of the CD neighborhood is not explicitly racialized yet the references to pimping and competition among "homies in the CD" easily fall into a common, even stereotypical definition of "the 'hood" that is pervasive throughout rap of the period.

The Attitude Adjuster states at one point that "it ain't nothing but the real up" that are evident in Seattle as well as the rest of the nation. Unlike most major American cities, Seattle's black presence does not have a huge defining influence on its urban character: black youths are a socially marginalized constituency within a geographically marginal city. The Attitude Adjuster's pronouncement may suggest a hint of defensiveness but it also gives voice to the region's black hip hop constituency that is, as the subtext implies, just as "hardcore" as that of other urban centers.

Having established his ghetto credentials, Mix-A-Lot expounds on several spatially oriented scenarios, shifting scale and perspective throughout the track with his descriptions of local, regional and national phenomena:

> So even though a lot of niggas talk shit
> I'm still down for the Northwest when I hit the stage
> Anywhere U.S.A.
> I give Seattle and Tacoma much play
> So here's to the Criminal Nation
> And the young brother Kid Sensation
> I can't forget Maharaji and the Attitude Adjuster
> And the hardcore brothers to the west of Seattle
> Yeah, West Side, High Point dippin' four door rides...

Mix-A-Lot adopts the role of Seattle's hip hop ambassador, acknowledging his own national celebrity profile while accepting the responsibilities of "representing" the Northwest, his record label and posse, and fellow rap artists from "Sea Town." Exploiting his access to the wider stage, he elevates the local scene, bringing it into focus and broadcasting the fact that hip hop is an important element of the Seattle lifestyle for young blacks living there as well.

The perspective shifts again as Mix-A-Lot adopts an intensely localized mode of description, recalling the days when he "used to cruise around Seward Park," moving out of the bounded territory of the city's Central District that is the posse's home base. Seattle is carto-graphically delineated here through the explicit naming of streets and civic landmarks that effectively identify the patterned mobility of the crew:

> Let's take a trip to the South End,
> We go west, hit Rainier Ave. and bust left,
> ...S.E.A. T.O.W.N., yo nigger is back again
> ...Gettin' back to the hood,
> Me and my boys is up to no good,
> A big line of cars rollin' deep through the South End,
> Made a left on Henderson,
> Clowns talkin' shit in the Southshore parking lot
> Critical Mass is begging to box

But we keep on going because down the street

A bunch of freaks in front of Rainier Beach

Was lookin' at us, they missed that bus

And they figure they could trust us...

With its references to the city's crosstown byways and meeting places, the track successfully communicates an image of the common, "everyday" leisure practices of the Rhyme Cartel posse while also retaining a privileged local or place-based perspective that resonates with greater meaning for all Seattle or Tacoma audience members. This audience will undoubtedly recognize its own environment and the track will consequently have a different and arguably more intense affective impact among Seattle's listeners and fans. Unlike Compton, which was popularized through a relentless process of reiteration by numerous artists, Seattle is represented much less frequently: "Seattle Ain't Bullshittin'" is a unique expression of Northwest identity. For example, there is no similar track on the Seattle-based Criminal Nation's *Trouble in the Hood* which was also released in 1992 (NastyMix/Ichiban), although references to the region are sprinkled throughout several tracks and on the liner sleeve one group member sports a Tacoma T-shirt identifying his home town.

In 1992, the trend towards such closely demarcated spatial parameters was not yet a common characteristic in rap, although it was increasingly becoming a factor in both lyrical and visual representations. Rather than an expression of a narrow social perspective celebrating the local to the exclusion of other wider scales, "Seattle Ain't Bullshittin' " demonstrates a rather successful method of representing the hometown local "flavor" on an internationally distributed recording.

Conclusion

Rap music's shift towards a self-produced discourse introducing the 'hood as a new spatial concept delimiting an "arena of experience" can be weighed against larger trends currently restructuring global and national economies, transforming national and regional workforces, and, often, devastating urban localities. As numerous supporters have suggested, rap emerges as a voice for black and Latino youth which, as a large subset of North America's socially disenfranchised population, is at risk of being lost in the combined transformations of domestic and global economies that are altering North America's urban cultures today. The discourse of space encompassed by the term "'hood" may in this context also be interpreted as a response to conditions of change occurring at a meta-level, far beyond the scale of the local (and the influence of those who inhabit it).

The requirement of maintaining strong local allegiances is a standard practice in hip hop that continues to mystify many critics of the rap genre. It is, therefore, imperative to recognize and understand the processes that are at work and to acknowledge that there are different messages being communicated to listeners who occupy different spaces and places and who identify with space or place according to different values of scale. It is precisely through these detailed image constructions that the abstract spaces of the ghetto are transformed into the more proximate sites of significance or places of the 'hood. Looking beyond the obvious, spatial discourse provides a communicative means through which numerous social systems are framed for consideration. Rap tracks, with their almost obsessive preoccupation with place and locality, are never *solely* about space and place on the local scale. Rather, they also identify and explore the ways in which these spaces and places are inhabited and made meaningful. Struggles and conflicts as well as the positive attachments to place are all represented in the spatial discourses of rap. This is not a display of parochial narrowness but a much more complex and interesting exploration of local practices and their discursive construction in the popular media.

NOTES

1. As an indication of the distinctions between rap and the more encompassing hip hop culture, rap artist KRS-One has said "rap is something you do, hip-hop is something you live" (quoted in *The Source*, June 1995, p. 40). Rap is the music of hip hop and its central form of articulation and expression.

2. Hip hop's timeline can be roughly divided into three general eras: old school refers to the period from 1978-86; middle school covers the period between 1987–1992; and new school extends from 1993–1999. In some cases, the present is referred to as "now school."

3. See Reebee Garofalo (1997, pp. 257–264); see also, Brian Ward (1998).

4. The factors leading to the demise of Death Row include the murder of its marquee star Tupac Shakur, Suge Knight's nine-year sentence for probation violations, an FBI investigation of possible gang-related enterprises including money laundering, and the desertion of its key producer Dr. Dre. In 1998, the artist Snoop Doggy Dogg defected to Master P's New Orleans-based No Limit Records.

5. The Flavor Unit posse at the time included such Rap notables as Queen Latifah, Monie Love, Apache, Lakim Shabazz, and Naughty By Nature who, perhaps more than the rest, explicitly refer to their origins as New Jersey rappers hailing from 118th Street, "Illtown," in East Orange. After internal restructuring, the posse's most bankable star, Queen Latifah, emerged as the executive head of Flavor Unit Management.

6. For a detailed examination of the Florida "bass" phenomenon, see the special feature of *The Source*, March 1994.

7. Addressing the relatively minor industry consideration for Seattle's black artists, Sir Mix-A-Lot's Rhyme Cartel Records released the conspicuously titled *Seattle...The Dark Side* in 1993. The cover prominently proclaims that the release "flips the script. No Grunge...just Rap and R&B...Sea Town Style."

REFERENCES

Chambers, Iain. 1985. *Urban Rhythms: Pop Music and Popular Culture* (London)

Cross, Brian. 1993. *It's Not About A Salary: Rap, Race, and Resistance in Los Angeles* (London)

Dery, Mark. 1990. "Public enemy: confrontation," *Keyboard*, September

Eure, Joseph and Spady, James (eds.). 1991. *Nation Conscious Rap* (New York)

Garofalo, Reebee. 1997. *Rockin' Out: Popular Music in the USA* (Boston)

George, Nelson. 1986. "The Rhythm and the Blues," in *Billboard*, May 31, p. 23

_____. 1992. *Buppies, B-Boys, Baps and Bohos: Notes on Post-Soul Black Culture* (New York)

_____. 1993. "Hip-hop's founding fathers speak the truth," *The Source*, November

Gilroy, Paul. 1992. "It's a Family Affair," in *Black Popular Culture*, (ed.) Gina Dent (Seattle)

Gunst, Laurie. 1995. *Born Fi Dead: A Journey Through the Jamaican Posse Underworld* (New York)

Hager, Steve. 1984. *Hip Hop: The Illustrated History of Break Dancing, Rap Music, and Graffiti* (New York)

Jones, Charisse. 1995. "Still hangin' in the 'hood: rappers who stay say their strength is from the streets," *The New York Times*, 24 September, pp. 43–46

Keith, Michael and Pile, Steve (eds.). 1993. *Place and the Politics of Identity* (New York)

Lipsitz, George. 1990. *Time Passages: Collective Memory and American Popular Culture* (Minneapolis)

Nelson, Havelock and Gonzales, Michael. 1991. *Bring the Noise: A Guide to Rap Music and Hip Hop Culture* (New York)

Pike, Jeff. 1990. "At long last, Seattle is suddenly hot," *Billboard*, 18 August, pp. 30–34

Rap Pages, 1991. "The world according to Ice-T," October, pp. 54–67

Rap Sheet, 1992. "The bloody 5: a day in the hood," October, pp. 18–26

Robins, Kevin. 1991. "Tradition and translation: national culture in its global context," in *Enterprise and Heritage Crosscurrents of National Culture*, (eds.) John Corner and Sylvia Harvey (New York)

Rose, Tricia. 1994. *BlackNoise: Rap Music and Black Culture in Contemporary America* (Hanover)

Samuels, David. 1991. "The rap on rap," *The New Republic*, 11 November

Shocked, Michelle, and Bull, Bart. 1992. "LA riots: cartoons vs. reality," *Billboard*, 20 June, p. 6

The Source, 1994. Special Issue: Miami Bass, March

Tate, Greg. 1992. "Posses in effect: Ice-T," in *Flyboy in the Buttermilk: Essays on Contemporary America* (New York)

Toop, David. 1984. *The Rap Attack: African Jive to New York Hip Hop* (Boston)

_____. 1991. *Rap Attack: African Rap to Global Hip-Hop* (New York)

Ward, Brian. 1998. *Just My Soul Responding: Rhythm and Blues, Black Consciousness, and Race Relations* (Berkeley)

Andy Bennett

Chapter 14

Hip-Hop Am Main, Rappin' on the Tyne

Aa dee it coz aa can green eggs and ham,

People always tell iz that am just like me mam,

Aa wuz born aa was bred in smelling distance

o the tyne,

An a couldn't give a toss that the fogs not mine,

Aa like me blaa an a like a pint,

But ave never needed speed for an alreet neet,

Aa divvent drive a car'coz they just get twoced,

Me ken's kanny safe it's on top of a shop...

— Ferank, Newcastle poet and rapper, 1994

Among contemporary youth cultural forms, hip hop has attracted a great deal of interest from academic theorists and researchers. It is also fair to say that hip hop is one of the most contested cultural forms from the point of view of its representation in academic texts. Much of the debate surrounding hip hop relates to the issue of authenticity. Thus, while some theorists maintain that the authenticity of hip hop remains firmly rooted in its origins and continuing significance as an African-American street culture, others suggest that the themes and issues expressed in hip hop contribute to the musicalized dialogue that is held to exist between those displaced peoples of African origin who collectively make up the African-diaspora. More recently, a new school of hip hop theorists, in considering the existence of hip hop culture outside the African-American and wider African-diasporic world, have contested earlier interpretations of hip hop, suggesting instead that hip hop is culturally mobile; that the definition of hip hop culture and its attendant notions of authenticity are constantly being "remade" as hip hop is appropriated by different groups of young people in cities and regions around the world.

In this chapter I want to consider some of the different sociological arguments that have been used to explain the cultural significance of hip hop. I will then offer my own interpretation of the cultural work performed by hip hop in the form of an ethnographic study that examines the local hip hop scenes in two European cities, Frankfurt am Main, Germany, and Newcastle upon Tyne, England. Through a consideration of hip hop's significance in these two cities, I will suggest that arguments and discussions among young people concerning the merits of hip hop as an authentic form of cultural expression correspond closely with the differing local contexts in which hip hop culture is played out. In exploring the relationship between hip hop and the local, I will also refer to comparable studies of "local" hip hop cultures in Italy, France, Southern Ireland, Sweden, Australia, New Zealand, and Japan.

The Origins and Sociological Representation of Hip Hop

There is a general consensus among both academic and non-academic accounts of hip hop that the style originated in the South Bronx area of New York during the early 1970s. A key figure in the creation of hip hop was an ex-street gang member known as Afrika Bambaataa. Aware of the inner-city tensions that were being created as a consequence of urban renewal programs and economic recession, Bambaataa formed "The Zulu Nation" in an attempt to "channel the anger of young people in the South Bronx away from gang fighting and into music, dance, and graffiti"[1] (Lipsitz, 1994, p. 26). Hip hop has since become more widely known because of rap, the aspect of its style that has been most successfully commercialized. Rap is a narrative form of vocal delivery in which rhyming lyrics are spoken or "rapped" in a rhythmic patois over a continuous backbeat. According to Keyes, the distinctive vocal technique employed in rapping "can be traced from African bardic traditions to rural southern-based expressions of African Americans—toast, tales, sermons, blues, game songs, and allied forms—all of which are recited in a chanted rhyme or poetic fashion" (1991, p. 40). The backbeat or "breakbeat" in rap is provided by a DJ who uses a twin-turntable record deck to "mix" sections of vinyl recordings together in a way that seamlessly recombines aspects of existing songs and instrumental passages into a new musical piece (Back, 1996a, p. 192). A further technique employed by rap DJs is "scratching," where the records themselves are used to a rhythmic, percussive effect by rapidly running their grooves to and forth against the record player's stylus to produce a scratching sound (Rose, 1994b).

If there is agreement among theorists as to hip hop's point of origin and the socio-economic conditions from which it emerged, there is much less agreement concerning the ethnic dimensions of hip hop and its significance as a form of cultural expression. Thus, according to one school of thought, the significance of hip hop as a cultural form orientates exclusively around its dialogue with the experience of African-American youth. Beadle, for example, has suggested that rap is "to the black American urban youth more or less what punk was to its British white counterpart" (1993, p. 77). Thus, argues Beadle, relying only upon the ability to "talk in rhythm," rapping has become the perfect "vehicle for pride and for anger, for asserting the self worth of the community" (ibid., p. 85). Similarly, Light defends the essential "blackness" of hip hop in the face of its commercialization and "white" imitations by groups such as the Beastie Boys. According to Light, hip hop "is about giving a voice to a black community otherwise underrepresented.... It has always been and remains (despite the curse of pop potential) directly connected with the streets from which it came" (1992, p. 232). The notion of hip hop as a purely African-American cultural form has been further fuelled by its reception among sections of white U.S. society. Rap music, and in particular *gangsta rap* with the often violent and misogynistic overtones of its lyrics, has instilled a form of moral panic among the U.S. white middle classes. According to Sexton, attempts by white institutions, notably the Parents Music Resource Center (see Epstein et al., 1990), to censor rap lyrics has led in turn to a form of "clinical paranoia" among black hip hop circles in the U.S. (1995, p. 2). Similarly, African-American writer Dyson argues that: "While gangsta rap takes the heat for a range of social maladies from urban violence to sexual misconduct, the roots of our racial misery remain buried beneath moralizing discourse that is confused and sometimes dishonest" (1996, p. 178). While debates concerning the legitimacy of such claims continue, the point remains that rap and hip hop are being discussed exclusively in African-American terms, a trope that also conveniently excludes the involvement of Puerto-Rican and white youth in the development of hip hop (Flores, 1994; Mitchell, 1998). Indeed, one could go as far as to say that such readings of hip hop historicize and sociologize the latter in a way that closes off any consideration of its significance in non-African-American contexts. This aspect of African-American-centered writing on hip hop is exemplified by Potter, who, in response to the growth of interest in hip hop outside the U.S., suggests that "there is always a *danger* that it will be appropriated in such a way that its histories are obscured and its message replaced by others" (1995, p. 146; my emphasis).

The implied notion in the work of Potter that hip hop's only authentic cultural resonance is with the experience of inner-city African-Americans is challenged by a number of theorists who argue that hip hop, while it may indeed have emerged from the ghettos of U.S.-America, is, like other aspects of African-American culture, historically rooted in the removal by force of native Africans from their homelands during the western slave trade of the sixteenth to nineteenth centuries (Lipsitz, 1994). Despite the gradual abolition of slavery in Europe and America during the nineteenth century, the African-diaspora created by the slave trade has continued to grow as people have left Africa and former slave colonies such as the West Indies in order to escape political and religious persecution or in an attempt to secure a better standard of living and better opportunities for themselves and their children (see, for example, Foner, 1978; Hebdige, 1987). Against this African-diasporic backdrop, it is suggested, cultural forms such as music function as "privileged site[s] for transnational communication, organization and mobilization" (Lipsitz: 1994, p. 34). This argument is central to a study by Cobley and Osgerby of Afro-Caribbean hip hoppers, in the Peckham district of London, whose attachment to hip hop, it is argued, is "engendered by diasporic identification" with African-Americans (1995, p. 11). The centrality of the African-diaspora to the cultural dialogue of hip hop is similarly emphasized in the work of Decker, who points to what he identifies as the Afro-centric sensibilities expressed in the work of U.S.-based rap groups such as Arrested Development. According to Decker, such Afro-centricism attempts "to reverse a history of Western economic dependency and cultural imperialism by placing a distinctly African value system...at the center of the worldview" (1994, p. 111).

Such work is arguably more useful in assessing hip hop's increasingly global significance than are studies that center exclusively around the latter's African-American properties. At the same time, however, there remains a danger of essentializing hip hop as a "black" cultural form. Indeed, it is increasingly evident that the appeal of hip hop is not merely limited to young people connected with the African-diaspora. On the contrary, hip hop and its various cultural activities appear to attract young people from very diverse socio-cultural backgrounds. Significant in this respect is the work of Gilroy, who challenges the contested blackness of hip hop through his positioning of the African-diaspora as a dynamic cultural force whose rootedness in the development of western capitalism has transformed it into a primary influence on global popular culture. Thus states Gilroy, "the transnational structures which brought the black Atlantic world into being have themselves developed and now articulate its myriad forms into a system of global communications constituted by flows" (1993, p. 80). In this way, argues Gilroy, "black" culture becomes a global culture, its styles, musics, and images crossing with a range of different national and regional sensibilities throughout the world and initiating a plurality of responses.

Gilroy's views and their implications for the interpretation of hip hop's cultural significance are developed in a new body of work that collectively examines the role of hip hop in a range of globally and culturally diffuse settings. Mitchell's research on hip hop in Europe and Oceania illustrates wide-ranging uses of rap and other aspects of the hip hop style in these areas of the world. Thus, in France and Italy hip hop has become a vehicle for the discussion of subjects such as "racism [and] police harassment," while in New Zealand Maori rap groups campaign for the rights of indigenous peoples around the world (1996, pp. 40, 244–50). Fillipa (1986) provides further insight into the localization of rap and hip hop in the context of Europe with an account of rap's incorporation into the suburban and rural cultures of southern Italy. Bjurström considers the significance of hip hop among the youth of ethnic minority groups in Sweden as a form of collective resistance to the white skinhead style, suggesting that hip hop and skinhead represent "the most conspicuous opposite poles in the ethnic-stylistic warfare of Swedish youth culture" (1997, p. 49). The diversity of hip hop culture at a global level is further illustrated by Harpin in a review of Southern Irish rap group Scary Eire, who, according to Harpin, "turn local problems, like high unemployment and the cost of everyday living, into sharp rhymes" (1993, p. 58). Finally, Condry's (1999) research into the significance of hip hop among Japanese youth illustrates how local hip hoppers use their musical and stylistic preferences as a means of marking themselves out from what they consider to be the "mainstream" youth of Japan. As such work begins to reveal, the commercial packaging of hip hop as a global commodity has facilitated its easy access by young people in many different parts of the world. Moreover, such appropriations have in each case involved a reworking of hip hop in ways that engage with local circumstances. In every respect then, hip hop is both a global and a local form.

Global, Local, and "Glocal" Cultures

There has been considerable debate among cultural theorists as to the effects of globalization on local cultures. One school of thought has maintained that globalization can have only a pathological effect on local differences, which are gradually eroded away by a one-directional flow of cultural commodities from the west, thus producing, according to Ritzer (1993), a gradual "McDonaldization" of the world. Such views have been challenged by theorists such as Lull (1995), whose concept of *cultural reterritorialisation* provides a framework for an understanding of cultural products as malleable resources that can be *reworked*, that is, inscribed with new meanings that relate to the particular local context within which such products are appropriated. Lull's approach is developed by Robertson who illustrates more graphically the interplay between the global and the local. Thus, argues Robertson:

> It is not a question of either homogenization or heterogenization, but rather the ways in which both of these tendencies have become features of life across much of the late-twentieth-century world. In this perspective the problem becomes that of spelling out the ways in which homogenizing and heterogenizing tendencies are mutually implicative. (1995, p. 27)

Robertson suggests that the crossing of such tendencies is best considered in terms of a process of *globalization*. While it could be argued that each of the musical forms and stylistic sensibilities considered in this study is in one way or another illustrative of such a process of glocalization, it seems to me that hip hop, particularly in view of the often fractious "in-scene" debates that accompany its appropriation in local contexts, provides an especially animated example of a "glocal" culture. Beginning with a study of the local hip hop scene in Frankfurt am Main, Germany, I will now consider how the localization of hip hop, rather than being a smooth and consensual transition, is fraught with tensions and contradictions as young people attempt to reconcile issues of musical and stylistic authenticity with those of locality, identity and everyday life.

Hip Hop Am Main

Frankfurt am Main is an international center. The city's population currently stands at around six hundred thousand people of whom approximately 25 per cent are foreign in origin. Many of Frankfurt's foreign residents, particularly the large Turkish and Moroccan populations, live in the city as "Gastarbeiter" (guest workers)[2] while many more have fled religious or political persecution in their home countries. Additionally, Frankfurt is the banking center of Germany and a central European base for a range of multinational companies. Consequently, the city's shopping areas, business quarters and suburbs are filled with the sights and sounds of a variety of different national cultures. Indeed, the Frankfurter Flohmarkt (flea market), held each Saturday on the south bank of the River Main, illustrates perfectly the mix of cultures that exist side by side in the city. To walk through the Flohmarkt is to experience at first hand the multicultural atmosphere of Frankfurt. Hip hop in Frankfurt also owes much to the international flavor of the city, albeit an internationalism borne out of somewhat different historical circumstances. As with other German cities, early experimentations with hip hop in Frankfurt were largely influenced by the African-American rap groups featured on American Forces Network (AFN), the radio station and TV channel established to serve personnel of the U.S. Army, which maintained a presence in central Germany between 1945 and 1996. Similarly, the presence of several large U.S. Army bases in and around Frankfurt meant that the local citizens were kept constantly in touch with many aspects of U.S. culture—particularly U.S. films, shown both in German and in their original English versions, U.S.-style diners and, most importantly, U.S. music and fashion. Thus, as one interviewee explained: "Frankfurt was introduced very early to soul, funk and so on. There were so many GIs here and they had such a great influence. So many new clubs opened while they were over here."

Similarly, a second interviewee gave the following account:

> When I was about seven years old my family moved to Ginnheim [a town just outside of Frankfurt]. On both sides of the apartment block where I lived were American Army quarters. The guys on one side used to listen to heavy metal music and the guys on the other played soul, funk and rap and stuff all the time.

It was due to this abundant supply of U.S. American cultural resources and information that the first Frankfurt hip hop "posses" and rap "crews" were formed. Sachsenhausen, a district in the south of Frankfurt and a principal location for live music venues in the city, is generally acknowledged as the place where the live hip hop scene in Frankfurt began. A local rapper of Spanish-German origin who worked in one of the district's bars remembers it thus:

> During the mid-1980s Sachsenhausen was a traditional meeting point for American GIs, many of whom were into hip hop. As a consequence, it was also the crystallization point for the local hip hop scene. And that set a precedent y'know. In the beginning the Frankfurt hip hop scene modeled itself very much on the example set by the GIs.

As a general trend, however, this stage in the development of Frankfurt hip hop was rather short lived. A large percentage of Frankfurt's hip hop following comprises young people from the city's numerous North African, South East Asian and southern European ethnic minority groups. In due course, a number of these young people, particularly those who came from Gastarbeiter families and whose social status in Germany remained decidedly unclear, began to make the realization that, as with African-Americans, theirs was a "distinct mode of lived [ethnicity]" which demanded its own localized and particularized mode of expression (Gilroy, 1993, p. 82). As a result of this, such groups began to seek ways in which to rework hip hop into a form that could be used as a vehicle for the expression of more locally relevant themes and issues.

The Localization of Hip Hop in Frankfurt

We've found our way of communicating...and now the German rappers have got to do that too [African-American rapper commenting upon rap in Germany].[3]

In Frankfurt, as with other German cities, an early attempt to rework hip hop into a medium for the expression of local themes and issues came as a number of local rap groups began incorporating German lyrics into their music. If much has been written about the cultural significance of popular music lyrics (see, for example, Denzin, 1969; Laing, 1971), rather less attention has been focused upon the cultural significance of the language in which they are sung. Arguably, however, language in popular music cannot be assessed merely in terms of the themes and issues that it conveys or in relation to the sound or "grain" of the voice (Barthes, 1977). Rather, the simple fact of language itself can also play a crucial role in informing the cultural sensibilities that become inscribed within conventions of musical taste. One might think, for example, of the nationalist sentiment encapsulated in the Welsh "Celtic rock" movement of the 1970s when the fact of performing and listening to lyrics written in Welsh became a form of political statement in itself (Wallis and Malm, 1984, pp. 139–143). Similarly, in many former Eastern bloc countries, English-language popular music became highly fashionable among young people, not primarily because the lyrical content of the songs was understood but because of the counter-cultural stance that could be implied through listening to such music (Easton, 1989; Pilkington, 1994).

Parallel notions of language as a signifier of particular cultural sensibilities can be identified with the turn towards German-language rap within the Frankfurt hip hop scene. In switching over from English to German-language rapping, it could be argued, a new measure of accuracy was made possible between localized social experience and linguistic representation. For many young Frankfurt hip hoppers, German, if not their mother tongue, had become their adopted tongue following many years of living in the country. Thus, at a fundamental level it was much easier for these young people to rap in German than in English, their knowledge of English being for the most part very limited. At the same time, however, a more ideological motive can also be seen to underpin the move towards German-language rap. Thus, among many Frankfurt rappers and rap fans whom I interviewed, it was argued that only when local rappers started to write and perform texts in the German language did their songs begin to work as an authentic form of communication with the audience. Frankfurt rap group United Energy gave me the following account of their own move towards rapping in German:

> In the beginning people didn't think that rapping would sound like it should if we tried to do it in German. But then people began to realise that it was too limiting rapping in English, because their knowledge of the language wasn't good enough. So now a lot of rappers have begun to rap in German and it's just better, more effective. Anyway, we're living in Germany, so we should rap in German.

Mitchell (1996) identifies similar motives underpinning the popularity of Italian-language rap. In particular, argues Mitchell, the use of regional dialect in Italian rap has become a dominant market of hip hop's significance in the articulation of local identity. Mitchell also illustrates how the turn towards rapping in Italian has facilitated rap's use as a means of engaging with more nationally felt issues such as neo-Fascism and racism. Comparable examples of such nationally felt issues, and their manifestation at local level, inform the move towards German language rap in Frankfurt and other German cities.

"Ich habe einen grünen Pass"

Two thematic issues that appear regularly in German-language rap songs concentrate respectively upon the fear and anger instilled in ethnic minority groups by racism and the insecurity experienced by many young members of such groups over issues of nationality. The first theme has in recent years become one of national concern in Germany. Since the German reunification in October 1990, there has been a steady rise in neo-Fascist attacks against Gastarbeiter and refugees in Germany[4] (Fekete, 1993, p. 162). This in turn has led to growing support in Germany for anti-Fascist movements such as "Rock gegen Rechts" (Rock Against Racism).[5] A point often made by German rappers, however, is that despite the well-meant intentions of antiracism concerns, neo-Fascists and other racist groups will not single out people on ideological grounds but will go for the easy targets, those who can be identified by the color of their skin. This was the theme of amateur Frankfurt rap band Extra Nervig's song "Gib die Glatzen keine Chance!"[6] (Stop the skinheads!).

> You tell me you're on my side,
> Well your fancy words are fine,
> But you're not kicked to the ground,
> Just because of the way you look...

While there are fewer incidents of racial violence in Frankfurt than in other German cities, although this is on the increase, racism is often experienced in other ways. As I have already pointed out, much of Frankfurt's non-German population is made up of Gastarbeiter (guest workers) who, as with the Asians and Afro-Caribbeans who emigrated to Britain from the 1950s onwards, were called upon to meet the increasing demand for manual laborers in post-war western Europe. Because many Gastarbeiter have a relatively poor command of the German language and occupy minor positions in the labor market, they are often regarded as second-rate citizens, a label that is also ascribed to their children despite the fact that they have been born and educated in Germany, speak the language fluently and often have a skilled trade and, increasingly, a college or university qualification. This problem is, in turn, compounded by the issue of citizenship, which, in contrast to many other countries, is not given automatically to any child who is born in Germany. As a consequence, those people who have acquired German citizenship often find that they are subject to the same sort of stigmatization as those who have not. The term "Asylant" or "Asylbewerber" (a person seeking political asylum) is often carelessly used in youth clubs, cafes and other public places and can be very offensive, especially to those in possession of German citizenship.

Rap group Advanced Chemistry's song "Fremd im eigenen Land" (A Foreigner in My Own Country), along with its simple yet effective promotional video, was one of the first German rap songs to underline the severity of this type of misunderstanding and the hurt that it can cause. Performed by three rappers, each holding German citizenship, but with respective origins in Haiti, Ghana and Italy, the song chronicles the struggle of each to be accepted as German and orientates around the phrase "Ich habe einen grünen Pass, mit einem Goldenen Adler drauf"—"I have a green passport, with a golden eagle on it" (this being the design of the old German passport). In the video, each member of the group is questioned about his nationality. On one occasion group member Frederick Hahn is approached by a white German youth who asks, "Where do you come from, are you African or American?" When Hahn replies that he is German the youth begins to ridicule him and accuses him of lying, only retreating when Hahn produces his passport and sarcastically retorts, "Is this the proof you're looking for?" In a further scene, another member of Advanced Chemistry is asked by a white girl if he is "going home later?," as in back to his "home" country, to which Hahn replies "always the same stupid questions...I've been living in this country for twenty years." In an interview with journalist Lee Harpin, Advanced Chemistry spoke of their concern to expose the racial exclusion suffered by Germany's ethnic minority groups. Thus, as one of the group explained:

> We rap in German in order to reach our own public, in order that they understand our problem...it's a fact of life that if you're not recognized as a full German citizen you face constant harassment and identity checks. (1993, pp. 59–60)

Since the release of "Fremd im eigenen Land," a number of German-language rappers in Frankfurt have endeavored to develop its theme and have also used the rap medium to explore a range of similar issues. The resulting work by groups such as United Energy and Extra Nervig has consolidated in the minds of many of those who attend their performances the link between rap as a politicized discourse and the various insecurities experienced by members of ethnic minority groups in Frankfurt. Indeed, the centrality of rap and hip hop within local strategies of resistance to issues such as racism and racial exclusion is not limited to Germany but can also be seen in a range of other European contexts. Mitchell, for example, has noted how French rap artists such as MC Solaar focus on issues of racism in their country while in Italy hip hop provides a powerful critique against the growing support for Fascist ideology and far right political groups (1996, pp. 40, 149–50). Similarly, Bjurström's work on ethnicity and identity in Sweden illustrates how local hip hop fans have embraced Swedish rapper Papa Dee's tongue-in-cheek claim to be an "Original Black Viking" as a means of negotiating the hostility exhibited by white racist agitators who "celebrate the mythical Viking as an ancestor to German Nazists [sic] and their modern counterparts" (1997, p. 54).

By the same token, however, to claim that hip hop's role in opposition to locally manifested instances of racism and Fascism must in each case involve such forms of dialogic engagement with issues of nation and national identity is oversimplistic. Thus, to return to the context of Germany, while the lyrical themes of groups such as Advanced Chemistry may find appeal among some sections of Germany's ethnic minority youth, for others the mutuality of German-language rap with the desire to be seen as "German" is viewed negatively and has resulted in alternative forms of local hip hop culture which actively seek to rediscover and, in many cases, reconstruct notions of identity tied to traditional ethnic roots.[7] This, is particularly so in the case of Frankfurt where the percentage of ethnic minority inhabitants is higher than in most other German cities. During a conversation with a group of hip hoppers from Nordweststadt, a particularly mul-tiethnic area of Frankfurt with a large number of Gastar-beiter families, I noted how German-language rap groups such as Advanced Chemistry were continually criticized for their failure to acknowledge any form of ethnic identification other than that symbolized by their German passports, a failure that was perceived to amount to a symbolic betrayal of the right of ethnic minorities to "roots" or to any expression of cultural heritage. Thus, as a young Turkish woman put it: "I think that they [Advanced Chemistry] should be proud of their roots. When people say to me 'are you German?', I say 'no I'm not' and I'm not ashamed to say that."

Such sentiments are encapsulated in the Turkish rap styles that are also an integral part of the Frankfurt hip hop scene. In the same way that Asian musicians in Britain have experimented with western popular music and traditional bhangra styles learned from cassette tapes acquired in Asian shops (see Banerji and Baumann, 1990, p. 144), so young Turkish people living in German cities are able to obtain cassette recordings of traditional songs and music very cheaply from local shops established to cater for their cultural needs. Using rhythms and melodies learned or sampled from such cassettes, traditional Turkish musical styles have been fused with African-American rap styles to produce a distinctive variation of the rap sound. If German-language rap has come to signify the voice of the second-generation immigrant attempting to integrate into German society, then Turkish rap works to a broadly opposite effect, the whole Turkish rap movement translating into a singly defiant message aimed at the Turk's white German hosts.

While employed as a youth worker in Frankfurt, I was invited to sit on the judging panel of a talent competition for local bands in the neighboring town of Schwalbach. As well as those bands taking part in the competition, a number of other local groups had been booked to provide entertainment between the various heats, including a Turkish rap group. Prior to the group's performance, an incident occurred in which some of the young Turkish people who had come specially to see the group began hurling eggs at a white group performing "Deutsch-rock" (rock music with German lyrics). The Deutsch-rock group's performance had to be temporarily interrupted while those responsible for the disruption were removed from the building. When the group returned to the stage their singer attempted to quell the situation by assuring the audience that, although the songs performed were in German, their lyrics were not racist and should not be regarded as such. Nevertheless, the young Turkish people remaining in the hall continued to act in a hostile fashion and accused the group of being Nazis. Later, as the Turkish rap group took to the stage, a large cheer went up and those who had come to see them moved onto the dance floor in a symbolic show of defiance regarding the incident that had occurred previously. Although many white Germans in the hall appeared to appreciate the music, few of them ventured onto the dance floor, wary of the nationalistic fervor that was manifesting itself there.

Scenes within Scenes

The two versions of hip hop examined above importantly illustrate how, even within the same city or region, hip hop scenes can be crossed by competing knowledges and sensibilities which, although working out of the same nexus of local experience, generate a multiplicity of musicalized and stylized solutions to the often problematic issue of place and identity. Interestingly, while researching in Frankfurt, I identified a third hip hop sensibility which, while also acting as a resource via which the youth of ethnic minorities are able to mark themselves out from the city's white population, relies upon an altogether different strategy to that of actively reworking hip hop. Rather, this realization of the hip hop identity relates to the possibility that it presents for the formulation of a romanticized association with the African-American experience. It is significant that in much of the work that focuses on non-U.S. examples of hip hop, there is an implication that "localization" necessarily involves some element of stylistic and musical transformation in hip hop. Thus, for example, Mitchell argues that the development of an Australian hip hop scene has been given some degree of "official recognition" by the release in 1995 of a compilation of rap tracks by Australian artists whose musical and stylistic direction indicates that the local hip hop scene "no longer needs 'supporting' " (1998, pp. 9–10). It seems to me, however, that there is a danger here of essentializing the process of localization so that it becomes synonymous with obvious innovation. In this way such an interpretation of "localization" overlooks some of the more subtly nuanced properties of appropriation and transformation for which Robertson (1995), as previously noted, coins the term *glocality*. Arguably then, the process of localization, as this relates to rap and hip hop, or indeed other forms of music and style, need not involve any obvious physical transformations of musical and stylistic resources but may, alternatively, rely on localized affinities, which are experienced more at the level of the experiential and which, in turn, demand a more abstract form of analytical engagement with the situating properties of local environments.

Thus, returning to the context of Frankfurt, I would argue that the African-American-based hip hop sensibility described above could also be seen as the expression of a "local" hip hop culture in that its origins are similarly rooted in the recent socio-historical context of Frankfurt. I have previously noted above how the Frankfurt hip hop scene developed in part because of the influence of African-American GIs whose impromptu rap performances in the city's clubs, bars and other public spaces encouraged imitation among local hip hop enthusiasts. Thus, in this sense, African-American representations of hip hop could be said to have been a "part" of the local scene from the outset. Furthermore, now that the U.S. army's occupation of central Germany has officially ended, there are clear indications that African-American hip hop will not only continue to be highly influential in Frankfurt but is also set to remain an integral part of the local hip hop scene. Thus, as a journalist working for a local hip hop magazine explained to me:

> Infrared [a small independent hip hop label in Frankfurt] have recently signed a U.S. rap group called Poverty. They were all stationed over here in the army and now they want to stay here and try and develop their career as a rap group. You get that quite a lot. Or American soldiers stationed over here invite relatives over who are into rap and hip hop and they like it here so they decide to stay. In the U.S. there's a lot of competition, very hard competition, between rappers...on every street corner there are ten rappers trying to get a recording deal. It's a lot easier for them over here, particularly if they come from the ghetto, the way of life is much less aggressive here...and the labels are often attracted to them, not least of all because they know that with any luck they can sell their records in the U.S. which means a lot of money for them.

The continuation of African-American hip hop's acutely physical presence within the local Frankfurt scene in turn ensures that it also continues to play a role in the formulation of local hip hop sensibilities. Thus, even today, for many enthusiasts hip hop continues to make "authentic" sense only in its African-American context. As one young hip hopper argued:

> How can you talk about German hip hop, what meaning does it have? What are you gonna do, sing about the ghetto? I'm into hip hop because of where it's at now y'know. It's a good style, you shouldn't mess with it. Some of those black guys are so cool. I look up to them and respect them.... When I go out on the street, they're the ones I'm thinking about, that's who I wanna be like y'know.

At the same time, however, it seems to me that this form of aesthetic attachment to the genre also derives from other distinctive forms of physical and visual experience acquired in Frankfurt's local environment. To put this another way, it could be argued that there is a direct correspondence between the significance of African-American-style hip hop as an authentic cultural practice in Frankfurt and the various terrains, both physical and symbolic, of the city itself. In many of the conversations I had with devotees of German-language rap, strong opinions were voiced against those who continue to listen to African-American rap artists. On one occasion, in speaking about the popularity of U.S.-style "gangsta rap" in Frankfurt, a German-language rapper explained to me:

> There are people who don't understand a word of English, but they like the music so they pretend that they understand what they're listening to and I personally have a problem with that. For a lot of people, the commercial side of it, the image and the clothes are more important than the music and I find that ridiculous. They pretend to be "gangsta" rappers from the USA and yet we've got enough social problems here which need to be addressed.

It is interesting to note the way in which the word "pretend" is used in the above account to denote a form of "playing" or "acting" out a role, which, according to the interviewee, is how those who favor the African-American style of hip hop must inevitably come to understand their aesthetic attachment to the hip hop genre. An interesting analogy between public life and the conventions of theatrical performance is offered by Chaney. It seems to me that Chaney's conceptualization of the modern city center as "a stage for public drama," together with its underlying implication that the modern urban experience, rather than complying with a commonly acknowledged and "objective" social narrative, comprises a series of competing fictive interpretations, provides a fitting theoretical starting point for a further exploration of the deeply ingrained visions of America that continue to inform much of the hip hop culture acted out in the streets of Frankfurt (1993, p. 68). If, on the one hand, Frankfurt's multiple fictions of collective life are sustained by the multicultural composition of the city, since 1945 the changing face of the city itself has increasingly enhanced the flow of public drama. In particular, U.S.-directed post-war redevelopment has brought with it a variety of structures, surfaces and images which have met head on with the increasing flow of popular culture resources from the U.S. to produce an enduring visage of America in Frankfurt.

The View from "Mainhatten"

During the Second World War, Frankfurt was heavily bombed by enemy aircraft and much of the city center completely destroyed. After the war, reconstruction work was facilitated in Frankfurt and other German cities with considerable financial assistance from the U.S. government in the form of an ambitious loan package known as the Marshall Plan (Mayer, 1969). While care was taken in certain parts of the city to restore buildings as they had appeared in the pre-war years, in other areas modern high rise constructions (Hochhäuse) replaced bomb damaged eighteenth- and nineteenth-century German architecture. In the city center, such redevelopment programs completely revised the appearance of the old business quarters and shopping districts. Indeed with its futuristic skyline, notably the Bundesbank, a high rise, glass fronted building with a twin tower design, and the more recently erected Messeturm (trade center), Frankfurt city center has taken on the look and feel of a modern North American city. It is perhaps of little surprise then that this part of Frankfurt has become known locally as "Mainhatten." Indeed, when such elements of local urban folklore are read in conjunction with a prolonged absorption in Frankfurt's impressive infrastructure of consumer, leisure and public transport facilities, the city center increasingly comes to resemble the physical realization of Baudrillard's (1988) "cinematographized" U.S., which, Baudrillard argues, has become the primary way in which non-Americans experience the U.S. and thus construct images and ideas concerning the nation, its people and culture (see also Smart, 1993 and Gane, 1993).

Such a visage is perhaps most evident in the pedestrianized shopping precinct known as the "Zeil" and two adjacent open areas, the "Konstablerwache" and the "Hauptwache," which are each built over main intersections of the Frankfurt underground system. Over the years, these locations have become central meeting places for young people, accommodating skate-boarders, breakdancers, buskers, street artists and the like. On either side of the "Zeil" familiar U.S. icons, such as the Disney Store and McDonald's, as well as a number of imitation U.S.-style fast food outlets, amplify the illusion that this is indeed a scene from a U.S. City. Similarly, the main entrance to Hertie, a large department store, is bedecked on either side and above with multiple TV screens which provide visitors to the Zeil with a twenty-four hour transmission of American MTV.

In the context of this scenario it is easy to see how a version of hip hop culture grounded in notions of African-American style and a form of romanticized association with African-American street culture has become as much a part of Frankfurt's convoluted urban narrative as the politicized German-language variation of hip hop considered above. Offering as they do, a sonic and visual backdrop of Americana, public spaces such as the Zeil provide a perfect stage for the acting out of a hip hop sensibility that imagines itself to be a part of the African-American experience. In this sense, the Zeil becomes simultaneously "both a real and an imaginary place" (Chambers, 1992, p. 188). Speaking about the popularity of U.S. rap in Frankfurt and attempting to account for this, the manager of a local independent record label specializing in rap made a number of points that add weight to the above observation. Thus, he argued:

> The thing about hip hop that people keep forgetting, is that it's not just one definite thing. It's a lot of things, different sounds, different styles, different feelings. You can basically do with it what you want.... A lot of kids here go for the groove and the image. They see the videos, they see the clothes and the "cool image" and the kids enjoy that, they want to be like that. They're just play acting the whole thing. And you know, Frankfurt is this big international city...there's lots going on here, movies, gigs. It's got really Americanized y'know. There's lots of places to go where you can hang out with your friends on the street, listen to your music real loud...just like in the States. English is used a lot here too and even if a lot of the kids don't know it so well they're used to the sound of it and they can pick out key phrases. And that influences tastes in rap music. English [that is, African-American] rap is simply cool, it's in, and you can relate it to what's going on in the street here.

In the social context of Frankfurt am Main then, collective notions of hip hop and its significance as a mode of cultural expression are governed by a range of differing local factors which have, in their turn, given rise to a number of distinctive localized variations in the formulation of hip hop authenticity. It follows, therefore, that if notions of hip hop authenticity are intimately bound up with forms of local knowledge and experience then, in the context of other urban and regional locations with differing social circumstances and conditions, versions of hip hop culture and debates concerning its authentic usage will be based around a rather different range of social and aesthetic criteria. In order to illustrate this point more conclusively, I want now to conduct a further examination of hip hop culture and its attendant notions of authenticity as these are realized in the context of a different local urban setting, Newcastle upon Tyne in northeast England.

Rappin' on the Tyne

In terms of both its socio-economic history and ethnic composition, the cultural context of Newcastle upon Tyne is markedly different to that of Frankfurt am Main. Newcastle is a predominantly white, working-class post-industrial city. Thus, although small Asian and Afro-Caribbean minorities do exist in Newcastle, their influence upon its cultural environment, including the local music and club scene, has been nominal as compared with other British cities with larger Asian and Afro-Caribbean populations. This is also true of the small hip hop scene that has grown up around Newcastle, the neighboring city of Gateshead and a number of outlying towns and villages, such as Blythe and Cramlington, this scene being dominated by white male enthusiasts. Indeed, the male-centered nature of the Newcastle hip hop scene is another factor that sets it apart from the Frankfurt scene which, although also largely male, is characterized by a growing number of female hip hop enthusiasts and rap groups. This is indicative of both the wider acceptance in Germany of women and girls taking part in music-making activities and the emphasis upon music as a learning resource, which has in turn led to the establishment of numerous community-based music-making projects, many of which offer courses and workshops exclusively for women and girls (see Meinig, 1993; Pohl, 1993; Bennett, 1998). In Britain, by contrast, it could be argued that women and girls wishing to become involved in music-making activities continue to be confronted by indifference and hostility from their male peers. Cohen, for example, notes that girls were discouraged from taking part in community music projects in Liverpool for fear of being "criticized for wanting to do something that was mainly a boy's activity" (1991, p. 204; see also Bayton, 1988). Similar sensibilities appear to prevent the participation of women in the Newcastle hip hop scene. Thus, although none of my male interviewees claimed to object to female hip hoppers, their code of speech contained a number of male-centered terms such as "new jack" and "homeboy," which suggested that they considered hip hop culture to be an essentially male-orientated pursuit.

Hip Hop and "Whiteness"

The issue of white British working-class youth appropriating African-American and other black musical forms is one that has long been addressed by theorists of youth culture and popular music. Significantly, however, there has been little attempt to study white appropriations of hip hop in the context of the UK. The essential "whiteness" of hip hop culture in Newcastle, in addition to providing an ideal setting for beginning such an enquiry, also casts further light on the micro-social issues that inform the "localization" of hip hop. In many parts of the UK, the localization of hip hop has involved its appropriation by Afro-Caribbean and Asian youth, whose collective use of the style has turned partly on its deemed failure to translate into white terms. Such a belief is manifest among Afro-Caribbean hip hoppers in Cobley and Osgerby's (1995) research on the hip hop scene in London's Peckham district. According to Cobley and Osgerby, while Afro-Caribbean hip hopper's acknowledged white appropriations of the hip hop style they refused to take such appropriations seriously, much less view them as authentic expressions of hip hop culture. Similarly, Ashwani Sharma's account of London and Midlands-based Asian rap groups, such as Asian Dub Foundation, Fun Da Mental, Hustlers HC and ADF, argues that these groups' bhangra—rap fusions—perform an instrumental function in the marking out of a *strategic* Asian identity" through their articulation of "significant dimensions of Asian cultural and political life in Britain" (1996, pp. 44–45). Finally, Back, in considering hip hop's translation in the context of south London, suggests that it has moved beyond its initial focus "on particular British circumstances" and now appropriates "the language of black New York…to document and mythologize happenings in South London" (1996, pp. 207–9). As will shortly become evident, such discourses and sensibilities of African-American hip hop also feature in the Newcastle hip hop scene but are translated into white terms. That such a translation is possible in Newcastle, while remaining problematic in other British cities, has much to do with the ethnic composition of the local urban population which, as previously noted, is predominantly white. Indeed it could be argued that the essential "whiteness" of Newcastle and, by definition, the local hip hop scene, facilitates a highly particularized series of responses to the "black" characteristics of the hip hop style which, among certain sections of the local hip hop community, amounts to a celebration of blackness in the absence of blackness.

A general supposition of those who have attempted to account for the appropriation of African-American musics by white British working-class youth is that the structural position of white working-class Britons and African-Americans is sufficiently similar to allow for African-American musics to perform a binary role in which the oppressions experienced by each group are simultaneously addressed. Thus, for example, Chambers has suggested that the "oppositional values" contained in African-American music also "symbolize and symptomatize the contradictions and tensions played out in [white] British working class youth" (1976, p. 166).[8] Certainly one could argue that sections of white working-class youth may appropriate black music and aspects of black style in symbolic recognition of their felt affinity with African-American and other black ethnic minority groups. At the same time however, it is also important to acknowledge the actively constructed nature of such a cultural association rather than viewing it simply as a product of structural circumstances. In this sense then, the use of black music and style on the part of the white working-class youth becomes a particular form of lived sensibility; a reflexive lifestyle "strategy" (Chaney, 1996, pp. 112–125). Moreover, if this line of argument is followed to its logical conclusion, it follows that a number of other actively constructed ideological positions may also be articulated by white working-class youth via their appropriation of black musical forms in which symbolic associations with the fact of "blackness" itself are considered to be less important. To this must be added the significance of place. It is often taken for granted that white British appropriations of black music and style routinely take place in settings where a prominent black population serves as a continual point of reference for such appropriations. This is the case with Jones's (1988) research on white appropriations of reggae, which was carried out in a mixed-race area of Birmingham, and is also evident in Hebdige's work on the origins of mod and skinhead culture (1976a, 1976b, 1979). In reality, however, white working-class youth's experimentation with black music and style occurs in a range of differing local contexts and thus against a variety of referential socio-cultural backdrops which may or may not include an established black population.

Black Music in the Northeast

The northeast region of England has a long established tradition of appropriation from African-American music. During the 1960s, Newcastle group the Animals achieved international success with a style of music based closely on the urban blues of African-American artists such as Robert Johnson (Gillett, 1983, pp. 269–272). Rhythm and blues continues to be immensely popular in the area with a significant number of local "R&B" groups performing in local pubs and clubs, while each August the County Durham town of Stanley plays host to an internationally renowned blues festival. Similarly, during the 1970s, a number of dance venues in small towns in the neighboring region of East Yorkshire featured "Northern Soul," an all-white "underground" soul scene that centers around rare black soul imports primarily from the U.S. (see Milestone, 1997). Significantly, in the case of northeast England, such white appropriations of black music and style have largely taken place without physical reference to a local black population. As such, the point raised above positing the issue of black "association" as something that is actively constructed by white youth in their appropriation of black music and style, rather than as a structurally determined "given" of such appropriation, is perhaps more clearly illustrated. Indeed, the consciously articulated nature of black association in the northeast region is particularly evident when one considers the competing sensibilities that characterize the local hip hop scene in Newcastle. At the center of this scene, a hardcore of hip hop enthusiasts share the belief that their intimate understanding of hip hop's essential "blackness" as the key to its relevance for the white working-class experience guarantees them a form of aesthetic supremacy over other local white hip hop fans who, according to this group, have no such understanding of the genre and thus no authentic claim to the African-American musics by white British working-class youth is that the structural position of white working-class Britons and African-Americans is sufficiently similar to allow for African-American musics to perform a binary role in which the oppressions experienced by each group are simultaneously addressed. Thus, for example, Chambers has suggested that the "oppositional values" contained in African-American music also "symbolize and symptomatize the contradictions and tensions played out in [white] British working class youth" (1976, p. 166).[8] Certainly one could argue that sections of white working-class youth may appropriate black music and aspects of black style in symbolic recognition of their felt affinity with African-American and other black ethnic minority groups. At the same time, however, it is also important to acknowledge the actively constructed nature of such a cultural association rather than viewing it simply as a product of structural circumstances. In this sense then, the use of black music and style on the part of the white working-class youth becomes a particular form of lived sensibility; a reflexive lifestyle "strategy" (Chaney, 1996, pp. 112–125). Moreover, if this line of argument is followed to its logical conclusion, it follows that a number of other actively constructed ideological positions may also be articulated by white working-class youth via their appropriation of black musical forms in which symbolic associations with the fact of "blackness" itself are considered to be less important. To this must be added the significance of place. It is often taken for granted that white British appropriations of black music and style routinely take place in settings where a prominent black population serves as a continual point of reference for such appropriations. This is the case with Jones's (1988) research on white appropriations of reggae, which was carried out in a mixed-race area of Birmingham, and is also evident in Hebdige's work on the origins of mod and skinhead culture (1976a, 1976b, 1979). In reality, however, white working-class youth's experimentation with black music and style occurs in a range of differing local contexts and thus against a variety of referential socio-cultural backdrops which may or may not include an established black population.

Black Music in the Northeast

The northeast region of England has a long established tradition of appropriation from African-American music. During the 1960s, Newcastle group the Animals achieved international success with a style of music based closely on the urban blues of African-American artists such as Robert Johnson (Gillett, 1983, pp. 269–272). Rhythm and blues continues to be immensely popular in the area with a significant number of local "R&B" groups performing in local pubs and clubs, while each August the County Durham town of Stanley plays host to an internationally renowned blues festival. Similarly, during the 1970s, a number of dance venues in small towns in the neighboring region of East Yorkshire featured "Northern Soul," an all-white "underground" soul scene that centers around rare black soul imports primarily from the U.S. (see Milestone, 1997). Significantly, in the case of northeast England, such white appropriations of black music and style have largely taken place without physical reference to a local black population. As such, the point raised above positing the issue of black "association" as something that is actively constructed by white youth in their appropriation of black music and style, rather than as a structurally determined "given" of such appropriation, is perhaps more clearly illustrated. Indeed, the consciously articulated nature of black association in the northeast region is particularly evident when one considers the competing sensibilities that characterize the local hip hop scene in Newcastle. At the center of this scene, a hardcore of hip hop enthusiasts share the belief that their intimate understanding of hip hop's essential "blackness" as the key to its relevance for the white working-class experience guarantees them a form of aesthetic supremacy over other local white hip hop fans who, according to this group, have no such understanding of the genre and thus no authentic claim to the title "hip hopper." Conversely, a number of other local hip hop enthusiasts firmly reject the notion that hip hop can be understood only in terms of its African-American context and attempt to rework it as a platform for the expression of issues that relate more directly to their own day to day experiences. I want now to consider each of these responses to hip hop in turn. In doing so, I hope to illustrate how, as with the various hip hop sensibilities examined in the case of Frankfurt, these responses, despite their obvious stylistic differences, are each intimately bound up with the particularities of local experience.

"You into That 'Nigger Music' Then?"

In his study of the music scene in Austin, Texas, Shank (1994) draws attention to the important role played by local independent record shops in authenticating particular scenes by providing a space for like-minded individuals to meet, discuss their tastes in music and argue over the merits of particular tracks and artists, thus positioning themselves in relation to other music scenes located in the same city or town. In the context of the Newcastle hip hop scene, a comparable role is performed by Groove. Groove is a tiny independent record shop in the center of Newcastle dealing exclusively in U.S. rap which is specially imported and, consequently, not readily available in the high street chain stores. The proprietor of Groove, a white Newcastle man named Jim, is a devotee of African-American rap music and hip hop culture. Having listened to soul music during his teens, he then turned to rap as it became more widely available in Britain during the 1980s. Groove has become something of a meeting point for those who believe, like Jim, that rap and hip hop can only be understood in terms of their African-American cultural context. On the surface, the group of local hip hop enthusiasts who frequent Groove appear to correspond unproblematically with the commonly expounded sociological thesis that African-American dance music is somehow able to connect with the experiential world of white working-class youth in Britain. Below is an extract from a discussion I conducted with Jim and several of the regular visitors to Groove during which I asked them to comment on the issue of *white* hip hop:

A.B.: *There are a lot of white rap fans in Newcastle who are using hip hop to talk about their own experiences.*

Jim: *There's no such thing as white hip hop.*

A.B.: *Why is that?*

Jim: *Because hip hop is a black music. As white people we should still respect it as black music.*

Jeff: *All the time before, white people were into, black music, hip hop's just the same. There's a message in black music which translates for white working-class people.*

A.B.: *What is that?*

Dave: *It's about being proud of where you come from...*

Jeff: *Yeah and because it [black music] offers a strength and intelligence which no British culture does.*

Jim: *The trend at the moment is to be real...to rap in your own accent and talk about things close to you...don't try to be American like. But that's why British hip hop will always be shite.... I went to New York, well actually to Cleveland near New York, and stayed with a black family. It was brilliant, it changed my life. You can't talk about white hip hop, it doesn't exist.*

Clearly then, among the Groove regulars there is a shared sense of belief that the essential blackness of hip hop is also the key to its use by white working-class youth as an authentic mode of cultural expression. Interestingly, however, when the wider cultural context of Groove and those who frequent it is studied in more detail, it becomes evident that such a belief in the nature of hip hop carries a level of symbolic importance that goes beyond a shared sense of affinity with the African-American experience. Within the local Newcastle music scene, Groove has a reputation for being one of the few "specialist" record shops in the city. As such the shop enjoys something of an "outsider" status. Indeed, as a local hairdresser and popular music enthusiast who is familiar with Groove suggested to me one day as I sat in his chair: "I can't see how he [Jim] makes any money from that business. It's more a labor of love for him really."

In many ways, the above observation constitutes a highly sensitive reading of Groove and the type of cultural work that it performs. In the context of Newcastle, Groove, although ostensibly a business venture, at the same time plays host to a type of self-styled local hip hop elite in which an intimate understanding of hip hop's black roots is combined with a comprehensive knowledge of rap music and what, on the basis of the group's understanding of the music's cultural significance, counts as good or bad rap. This form of local "cultural capital," into which the local reputation of Groove is included, is then used as a way of articulating the group's difference from the "new jacks," a term given to those who are considered to be hip hop "tourists," that is, those who listen indiscriminately to rap music before moving on to a new trend. Thus, as Jim pointed out:

> These new jacks, you can spot them a mile off. They're just into hip hop 'cause it's trendy like. They come in here and they don't know what the fuck they're talking about. They'll buy about one record a month for a year or something and then get into something else, house or something.

Marks has suggested that white appropriations of black musical forms are often symbolically transformed into "badge[s] of exclusivity," particularly if such conspicuous displays of black taste on the part of young whites enable them to "manifest their difference from the cultural mainstream" (1990, p. 105). Clearly, this observation goes some way towards explaining the shared sensibility of those local hip hop enthusiasts who frequent Groove and their collective response towards the perceived fickleness of the new jacks' attachment to the genre.

Arguably, however, there is a further reason why these and other like-minded local hip hop enthusiasts are so passionate in their symbolic association with African-American culture. In a Birmingham-based study Jones has noted how young whites' "displays of affiliation to black culture" result on occasion in them becoming "the objects of a 'deflected' form of racism" (1988, p. 199). In the social context of Newcastle, perhaps because of the city's predominately white populace, such physical challenges to forms of black association occur more frequently. On one particular evening, I accompanied a group of local hip hop enthusiasts, several of whom were regular customers at Groove, to a bar in the center of Newcastle where a weekly "hip hop" night was being held. On the way to the bar the group, who were dressed in typical African-American hip hop style clothes such as loose fitting shorts, basketball caps, designer training shoes and sunglasses, attracted comments such as "are you going to a fancy dress party?" and were also subject to several shouts of "wigger" (white nigger) from other young club and pub-goers. The use of "wigger" in this context is particularly significant in that it involves a localized reworking of the term. Cobley and Osgerby note how in London, Afro-Caribbean hip hop enthusiasts use "wigger" as a way of marking out the deemed inauthenticity of "white youth [who] appropriate 'black' styles" (1995, p. 6). In the context of Newcastle, however, "wigger's" white on white application suggests that it is being used as a way of stigmatizing those who are seen as "wanting to be black" and thus deviating from the locally established norm. Clearly, such "deflected" racism cannot be equated with the systematic abuse and physical violence that continues to be directed at ethnic minorities in Britain by white racist groups. It does, however, suggest the need for a broader consideration of the factors contributing to racist behavior and the ways in which the symbolic alliance of whites with African-American and other ethnic minority groups, through mediums such as music and style, might be viewed as a form of cultural betrayal by other sections of white youth.

Such a view is substantiated via other accounts I received of the deflected racism encountered by hip hop enthusiasts in Newcastle. Thus, for example, as another Groove regular explained: "I used to work in a record shop and I'd always be getting loads of shit from the customers…they'd say 'what do you like this nigger music for?' Or, 'you only like this music 'cause it's black.'" The particular hostility of deflected racism in "white" settings is graphically portrayed in the following account by a white hip hop enthusiast from Glasgow, another British city with a predominantly white population, whose expertise in breakdancing had led him to move down to Newcastle where he worked part-time in a local dance school. This hip hopper's account of his experiences in Glasgow is comparable with those of the Newcastle hip hoppers noted above. Thus, he explained:

We were always different like...'cause we always used to go in the park and that and you'd get these idiots comin' up and saying "what yoos doin' there, that breakdancin'?"...and they'd do us in.... And we used to go to nightclubs and that and the DJ was one of our mates. He'd clear the floor and say "right we're havin' some breakdancers up now, some really hardcore hip hoppers," and they'd all start spittin' on us.

If the essential whiteness of given local settings can lead to such expressions of prejudice and hostility regarding white associations with "blackness," at the same time those who are stigmatized for their "deviant" identity politics often use the fact of such negative responses as a key resource when marking out a cultural territory for themselves. Thus, in the case of the Newcastle hip hoppers, the displays of hostility that they encountered resulted in them becoming even more forthright in terms of their "black association," this symbol of "exclusivity" being turned around and worn with an air of defiance in the face of a crowd whose racism, it was argued, went hand in hand with its small-mindedness and conservative tastes in music and fashion. Thus, as one of the group exclaimed: "I fucking hate the town scene, all that crap commercial music and fashion stuff. As far as I'm concerned it has nothing to do with my life whatsoever!" Within the group then, there was a carefully fashioned sensibility which dictated that in being frank about their dedication not only to African-American hip hop but also to the stylistic and ideological forms of address they deemed to be a part of it, they were in turn revealing an honesty and integrity within themselves, thus setting the group apart from the small town mentality that was deemed to prevail in Newcastle. Indeed, one could go as far as to argue that for this particular group of hip hoppers, their staunchly adhered-to hip hop identity had become a form of external faith, the latter being reconfirmed each time the group was subject to abuse by "non-believers." As such, incidents of abuse had become not so much insulting experiences or tests of patience, but rather provided the group with a platform for displays of collective martyrdom to their cause. This "localized" response on the part of white youth to African-American hip hop style further emphasizes the point made in relation to the continuing significance of African-American hip hop in Frankfurt. Thus, in relation to Groove and those hip hop enthusiasts whose shared discourse of authenticity and integrity revolves around being a part of the Groove "scene," the local significance of rap and hip hop derives not from any obvious physical reworking of the latter but more from a locally forged sense of affinity with hip hop based upon a sense of its *strength and intelligence* in comparison to what is seen as a fickle and undiscerning local mainstream youth culture.

A "Street Thing!"

A somewhat different if equally constructed hip hop sensibility can be seen in relation to those individuals who make up what could be termed Newcastle's *white* hip hop culture. For these local enthusiasts, hip hop's use as an authentic mode of expression does not center around the form of felt association with the African-American experience shared by those individuals who frequent Groove. Rather, there is a commonly held view among *white* hip hoppers that the essence of hip hop culture relates to its ready translation into a medium that directly bespeaks the white British working-class experience. Thus as one self-styled "Geordie" rapper explained to me:

Hip hop isn't a black thing, it's a street thing y'know, where people get so pissed off with their environment that they have to do something about it. And the way to do it and get the word to the people is to do it creatively, be it writing on a wall or expressing it in a rap...or wearing baggy clothes y'know. It's all part of this one thing of going "oh look man, we've had enough of this and we're gonna change it in our way."

An interesting comparison here is a study by Maxwell of the hip hop scene in Sydney, Australia. According to Maxwell, although the Sydney hip hoppers' realization of their scene involved taking "the simulacrum of a culture which they had accessed through the electronic media" the physical realization of this simulacrum brought it into contact with a new reality, one located in the streets and neighborhoods of Sydney (1994, p. 15). In a similar fashion *white* hip hop enthusiasts in Newcastle are attempting to rework the hip hop style so that it becomes a form of address that resonates intimately with the nature of their own particular local circumstances. I want now to consider two specific examples of the way in which hip hop has been taken up by white working-class youth in Newcastle as a way of addressing issues encountered on a day to day basis in the city.

"Am That Dreadlock Hippy Bastard That Comes from the Toon"

This chapter begins with an extract from "Aa dee it coz aa can" (I do it because I can) by Ferank, a Newcastle poet and rapper. Originally written as a poem, "Aa dee it coz aa can" was later recorded as rap. As with much of Ferank's work, this rap deals directly with his own experiences of living in Newcastle and is performed in a local Geordie accent, a feature that Ferank feels adds an important element of authenticity to his style. Thus, he argues: "I'm not American, so it's pointless for me to do a rap in an American accent…. Anyway, the Geordie accent that myself and other rappers up here are using is a dialect, just like patois, and so it should be used." "Aa dee it coz aa can," which is essentially a commentary on aspects of Newcastle life and the local Geordie culture, works at a number of different levels. Thus, in one sense the rap is intended to deliver a firm message to those living in other places, both in Britain and abroad, whose impressions of Newcastle are dominated by the notion of the typical Geordie stereotype. Using his own starkly profiled local identity as a springboard, Ferank attempts to demonstrate, through the medium of his informed reading and poetical summary of the local situation, that the stereotypical image of the Geordie character is erroneous. As Ferank explained to me:

I was tryin' to change people's perceptions of what they think o' Geordies. Flat caps and this Geordie pride thing which I don't feel. Eh, I'm proud o' where I come from and of the people that I care for and who care for me. But eh, there's a lot of malice in this town and a lotta people who need an education. And I'd like to think that I've had one of sorts, and I've always been from here. So it was kinda sayin' "oh look man for fuck's sake, I might be from here but I'm not your typical Geordie!." While I am...while I should be accepted as the most typical Geordie.

At the same time, however, "Aa dee it coz aa can" also criticizes the cultural conservatism that Ferank identifies with sections of Newcastle's population, especially when confronted with someone who fails to conform with accepted conventions of appearance such as dress and hairstyle. It is Ferank's opinion that such conservatism is destined to remain a part of the city's character for a long time to come as, from a very early age, children are indoctrinated by their parents into believing that those who are in some way "individual" or "eccentric" in their appearance or manner are misfits and should therefore be subject to a form of systematic stigmatization. Again, as Ferank himself explained to me:

> When I'm out in the street I'll get someone pass a comment on how I look, within earshot of myself and they don't mind if I hear. Y'know...and that's their attitude to everything here.... Like I'll walk past kids in the street and they'll be with their parents and that and even the parents'll join in wi' like "look at the state o' him, they look like bloody rats' tails in 'is hair." Y'know, they're really blatant about it.... These people need an education. You can't get away with that, you gotta expect a reaction. And they normally get one from me.... They get it in a rhyme, they're there y'know. And maybe they'll see themselves and go "oh hang on a sec...I need to think a little differently about what I'm sayin."

Ferank's visual image combines a dreadlock hairstyle with a broadly eclectic if eccentric dress sense in which brightly colored garments are often combined to dazzling effect. Thus, as he explains: "I love to dress up myself, I always have. So amongst my mates it's like, 'whoa fuckin' hell, look what Ferank's got on!' " In his rap, Ferank contrasts the playfulness implied in his own chosen image with the harsh reactions which this image often elicits and makes it pointedly clear that, whatever others may think of him, he is determined to stand by his right to be an individual.

> It shouldn't really matter that me skeets are aal tatty, An a wear funny clothes wi' me dreads aal natty, 'Coz underneath am just like yeez, Or have aa just managed to outrun the disease...An me eyes just sing the sad, sad song, Of the hatred the parents install in tha young...aal never shaddap an aal never siddoon, 'Am that dreadlock hippy bastard that comes from the toon.

While Ferank describes his work as a form of protest against the conservatism he encounters on the streets of Newcastle, there is a clear sense in which, at a deeper level, he is also exposing the contradictions inherent in the sensibilities of a local white youth culture that collectively appropriates black cultural resources while simultaneously stigmatizing certain individual experimentations with black style as in some way going "too far." In many respects, Ferank's personal battle for self-expression serves to reconfirm the fact that many young whites, especially those who live in predominantly white areas, maintain a double standard in which an acceptance of black music and style goes hand in hand with an intolerance of black minority groups. While Ferank, who is regarded as a white "imitator," remains untouched by the more brutal and disturbing aspects of such intolerance, the reactions of local white youth to his experiments with aspects of black style serve as telling reminders of considerable local variations which characterize racial tolerance and multiculturalism in Britain.

At the same time, Ferank's work illustrates another of the ways in which hip hop is being modified or reworked by white working-class youth in Newcastle so that it becomes a more localized and, in Ferank's case, highly personalized mode of expression. Indeed, it is clear from Ferank's own account of the meanings underlying his work that his personal attachment to hip hop results directly from the artistic license it grants him. Through the medium of hip hop Ferank is able to publicly voice feelings and opinions that would otherwise find little scope for expression. In this sense, a further similarity can be seen between the *white* hip hop culture of Newcastle and the German-language rappers of Frankfurt in that both of them consider hip hop's value as an authentic mode of expression to be primarily rooted in the power it gives them as individuals to comment upon the nature of their own day to day experiences. This form of attachment to hip hop is further illustrated below where a second "Geordie" adaptation of the hip hop sensibility is considered.

The "Broon Ale" Ward

Ferank is often to be heard performing his raps at Mac's Bar, one of the few venues in Newcastle that provides an opportunity for local rappers to air their skill in a live situation. While much of Ferank's work is composed beforehand, many of the rappers who frequent Mac's Bar engage in a form of rapping known as "freestyle." Basically, this involves taking a particular theme and verbally improvising a series of ideas and points of view around the chosen theme. This form of rapping has also become a primary way in which local *white* rappers address issues that are particular to Newcastle and its people. Indeed, in many ways, "freestyling" provides a more effective form of local address than written rap as it enables the rapper to engage in a relatively spontaneous form of discourse. Thus, snippets of local "street" gossip and more widely acknowledged local themes and issues can be verbally woven together with pieces of local urban folklore to produce particularly pointed, hard-hitting and, on occasion, humorous cameos of local social life. The following account is drawn from a conversation with a member of one particular group of freestyle rappers who regularly perform at Mac's Bar:

> We used to use a lot of "Americanisms" in our raps, but then when we started comin' down here we heard pure Geordie rap. Like with Ferank...it was just like "oh yeah check out Ferank's flow." And then people'd be sayin' to us "why don't you do a rap theme about like eh, like an American rap crew would do a song about Crack and about how it's affecting their city an' that?" An' we started thinkin' "well aye why not, let's 'ave a go at doin' something about Newcastle Brown Ale" because there's lots of "isms" for Newcastle Brown Ale. "The Dog," "Geordie into space," all these different names and it's...y'know all these different reputations it's got. They used to have a ward up at the General [hospital] which was the "Broon Ale" ward [owing to the number of people admitted with injuries caused through fighting when drunk]. So we thought, "yeah, that's the stuff we should be rappin' about," it's like our version of "Crack on the streets" with a bit a' humour in there an' all y'know.

While the notion of a white Newcastle rap group rapping about the local drinking culture may initially seem rather comical, it is important to understand the local circumstances to which the group is responding. As with many of those young people involved in the Newcastle dance music scene, there is growing cynicism among local hip hoppers concerning the city center pub and club scene and the aggressive, masochistic atmosphere that often manifests itself there. Thus, in a very real sense, by rapping about the problems of excessive drinking and alcohol-related violence, the white rap group quoted above are addressing an aspect of their local environment which, they feel, needs to be acknowledged and changed. Additionally, it is also widely held among members of Newcastle's hip hop scene that the possibility of staging hip hop nights in the city is being continually reduced because of the more commercially successful mainstream club nights that increasingly dominate Newcastle's night-time economy. Consequently, the freestyle raps heard in Mac's Bar assume a dual resonance in that they not only attack the senseless violence that characterizes the local mainstream club scene but also deal with the latter's steady encroachment on the hard-won club space of Newcastle's more underground and alternative youth cultures.

The obvious connection of such "home grown" rap with the shared sensibilities of local hip hoppers is clearly evidenced by the particular type of listening sensibility that it appears to invoke in Mac's Bar. When the "freestylers" take to the floor, usually towards the end of the evening, the audience, who have up to that point been lazily dancing to a mix of mainly U.S. rap sounds, stop dancing and gather around the performers to listen to their raps. In doing so they are acknowledging the fact that the improvised stories these local rappers are relating work out of a shared stock of local knowledges and experiences that are in many ways uniquely relevant to Newcastle and the surrounding area. In listening to the "freestylers," regulars at Mac's Bar are receiving accounts of their own lives depicted via a form of quickfire verbal reference to locations and events, names and faces with which they are all intimately familiar. Again, this instance of local hip hop activity is indicative of the close links that prefigure collective notions of authenticity, identity and local experience in hip hop. When the Geordie rappers take to the floor, there is an obvious shift in the audience's response. From the point of view of the audience, the music ceases to provide purely a rhythm for dancing or a background noise over which to talk and becomes something to be listened to, something that actively involves them. In drawing around the stage to listen to the Geordie rappers, the audience collectively endorse the more locally relevant focus of the rappers' messages, thus celebrating its particularized "authenticity."

The purpose of this chapter has been to demonstrate how hip hop cultures and attendant notions of authenticity are in each case a product of locality, that is to say, the particular local circumstances under which hip hop is appropriated and subsequently used as a collective form of expression. Using examples of different local hip hop scenes, I have attempted to illustrate how, in each instance, the particular version, or versions, of hip hop culture created, together with attendant debates as to which individuals are *authentically* portraying the hip hop sensibility, is underpinned by a stock of distinctive local knowledges. In each of the local hip hop cultures examined here, the particular characteristics of the wider social context have been shown to greatly influence the manner in which enthusiasts frame their association with the hip hop genre. In addition to looking at localized receptions of recorded rap music, during the course of this chapter I have also made some consideration of how live performances by local rappers can similarly serve to articulate notions of local identity. If "recorded" musical texts can be reworked by audiences to act as powerful statements of regional place and identity, then local "live" music scenes and the musicians who participate in them can also play a crucial role in the communicating such themes and issues to local audiences.

NOTES

1. Aside from rap music, "graffiti" is perhaps the most characteristic aspect of hip hop culture. However, because of the nature of this chapter's enquiry, which focuses primarily upon the local significance of rap, it will not be possible to engage in any in-depth discussion of hip hop graffiti. For a more informed analysis of the latter, see Lachmann (1988), Brewer and Miller (1990) and Deppe (1997).

2. Gastarbeiter" is the term applied to those individuals, typically from Turkey and Morocco, who have been granted special permission to enter Germany in order to meet the country's demand for unskilled manual labor.

3. Excerpt from the documentary *Lost in Music* broadcast on ZDF, March 1993.

4. This is particularly so in the former East Germany where the influx of capitalism from the west has not, as was expected, led to a better quality of life but has rather resulted in high levels of unemployment and related social problems such as homelessness.

5. For an account of the Rock gegen Rechts movement see de Cologne (1980).

6. The term "*Glatzen*" (plural of *Glatze*) derives from the German adjective *glatt* which means "smooth" "*Glatze*" is a slang term often applied to a bald person. In the wake of the neo-Fascist movement in Ger-

many the term has been appropriated by opposers of the movement and used in relation to all German skinheads as a way of linking them with neo-Nazi ideology. This automatic association of "skinhead" culture with the neo-Fascist movement is, however, largely inaccurate. In Germany, as in Britain, many skinheads are themselves anti-Facists. For a fuller account of this general misunderstanding and the special problems it has caused for skinheads in Germany, see Farin and Seidel-Pielen (1994).

7. It should be pointed out that German-language rap is almost exclusively performed by groups who originate in whole or in part from Germany's ethnic minorities. "All white" German-language rap groups, the most famous example of which is Die Fantastichen Vier, remain conspicuously apolitical in their music. This has lead to criticism from more politicized German-language rap groups such as Advanced Chemistry, who have suggested in a TV interview that Die Fantastichen Vier are a "hit pop" group whose style is little more than a fashionable pastiche of hip hop culture.

8. For historical accounts of white appropriations of black music in Britain, see Oliver (1990) and Fryer (1998).

REFERENCES

Back, L. (1996) *New Ethnicities and Urban Culture: Racisms and Multiculture in Young Lives*, UCL Press, London.

Banerji, S. and Baumann, G. (1990) Bhangra 1984–88: Fusion and Professionalisation in a Genre of South Asian Dance Music in P. Oliver (ed.) *Black Music in Britain: Essays on the Afro-Asian Contribution to Popular Music*, Open University Press, Milton Keynes.

Barthes, R. (1977) The Grain of the Voice in S. Frith and A. Goodwin (eds) (1990) *On Record: Rock, Pop and the Written Word*, Routledge, London.

Bayton, M. (1988) How Woman Become Rock Musicians in S. Frith and A. Goodwin (eds) (1990) *On Record: Rock, Pop and the Written Word*, Routledge, London.

Beadle, J.J. (1993) *Will Pop Eat Itself?: Pop Music in the Sound Bite Era*, Faber & Faber, London.

Bennett, A. (1988) The Frankfurt Rockmobil: A New Insight into the Significance of Music-Making for Young People, *Youth and Policy*, 60: 16–29.

Bjurström, E. (1997) The Struggle for Ethnicity: Swedish Youth Styles and the Construction of Ethnic Identities, *Young: Nordic Journal of Youth Research*, 5(3): 44–58.

Brewer, D.D. and Miller, M.L. (1990) Bombing and Burning: The Social Organization and Values of Hip Hop Graffiti Writers and Implications for Policy, *Deviant Behavior*, 11: 345–69.

Chambers, I. (1976) A Strategy for Living: Black Music and White Subcultures in S. Hall and T. Jefferson (eds) *Resistance Through Rituals: Youth Subcultures in Post-War Britain*, Hutchinson, London.

Chambers, I. (1992) Cities Without Maps in J. Bird, B. Curtis, T. Putnam, G. Robertson, and L. Tickner (eds) *Mapping the Futures: Local Cultures, Global Change*, Routledge, London.

Chaney, D. (1993) *Fictions of Collective Life: Public Drama in Late Modern Culture*, Routledge, London.

Chaney, D. (1996) *Lifestyles*, Routledge, London.

Cobley, P. and Osgerby. W. (1995) Peckham Clan Ain't Nothin' to Fuck With: Urban Rap Style in Britain' unpublished paper presented at the Youth 2000 conference, University of Teesside, Middlesborough.

Cohen, Sara (1991) *Rock Culture in Liverpool: Popular Music in the Making*, Clarendon Press, Oxford.

de Cologne, F. (1980) *Rock gegen Rechts: Beitrage zu einer Bewegung*, Weltkreis, Dortmund.

Condry, I. (1999) The Social Production of Difference: Imitation and Authenticity in Japanese Rap Music in H. Fehrenbach and U. Poiger (eds) *Transactions, Transgressions, Transformations American Culture in Western Europe and Japan*, Providence, RI, Berghan Books.

Decker, J.L. (1994) The State of Rap: Time and Place in Hip Hop Nationalism in A. Ross and T. Rose (eds) *Microphone Fiends: Youth Music and Youth Culture*, Routledge, London.

Denzin, N.K. (1969) Problems in Analyzing Elements of Mass Culture: Notes on the Popular Song and Other Artistic Productions, *American Journal of Sociology*, 75: 1035–38.

Deppe, J. (1997) *Oden: On the Run—Eine Jugend in der Graffiti-Szene*, Schwarzkopf & Schwarzkopf, Berlin.

Dyson, M.E. (1996) *Between God and Gangsta Rap: Bearing Witness to Black Culture*, Oxford University Press, New York.

Easton, P. (1989) The Rock Music Communit' in J. Riordan (ed.) *Soviet Youth Culture*, Indiana University Press, Bloomington and Indianapolis.

Epstein, J.S., Pratto, D.J. and Skipper Jr., J.K. (1990) Teenagers, Behavioral Problems, and Preferences for Heavy Metal and Rap Music: A Case Study of a Southern Middle School, *Deviant Behavior*, 11: 381–94.

Farin, K. and Seidel-Pielen, E. (1994) *Skinheads*, Verlag C.H. Beck, München.

Fekete, L. (1993) Inside Racist Europe in T. Bunyan (ed.) *Statewatching the New Europe: A Handbook on the European State*, Statewatch, London.

Filippa, M. (1986) Popular Song and Musical Cultures in D. Forgacs and R. Lumley (eds) *Italian Cultural Studies: An Introduction*, Oxford University Press, Oxford.

Flores, J. (1994) Puerto Rican and Proud, Boyee!: Rap Roots and Amnesia in A. Ross and T. Rose (eds) *Microphone Fiends: Youth Music and Youth Culture*, Routledge, London.

Foner, N. (1978) *Jamaica Farewell: Jamaican Migrants in London*, Routledge & Kegan Paul, London.

Gane, M. (ed.) (1993) *Baudrillard Live: Selected Interviews*, Routledge, London.

Gillett, C. (1983) *The Sound of the City: The Rise of Rock and Roll*, 2nd edn, Souvenir Press, London.

Gilroy, P. (1993) *The Black Atlantic: Modernity and Double Consciousness*, Verson, London.

Harpin, L. (1993) One Continent Under a Groove, *ID: The Europe Issue*, 16 May: 58–60.

Hebdige, D. (1976a) The Meaning of Mod in S. Hall and T. Jefferson (eds) *Resistance Through Rituals: Youth Subcultures in Post-War Britain*, Hutchinson, London.

Hebdige, D. (1976b) Reggae, Rastas and Rudies in S. Hall and T. Jefferson (eds) *Resistance Through Rituals: Youth Subcultures in Post-War Britain*, Hutchinson, London.

Hebdige, D. (1979) *Subculture: The Meaning of Style*, Routledge, London.

Hebdige, D. (1987) *Cut 'n' Mix: Culture, Identity and Caribbean Music*, Routledge, London.

Jones, S. (1988) *Black Culture, White Youth: The Reggae Tradition from JA to UK*, Macmillan, London.

Keyes, C.L. (1991) Rappin' to the Beat: Rap Music as Street Culture Among African Americans, Doctoral thesis published by University Microfilms International, Ann Arbor, Michigan.

Lachmann, R. (1988) Graffiti as Career and Ideology, *American Journal of Sociology*, 94(2): 229–50.

Laing, D. (1971) Listen to Me in S. Frith and A. Goodwin (eds) (1990) *On Record: Rock, Pop and the Written Word*, Routledge, London.

Light, A. (1992) About a Salary or Reality?: Rap's Recurrent Conflict in A. DeCurtis (ed.) *Present Tense: Rock and Roll and Culture*, Duke University Press, London.

Lipsitz, G. (1994) *Dangerous Crossroads: Popular Music, Postmodernism and the Poetics of Place*, Verso, London.

Lull, J. (1995) *Media, Communication, Culture: A Global Approach*, Polity Press, Cambridge.

Marks, A. (1990) Young, Gifted and Black: Afro-American and Afro-Caribbean Music in Britain 1963–88 in P. Oliver (ed.) *Black Music in Britain: Essays on the Afro-Asian Contribution to Popular Music*, Open University Press, Milton Keynes.

Maxwell, I. (with Bambrick, N.) (1994) Discourses of Culture and Nationalism in Contemporary Sydney Hip Hop, *Perfect Beat*, 2(1): 1–19.

Mayer, H.C. (1969) *German Recovery and the Marshall Plan, 1948–1952*, Edition Atlantic Forum, New York.

Meinig, U. (1993) Von "e-Moll" und "langen Fingernägeln"—eine Mädchen-Rockband in Hamburg-Eidel-stadt in W. Hering, B. Hill, and G. Pleiner (eds) *Prasixhandbuch Rockmusik in der Jugendarbeit*, Leske & Budrich, Opladen.

Milestone, K. (1997) Love Factory: The Sites, Practices and Media Relationships of Northern Soul in S. Redhead, D. Wynne and J. O'Connor (eds), *The Clubcultures Reader: Readings in Popular Cultural Studies*, Blackwell, Oxford.

Mitchell, T. (1996) *Popular Music and Local Identity: Rock, Pop and Rap in Europe and Oceania*, Leicester University Press, London.

Pilkington, H. (1994) *Russia's Youth and its Culture: A Nation's Constructors and Constructed*, Routledge, London.

Pohl, M. (1993) Mädchen—und Frauenrockbands in der Jugendarbeit in W. Hering, B. Hill, and G. Pleiner (eds) *Praxishandbuch Rockmusik in der Jugendarbeit*, Leske & Budrich, Opladen.

Potter, R. (1995) *Spectacular Vernaculars: Hip hop and the Politics of Postmodernism*, State University of New York Press, New York.

Ritzer, G. (1993) *The McDonaldization of Society: An Investigation into the Changing Character of Contemporary Social Life*, Pine Forge Press, London.

Robertson, R. (1995) Glocalization: Time-Space and Momogeneity-Heterogeneity in M. Featherstone, S. Lash and R. Robertson (eds) *Global Modernities*, Sage, London.

Rose, T. (1994) *Black Noise: Rap Music and Black Culture in Contemporary America*, Wesleyan University Press, London.

Sexton, A. (1995) Don't Believe the Hype: Why Isn't Hip-Hop Criticism Better? in A. Sexton (ed.) *Rap on Rap: Straight-Up Talk on Hip-Hop Culture*, Delta, New York.

Shank, B. (1994) *Dissonant Idententies: The Rock 'n' Roll Scene in Austin, Texas*, Wesleyan University Press, London.

Sharma, A. (1996) Sounds Oriental: The (Im)possibility of Theorizing Asian Music Cultures in S. Sharma, J. Hutnyk and A. Sharma (eds) *Dis-Orienting Rhythms: The Politics of the New Asian Dance Music*, Zed Books, London.

Smart, B. (1993) Europe/America: Baudrillard's Fatal Comparison in C. Rojek and B.S. Turner (eds) *Forget Baudrillard?*, Routledge, London.

Wallis, R. and Malm, K. (1984) *Big Sounds from Small Peoples: The Music Industry in Small Countries*, Constable, London.

Thomas G. Schumacher

Chapter 15

"This Is a Sampling Sport"

Everyday life invents itself by poaching in countless ways on the property of others.

— de Certeau, 1984: xii

Introduction

Digital audio sampling poses several interesting challenges to existing intellectual property right laws, and by looking at the specific case of rap music, a form that is in many ways based on the opportunities presented by sampling technology, these confrontations are highlighted.[2] This article questions both the philosophical bases and common law decisions surrounding intellectual property through a critique of their understanding of individual authorship and creativity. Ultimately, copyright law is *property* law, and its foundation in notions of creativity and originality therefore have to be seen within the complex of capitalist social relations. Even so, because much of the discourse surrounding the question of copyright concerns itself with the creative process and the circulation of cultural products, it becomes necessary to address the ways in which sampling technology is able to highlight some of the contradictions in the foundational principles of jurisprudence. Sampling, in general and here in the particular case of rap music, forces us to reconceptualize these bases of copyright doctrine for both technological and cultural reasons—the former because digital reproduction accentuates existing understandings of "copying" and poses its own challenge to the ways in which we have to think about the process of production, the latter because rap highlights how different cultural forms and traditions are founded on different understandings of creativity and originality. Finally, because under capitalism the cultural form is necessarily the commodity form, because "the real creative subject within copyright law…is capital" (Bettig, 1992: 150), current intellectual property rights articulate the limits of the cultural raw materials available for musical production as well as defining the formal boundaries of acceptable end-products. Gaines (1991: 9) points out that this limitation is "self-correcting" through the "double movement of circulation and restriction." Copyright is enabling of certain forms of discourse while prohibiting others in the ideological balance of "free expression" and profitability. Therefore, copyright becomes an issue for discussions of so-called free expression. In order to enter the fray, it is necessary to look at existing definitions of copyright within legal discourse.

Copyright and the Structuring of Noise in Legal Discourse

The authority of the sovereign's law depends on the establishing of unambiguous proper meanings for words…. Such absolute meaning requires the possibility of absolute knowledge, of a logos in which meaning and word coalesce as law. The absolute political state is necessarily logocentric because it depends on law, which in turn depends on the univocal meaning of words,…a point at which knowledge and language attain an identity that can serve as an absolute authority.

— Ryan, 1982: 3

Music, the quintessential mass activity, like the crowd, is simultaneously a threat and a necessary source of legitimacy; trying to channel it is a risk that every system of power must run.

— Attali, 1985: 14

The copyright problems caused by digital audio sampling concern basically those inhering in the sound recording (McGraw, 1989). Copyright protection for music is divided between the underlying composition and the sounds "fixed in a tangible medium." The latter received protection only in 1971 as an amendment to the 1909 Copyright Act in an effort to control widespread record piracy, and are defined as:

> works that result from the fixation of a series of musical, spoken, or other sounds, but not including the sounds accompanying a motion picture or other audio visual work, regardless of the nature of the material objects, such as disks, tapes, or other phonorecords, in which they are embodied. (17 USC, s.101)

Under the 1976 Copyright Act, only those sounds which were "fixed" on or before 15 February 1972 are protected (17 USC, s.102(a)) and protection subsists only in "original works of authorship." Authorship is the capturing of sound in a tangible medium, not the production of those sounds. Importantly, most musicians or performers as well as engineers and producers contractually deliver the right of authorship to the record company (this is the "circle-p" copyright).[3] The originality required for copyright protection is *de minimis* and does not have to be novel, ingenuous or aesthetically meritorious (HR Rep. No. 94–1476, 94th Cong., 2d Sess. 1, 51 (1976); Fishman, 1989: 205). Originality means nothing more than a designation of origin with a particular author (*Burrow-Giles Lithographic Co. v. Sarony*, 111 US 53, 57–58 (1884)). As Gaines (1991: 63) has stated it, "all works originating from an individual are individual works of authorship." Hence, in order for a sample to be copyrightable, it must be original. While simple sounds of a snare drum may not be protected,

> the "signature sample," an identifiable sound of an artist taken live or from a recording, which is then dropped into a musical composition, may possess the required degree of personality to warrant copyrightability. (McGraw, 1989:159)

Prevost (1987: 8) has stated that "it is difficult to imagine a musical performance that does not have originality sufficient to qualify for copyright."[4]

After proving copyrightability and the ownership of copyright, the plaintiff must show that there was an actual "recapture of original sounds" (Prevost, 1987: 9) and that the taking was more than *de minimis*, i.e., that it was substantially similar. In the case of sampling, however, the taking is exactly similar (an exact reproduction), so the question becomes one of determining if the taking was significant. This leads back to the protectability of sounds—if a sound is copyrightable, it will probably be substantial enough to be infringed. Thom has rather crassly suggested that the extent of the taking be judged by looking at "the artistic and *financial* importance of the portion(s) copied or appropriated" (Thorn, 1988: 324; emphasis added). In any event, "the question turns on whether the similarity relates to a substantial portion of the plaintiff's work, not whether the material constitutes a substantial portion of the defendant's work" (Mc-Graw, 1989: 164).

With these foundational points of law in mind, the three extant U.S. court decisions on sampling and copyright provide another segue into legal doctrine. The first case to be decided on the subject of sampling and copyright was *Acuff-Rose Music Inc. v. Campbell* (754 F.Supp. 1150 (MD Tenn. 1991)) in which the holders of the copyright of Roy Orbison's "Oh, Pretty Woman" enjoined Luther Campbell of the rap group 2 Live Crew for their use of a sample in the song "Pretty Woman" from the album *As Clean As They Wanna Be*. Acuff-Rose Music denied 2 Live Crew's management the license request to parody the Orbison song and sued Luther Campbell and 2 Live Crew's record company, Luke Skyywalker Records, after the release of "Pretty Woman" for copyright infringement and two tort claims of interference with business relations and prospective business advantage (under Tennessee state law), in spite of the fact that the album acknowledged Orbison and Dees (the co-writer) and Acuff-Rose as holding rights to the song. The defendants argued that their use of "Oh, Pretty Woman" was a parody and was therefore protected as fair use under 17 USC, s.107 of the Copyright Act (754 F.Supp. at 1152). While the tort claims are less important for this article's purposes, the claim of fair use as a defense in sampling cases is an important one. The statutory law of copyright in s.107 suggests that the courts consider four factors in determining a fair use defense:

> *The purpose and character of the use, including whether such a use is of a commercial nature or is for non-profit educational purposes;*
>
> *The nature of the copyrighted work;*
>
> *The amount and substantiality of the portion used in relation to the copyrighted work as a whole; and*
>
> *The effect of the use upon the potential market for or value of the copyrighted work.*

The courts have indicated that these factors are minimally required but are not exclusive in determining fair use (see *Harper & Row Publishers, Inc. v. Nation Enterprises*, 471 US 539, 560).

In deciding the *Acuff-Rose* case, the court considered each of these points in turn. First, Congress listed parody as one of the purposes of fair use which might be granted and common law has traditionally allowed this. Because 2 Live Crew's record was sold for profit, this is an important point. However, a finding of parody is not a presumptive finding of fair use; therefore, the other factors have to be weighed as well (745 F.Supp. at 1115, quoting *Fisher v. Dees*, 794, F.2d 432, 435 (9th Cir. 1986)). The second factor in fair use determines whether the copyrighted work (not the subsequent work) is "creative, imaginative, and original,...and whether it represented a substantial investment of time and labor made in anticipation of financial return" (quoting MCA, *Inc. v. Wilson*, 677 F.2d 180, 182). The original can be (must be?) for profit, the derivative work cannot. The court in *Acuff-Rose* decided that "since 'Oh, Pretty Woman' is a published work, with creative roots, this factor weighs in favor of the plaintiff" (754 F. Supp. at 1156). In other words, it is impossible to infringe on a work which is not original itself. Third, the courts addressed the question of the substantiality and amount of quotation. While the 2 Live Crew song was a substantial use, the court maintained that "the question about substantial similarity cannot be divorced from the purpose for which the defendant's work will be used" (754 F.Supp. at 1156). Because the defendant's work was a parody, the court maintained that a greater use was allowed. In *Elsmere Music v. National Broadcasting Co.* (623 F.2d 252 (1980)) the court held that "a parody frequently needs to be more than a fleeting evocation of the original in order to make its humorous point" (at 253). The courts maintained in *Acuff-Rose* that 2 Live Crew's parody did not invoke too much of the original. Lastly, the court held that the defendant's work would not have a detrimental effect on the market of the original, perceptively noting that "the intended audience for the two songs is entirely different" (754 F. Supp at 1158).

The decision in *Acuff-Rose* was appealed to the Sixth Circuit Court of Appeals and was reversed and remanded because it held that "Pretty Woman" was not a fair use (972 F.2d 1429 (6th Cir. 1992)). Even if "Pretty Woman" is a parody (which the Circuit Court had difficulty granting), its purpose as a for-profit song (i.e. its commodity status) outweighed its character as parodic (972 F.2d at 1437). The Appellate Court also held that "Oh, Pretty Woman" was a copyrightable work, but reversed the District Court's decision that the amount of the taking was not an infringement. Here, the Circuit Court's opinion becomes convoluted as they argue that "near verbatim taking of the music and meter of a copyrighted work without the creation of a parody is excessive taking" (at 1438) even though they admit that "we will assume...that 2 Live Crew's song is a parody" (at 1435). The court then held, following *Sony Corp. of America v. Universal City Studios, Inc* (464 US 417, 451), that it is not necessary to show any certain future harm and that a commercial use is presumptively unfair (972 F.2d at 1438). However, as Judge Nelson states in his dissenting opinion, the "Betamax" case cited above involved a copying which did not involve any "alteration of the copied material" (972 F.2d at 1443). A commercial use which transforms the original is different from one which does not. Overall, the result of this appeal has been that sampling has not been afforded a fair use defense on the grounds of parody (keeping in mind that each instance would still have to be decided on a case-by-case basis). Luther Campbell has had a writ of certiorari granted by the Supreme Court to finally decide whether or not 2 Live Crew's parody was a fair use under s.107 (123 L.Ed.2d 264), and the outcome of this case will be significant for future sampling parody claims.

Before the *Acuff-Rose* Circuit Court decision, a second case was handed down by the U.S. District Court in New York. In *Grand Upright Music v. Warner Bros Records* (780 F.Supp. 182 (SDNY 1991)), the court held that Biz Markie's sample of three words and portions of music from Gilbert O'Sullivan's "Alone Again (Naturally)" was an infringement of copyright. The case does not present the legal problems that arose in *Acuff-Rose* because quite simply the clearance was not obtained for the use of the samples and there was no formal fair use defense, and Warner Brothers was ordered to discontinue the sale of the Biz Markie recording. However, the defense's claim that "because others in the 'rap music' business are also engaged in illegal activity" they should be excused, although dismissed as "totally specious" by the judge, is an interesting comment on widespread musical practice. Perhaps buoyed by the preliminary success of 2 Live Crew at the District Court level, this line of argument suggests that the counsel may have been hoping for an even wider interpretation of originality for sampling. The ruling in favour of the plaintiffs, however, had wide effect and was reported extensively in the popular press (*New York Times*, 8 January 1992: C13, 21 April 1992: C13, for example).[5]

The most recent sampling case to be decided is *Boyd Jarvis v. A&M Records et al.* (1993 US Dist. LEXIS 10062, filed 27 April 1993; 827 F.Supp. 282). In this case, Robert Clivilles and David Cole used samples of Boyd Jarvis's song "The Music's Got Me" in their "Get Dumb! (Free Your Body)." Interestingly in this case, the court considered the specific issue of the digital audio sampling of uncopyrightable portions of an original. The court points out that "the simple fact of copying is not enough to prove an improper appropriation" (note 2 in text). Because in the case of sampling there is not a question that copying took place, the courts have to determine whether the sample is an unlawful one. Infringement is decided if "the value of a[n original] work may be substantially diminished even when only a part of it is copied, if the part that is copied is of great qualitative importance to the work as a whole"(*Werlin v. Reader's Digest Association*, 528 F.Supp. 451, 463 (SDNY 1981)) and, as in *Grand Upright*, if the defendants appropriated elements that are "original." While the court held that non-copyrightable elements of a song should be factored out in determining the extent of appropriation, it ruled that the series of "oohs" and "moves" and the phrase "free your body" were in fact copyrightable expressions. The court concluded that the fact this was a sampling case in which direct appropriation took place "says more than what can be captured in abstract legal analysis." The court ultimately agreed with the judge in *Grand Upright* when it found here that "there can be no more brazen stealing of music than digital sampling."

This sentiment is the same as that expressed in the vast majority of legal literature on the subject of audio sampling. The subject first emerged for legal scholars with the "problems" of mastermix recordings in which DJs would spin different records together over borrowed beat tracks (Prevost, 1987). Since then, more than a dozen law review articles have appeared addressing the challenges of sampling to copyright doctrine—even before the courts supplied a case on which to comment. While McGraw's (1989) study presents a fairly even-handed investigation of the relevant portion of the Copyright Act, most others have been less sympathetic to samplers.[6] A number of the articles worry about the future place of "live" musicians and the general impact of sampling on presumably more "authentic" musical creators. Wells (1989: 705) is characteristic in his quip that "ultimately, digital samplers are thieves" (see also McGiverin, 1987; Thorn, 1988; Newton, 1989; Moglovkin, 1990; Small, 1991). The other primary concerns of legal theorists has been the economics of sampling. Authors have drawn attention to the ways in which sampling is seen as a threat to the livelihood of record companies, and this is seen as a motivation to prosecute samplers (Giannini, 1990; Houle, 1992). Characteristic of this view is Fishman who argues that while the courts have successfully balanced free speech interests against those of profitability in the past, sampling upsets that balance and is therefore "a substantial economic threat" to musicians and the industry (Fishman, 1989: 223). The other concern is that sampling upsets the balance of copyright doctrine itself: "the law can ill afford to linger during the exponential growth of the legal complexities that encompass this technology" (Moglovkin, 1990: 174). Finally, Houle (1992: 902) has expressed the underlying belief of these authors when he states that only through prosecuting samplers "will the true creativity be spawned and true genius discovered."

What this article maintains is that legal doctrine, through its assigning of copyrights to corporate subjects and its definition of originality as origin in the individual author, is a contradictory discourse—one that allows for its own contradiction even as it seeks to secure unambiguous meanings. Even though, after *Bleistein v. Donaldson Lithographing Co.*, authorship can now be assigned to corporate entities instead of artists, and even though originality has come to mean origination (here, the "fixing" of sound), copyright is still influenced by the ideological construct of the "author" as a singular "origin" of artistic works (Jaszi, 1991).[7] As the three extant cases show, these contradictions have been consistently resolved in the interests of copyright holders. The significance of copyrights to further accumulation by record companies is being supported at the expense of more dialogic forms of cultural production. The technological practice of sampling and the specific case of rap music highlight these issues.

Looking for Benjamin's Orchid: Technology, Authenticity and Authorship in Popular Music

That is to say, in the studio the mechanical equipment has penetrated so deeply into reality that its pure aspect freed from the foreign substance of equipment is the result of a special procedure.... The equipment-free aspect of reality here has become the height of artifice; the sight of immediate reality has become an orchid in the land of technology.

— Benjamin, 1968: 233

Walter Benjamin early on argued that the technological reproduction of artistic works has an impact on them. His argument is that through the process of mechanical reproduction, the artifact loses its "aura" and "detaches the reproduced object from the domain of tradition." Instead of a single art object, there now exists "a plurality of copies" (Benjamin, 1968: 221). One effect of this is that the copy can then be used in different ways than the original could have been "and in permitting the reproduction to meet the beholder or listener in his own particular situation, it reactivates the object reproduced" (Benjamin, 1968: 221). This "shattering of tradition" takes the object of art and moves it from both the realm of cult-inspired awe and artistic authenticity to a new social function:

for the first time in world history, mechanical reproduction emancipates the work of art from its parasitical dependence on ritual. To an ever greater degree the work of art reproduced becomes the work of art designed for reproducibility.... But the instant the criterion of authenticity ceases to be applicable to artistic production, the total function of art is reversed. Instead of being based on ritual, it begins to be based on another practice—politics. (Benjamin, 1968: 224)

The work of art is now seen as having lost an aura of authenticity and as having gained a foundation in relations of power. However, the structures of intellectual property rights are founded on notions of the work of art that has its aura intact. Statute and common law definitions of originality and authenticity still presume that the aura of the author remains intact after the processes of technological mediation. In order to understand Benjamin's point about artifice and reality in technologized art, it becomes necessary to look at the practices of musical production.

As Steve Jones has pointed out, the different technical apparatuses like sampling that are available and are used in the making of popular music are an important part of that process and need to be part of an understanding of musical production:

The effects those [sonic and compositional] limitations [of equipment used for the fixation of sound] have on the composition and realization...of music play a critical role in the production of popular music. Therefore, it is at the level of composition and realization that one should begin to analyze the relationship of technology and popular music, for it is at that level that popular music is formed. (Jones, 1993: 7)

However, the relationship between technology and music is not altogether obvious: for one thing, the precise moment of realization becomes less clear (Frith, 1987a: 65). Clearly, no recorded music is simply the recording of a live event—even "live" recordings are the product of mixing and post-production work. The very uncertainty of the precise musical moment is a product of the ideological mystification of the production process that conceals the constructedness of musical sound. As Doane explains in the context of recorded sound in film,

> the rhetoric of sound is the result of a technique whose ideological aim is to conceal the tremendous amount of work necessary to convey an effect of spontaneity and naturalness. What is repressed in this operation is the sound which would signal the existence of the apparatus. (Doane, 1980: 55)

The arrival of the apparatus in the form of sampling is a reminder that there is more to a recording than simply the virtuosity of the performers.[8]

There is a need to reconceptualize the musical process to include an understanding that technological knowledge, not just knowledge of particular instruments, is now an integral part of the process of popular music production (Jones, 1993). The sounds that we think of as original or authentic are themselves the product of the production process. As Tankel (1990) has shown, the process of remixing is a recoding of the musical text and engineers are as much a part of the recorded sound as musicians. One engineer put it this way:

> I don't know if you've ever tried to make a sample, but making one is a real pain in the ass. Everybody thinks, oh, sample, oh, I just play a note and that's it. It's a lot harder than that, because of the vagaries of the machine once you get it in and once you get it out. (Jones, 1993: 108)

This engineer goes on to explain the different procedures for refining the sample in order to put it into a usable form and points out "it's just not as easy as it *sounds*" (Jones, 1993: 109; emphasis added). Durant (1990) points out that sampling has created a new technological literacy that is necessary for modern musical production. Indeed, Porcello (1991) notes that engineers are unemployable if they do not know how to sample effectively.[9]

The production of music is not something that is tainted by the effects of technology; rather, music is constituted by technology through and through. As Frith explains,

> The "industrialization of music" can't be understood as something that happens *to* music but describes a process in which music itself is made—a process, that is, which fuses (and confuses) capital, technical, and musical arguments. (Frith, 1987b: 54)

All of popular music is the product of technology, and it becomes important to look at those "relations [which] exist between different technical and practical elements at play in any changing context of musical production" (Durant, 1990: 180). By looking at the process of production, we see that technologized music is the product of not just auteur-musicians but of the work of musicians and engineers alike. We cannot go back to some pre-industrial form of music. The "demand for authenticity in popular music is a false request, because such a demand is made with the assumption that music exists in some pure form"

(Jones, 1993:208). The practices of making music cannot be usefully detached from the conditions of their existence; therefore, in the age of digital reproduction, the search for a singular musical moment is a search in vain. Gaines points out that,

> while sound recording is certainly mechanical or electronic "copying," it produces neither a "copy" of the acoustic event nor a "copy" of the notational system in which the underlying composition has been encoded. It is more likely a "sample" of an acoustic event stored in another form such as paper roll, magnetic tape, pressed vinyl, or compact disc. (Gaines, 1991:131)

As with Benjamin's orchid, popular music is now so imbricated with technology that its "reality" can no longer be assigned to a pre-industrial authenticity but is instead constituted by its technical processes.[10]

Frith and Durant's understanding above of the connection between popular music and technology (i.e. that music is part of a productive process that necessarily involves the engagement of the productive apparatus) forces us to interrogate the role of the author or musician in the productive process itself. Traditional aesthetics and copyright philosophy depend on a strong notion of authorship and are situated within humanist ideologies of the creative *artiste*. However, after the industrialization of art, as described by Benjamin for cinema, the role of the Producer has changed. As Lyotard has argued,

> that the mechanical and the industrial should appear as substitutes for hand and craft was not in itself a disaster—except if one believes that art is in its essence the expression of an individuality of genius assisted by an elite craftsmanship. (Lyotard, 1984: 74)

That is, the end of the dominance of the aura of a work of art is only a problem insofar as this end further discredits the myth of the individual creator. In the case of sampling technology in musical production, the abolition of the aura signals the insertion of different subjects into the creative process, namely those of DJs, engineers and producers.

Foucault (1977) provides some interesting comments on the social function of the author. He points out that the role of the name of an author is not simply that of the proper name, which distinguishes between different subjects; rather the name of an author serves to distinguish between different texts, separating them and marking them distinct from others. Moreover, not all texts (e.g., bureaucratic forms, receipts, now the post-it note) necessarily require (or are granted) authorship. For Foucault, the question becomes one of understanding not only which texts are designated as authored, but also analyzing the conditions for authorial discourse. Thus Foucault says that "the function of an author is to characterize the existence, circulation, and operation of certain discourses within society" (Foucault, 1977: 124). The designation of authorship for a text signifies for that text a certain social significance that the anonymous text does not possess. The author then becomes a function of social discourses.

According to Foucault, there are four characteristics of the "author-function" in discourse. One is that it is not universal or constant, that is, certain forms of discourse do not always require authorship for validity (e.g., the use of authorship in scientific discourse over time has generally changed to one of anonymity). Second, the attribution of authorship is not automatic or "spontaneous" simply by connecting individuals and discourses. Instead, it is a result of a "complex operation whose purpose is to construct the rational entity we call an author" (Foucault, 1977: 127). The characteristics that we localize as belonging to an author of a particular type are for Foucault projections onto that individual of our interaction with the text. Thus the qualities that we would characterize as constituting the author of a musical piece are those that we choose to locate in the individual to whom authorship is attributed. Combined with the first characteristic, it is important to remember that these characteristics are not transhistorical or culturally universal but rather are transformed over time. The next characteristic of the author-function concerns the presence of the author in the text. In discourses that do not have authorship, the use of personal pronouns points directly towards the writer; however, in authored texts, the reference to "I" is never exact and therefore signals a generality of the text which the reader encounters. Thus the author-function in an authored text does not refer to an actual individual but to a subject position that remains open to the reader.

Most importantly for purposes of understanding authorship and copyright, however, is the characteristic of authored discourse that Foucault (1977: 130) says "is tied to the legal and institutional systems that circumscribe, determine, and articulate the realm of discourses." Authored texts are always a form of property—they are "objects of appropriation" (Foucault, 1977:124). Foucault notes that this author-function has been linked to transgression, first by assigning authorship to discourses that were to be punished—misappropriation. He goes on to say that

it was a gesture charged with risks long before it became a possession caught in a circuit of property values. But it was at the moment when a system of ownership and strict copyright rules were established...that the transgressive properties always intrinsic to the act of writing became the forceful imperative of writing. (Foucault, 1977:125)

Now writing, in general, again becomes a dangerous activity through conferring "the benefits of property" (Foucault, 1977: 125). What this analysis of authorship provides for a current understanding of copyright law is in its approach to the category of author as historically situated and constructed. Moreover, it is the granting of copyright to authors that situates them in the dynamics of power. From Benjamin we see that the work in the age of reproduction is no longer authentic, but it is firmly situated in politics. This politics is the politics of authorship, and from Foucault we see that not every discourse stands equal before the law.

Sampled recordings are not granted an author-function the way that supposedly individually created recordings are. Given that the myth of the pre-technological musician is abolished in the age of electronic reproduction, the specific practices of sampling become transgressive.[11] Porcello notes also the problems of authorship and copyright when he states that

after Foucault, it is hard to imagine how any particular instance of interaction with a text does not itself create a new text (thus satisfying the conditions of the older aesthetic anyway), which is why the author is a spurious category for Foucault, and why the sampler's physical and functioning fusing of documentary and reproductive capabilities—which serves to throw the authorial producer of sound into a binary electronic limbo—has so thoroughly frustrated a legal model of copyright which is based on assumptions that one can clearly separate producers from consumers and texts from their readings. (Porcello, 1991: 77)

The DJ's interaction with the prerecorded sound of another unsettles the idea of the audio text as sealed and final to be consumed in preordained ways. The text is now part of the aural collage (Korn, 1992) as it becomes temporarily fixed to other samples in the record.

Transgression on the Turntable: Rap and Intertextuality

I found this mineral that I call a beat

I paid zero

I packed my load 'cause it's better than gold

People don't ask the price, but its sold

They say that I sample, but they should

Sample this, my pit bull

We ain't goin' for this

They said that I stole this

Can I get a witness?

— Public Enemy, "Caught, Can We Get A Witness?"

The Foucauldian analysis of authorship reveals the intertextuality of the text, i.e., the connections between texts that are (arbitrarily) separated from one another by the name of the author. As Gaines (1991: 77) has stated, "the very concept of authorship overrides the generic and conventional indebtedness that would mark words as the product not so much of individuals as of societies." The text is historically suited within aesthetic traditions which contextualize cultural production. Rap music can be seen as part of a tradition of Black culture that Gates (1988) has drawn attention o as being double-voiced and which he calls "Signifyin(g)." Signifyin(g) is the practice of formal revision and intertextual relation between texts and refers to "the manner in which texts seem concerned to address their antecedents. Repetition, with a signal difference, is fundamental to the nature of Signifyin(g)" (Gates, 1988: 51). Meaning is created in the tradition of Signifyin(g) through the formal revision of patterns of representation, i.e., through the inflection of previous texts in new texts. Further, Gates states that

> Signifyin(g), in other words, is the figurative difference between the literal and the metaphorical, between surface and latent meaning.... Signifyin(g) presupposes an "encoded" intention to say one thing but to mean quite another. (Gates, 1988: 82)

That is to say, meaning operates at several levels and does not lend itself to surface-level decodings. Signifyin(g) is a form of Black discourse, one that significantly relies on the intertextual referencing of previous texts in its making of meaning.[12] Rap's "double-voiced discourse" (Stephens, 1991) is premised on the practices of intertextuality such that the rap song (through both aural and verbal cues) contains within it the inflected "voice" of its antecedent "other" (Bakhtin, 1981; Volo_inov, 1973).[13]

The case of rap also highlights the ways in which notions of authorship and originality do not necessarily apply across forms and cultural traditions—not because of any inherent worth or quality of different musics, but because different musical practices defy the universals of legal discourse. Frith (1987a: 63) points out that "copyright law defines music in terms of nineteenth-century Western conventions and is not well suited to the protection of Afro-american musicians' improvisational art." The formal practices of Signifyin(g) in rap music defy traditional definitions of authorship because they are ultimately premised on referencing the other and by explicitly relying on previous utterances.

The specific case of rap music challenges both the accepted understandings of musical practice and the dominant definitions of pop form, both of which are situated within capitalist social relations. Gaines's analysis presents the development of technological means for capturing sound—for giving sound its materiality—as one way in which sound has been able to become copyrightable, hence its status as a "protected property-appendage" (Gaines, 1991: 119). Sampling is a way of appropriating this property, of subverting the proprietary status of sound and allows for a new kind of poaching on the aural commons. Toop notes that scratching and sampling have "led to creative pillage on a grand scale and [have] caused a crisis for pre-computer-age concepts of artistic property" (Frith, 1986: 276). By selecting recorded sounds and reusing them in new recordings, rap music offers its critique of the ownership of sound. Porcello (1991: 82) argues that "rap musicians have come to use the sampler in an oppositional manner which contests capitalist notions of public and private property by employing previously tabooed modes of citation." It is rap's very flaunting of its intertextuality that poses the challenge to copyright law. Porcello continues:

> Rap musicians may be engaging in opposition at the level of praxis, but there is an ideological war occurring over the sign as well. The connotative meanings behind each term may be read as attempts to define appropriate sampling practice, at a discursive level, within both industry structures and pop aesthetics. (Porcello, 1991: 84, n.5)

As the DJ samples, there is a simultaneous critique of the ownership of sound and "Rockist"[14] aesthetics that remain tied to the romantic ideals of the individual performer. Rap forces an expansion of these definitions of musicality. Its meaning-making practices that rely on intertextual referencing via the sample demonstrate the different ways in which the struggle over originality is waged in divergent musical traditions. Because rap music and the practice of sampling change the notion of origin (the basis of copyright) to one of origins, it becomes transgressive in the Foucauldian sense and an infringement of copyright law in the eyes of the courts.

Intellectual Property Is Theft: Copyright and "Free Speech"

> In society, however, the producer's relation to the project, once the latter is finished, is an external one, and its return to the subject depends on his [sic] relations to other individuals. He does not come into possession of it directly. Nor is its immediate appropriation his purpose when he produces in society. Distribution steps between the producers and the products, hence between production and consumption, to determine in accordance with social laws what the producer's share will be in the world of products.
>
> — Marx, 1973: 94

Copyright is a political and economic not a moral matter.

— Frith, 1987a: 73

As Marx states here, the relationship between a musician and her or his musical product is not a natural one but is determined by social relations. The first step towards a critical understanding of copyright is to acknowledge that "copyright law is not a statement of ethical principle but a device to sustain a *market* in ideas" (Frith, 1988: 123). As Bettig (1992) has shown, the development of copyright philosophy has been more to secure the rights of capital in the sphere of cultural production. In the decisions that have come down on digital audio sampling, the courts have ruled consistently in favor of the owners of intellectual property, thereby reinscribing the relation of exteriority between producers and capital and securing the rights of the corporate legal subject over the concerns of cultural expression. Bettig (1992: 152) comments that "intellectual property rights continue to be utilized to gain or maintain market advantages by an increasingly oligopolistic and multinational culture industry." It is this development that has concerned many observers.

Rosemary Coombe has shown how the organization of intellectual property law (and its interpretation in the courts) is a limiting force on the free expression of ideas.[15] She echoes Frith when she points out that copyright and intellectual property in general functions solely to secure the market values of cultural artefacts.[16] Ultimately, however, this function limits the possible forms of expression. While certain signs retain cultural meanings even after (or in spite of the fact that) they are owned as intellectual property, the law prevents the free circulation of those signs. Coombe charges that

> by objectifying and reifying cultural forms—freezing the connotations of signs and symbols and fencing off fields of cultural meaning with "no trespassing" signs—intellectual property laws may enable certain forms of political practice and constrain others. (Coombe, 1991: 1866)

This brings us back to Gaines's point about the double movement of circulation and restriction in the law. While allowing certain forms of cultural expression to exist, others are restricted. As Coombe's study of trademark shows, the determination of this process is not innocent:

> the more powerful the corporate actor in our commercial culture, the more successfully it may immunize itself against oppositional (or ironic or simply mocking) cultural strategies to "recode" those signifiers that most evocatively embody its presence in postmodernity. (Coombe, 1991: 1874)

In other words, capital is able to control the patterns of signification that are most suited to its needs. While it is easy at this point to lapse into an instrumentalist or reductive argument about base and superstructure, even a careful analysis reveals that the political and economic structures are in place which facilitate the interests of capital. Durant gloomily suggests that if the issues of copyright are not resolved favorably, then the production knowledges involved in sampling will be "largely *cut off from* the possibility of responding to developments in musical culture expressed in the form of quotation or imitation" (Durant, 1990: 195). This appears to be true.

However, an analysis of sampling also draws our attention to other issues of critical importance. Digital technology is:

disrupting the implicit equation of artists' "ownership" of their creative work and companies' ownership of the resulting commodities—the latter is being defended by reference to the former. (Frith, 1986:276)

As I have shown in this article, sampling technology challenges the concept of the singular artist as the only embodied voice in the text. The ways in which copyright law understands the creative process and its assigning of property on that basis is confronted by the intertextual artifact. Jaszi points to this as a central contradiction in copyright doctrine when he states that

the overall incoherence of the law's account of "authorship" may be best understood as reflecting a continuing struggle between the economic forces that (at least in the abstract) would be best served by the further depersonalization of creative endeavor and the ideological persistence of an increasingly inefficient version of individualism. (Jaszi, 1991: 501–2)

It is not altogether clear that the interests of the record companies would not be served by the widespread use of samplers, given their status as commodities whose profits are generated for these corporations (McGiverin, 1987: 1730); the struggle over appropriate sampling practices in rap and other dance-based forms is currently seeking to resolve this contradiction in the dance halls over the court rooms.

Gaines points out that sometimes the very ways in which capital seeks to realize its accumulation may actually speed up the "production of a common culture, a culture which can be inflected oppositionally" (Gaines, 1991:228). As the culture industries seek the widest possible circulation of their products, the meanings of those products then gain such a purchase that they become part of the public domain: "what the proprietors of popular signs will always come up against is the predictable and desired result of their own popularity—imitation, appropriation, re-articulation" (Gaines, 1991: 232). The litigation surrounding sampling has been an effort to prevent just this. Record companies, as owners of the copyrights to the recorded sounds, have tried to take back what have become widely popular tracks from the DJs and engineers who are using them in new mixes.

Collins and Skover (1993) present a "cultural" analysis of free expression that they call "pissing in the snow." They suggest that actual speech practices (not idealized ones from legal theory) assume a Carnivalesque quality in that they tend not to abide by existing rules or laws. In the Carnival of popular culture, speech is directed more by the demands of listeners than by a fear of infringement:

The "anarchistic" quality of the Carnival is fundamentally at war with the notion of a government of laws. The very character of the Carnival is to push all boundaries, including the fixed lines of law. (Collins and Skover, 1993: 802).

The other thing that this article has tried to show, however, is that the Carnival is also often at odds with the very medium of its circulation—the market. This article has advocated (at least implicitly) the freedom of unauthorized sampling, much in the spirit of the Carnival that respects no boundaries. What it has also shown is that "what cannot be tolerated by the gatekeepers of the Carnival, however, is dissent which poses a clear and present danger to the amusement culture and its economy" (Collins and Skover, 1993: 802).

NOTES

1. Public Enemy, "Caught, Can We Get a Witness" (*It Takes a Nation of Millions to Hold Us Back*, Def Jam Records, 1988).

2. I would like to thank Priyadarshini Jaikumar-Mahey and Joseph Foley for their comments on an earlier version of this paper.

3. The ownership of the copyright of a sound recording grants three rights:

   to reproduce the copyrighted work in copies or phonorecords (the right to duplicate the sound recording in a fixed form that directly or indirectly recaptures the actual sounds fixed in the recording);

   to prepare derivative works based on the copyrighted work (the right to create a derivative work in which the actual sounds fixed in the sound recording are rearranged, remixed, or otherwise altered insequence or quality); and

   to distribute copies or phonorecords of the work to the public by sale or other transfer of ownership, or by rental, lease, or lending. (17 USC ss. 106 and 114)

   This excludes the right to control public performance that is attached to the copyright of the underlying composition (and hence why it is ASCAP and BMI which are involved in litigation in public performance cases, not the record companies; see Morgan, 1980).

4. As Frith (1987a: 64) points out, "originality, in short, can be difficult to define in a business in which similarity (the hit formula) is at a premium." That is, record companies do not have an interest in a record being so "original" that it does not attract a wide audience! The avant-garde, while "original" by romantic definitions, has not always proved commercially viable.

5. Indeed, the success of Grand Upright Music spurred on other suits to recover from unauthorized samples. In a significant case, Aaron Fuchs of Tuff City Records tried to sue Sony and Def Jam Records for the unauthorized use of drum beats from a song by the Honeydrippers. This case, although it was settled out of court, is significant because most drum beat samples are not cleared. Should this decision have come down in favour of Fuchs, rap music would have become prohibitively expensive because it would have required the clearance of all samples used, no matter how small (see *Billboard*, 11 January 1992: 71, 23 May 1992:4, 30 May 1992: 8, 6 June 1992:6).

6. For a sympathetic reading of sampling and copyright, see Marcus (1991) who suggests a licensing scheme to alleviate the problem; Hempel (1992) who argues that being sampled does not necessarily deprive the original author the rights of copyright; Korn (1992) who advocates a fair use defense for samples as parodies of pre-existing texts; and Brown (1992) who suggests amending the Copyright Act to allow for short samples.

7. Jaszi (1991:459) argues that:

   Legal scholars' failure to theorize copyright relates to their tendency to mythologize "authorship," leading them to fail (or refuse) to recognize the foundational concept for what it is—a culturally, politically, economically, and socially constructed category rather than a real or natural one.

8. Some critics of sampling maintain that the sampler is still invisible. Small (1991: 108) claims that "the practice of digital sampling is not common knowledge to the untutored public at this time" and therefore is guilty of unfair competition by confusion of origin. On the other hand, Goodwin (1990: 263) maintains that pop fans "have grown used to connecting *machines* and *funkiness*" suggesting that their presence is recognized by audience members. Ultimately, listeners' perceptions remain an empirical question, but the theoretical point that sampling practice challenges traditional understandings of the productive process still obtains.

9. It is important to remember the distinction between the "threat" of "piracy" of recordings and the practice of sampling. As Jones (1993:117) points out, "even though it appears that sampling allows artists to reclaim or recontextualize sound, it must be remembered that sampling is a *production* method and not a means of distribution" and is therefore distinct from the challenge of "piracy" to corporate profits. Sampling's recording is quite distinct from the practices of illegal record pressing (the problem which brought the 1971 amendment to the 1909 Copyright Act) and home-taping—the industry's menace in the 1980s. This point is missed sorely by Thorn (1988) who confuses the two in making points of law.

10. Andrew Goodwin's (1990:259) assertion that digital reproduction allows a "mass production of the aura" in which "*everyone* may purchase an 'original' " seems to me to miss the point. Benjamin's argument is that the performer's presence is lost in technological mediation; even under conditions where the studio performance is reproduced "exactly" using digital technology (disregarding contentions about the "warmth" of analogue recordings), the performer is still absent. It may be that the affect of popular music no longer relies exclusively on the presence of the author, as in the ways in which DJ-based musical cultures upset the meaning of "live" performances.

11. It is important to remember that copyright needs an "author-function" but not necessarily an "author." Gaines points this out when she states that:

> we should not be surprised that Anglo-American intellectual property law is formally unaccommodating to the human subject bearing natural rights, because copyright doctrine is nothing more or less than a right to prohibit copying by others. Actual authors, in other words, are irrelevant to the operation of a copyright system. (Gaines, 1991: 64)

It is the record companies as rights-holders who are enjoining samplers, not necessarily individual author-subjects. This is one of the fundamental contradictions in legal theory: its reliance on the myth of the original, individual author coupled with the abandonment of the author-subject for the corporate rights-holding-subject.

12. Importantly, Gates does not maintain that the tradition of signifyin(g) is metaphysically connected to conditions of race, nor is it part of an essential nature outside of history. Instead, "blackness" for Gates (1988:121) means "the specific uses of literary language that are shared, repeated, critiqued, and revised."

13. For a descriptive presentation of the ways in which reggae DJs are also part of a multi-voiced Black discourse, see Hebdige (1987). A more analytical presentation of the position of reggae within Black diasporic culture is provided by Gilroy (1987).

14. Most criticism of popular music remains firmly tied to the aesthetics and affects of rock music—a form which is facilitated by copyright doctrine through its reliance on virtuosity and artistry, especially in the excesses of 1970s progressive rock and its aftermath. The implications of this are that different forms are judged by rock's presumed universal standards to be "less creative" as a new high culture/low culture divide is instituted between the more "serious" rock and pop (or other dance-based forms).

Bradby (1993:156) has recently pointed out how rock's ideology of virtuosity has not applied equally to men and women performers and has not allowed "women's performances to be 'authentic' in the ways that men's are." Moreover, she argues that modernist ideologies of the creative process "are kept alive especially by the 'expert' writing of the male rock press and among male groups and producers" (Bradby, 1993: 164). In this way, the discourse of authorship and originality can be seen as gendered.

15. Coombe points out that legal theory does not address the problem of how meanings are fixed and dialogue is prevented. Legal theorists she says,

> fail to examine the differential power that social agents have to make their meanings mean something and the material factors that constrain signification and its circulation in the late twentieth-century. Legal theory perhaps defines itself as theory by its loathing to address specific processes of hegemonic struggle or the political economies of communication in a late capitalist era. (Coombe, 1991: 1860).

16. See also Helfand (1992) who points to the convergence in court interpretations of the logics of copyright, trademark, and Lanham Act s. 43 (a) which, "led by a small handful of major character owners" (Helfand, 1992: 627), has had the effect of preventing fictional characters from falling into the public domain and therefore "unavailable for new expressive uses" (Helfand, 1992: 654).

REFERENCES

Attali, J. (1985) *Noise: The Political Economy of Music* (trans. by B. Massumi). Manchester: University of Manchester Press.

Bakhtin, M.M. (1981) in M. Holquist (ed.), *The Dialogic Imagination* (trans. by C. Emerson and M. Holquist). Austin: University of Texas Press.

Benjamin, W. (1968) "The Work of Art in the Age of Mechanical Reproduction," pp. 217–51 in H. Arendt (ed.), *Illuminations*. New York: Schocken.

Bettig, R. V. (1992) "Critical Perspectives on the History and Philosophy of Copyright," *Critical Studies in Mass Communication*, 9(2): 13–55.

Bradby, B. (1993) "Sampling Sexuality: Gender, Technology and the Body in Dance Music," *Popular Music*, 12(2): 155–76.

Brown, J.H. (1992)" 'They Don't Make Music the Way They Used To': The Legal Implications of 'Sampling' in Contemporary Music," *Wisconsin Law Review*, No. 6:1941–91.

Collins, R.K.L. and D.M. Skover (1993) "Pissing in the Snow: A Cultural Approach to the First Amendment," *Stanford Law Review*, 45(3): 783:80.

Coombe, R.J. (1991) "Objects of Property and Subjects of Politics: Intellectual Property Laws and Democratic Dialogue," *Texas Law Review*, 69(7): 1853–80.

de Certeau, M. (1984) *The Practice of Everyday Life* (trans, by S. Rendall). Berkeley, CA: University of California Press.

Doane, M.A. (1980) "Ideology and the Practice of Sound Editing and Mixing," pp. 47–56 in T. DeLaurentis and S. Heath (eds.), *The Cinematic Apparatus*. New York: St. Martin's.

Durant, A. (1990) "A New Day for Music? Digital Technologies in Contemporary Music-Making," pp. 175–96 in P. Hayward (ed.), *Culture, Technology, and Creativity in the Late Twentieth Century*. London: John Libbey.

Fishman, L.D. (1989) "Your Sound or Mine?: The Digital Sampling Dilemma," *St John's Journal of Legal Commentary*, 4(2): 205–23.

Foucault, M. (1977) "What Is an Author"," pp. 113–38 in D.F. Bouchard (ed. and trans.), *Language, Counter-memory, Practice*. Ithaca, NY: Cornell University Press.

Frith, S. (1986) "Art versus Technology: The Strange Case of Popular Music," *Media, Culture, and Society*, 8(3): 263–79.

Frith, S. (1987a) "Copyright and the Music Business," *Popular Music*, 7(1): 57–75.

Frith, S. (1987b) "The Industrialization of Popular Music," pp. 53–77 in J. Lull (ed.), *Popular Music and Communication*. Newbury Park, CA: Sage.

Frith, S. (1988) "Video Pop: Picking up the Pieces," pp. 88–130 in S. Frith (ed.), *Facing the Music*. New York: Pantheon.

Gaines, J.M. (1991) *Contested Culture: The Image, the Voice, and the Law*. Chapel Hill, NC: University of North Carolina Press.

Gates, H.L., Jr. (1988) *The Signifying Monkey: A Theory of African-American Literary Criticism*. New York:Oxford University Press.

Giannini, M. (1990) "The Substantiality Similarity Test and its Use in Determining Copyright Infringement Through Digital Sampling," *Rutgers Computer and Technology Law Journal*, 16(2): 509:30.

Gilroy, P. (1987) *There Ain't No Black in the Union Jack': The Cultural Politics of Race and Nation*. Chicago, IL: University of Chicago Press.

Goodwin, A. (1990) "Sample and Hold: Pop Music in the Digital Age of Reproduction," pp. 258–73 in S. Frith and A. Goodwin (eds.), *On Record: Rock, Pop, and the Written Word*. New York: Pantheon.

Hebdige, D. (1987) *Cut 'n' Mix*. New York: Routledge.

Helfand, M.T. (1992) "When Mickey Mouse Is as Strong as Superman: The Convergence of Intellectual Property Laws to Protect Fictional Literary and Pictorial Characters," *Stanford Law Review*, 44(3): 623–74.

Hempel, S.C. (1992) "Are Samplers Getting a Bum Rap?: Copyright Infringement or Technological Creativity," *University of Illinois Law Review*, No. 2: 559–91.

Houle, J.R. (1992) "Digital Audio Sampling, Copyright Law and the American Music Industry: Piracy or Just a Bad 'Rap'?," *Loyola Law Review*, 37(4): 879–902.

Jaszi, P. (1991) "Toward a Theory of Copyright: The Metamorphoses of 'Authorship,' " *Duke Law Journal*, No.2: 455–502.

Jones, S. (1993) *Rock Formation: Music, Technology, and Mass Communication*. Newbury Park, CA: Sage.

Korn, A. (1992) "Renaming that Tune: Aural Collage, Parody and Fair Use," *Golden Gate University Law Review*, 22(3): 321–70.

Lyotard, J.-F. (1984) *The Postmodern Condition: A Report on Knowledge* (trans. by G. Bennington and B. Massumi).Minneapolis, MN: University of Minnesota Press.

McGiverin, B.J. (1987) "Digital Sound Sampling, Copyright and Publicity: Protecting Against the Electronic Appropriation of Sounds," *Columbia Law Review*, 87(8): 1723–45.

McGraw, M. (1989) "Sound Sampling Protection and Infringement in Today's Music Industry," *High Technology Law Review*, 4(1): 147–69.

Marcus, J. (1991) "Don't Stop that Funky Beat: The Essentiality of Digital Sampling to Rap Music," *Hastings Communications and Entertainment Law Journal*, 13(4): 767–90.

Marx, K. (1973) *Grundrisse* (trans. by M. Nicolaus). New York: Penguin.

Moglovkin, T.C. (1990) "Original Digital: No More Free Samples," *Southern California Law Review*, 64(1): 135–74.

Morgan, B. (1980) "Sound Recording Copyright Law—Its Application to the Performance of Records andTapes," *Cumberland Law Review*, 11(1): 447–63.

Newton, J.S. (1989) "Digital Sampling: The Copyright Considerations of a New Technological Use of Musical Performance," *Hastings Communications and Entertainment Law Journal*, 11 (4), 671–713.

Porcello, T. (1991) "The Ethics of Digital Audio-Sampling: Engineers Discourse," *Popular Music*, 10(1): 69–84.

Prevost, J.V.A. (1987) "Copyright Problems in Mastermixes," *Communication and Law*, 9(4): 3–30.

Ryan, M. (1982) *Marxism and Deconstruction: A Critical Articulation*. Baltimore, MD: Johns Hopkins University Press.

Small, D. (1991) "To Catch a Thief: Unauthorized Digital Sampling of Copyrighted Musical Works," *Thurgood Marshall Law Review*, 17(1): 83–112.

Stephens, G. (1991) "Rap Music's Double-voiced Discourse: A Crossroads for Interracial Communication," *Journal of Communication Inquiry*, 15(2): 70–91.

Tankel, J.D. (1990) "The Practice of Recording Music: Remixing as Recording," *Journal of Communication*, 40(3): 34–46.

Thom, J.C. (1988) "Digital Sampling: Old-fashioned Piracy Dressed Up in Sleek New Technology," *Loyola Entertainment Law Journal*, 8(2): 297–336.

Volo_inov, V.N. (1973) *Marxism and the Philosophy of Language* (trans, by L. Matejka and I.R. Titunik). Cambridge, MA: Harvard University Press.

Wells, R.M. (1989) "You Can't Always Get What You Want But Digital Sampling Can Get You What You Need!," *Akron Law Review*, 22(4): 691–706.

Chapter 16

Civil Disobedience

Amaya: *Yeah, you hit the nail on the head. People have this perception "yeah, you know, I'm from Los Angeles, Hispanic, goatee, you know, typical stereotype Mexican cholo." I was brought up in that from Los Angeles, from Compton California. I saw that everywhere around. It's either gangs, drugs, prison, or death, you know? I chose arts and started going a completely opposite direction. Going to family's funerals, I learned at a young age, I don't want to end up like my uncle, banging for a neighborhood that I don't even own, because every time the sheriff or police come through, they have us sitting down taking our shoes off, stripping us, patting us down. They're the ones that control the neighborhoods. The gangs don't. I saw that at a young age, so I started pushing graffiti, you know? It's a difficult game, it's the streets. There's nothing fair in life, so we're constantly fighting the system as graffiti writers and still struggling to be accepted.*

Mook: *I see some heads nodding. Mattlox and KRS-One, you guys are nodding. Would you like to comment on your views on what's been said.*

KRS-One: *Yeah, graffiti writing in and of itself-let me comment on New York Graffiti. This is where I started in the early 1980s... This is when we had no money. I remember when BG-you were speaking about buying paint,*

Justus: *We used to rack 'em.*

KRS-One: *You know the deal. We used to rack paint - I'm sorry, for those of you who aren't bilingual, we used to steal paint. And we would go down to Canal Street in Manhattan, lower east side of Manhattan, and basically walk out of the store with 25 cans, and go to the train yards, put up our pieces on the train so that New York City could see that we exist. And this is the point I wanted to make - graffiti writing in the beginning was about existence. It was about "you're not hearing me. You're not seeing me. You're not speaking to me. You're actually trying to ignore me. So I'm going to make myself heard." And it starts with your name. There was a crew I used to be with called Out For Fame, OFF, Out For Fame crew. There's another called Down To Bomb. Bombing, tagging, burners, pieces. Tagging is considered vandalism, even by graffiti writers. Certain writers write sloppily. They're called "toys." Just because you tag don't make you a graf writer, make you an aerosol artist. You have to put pieces up, full murals, that tell stories about your neighborhood, about what you're going through in your life. This is an ancient practice that goes back to prehistoric times.*

And this is my last point about graffiti writing, is that graffiti writing answers the question that hip hop itself asks, and that question is "what does it mean to be human?" Not only does hip hop answer that question, but graffiti writing answers that question. And it answers it in this way: first, why is it important to even be a graffiti writer? Why is it even important? It's your self expression! If you can't express yourself in a society, you are oppressed. We were oppressed until we racked some paint, and put our names on the sides of trains and busses, which by the way Coca-Cola, McDonalds and others have now bit our style, and they use it in marketing, promotion, and all that. But that's my last point. What does it mean to be human? What does it actually mean to self-express? And graffiti writing is the story of people who beyond all odds be it even in the face of the most powerful government on earth, the American government, we said we don't care about all that, we're going to write on your property. I used to write on police cars.

Mook: *For those of you who were at the alley last night, there was one piece in particular that had a shout out on the upper right that said "for my unborn child."*

KRS-One: *Oooh.*

Mook: *Those kinds of profound, personal statements that I hope most of you got a chance to see last evening. Mattlox, did you have something you wanted to add?*

Mattlox: *For me, I'm not a graf writer, but I've hung out with most of - most of my friends are. And being from San Diego, California - that's where I was born and raised, I moved out here to Arizona about 8 years ago - seeing the struggle for them to try to exercise their craft and get their art out, while running from the police, it's crazy. I've been out, I've done the train yard run and I've had to be lookout and it's intense. You're looking out while your boy's trying to do a piece, and looking for the yard guy, looking for the police, and any slight thing you're ready to drop it and run, to try to put that piece up that runs on that train and that joy that artist gets. It's sad that even when you go through the proper channels to get the permits or to get the approvals from somebody to do it on a wall that the police will come by and "no, that's alright, you can't do it" and go over it, it's sad.*

Mook: *I should note that the [Graffiti Busters] several times tried to shut down the graffiti alley that you all saw last night. And, Michael, I believe they were minutes away from painting it over on a number of occasions. And -*

Amaya: *Yes.*

Mook: *And do you carry a permission slip?*

Amaya: *Yeah, I had to carry permission slips on that entire alley. I just caught the buff back there, the guys that paint over all graffiti, about to go over the stuff. And it was funny, he wasn't actually, he wasn't going to start painting the entire wall, but since he's an art critic and all he started painting over what he thought was random acts of vandalism and choosing what he wanted to paint over in my alley, and I told him pretty much "take a hike." You know, I went back at him like "yo, you're going to come here without permission from the owners painting over something I got permission for, you're the one that's a vandal. You're going to point fingers at me and tell me I'm a vandal? You're the vandal.*

[Applause]

Mook: *So, I'd like to shift the discussion at this point from graffiti to hip hop in general because, as the panel has already noted, graffiti is particularly problematic in terms of its status in America right now, but it's also part of hip hop culture. It has deep connections, many of the early DJs and b-boys and MCs were also writers. Many of these gentlemen here participated in more than one element of hip hop.*

Justus: *We all started writing graffiti. That's the foundation for hip hop was MCing, graffiti, and beat boxing, all the four elements. I was basically a vandal. I just tagged my name everywhere, anywhere. And that's how it starts. You get that bug, that spark and you're addicted. And then it just snowballs.*

Mook: *So Justus, comment on that a little bit more. How do you see Phoenix graffiti writing fitting into Phoenix hip hop? And a related question: what's the status of the Phoenix hip hop community? Is it big, is it small, is it active, is it growing? What's going on there?*

Justus: *The status of the Phoenix hip hop scene is it's about to explode. It's about to get national recognition. People like Rocadolla have national distribution and are getting recognized worldwide. With community acts like Dose's alley downtown, you cleaned up an alley that* was drug infested and homeless infested, and you got bums cleaning it for a burrito and a 40. It may not be much but it's food, and it's giving back and letting it grow, watching these young MCs come up and teaching kids how to rap and teaching kids how to write, and seeing the next generation come up. We started it because he started it and we followed in his footsteps because he is our teacher ultimately. But we want to teach these kids and keep passing that torch because it's just going to continue to grow.

Mook: House, I'd like to get your thoughts on where Phoenix hip hop is at.

House: It's good. When you're here in Arizona we tend to complain a lot about what we have here in our hometown. It's like anything else - we don't appreciate what we have right in front of us. And I've been able to travel all over the world and even anywhere in the States. When I go places, I miss Arizona. I go to other places, I check out their hip hop spots, check out their scene, and it's just not the same. So to me it's really good. It's still smaller than we'd like it to be. We need to work on longevity and not losing our kids. A lot of kids get into a lot of the elements and we lose them. There's not a lot of older guys in Arizona. But it's a good thing. It's small, but everybody knows each other. Everybody's kind of gone through their trials and tribulations with each other. Some of us up here have deeds in the past, but we've gotten past that and right now we're in a really good time. Right now we're getting more established and we're getting older heads that are there to school the kids hopefully produce more things to keep everybody going. I like hip hop in Arizona, and I know people don't think of Arizona in that way still, but it's come a long way. I remember going to my first b-boy event in LA b-boys were asking "where you from" and I was like "Arizona," and they were like "Arizona? You guys break there? There's people there?" I'm like "yeah." But now half the team that went on Team USA was from Arizona. So Arizona's still not getting the credit it needs to, but there's a lot of talent and it's a great place and people are going to recognize it.

Mook: Roca Dolla you've been in this from the beginning, What are your thoughts on where we're at?

Roca Dolla: I think I've talked to you about this on the phone a little bit, when in the 80s when I was one of the - in the 80s there was just a few groups that rapped, and I can name them on probably one hand. And now I look up and see five or ten thousand MCs at a time hitting me up on Myspace, we've progressed a long way. One of the things that I talk about, and I talked with you about it, is just the negative image that the fact that we didn't get Martin Luther King holiday. We were the last state to have the Martin Luther King holiday. I think that put a negative stigma on Arizona hip hop. We had Public Enemy speak about it, big acts like Steve Wonder that wouldn't come up here, Superbowls, we didn't get any Superbowls or all star events because we were the last state to have the Martin Luther King holiday because of different people who opposed that holiday. I think that set the entertainment period, not only hip hop but just entertainment period, set it back maybe about ten years. It took, it's taken us this long and back then you had to do it for the love. Now there's a lot of cats out here, a lot of talent. We're defining the sound of the Southwest because Arizona, hip hop in Arizona is bigger than Arizona. And I always equate it to the southwest. Southwest is a new east - hip hop started in the East coast, moved to West coast, and then it's jumped to the midwest, dirty south, and now we're building a new coast basically. Which includes Vegas and some of these other cities, and it's come a long way. We're actually defining the actual figurative coast, you could say. So it's slow motion, but it's definitely come a long way.

Mook: *KRS-One, I'd love to get your thoughts on this. As someone who comes in and out of the Arizona and Southwest hip hop community, what's your sense of what's happening here and what might make it distinctive, and how it stands relative to national and international hip hop culture.*

KRS-One: *The one thing to realize is that hip hop is an idea. It's not a physical thing. So anybody on this planet that understands the idea can be hip hop. Hip hop didn't start in New York. It didn't start in the Bronx. Rap started in the Bronx. No, that's not even true. No, that's not true. I put it this way: a lot came to the Bronx. And we credit hip hop for starting in the Bronx, but hip hop is a world culture. It is a global culture. The whole world gave to it, for it to be what it is. Just as an example, to give you some background: graffiti writing is said to come out of Philadelphia with a guy named Cornbread. Breaking - we look at b-boying today and we see a b-boy may do 4, 5 different moves like uprocking, popping, locking, windmill, breaking, traditional breaking, but each of these moves were at one time sepa-rate cultures unto themselves. Like popping and locking is west coast. Oakland, California. Uprocking, New York. But today, it's all combined. So you see a b-boy coming in there and do all of it. He may give you a little bit of LA, a little bit of New York, a little bit of France and Germany even. Because they're coming up with styles and stuff like that. So the point is that first understand hip hop is an idea. When you know the idea, you progress the idea. Now, progressing the idea. Tempe should battle Phoenix, and this whole region will be rich. That's my advice.*

Justus: *Tempe battles Phoenix all the time, and they usually loose.*

Mook: *Uh-oh!*

KRS-One: *Phoenix battles Tempe, Tempe battles Phoenix, and you create your own market.*

Mook: *Now I want to clarify, cause I also hear something really deep in there which is this idea that's at the core of hip hop, which is the battle, the notion that someone puts something out there, and you have this visceral need to respond to it, and to show it up. This gets com-pared to cutting contests among jazz musicians in the 1940s and there are many, many precedents for this, but it's a core idea of hip hop, that you have to answer what's out there. So that's good advice, I think.*

KRS-One: *Balance it, balance it. Because in one breath battling is - really competition - is - let me say this: scientifically, competition is the seat of market, of society, all of the capitalism that makes us better, all of that. But competition is also very immature as well. And it's the im-maturity that brings out your art. It's hurt that brings out your art. It's the fact that they want to go over your piece that makes your piece brighter. The fact that when you do a piece you know there's opposition, that right there - even if there is none, you know that what you're doing, there's an opposing force to it, and that makes you put your art forward. If there's no opposing force, your art becomes very stale, like Michelangelo.*

Mook: *Wow, that's a provocative statement.*

KRS-One: *Michelangelo's art, one of the greatest minds in art, Michelangelo, Leonardo Da Vinci, they were more scientists even than artists. And I mention that because art needs conflict. And if you don't have no conflict in your life, it's not that you're not an artist, but you may not rise to the heights that your soul can produce. You gotta have some conflict. But it's imma-ture, it's destructive, we need to be careful, but it is a necessary part of art development.*

Mook: *Thoughts? Unanimous agreement? Do we have consensus?*

KRS-One: *Someone disagree!*

RM: *Otherwise his soul won't rise to the heights that it might have. [Laughter] I would like at this point to open it up to questions and comments from our eager audience here. Yes, you sir: third row.*

Q: *Well, you guys are talking about writing being about expressing, but I think that it's different for every writer so I'd be interested, anybody, whether or not they're current or active graf writers, what personally motivates you writing. I think, like he said, some are vandalizing, you know, "get up," and some people are more artistic. So I'd just be interested - and then for KRS and the whole panel, you're talking about hip hop and how it fits into Phoenix. But at the same time, you turn on the TV, you go down to Best Buy and look at the record sales, the hot selling stuff is people rapping, people doing, producing beats. So I'm interested in how you see with hip hop selling McDonalds and beer, how does graf fit into hip hop 'cause there's a lot of people now who are, the newer generation coming in and going "well, I listen to punk rock and graf has nothing to do with hip hop. To me it's just art, and what's that got to do with hip hop," which they see as musically based, not a larger culture... And so how does that fit into hip hop and how does what we're defining as the hip hop scene where everybody sees each other and knows each other, how does that fit into the fact that probably most of the kids under 18 in the larger valley of the sun are consuming what I would consider to be hip hop?*

KRS-One: *First point: I write because it is my self-expression. I was born to write. Second point: how does graf fit into hip hop? Graffiti writers should consider motion picture development, graphic design, website design, all forms of graphic advertisement - flyers, even calligraphy in the sense of develop and new language. Let me recoil - that's too far. Think about the every young graf writer should think about themselves doing graf at 50 or 60. Never live as an 18-year-old. Think of yourself right now at 50 and say, what do I look like? What am I doing as a graffiti writer? This is the question we asked ourselves in the early 80s. TAK's crew answered it. They formed a business - a straight business. They're very successful. They're called all over the world to do graffiti writing. And this also answers - to do aerosol art - this also answers the forward movement of graffiti writing, is that this is a power struggle. This is a power issue. What art isn't vandalism? What art did not start off as an offense to somebody else? It's just that when your [inaudible] comes into power then you become legitimized.*

So, maybe with Barack Obama in office graffiti writing may be more legitimized. And here's why: not that he has anything to do with that, but the American people as well as the world are now ready for new ideas. Graffiti writers might want to seize on that, and do things like run for office. Do things like support candidates who are running for office. If the graffiti community voted more in Arizona you wouldn't have a problem. If you took your money and paid for a politician to go into office, which is what politics is, you wouldn't have a problem... I'm going the easy route. The easy route is just pay 'em. Or, here's something even more than - we say "steal 'em." Here's how you steal a politician: graffiti writers should do campaigns of graffiti writing for their favorite candidate. Then their candidate will defend them. Put your candidate's face on the wall illegally. And that's how you steal a candidate.

Justus: *Speaking of Barak, he was probably the first presidential candidate to have pieces across the nation with his face murals. So what he just said is, did we steal it? Yes, we took that presidency, yes we did. Yes we can. And we will. You know what I'm sayin'?*

Amaya: *And to go a little bit further, you figure the person that did that mural for him and did that stuff is one of my boys from Phoenix, the MACK, from NG crew, from Phoenix, Arizona. [Applause]*

House: *I just want to give an example of that. When we went to Germany, the thing we went to is called "Battle of the Year," which is an event that's been going on forever, we didn't win, obviously - we came in 8th out of 19 countries, but we were cool with that for a lot of different reasons. Our intro to our show, everybody was kinda like "you guys are crazy. What are you guys doing? Just go out there and break." Our intro to our show started with an Obama speech. And we had Obama up in the DJ booth in an Obama mask, since we couldn't have him. It would have been good - maybe we would have won. But then in the intro to the show we had an Obama in the middle, and a bunch of guys around him with Bush masks. And we went and did this whole Obama intro and eventually Obama was killing all the Bushes off one by one. But we were doing our routines and Bush was up there rocking it for a minute. So people were like - better than the youtube video - so people were out there like "I don't know how these people are gonna take it out there. It's kinda crazy." But it's all right. The feeling that you get is a change of direction. And so that was the theme of our entire show. And we just jumped on with the whole Obama thing and took it there. So in any aspect whether it's graffiti or b-boy you guys can - you can get out there. You just gotta shake some heads sometimes, you gotta shake some people up.*

Amaya: *You asked too, there are graffiti writers I know out there that could really not even care about hip hop. Personally me, just style-wise you can completely see the difference from East to West coast. West coast, my whole style of how I rock stuff is calligraphy. Cholo influenced, gang writing from Chicano influence in LA, which started way before even graffiti in Philadelphia started. You're talking about writings on the walls from the 30s, the 40s, zoot suit era. A lot of people don't understand that. So I grew up on oldies, I never knew what hip hop was, coming out of Compton, California. The first taste of it really was gangsta rap, Public Enemy, you're talking about in the 90s, Dre and stuff like that was built on gangsta stuff. But when it came to punk rock you have nowadays all these kids that are skaters that listen to punk music. Myself I listen to death metal I listen to all kinds of different music. It's not just one specific thing. But for them to forget the root of where something started, they've got to understand the beginning of it before you can get to the end. If you try to already-if you're trying to grab a can and go to a wall and do a piece and you don't even know how to do a tag you're doing it completely backwards. You've gotta crawl before you can walk and you gotta walk before you can run, period.*

Mook: *A question from a student in MUS 354: "Did you ever think hip hop was just a fad, and that it would fade away in the future."*

Justus: *They did. They were wrong.*

Mook: *Which they? Who is "they?"*

Justus: *They got a lot to say but they were wrong. They said in the 70s and the 80s that it was gonna die. It never died. It will never die. It will always be alive through the writer and the MC that passes that bug on to, say, his godson who's watching a video and sees his uncle* rapping, and he's like "I'm gonna do that one day." Somebody inspired me, and he's sitting next to me right now. I'm gonna do that one day and I'm doing it now for Phoenix, for hip hop.

Amaya: *Parents in general told me that hip hop's just a fad. "Graffiti writing? Why are you writing on people's stuff?" They constantly knocked it and told me I was dumb for doing it. Now finally I'm pulling sponsorships from Red Bull and corporate gigs and doing stuff for ESPN, next thing you know my dad's giving me a pat on the back saying "you can do it."*

KRS-One: *You know what? That's the answer. Coming back to the answer I was giving you, after he received success his father said "this is good now. I've been taught." And this - I think this is the symbol of hip hop world wide. Once we - and let me say this too: corporate America is a funny place. Whenever you have intercourse with corporate America use your culture as a condo. And this is very important. Because this is the answer - this is the answer right here. Red Bull pays heavily for graf, breaking, rap, DJ-ing - Pepsi just opened an entire DJ-ing division, with –*

Amaya: *You've got to embrace that.*

KRS-One: *Well we're, controversial right now. Because, yes, I agree, we have to embrace that. But, in early 90s when we first embraced it, we were called sellouts. The early Nike commercials.*

Mook: *Tipper Gore called you something else.*

KRS-One: *What was that?*

Mook: *You know, the whole parental advisory label.*

KRS-One: *Right, which actually worked it our favor. That explicit lyrics sticker? That sold billions of records. Billions. Just to put a period on that - that last point you just made was profound. Once you have success, the world is more likely to deal with you. And so that's where it is. Graffiti writers need to seize that success. Red Bull is not the beacon of success. Neither is any of these corporations. But the fact that you can actually do business with a corporation like that means that really, we're pushing facism here. We're pushing globalization here. We're pushing federal globalization here. We're pushing the new world order here. This is what hip hop should really pay attention to. We are actually part of everything we said we didn't want to be about. And our parents went through the same thing as well. Bill and Hilary Clinton is the symbol of that - fighting against the Vietnam War and railing against government and this that and the other, then you become the government. And now hip hop starts this path as well. We railed against corporate America, they were ignoring us, they didn't want to deal with us. Now we are corporate America. And not "we do business with -" we are corporate America.*

Justus: *So where do we go next?*

KRS-One: *See this is where I bring spirituality into the picture. Because materially there is no answer as to where we go next. We just have to wipe each other out materially. You say "where should hip hop go next?" We should conquer jazz. No, seriously! I know it sounds crazy. But we should conquer rock, conquer reggae, conquer classical, conquer - you know, and what does that mean? That means we master them. We understand it so well that we are able to do it better than the originators. And so that's the other - but I bring spirituality into it. We need some virtues in hip hop. We need some standard principles.*

Civil Disobedience   331

Mook: *Wow. I think that speaks to a problem that I've heard some buzz about in the last five years or so, this notion that hip hop is now so diffused into all these other genres - you have acid jazz, you even have concertos for turntable now - in a way hip hop has conquered. It has certainly conquered R+B.*

KRS-One: *Oh yeah, no doubt.*

Mook: *And rock, and most other - it's conquered heavy metal.*

KRS-One: *Rock has turntables. Rock musicians have turntables.*

Mook: *And you look at a group like Limp Bizkit and...*

KRS-One: *It's crazy. I never got over that.*

Mook: *So are you talking about a crisis of identity here? Now that we're spread really thin, what do we draw on to move forward as hip hop? Is that what you're articulating?*

KRS-One: *Yeah, and not to move the discussion in a political, spiritual, metaphysical mode here, but yeah. Where is the hip hop government? The council? The leadership? I've been preaching about this for 20 years. We started the stop the violence movement and education against lies, all in the same gang, all with the notion of uniting hip hop. This goes back to Afrika Bambaataa and Zulu Nation that first called hip hop a culture. It was Afrika Bambaataa that said we are a community of specialized people. And that blew my mind in 1985 when I first heard it. And so we were inspired and then we went on. But I think we are afraid of ourselves. I think we are more afraid of our success than we are our failure. So I think that the real hip hopers are not even born yet. Or they are Barack Obama's daughters. Or my young children, the five and six year olds today are the real hip hopers. We are still creating hip hop. Hip hop hasn't even really begun yet, really. And I say that to say that I question the notion of being spread to thin. I understand what you're saying now. We're all over the place. But how do you know that we're spread thin? I think we may be transforming-we are in an identity - it's not a crisis - I dont know what the word is, but it's an identity something that equates to growth and maturity and - we're in identity architecture. We are building our identity. And I don't think any of us are in crisis about it, but I think America is. I think America is in crisis about hip hop's identity, and people like Lil Wayne for instance, that must totally frighten the United States. But then again, look at that - is that art? That's the question. That's the question, and all answers are right. Can you imagine? All answers are right. Is that art? No. You're right! Is that art? Yes. You're right. So I guess going back to identity, this is one of those metaphysical arguments when you deal with identity. Cause, substance, essence, those things. So, yeah. Just put a period there.*

Q: *[Inaudible]*

KRS-One: *It's controversy I would say. Nas should continue to say hip hop is dead. Because the more he says that, and the more we say "no it's not" the brighter it gets. As a matter of fact it was a weird thing - just before Nas said that on his last album, a 2007 album "hip hop is dead," hip hop was dead. Or at least sleeping. And Nas said "it's over." And everyone said "No-no-no-no, no it's not! No it's not!" And right there, it became alive. So again go back to that opposition. Without that conflict you cannot live. You can survive, but you cannot live. And so yeah, I would say Nas, he is right in one breath to say that hip hop is dead. The hip hop of Kool Herc is dead. The hip hop of Afrika Bambaataa is dead. My hip* hop is dead. My era - 80s, Big Daddy Kane, those guys are gone. Not Kane, Kane's still working.

So, I think it's more like an inhale - exhale thing, not death and life. More like rest and wake. Hip hop was asleep for like - Ten - the whole Bush administration. I mean seriously, look back on it. We're in an academic environment here. Empirical data is important. And look at the data. In the early 90s, in fact 1989 you had the Stop The Violence movement. 1990 you get All In The Same Gang. Gangs on the west coast actually took off the colors and said "it's over." But then the gulf war was announced in '91. And right then in 91 all the radio stations changed, all the movies started-war movies started coming out more prevalently, television, violence went up, all of that I think it was orchestrated personally. Because the few times I took my songs to BET, MTV, VH1, radio stations, and they would just flatly not play KRS-One, just outright say I can't play your music. I'd say "why?" They say, well you don't fit our demographic. I say "what's your demographic? Seven to seventeen. So I said, okay, what you're pushing right now on BET is seven to seventeen? And their answer is yes." That's what it is.

Mook: The Chronic.

KRS-One: Yeah, to seven to seventeen. So this is where we are. Hip hop is not dead. It sleeps, it awakens, and it will go to sleep again.

Mook: I have a list of questions here. The questions are getting better and better as you guys talk, which tells me that - and I think the audience would share this opinion - the discussion is raising some more and more interesting issues. Alright, so you mention the University environment: this is something that Mike and I were talking about last night. "To the panel: do you think that graffiti art will ever by taught and respected at the University level?"

Amaya: Well we're doing it now. This is the first time that I've heard of it at ASU, getting this big or any type of notoriety, so proof's right here in front of you - this panel. It's just a matter of how far you guys want to take it.

KRS-One: Can I probe that?

Mook: Please!

KRS-One: Another question: why should hip hop be taught in universities?

Amaya: Better yet, why do we have to wait until it gets to universities? Why aren't we doing it at a young age in Elementary schools or junior highs?

KRS-One: Any of these questions have answers.

House: There are programs like that. I have a friend in California with an after school program and she showed me their - she had like a coloring workbook and it was all pictures of b-boys and they were coloring their boom box and cutting it out and making medallions and it was like hip hop 101 afterschool program in Cali. Asia 1 who started b-boy summit back in the day, she has that afterschool program going on. So it is getting taught. When I - I worked at City of Phoenix for a long time at a teen center and that's where I met a lot of the guys that are still in my crew now. We taught all the elements there at the teen center. So it does happen, it just doesn't get the exposure. You gotta spoon-feed America, obviously, you gotta spoon-feed the masses. And should it be taught? I that's again yes and no.

Westenberg: May I respond to that?

Mook: *Please*

Westenberg: *It should be in higher education because the university is there to look at and address everything that is there in the world. Everything. And we are about extending and growing and knowing about ourselves and the world in every respect. And hip hop is a part of that, and thus it belongs in the university.*

Mook: *That sounds like a period to me.*

KRS-One: *No, she actually complicated it more. But does the university, or does the academic system, the environment, the university environment, does the university environment have the methodology for teaching hip hop?*

Westenberg: *There are individuals that are actively working. There are individuals who want this treated properly.*

KRS-One: *But will Arizona State itself give you the tools to probe hip hop for - in other words do we have to put on a different garment to come into the university.*

Westenberg: *I'm not at a university, I'm at a community college. But you don't have to [inaudible].*

Q: *So here's the question - you're saying you have to put on a different garment to enter community colleges, so where's the KRS-One university? Where are these hip hop artists that are gonna start taking this money that they're making and -*

KRS-One: *Let me - thank you for that - that is exactly what we're looking to do. And that is exactly why I asked - not exactly, that's part of the reason why I asked that question. I appreciate your answers. I hope we're all learning something here. But that's the point. A hip hop university should be started by hip hoppers. And does the traditional university setting-is it even capable of holding hip hop? Hip hop I think is bigger than the university system. For instance, if I said to you, well I can't say it we have kids in the audience. If I used expletives, the university may not deem me scholarly. If I use the language we use on the streets, let's say I used the N-word. And in hip hop we use the n-word freely. People disagree - the African American community is totally against that. Will African American academicians even be able to hear us?*

Roca Dolla: *I want to add one thing.*

Q: *[inaudible]*

Mook: *Two comments that I want to raise. One is there's an argument that's been made by Mark Anthony Neal and others that scholarship has actually been a part of hip hop from the beginning. Journalists writing critically about the evolution of the genres, scholars who were also hip hoppers writing pieces, pieces of scholarship about the evolution of hip hop and they make the argument that criticism and literature and journalism have been a part of the hip hop movement, again, because of this intrinsic interest in call and response where someone says something and you answer back, which is how scholarship works. Second point I'd like to make - Dean Kim who said hello to you all at the beginning, what you have just articulated, this problem of who should teach and can the traditional university methodology encompass the arts, that's something that all of the Schools within the College of the Arts are wrestling with madly right now. Can we teach music the way it's been taught since the middle ages? Can - if we produce a musician who can imitate Paganini, does that really get us anywhere? Right? If we produce these students who can imitate previous performances or* emulate their teachers, is that what we want? Or should they be able to improvise? Should they transform their thinking through music? Should they be able to apply musical ideas to medicine? Right? So, the statements that you're making are in fact the same concerns that the university has as well. In other words, you're already here! And you're already here! So, and do you have to be a hip hopper, well I'm not one.

KRS-One: Yeah, you are... You are hip hop.

Mook: I want to move back to another question and this is political. Specifically for KRS-One and for the panel as well: Do you believe that rap music is still the voice of the people? That's a loaded question. Do you think that MCs today make the best use of technology available to them, for example, only distributing music online with success. Why don't more rappers do that?

KRS-One: The first question is a no. Rap music does not represent the voice of the people today. Mainstream rap music represents the voice of some people. A large percentage of the American populace is represented by rap music today. By Lil Wayne, Ludacris, Snoop Dogg, 50 Cent, and all the rest. Americans like this. We produce it, we buy it, we want it. But does it speak to the people with a capital P? No, not at all. Even those people who buy the music will tell you "no. This is not speaking to my political views or my spiritual socio-economic, whatever. No. This is - I'm using this as an escape, this is my chance to bug out, this is my chance to just go free and happy and when the song is over I click it off and I get back to my serious life." So, and then the other part of the question?

Mook: Do you think that MCs today make the best use of technology available?

KRS-One: No. Next question.

Mook: Before we depart too far, I want to give Roca Dolla a chance to say one thing about hip hop in the university.

Roca Dolla: Well, not hip hop in the University. I just wanted to say that Dr. Westenberg teaches a hip hop 101 class at the Phoenix College, but I wanted to - I happened to be in one of her classes. I used to teach at Phoenix College but I also took one of her classes and I have some friends that came in, I think they call their group Fundamentals, is that what they call themselves? But what they do is they have - they educate youngsters. We were talking about hip hop as far as education. And using education they rap continents because it's easy for young kids to remember rap songs. So they rap about the continents and rap about math equations and various things and interject hip hop into the education and the education system. In a political system, in an educational system in the streets. So I just wanted to add that.

Mook: I'm going to fold another layer into this. We have in the audience today a new music education professor here at ASU. One of the things that he studies is how students learn through hip hop music, and that's Evan Tobias. So now we have a school of education actually studying how hip hop teaches, and doing scholarship on that, which then informs teaching again. It's a layered thing. We're getting all tied up together.

Q: [inaudible]

KRS-One: You know, you raise several complex issues. One: the idea of virtue. Virtue and morality are opinions. If we constantly use the B-word, N-word, H-word, MF, blah blah, and you can even see, even as I think about my language I get happy. Now if I came into a University and I started speaking in my language, my coded language, when you say there are people who will not accept hip hop because of its language, that's the problem right there. We're not giving up our language. We will respect other people's wishes though, no doubt. We don't have to use the N-word around you. We don't have to use the B-word around you. But for us, these words don't have negative connotations. They're not negative at all in our culture. So again, I don't know that you can teach an authentic hip hop class in a University that doesn't respect its language. So that's the first part. I don't have an answer. I'm raising more problems to the questions you - I'm just raising more problems here. Because I would like to teach a class where I can use expletives, I can do things that may even be obscene, to teach. Go back to what you was mentioning about Lil Wayne and that. As long as that is the face of hip hop, academia will not respect it or bring it in for critical analysis.

Martin Luther King, Dr. Martin Luther King Jr. had a concept called creative dissatisfaction. He spoke about it often. It was supposedly a part of the I have a Dream speech but it didn't make it. But he spoke about this thing called creative dissatisfaction that you are to express creatively your dissatisfaction. You are not to pick up a gun and go shoot. You're not to rob, steal, and kill to express your dissatisfaction. You are to express your dissatisfaction creatively. That's what Lil Wayne is. He is expressing the dissatisfaction that he feels with the United States of America, that's what all street culture really is. If the United States embraced the streets there would be no streets. there'd be no crack dealers and all this stuff. None of this would exist. But the more you ignore a population not only the stronger they get, but you yourself don't learn. And this is how we conquered the American mainstream of the 70s and 80s and 90s. When we first started our whole way of being was illegal. Rap music - I remember getting arrested in - not arrested, we weren't arrested, they just took our equipment and threw us out of the park. And we would go through this often because we didn't have permits to be in the park. We didn't even know we was supposed to have permits to be in the park. We just went out with our equipment, set it up in the park, we plugged into the light pole at the bottom. You break in to the light, and right away, that got the cops attention right there. There's a fuse in the light. You unscrew the fuse and you put in a - I don't know if you guys have seen this, it has a bulb and two outlets on the side. We used to get one of those, put it in to the light pole, and that's where we got power from. And I mention that because what if we teach today that that's what you should be doing to be hip hop.

Q: *[inaudible]*

KRS-One: *Hip hop is not misogynistic. Misogyny means hatred for women. It's a mental disease. Hip hop never ever in its thirty year history ever was misogynistic. There is no rap artist that will tell you that he hates women. Or even have participated in some sort of hatred toward women. No major rap - I wouldn't say anybody in hip hop is with that. The other part though -*

Q: *[inaudible]*

KRS-One: *True, but the images you see on television is what women are doing. And women are the ones who market promote and profit from hip hop. The biggest executives in hip hop are women. The one who produces the videos - women. The one who puts the short skirt on the other woman is a woman stylist. Women are in complete control of their destiny and of their image in hip hop - complete. It's women that are trying to compete with men that gives* you the image that you see. If women in hip hop would be women, we wouldn't have this problem. But women are trying to be men. Or compete with men in hip hop. And so we're not even getting a female voice.

Mook: *This is a very provocative comment that you're making I think because it sounds an awful lot like blaming the victim... Because we look at, or we hear the lyrics of many rap artists, yeah, it's pretty rough stuff.*

KRS-One: *Ever been to a strip club.*

Mook: *Well yeah, I see your point. No, I haven't, but I get the point. So I wanted to give you a chance to clarify what you're saying because I don't want to give our audience the impression that you're blaming a victim in this situation.*

KRS-One: *No, I thank you for that. This is a very collegiate conversation. We're tackling concepts that are controversial. And so let me try to be even more clear. We are not the victim, which is why I invite the criticism. By no means am I saying here that we are not at fault. We are. By no means am I saying that hip hop is perfect. It is not. But there is something to be said about our independence. And our right to exist. Just that. And that's the perspective that I come from. Not only that, a historical perspective as well. You're talking to a person that has seen hip hop from the beginning. Kool Herc, I lived across the street from Kool DJ Herc. 1972 he pulled his turntables out, at the request of his sister, by the way - Cindy. Cindy said Herc, bring your equipment out. I was right outside, me and my brother Kenny, we were right there. And we didn't know what we were listening to. We didn't know what anything was. But what we knew was: these people in this environment is our crew. This is our family. Take this, you might be able - not you - We might be able to understand this understanding how human beings in family, like the psychology of family is that my family does no wrong. I can criticize my family but you cannot. My family is crazy, no doubt, but it's my family and so I will defend it with my life. It's that psychology that I actually come from. I'm not saying that's even right, but I'm being honest about the way I feel.*

This is also, let me also put a disclaimer on it, this is how people join like the Nazi party, and justify it. This is how people join terrorist groups and justify it. This is how people join conservative parties, or democratic parties, or religious groups, even the police department if I may be so disrespectful. People join the police department and will defend it even though they know what's going on, even in their own precinct. But it's the fact that they're a cop and these are their boys and they understand. So the question then becomes in my mind: what is hip hop doing for itself internally, which is the judgment like: do you see us trying? Or are we just B-s, Hos, and N-s. "Accept us for who we are or don't listen to the music." We're not into that either. But what is the question - how do we live as ourselves?? We don't want to put another suit on. We don't want to put another hat on. We don't want to-we want to be ourselves. And that may mean starting our own institutions. I don't know that the University is worthy of hip hop.

Sponsors:
Herberger College
School of Music
Future Arts Research

Participants: Richard Mook

Michael Amaya is a graffiti writer originally from LA. He has moved between LA and Phoenix for decades, and has been writing graffiti since 1989. He is the founder of Forever In Control, a street art collective in Phoenix.

IRoc, AKA Rocadolla is a producer and director. Known as Arizona's Godfather of hip hop music, he teaches music business at ASU West, Phoenix College, and Collins College. He operates Clear Image Media Group, also known as Fifth Coast Records, which just won the New Times Best of Award for Hip Hop Recordings.

B-Boy House is a founding member of Furious Styles Crew. He has taught hip hop dance at colleges and universities including ASU. He just returned from Germany, where he competed with Team USA at a major competition. He is in demand as a dancer for music videos and other productions.

MC Justus is a member of Cut Throat Logic, and a solo artist. A rising star in Arizona hip hop, his performance with KRS-One was acclaimed in 2007 as one of the best collaborations of the year.

Mattlocks is a DJ in Phoenix, an experienced and knowledgeable voice in the Phoenix hip hop community.

Doug is a very experienced graffiti writer, and an important figure in the events of Civil Disobedience 2008, with a very distinctive graffiti style.

KRS-One is a founder of hip hop culture and a very accomplished recording artist with an international reputation. He has a prominent place in the history of American Popular Music, and is an expert on the history of hip hop as a cultural and political movement.

-lack of women on the panel

-microphones did not capture questions and comments from the audience, all of which were outstanding.

> **Mook:** *The first question that I'd like to start with: I'd like to address to the artists from Phoenix, the graffiti writers from Phoenix, if you'd be willing to comment for us on the status of graffiti in Phoenix in particular. What kinds of challenges do you face? How are you celebrated? How are you persecuted? What's your life like here as a graffiti artist?*

> **Amaya:** *Wow. Where do I start? Obviously graffiti in Arizona isn't accepted at all. People look at it as blight, just vandalism. They don't understand the motive behind it. When I got out of the marine corps and came back to Phoenix I had legal walls, I started doing stuff the legal way. I've been shut down on several walls that we got legally from the business owners and the property owners, so all the City has been doing is pushing us back into the streets. Graffiti came from the streets, it's gonna stay streets. But if you try to do something like we've been doing and get the community involved, get kids involved, start doing positive things and be role models for these people and the City pushes it out, they're not really giving us a chance to do anything. So I think we're highly persecuted. Out of all of hip hop, from what*

I understand and what I know, graf is still the only thing out of hip hop that's still illegally done in society's eyes on the streets.

Mook: *What do you mean by shut down? When the City shuts down a wall, what does that mean for you guys?*

Doug: *Even though we spend our own money, and sometimes we'll get people from the neighborhood to donate some money for us for paint, because it's expensive. It costs a lot of money. We'll sit at a wall for 20 or more hours and do a nice production, and the city will come and just paint over it. And they'll call it vandalism because it's done with aerosol. And if we were out there with paint brushes they wouldn't say a word. So there's a big taboo just with graffiti in general.*

Mook: *What kinds of things are you associated with maybe that you're not a part of? Are you often equated with gang culture to some degree? What kinds of representations are there that don't fit who you are as artists?*

Amaya: *Yeah, you hit the nail on the head. People have this perception "yeah, you know, I'm from Los Angeles, Hispanic, goatee, you know, typical stereotype Mexican cholo." I was brought up in that from Los Angeles, from Compton, California. I saw that everywhere around. It's either gangs, drugs, prison, or death, you know? I chose arts and started going a completely opposite direction. Going to family's funerals, I learned at a young age, I don't want to end up like my uncle, banging for a neighborhood that I don't even own, because every time the sheriff or police come through, they have us sitting down taking our shoes off, stripping us, patting us down. They're the ones that control the neighborhoods. The gangs don't. I saw that at a young age, so I started pushing graffiti, you know? It's a difficult game, it's the streets. There's nothing fair in life, so we're constantly fighting the system as graffiti writers and still struggling to be accepted.*

Mook: *I see some heads nodding. Mattlocks and KRS-One, you guys are nodding. Would you like to comment on your views on what's been said?*

KRS-One: *Yeah, graffiti writing in and of itself—let me comment on New York Graffiti. This is where I started in the early 1980s... This is when we had no money. I remember when BG—you were speaking about buying paint...*

Justus: *We used to rack 'em.*

KRS-One: *You know the deal. We used to rack paint—I'm sorry, for those of you who aren't bilingual, we used to steal paint. And we would go down to Canal Street in Manhattan, lower east side of Manhattan, and basically walk out of the store with 25 cans, and go to the train yards, put up our pieces on the train so that New York City could see that we exist. And this is the point I wanted to make—graffiti writing in the beginning was about existence. It was about "You're not hearing me. You're not seeing me. You're not speaking to me. You're actually trying to ignore me. So I'm going to make myself heard." And it starts with your name. There was a crew I used to be with called Out For Fame, OFF, Out For Fame crew. There's another called Down To Bomb. Bombing, tagging, burners, pieces. Tagging is considered vandalism, even by graffiti writers. Certain writers write sloppily. They're called "toys." Just because you tag don't make you a graf writer, make you an aerosol artist. You have to put pieces up—full murals—that tell stories about your neighborhood, about what you're going through in your life. This is an ancient practice that goes back to prehistoric times.*

And this is my last point about graffiti writing, is that graffiti writing answers the question that hip hop itself asks, and that question is "What does it mean to be human?" Not only does hip hop answer that question, but graffiti writing answers that question. And it answers it in this way: first, why is it important to even be a graffiti writer? Why is it even important? It's your self expression! If you can't express yourself in a society, you are oppressed. We were oppressed until we racked some paint, and put our names on the sides of trains and busses, which by the way Coca-Cola, McDonalds and others have now bit our style, and they use it in marketing, promotion, and all that. But that's my last point. What does it mean to be human? What does it actually mean to self-express? And graffiti writing is the story of people who beyond all odds be it even in the face of the most powerful government on earth, the American government, we said we don't care about all that, we're going to write on your property. I used to write on police cars.

Mook: *For those of you who were at the alley last night, there was one piece in particular that had a shout out on the upper right that said "for my unborn child."*

KRS-One: *Oooh.*

Mook: *Those kinds of profound, personal statements that I hope most of you got a chance to see last evening. Mattlocks, did you have something you wanted to add?*

Mattlocks: *For me, I'm not a graf writer, but I've hung out with most of—most f my friends are. And being from San Diego, California—that's where I was born and raised, I moved out here to Arizona about 8 years ago—seeing the struggle for them to try to exercise their craft and get their art out, while running from the police, it's crazy. I've been out, I've done the train yard run and I've had to be lookout and it's intense. You're looking out while your boy's trying to do a piece, and looking for the yard guy, looking for the police, and any slight thing you're ready to drop it and run, to try to put that piece up that runs on that train and that joy that that artist gets. It's sad that even when you go through the proper channels to get the permits or to get the approvals from somebody to do it on a wall that the police will come by and "no, that's alright, you can't do it" and go over it, it's sad.*

Mook: *I should note that the [Graffiti Busters] several times tried to shut down the graffiti alley that you all saw last night. And, Michael, I believe they were minutes away from painting it over on a number of occasions. And—*

Amaya: *Yes.*

Mook: *And do you carry a permission slip?*

Amaya: *Yeah, I had to carry permission slips on that entire alley. I just caught the buff back there, the guys that paint over all graffiti, about to go over the stuff. And it was funny, he wasn't actually, he wasn't going to start painting the entire wall, but since he's an art critic and all he started painting over what he thought was random acts of vandalism and choosing what he wanted to paint over in my alley, and I told him pretty much "take a hike." You know, I went back at him like "yo, you're going to come here without permission from the owners painting over something I got permission for, you're the one that's a vandal. You're going to point fingers at me and tell me I'm a vandal? You're the vandal.*

[Applause]

Mook: *So, I'd like to shift the discussion at this point from graffiti to hip hop in general because, as the panel has already noted, graffiti is particularly problematic in terms of its status in*

America right now, but it's also part of hip hop culture. It has deep connections, many of the early DJs and b-boys and MCs were also writers. Many of these gentlemen here participated in more than one element of hip hop.

Justus: We all started writing graffiti. That's the foundation for hip hop was MCing, graffiti, and beat boxing, all the four elements. I was basically a vandal. I just tagged my name everywhere, anywhere. And that's how it starts. You get that bug, that spark and you're addicted. And then it just snowballs.

Mook: So Justus, comment on that a little bit more. How do you see Phoenix graffiti writing fitting into Phoenix hip hop? And a related question: what's the status of the Phoenix hip hop community? Is it big, is it small, is it active, is it growing? What's going on there?

Justus: The status of the Phoenix hip hop scene is it's about to explode. It's about to get national recognition. People like Rocadolla have national distribution and are getting recognized worldwide. With community acts like Dose's alley downtown, you cleaned up an alley that was drug infested and homeless infested, and you got bums cleaning it for a burrito and a 40. It may not be much, but it's food, and it's giving back and letting it grow, watching these young MCs come up and teaching kids how to rap and teaching kids how to write, and seeing the next generation come up. We started it because he started it and we followed in his footsteps because he is our teacher ultimately. But we want to teach these kids and keep passing that torch because it's just going to continue to grow.

Mook: House, I'd like to get your thoughts on where Phoenix hip hop is at.

House: It's good. When you're here in Arizona we tend to complain a lot about what we have here in our hometown. It's like anything else—we don't appreciate what we have right in front of us. And I've been able to travel all over the world and even anywhere in the States. When I go places, I miss Arizona. I go to other places, I check out their hip hop spots, check out their scene, and it's just not the same. So to me it's really good. It's still smaller than we'd like it to be. We need to work on longevity and not losing our kids. A lot of kids get into a lot of the elements and we lose them. There's not a lot of older guys in Arizona. But it's a good thing. It's small, but everybody knows each other. Everybody's kind of gone through their trials and tribulations with each other. Some of us up here have deeds in the past, but we've gotten past that and right now we're in a really good time. Right now we're getting more established and we're getting older heads that are there to school the kids, hopefully produce more things to keep everybody going. I like hip hop in Arizona, and I know people don't think of Arizona in that way still, but it's come a long way. I remember going to my first b-boy event in LA. B-boys were asking "Where you from?" and I was like "Arizona," and they were like "Arizona? You guys break there? There's people there?" I'm like "Yeah." But now half the team that went on Team USA was from Arizona. So Arizona's still not getting the credit it needs to, but there's a lot of talent and it's a great place and people are going to recognize it.

Mook: Roca Dolla you've been in this from the beginning. What are your thoughts on where we're at?

Roca Dolla: I think I've talked to you about this on the phone a little bit, when in the 80s when I was one of the—in the 80s there was just a few groups that rapped, and I can name them on probably one hand. And now I look up and see five or ten thousand MCs at a time hitting me up on Myspace; we've progressed a long way. One of the things that I talk about, and

I talked with you about it, is just the negative image that the fact that we didn't get Martin Luther King holiday. We were the last state to have the Martin Luther King holiday. I think that put a negative stigma on Arizona hip hop. We had Public Enemy speak about it, big acts like Steve Wonder that wouldn't come up here, Superbowls, we didn't get any Superbowls or all star events because we were the last state to have the Martin Luther King holiday because of different people who opposed that holiday. I think that set the entertainment period, not only hip hop but just entertainment period, set it back maybe about ten years. It took—it's taken us this long and back then you had to do it for the love. Now there's a lot of cats out here, a lot of talent. We're defining the sound of the Southwest because Arizona, hip hop in Arizona is bigger than Arizona. And I always equate it to the southwest. Southwest is a new east. Hip hop started in the East coast, moved to West coast, and then it's jumped to the midwest, dirty south, and now we're building a new coast basically. Which includes Vegas and some of these other cities, and it's come a long way. We're actually defining the actual figurative coast, you could say. So it's slow motion, but it's definitely come a long way.

Mook: KRS-One, I'd love to get your thoughts on this. As someone who comes in and out of the Arizona and Southwest hip hop community, what's your sense of what's happening here and what might make it distinctive, and how it stands relative to national and international hip hop culture?

KRS-One: The one thing to realize is that hip hop is an idea. It's not a physical thing. So anybody on this planet that understands the idea can be hip hop. Hip hop didn't start in New York. It didn't start in the Bronx. Rap started in the Bronx. No, that's not even true. No, that's not true. I put it this way: a lot came to the Bronx. And we credit hip hop for starting in the Bronx, but hip hop is a world culture. It is a global culture. The whole world gave to it for it to be what it is. Just as an example, to give you some background: graffiti writing is said to come out of Philadelphia with a guy named Cornbread. Breaking—we look at b-boying today and we see a b-boy may do 4, 5 different moves like uprocking, popping, locking, windmill, breaking, traditional breaking, but each of these moves were at one time separate cultures unto themselves. Like popping and locking is west coast. Oakland, California. Uprocking, New York. But today, it's all combined. So you see a b-boy coming in there and do all of it. He may give you a little bit of LA, a little bit of New York, a little bit of France and Germany even. Because they're coming up with styles and stuff like that. So the point is that first understand hip hop is an idea. When you know the idea, you progress the idea. Now, progressing the idea. Tempe should battle Phoenix, and this whole region will be rich. That's my advice.

Justus: Tempe battles Phoenix all the time, and they usually loose.

Mook: Uh-oh!

KRS-One: Phoenix battles Tempe, Tempe battles Phoenix, and you create your own market.

Mook: Now I want to clarify, cause I also hear something really deep in there which is this idea that's at the core of hip hop, which is the battle, the notion that someone puts something out there, and you have this visceral need to respond to it, and to show it up. This gets compared to cutting contests among jazz musicians in the 1940s and there are many, many precedents for this, but it's a core idea of hip hop, that you have to answer what's out there. So that's good advice, I think.

KRS-One: Balance it, balance it. Because in one breath battling is—really competition—is—let me say this: scientifically, competition is the seat of market, of society, all of the capitalism that makes us better, all of that. But competition is also very immature as well. And it's the immaturity that brings out your art. It's hurt that brings out your art. It's the fact that they want to go over your piece that makes your piece brighter. The fact that when you do a piece you know there's opposition, that right there—even if there is none—you know that what you're doing, there's an opposing force to it, and that makes you put your art forward. If there's no opposing force, your art becomes very stale, like Michelangelo.

Mook: *Wow, that's a provocative statement.*

KRS-One: *Michelangelo's art, one of the greatest minds in art, Michelangelo, Leonardo Da Vinci, they were more scientists even than artists. And I mention that because art needs conflict. And if you don't have no conflict in your life, it's not that you're not an artist, but you may not rise to the heights that your soul can produce. You gotta have some conflict. But it's immature, it's destructive, we need to be careful, but it is a necessary part of art development.*

Mook: *Thoughts? Unanimous agreement? Do we have consensus?*

KRS-One: *Someone disagree!*

RM: *Otherwise his soul won't rise to the heights that it might have. [Laughter] I would like at this point to open it up to questions and comments from our eager audience here. Yes, you sir: third row.*

Q: *Well, you guys are talking about writing being about expressing, but I think that it's different for every writer so I'd be interested, anybody, whether or not they're current or active graf writers, what personally motivates you writing. I think, like he said, some are vandalizing, you know, "get up," and some people are more artistic. So I'd just be interested—and then for KRS and the whole panel, you're talking about hip hop and how it fits into Phoenix. But at the same time, you turn on the TV, you go down to Best Buy and look at the record sales, the hot selling stuff is people rapping, people doing, producing beats. So I'm interested in how you see with hip hop selling McDonalds and beer, how does graf fit into hip hop 'cause there's a lot of people now who are, the newer generation coming in and going "Well, I listen to punk rock and graf has nothing to do with hip hop. To me it's just art, and what's that got to do with hip hop," which they see as musically based, not a larger culture . . . And so how does that fit into hip hop and how does what we're defining as the hip hop scene where everybody sees each other and knows each other, how does that fit into the fact that probably most of the kids under 18 in the larger valley of the sun are consuming what I would consider to be hip hop?*

KRS-One: *First point: I write because it is my self-expression. I was born to write. Second point: how does graf fit into hip hop? Graffiti writers should consider motion picture development, graphic design, website design, all forms of graphic advertisement -flyers, even calligraphy in the sense of develop and new language. Let me recoil — that's too far. Think about the — every young graf writer should think about themselves doing graf at 50 or 60. Never live as an 18-year-old. Think of yourself right now at 50 and say, what do I look like? What am I doing as a graffiti writer? This is the question we asked ourselves in the early 80s. TAK's crew answered it. They formed a business — a straight business. They're very successful. They're called all over the world to do graffiti writing. And this also answers — to do aerosol art — this also answers the forward movement of graffiti writing, is that this is a power struggle. This is a power issue. What art isn't vandalism? What art did not start off as an offense to somebody else? It's just that when your [inaudible] comes into power then you become legitimized.*

So, maybe with Barack Obama in office graffiti writing may be more legitimized. And here's why: not that he has anything to do with that, but the American people as well as the world are now ready for new ideas. Graffiti writers might want to seize on that, and do things like run for office. Do things like support candidates who are running for office. If the graffiti community voted more in Arizona you wouldn't have a problem. If you took your money and paid for a politician to go into office, which is what politics is, you wouldn't have a problem... I'm going the easy route. The easy route is just pay 'em. Or, here's something even more than — we say "steal 'em." Here's how you steal a politician: graffiti writers should do campaigns of graffiti writing for their favorite candidate. Then their candidate will defend them. Put your candidate's face on the wall illegally. And that's how you steal a candidate.

Justus: Speaking of Barak, he was probably the first presidential candidate to have pieces across the nation with his face murals. So what he just said is, did we steal it? Yes, we took that presidency, yes we did. Yes we can. And we will. You know what I'm sayin'?

Amaya: And to go a little bit further, you figure the person that did that mural for him and did that stuff is one of my boys from Phoenix, the MACK, from NG crew, from Phoenix, Arizona. [Applause]

House: I just want to give an example of that. When we went to Germany, the thing we went to is called "Battle of the Year," which is an event that's been going on forever, we didn't win, obviously - we came in 8th out of 19 countries, but we were cool with that for a lot of different reasons. Our intro to our show, everybody was kinda like "you guys are crazy. What are you guys doing? Just go out there and break." Our intro to our show started with an Obama speech. And we had Obama up in the DJ booth in an Obama mask, since we couldn't have him. It would have been good - maybe we would have won. But then in the intro to the show we had an Obama in the middle, and a bunch of guys around him with Bush masks. And we went and did this whole Obama intro and eventually Obama was killing all the Bushes off one by one. But we were doing our routines and Bush was up there rocking it for a minute. So people were like - better than the youtube video—so people were out there like "I don't know how these people are gonna take it out there. It's kinda crazy." But it's all right. The feeling that you get is a change of direction. And so that was the theme of our entire show. And we just jumped on with the whole Obama thing and took it there. So in any aspect whether it's graffiti or b-boy you guys can—you can get out there. You just gotta shake some heads sometimes, you gotta shake some people up.

Amaya: You asked too, there are graffiti writers I know out there that could really not even care about hip hop. Personally me, just style-wise you can completely see the difference from East to West coast. West coast, my whole style of how I rock stuff is calligraphy. Cholo influenced, gang writing from Chicano influence in LA, which started way before even graffiti in Philadelphia started. You're talking about writings on the walls from the 30s, the 40s, zoot suit era. A lot of people don't understand that. So I grew up on oldies, I never knew what hip hop was, coming out of Compton, California. The first taste of it really was gangsta rap, Public Enemy, you're talking about in the 90s, Dre and stuff like that was built on gangsta stuff. But when it came to punk rock you have nowadays all these kids that are skaters that listen to punk music. Myself I listen to death metal I listen to all kinds of different music. It's not just one specific thing. But for them to forget the root of where something started, they've got to understand the beginning of it before you can get to the end. If you try to already-if you're trying to grab a can and go to a wall and do a piece and you don't even know how *to do a tag you're doing it completely backwards. You've gotta crawl before you can walk and you gotta walk before you can run, period.*

Mook: *A question from a student in MUS 354: "Did you ever think hip hop was just a fad, and that it would fade away in the future."*

Justus: *They did. They were wrong.*

Mook: *Which they? Who is "they?"*

Justus: *They got a lot to say but they were wrong. They said in the 70s and the 80s that it was gonna die. It never died. It will never die. It will always be alive through the writer and the MC that passes that bug on to, say, his godson who's watching a video and sees his uncle rapping, and he's like "I'm gonna do that one day." Somebody inspired me, and he's sitting next to me right now. I'm gonna do that one day and I'm doing it now for Phoenix, for hip hop.*

Amaya: *Parents in general told me that hip hop's just a fad. "Graffiti writing? Why are you writing on people's stuff?" They constantly knocked it and told me I was dumb for doing it. Now finally I'm pulling sponsorships from Red Bull and corporate gigs and doing stuff for ESPN, next thing you know my dad's giving me a pat on the back saying "you can do it."*

KRS-One: *You know what? That's the answer. Coming back to the answer I was giving you, after he received success his father said "this is good now. I've been taught." And this -I think this is the symbol of hip hop world wide. Once we - and let me say this too: corporate America is a funny place. Whenever you have intercourse with corporate America use your culture as a condom. And this is very important. Because this is the answer—this is the answer right here. Red Bull pays heavily for graf, breaking, rap, DJ-ing—Pepsi just opened an entire DJ-ing division, with –*

Amaya: *You've got to embrace that.*

KRS-One: *Well, we're, controversial right now. Because, yes, I agree, we have to embrace that. But, in early 90s when we first embraced it, we were called sellouts. The early Nike commercials.*

Mook: *Tipper Gore called you something else.*

KRS-One: *What was that?*

Mook: *You know, the whole parental advisory label.*

KRS-One: *Right, which actually worked it our favor. That explicit lyrics sticker? That sold billions of records. Billions. Just to put a period on that—that last point you just made was profound. Once you have success, the world is more likely to deal with you. And so that's where it is. Graffiti writers need to seize that success. Red Bull is not the beacon of success. Neither is any of these corporations. But the fact that you can actually do business with a corporation like that means that really, we're pushing facism here. We're pushing globalization here. We're pushing federal globalization here. We're pushing the new world order here. This is what hip hop should really pay attention to. We are actually part of everything we said we didn't want to be about. And our parents went through the same thing as well. Bill and Hilary Clinton is the symbol of that—fighting against the Vietnam War and railing against government and this that and the other, then you become the government. And now hip hop starts this path as well. We railed against corporate America, they were ignoring us, they* *didn't want to deal with us. Now we are corporate America. And not "we do business with - " we are corporate America.*

Justus: *So where do we go next?*

KRS-One: *See this is where I bring spirituality into the picture. Because materially there is no answer as to where we go next. We just have to wipe each other out materially. You say "where should hip hop go next?" We should conquer jazz. No, seriously! I know it sounds crazy. But we should conquer rock, conquer reggae, conquer classical, conquer—you know, and what does that mean? That means we master them. We understand it so well that we are able to do it better than the originators. And so that's the other—but I bring spirituality into it. We need some virtues in hip hop. We need some standard principles.*

Mook: *Wow. I think that speaks to a problem that I've heard some buzz about in the last five years or so, this notion that hip hop is now so diffused into all these other genres—you have acid jazz, you even have concertos for turntable now—in a way hip hop has conquered. It has certainly conquered R+B.*

KRS-One: *Oh yeah, no doubt.*

Mook: *And rock, and most other—it's conquered heavy metal.*

KRS-One: *Rock has turntables. Rock musicians have turntables.*

Mook: *And you look at a group like Limp Bizkit and. . .*

KRS-One: *It's crazy. I never got over that.*

Mook: *So are you talking about a crisis of identity here? Now that we're spread really thin, what do we draw on to move forward as hip hop? Is that what you're articulating?*

KRS-One: *Yeah, and not to move the discussion in a political, spiritual, metaphysical mode here, but yeah. Where is the hip hop government? The council? The leadership? I've been preaching about this for 20 years. We started the stop the violence movement and education against lies, all in the same gang, all with the notion of uniting hip hop. This goes back to Afrika Bambaataa and Zulu Nation that first called hip hop a culture. It was Afrika Bambaataa that said we are a community of specialized people. And that blew my mind in 1985 when I first heard it. And so we were inspired and then we went on. But I think we are afraid of ourselves. I think we are more afraid of our success than we are our failure. So I think that the real hip hopers are not even born yet. Or they are Barack Obama's daughters. Or my young children, the five and six year olds today are the real hip hopers. We are still creating hip hop. Hip hop hasn't even really begun yet, really. And I say that to say that I question the notion of being spread to thin. I understand what you're saying now. We're all over the place. But how do you know that we're spread thin? I think we may be transforming—we are in an identity—it's not a crisis—I don't know what the word is, but it's an identity something that equates to growth and maturity and—we're in identity architecture. We are building our identity. And I don't think any of us are in crisis about it, but I think America is. I think America is in crisis about hip hop's identity, and people like Lil Wayne for instance, that must totally frighten the United States. But then again, look at that—is that art? That's the question. That's the question, and all answers are right. Can you imagine? All answers are right. Is that art? No. You're right! Is that art? Yes. You're right. So I guess going back to identity, this is one of those metaphysical arguments when you deal with identity. Cause, substance, essence, those things. So, yeah. Just put a period there.*

Q: *[Inaudible]*

KRS-One: *It's controversy I would say. Nas should continue to say hip hop is dead. Because the more he says that, and the more we say, "no, it's not," the brighter it gets. As a matter of fact it was a weird thing—just before Nas said that on his last album, a 2007 album "hip hop is dead," hip hop was dead. Or at least sleeping. And Nas said "it's over." And everyone said "No-no-no-no, no, it's not! No, it's not!" And right there, it became alive. So again go back to that opposition. Without that conflict you cannot live. You can survive, but you cannot live. And so yeah, I would say Nas, he is right in one breath to say that hip hop is dead. The hip hop of Kool Herc is dead. The hip hop of Afrika Bambaataa is dead. My hip hop is dead. My era - 80s, Big Daddy Kane, those guys are gone. Not Kane, Kane's still working.*

So, I think it's more like an inhale - exhale thing, not death and life. More like rest and wake. Hip hop was asleep for like - Ten - the whole Bush administration. I mean seriously, look back on it. We're in an academic environment here. Empirical data is important. And look at the data. In the early 90s, in fact 1989 you had the Stop the Violence movement. 1990 you get All in the Same Gang. Gangs on the west coast actually took off the colors and said "it's over." But then the gulf war was announced in '91. And right then in 91 all the radio stations changed, all the movies started—war movies started coming out more prevalently, television, violence went up, all of that I think it was orchestrated personally. Because the few times I took my songs to BET, MTV, VH1, radio stations, and they would just flatly not play KRS-One, just outright say I can't play your music. I'd say "why?" They say, well you don't fit our demographic. I say "what's your demographic? Seven to seventeen. So I said, okay, what you're pushing right now on BET is seven to seventeen? And their answer is yes." That's what it is.

Mook: *The Chronic.*

KRS-One: *Yeah, to seven to seventeen. So this is where we are. Hip hop is not dead. It sleeps, it awakens, and it will go to sleep again.*

Mook: *I have a list of questions here. The questions are getting better and better as you guys talk, which tells me that—and I think the audience would share this opinion—the discussion is raising some more and more interesting issues. Alright, so you mention the University environment: this is something that Mike and I were talking about last night. "To the panel: do you think that graffiti art will ever be taught and respected at the University level?"*

Amaya: *Well we're doing it now. This is the first time that I've heard of it at ASU, getting this big or any type of notoriety, so proofs right here in front of you—this panel. It's just a matter of how far you guys want to take it.*

KRS-One: *Can I probe that?*

Mook: *Please!*

KRS-One: *Another question: why should hip hop be taught in universities?*

Amaya: *Better yet, why do we have to wait until it gets to universities? Why aren't we doing it at a young age in Elementary schools or junior highs?*

KRS-One: *Any of these questions have answers.*

House: *There are programs like that. I have a friend in California with an after school program and she showed me their — she had like a coloring workbook and it was all pictures of* *b-boys and they were coloring their boom box and cutting it out and making medallions and it was like hip hop 101 afterschool program in Cali. Asia 1 who started b-boy summit back in the day, she has that afterschool program going on. So it is getting taught. When I — I worked at City of Phoenix for a long time at a teen center and that's where I met a lot of the guys that are still in my crew now. We taught all the elements there at the teen center. So it does happen, it just doesn't get the exposure. You gotta spoon-feed America, obviously, you gotta spoon-feed the masses. And should it be taught? I that's again yes and no.*

Westenberg: *May I respond to that?*

Mook: *Please.*

Westenberg: *It should be in higher education because the university is there to look at and address everything that is there in the world. Everything. And we are about extending and growing and knowing about ourselves and the world in every respect. And hip hop is a part of that, and thus it belongs in the university.*

Mook: *That sounds like a period to me.*

KRS-One: *No, she actually complicated it more. But does the university, or does the academic system, the environment, the university environment, does the university environment have the methodology for teaching hip hop?*

Westenberg: *There are individuals that are actively working. There are individuals who want this treated properly.*

KRS-One: *But will Arizona State itself give you the tools to probe hip hop or — in other words do we have to put on a different garment to come into the university.*

Westenberg: *I'm not at a university, I'm at a community college. But you don't have to [inaudible].*

Q: *So here's the question — you're saying you have to put on a different garment to enter community colleges, so where's the KRS-One university? Where are these hip hop artists that are gonna start taking this money that they're making and —*

KRS-One: *Let me — thank you for that — that is exactly what we're looking to do. And that is exactly why I asked — not exactly, that's part of the reason why I asked that question. I appreciate your answers. I hope we're all learning something here. But that's the point. A hip hop university should be started by hip hoppers. And does the traditional university setting — is it even capable of holding hip hop? Hip hop I think is bigger than the university system. For instance, if I said to you, well I can't say it we have kids in the audience. If I used expletives, the university may not deem me scholarly. If I use the language we use on the streets, let's say I used the N-word. And in hip hop we use the n-word freely. People disagree — the African American community is totally against that. Will African American academicians even be able to hear us?*

Roca Dolla: *I want to add one thing.*

Q: *[inaudible]*

Mook: *Two comments that I want to raise. One is there's an argument that's been made by Mark Anthony Neal and others that scholarship has actually been a part of hip hop from the beginning. Journalists writing critically about the evolution of the genres, scholars who were also hip hoppers writing pieces, pieces of scholarship about the evolution of hip hop and* *they make the argument that criticism and literature and journalism have been a part of the hip hop movement, again, because of this intrinsic interest in call and response where someone says something and you answer back, which is how scholarship works. Second point I'd like to make — Dean Kim who said hello to you all at the beginning, what you have just articulated, this problem of who should teach and can the traditional university methodology encompass the arts, that's something that all of the Schools within the College of the Arts are wrestling with madly right now. Can we teach music the way it's been taught since the middle ages? Can — if we produce a musician who can imitate Paganini, does that really get us anywhere? Right? If we produce these students who can imitate previous performances or emulate their teachers, is that what we want? Or should they be able to improvise? Should they transform their thinking through music? Should they be able to apply musical ideas to medicine? Right? So, the statements that you're making are in fact the same concerns that the university has as well. In other words, you're already here! And you're already here! So, and do you have to be a hip hopper, well I'm not one.*

KRS-One: *Yeah, you are ... You are hip hop.*

Mook: *I want to move back to another question and this is political. Specifically for KRS-One and for the panel as well: Do you believe that rap music is still the voice of the people? That's a loaded question. Do you think that MCs today make the best use of technology available to them, for example, only distributing music online with success. Why don't more rappers do that?*

KRS-One: *The first question is a no. Rap music does not represent the voice of the people today. Mainstream rap music represents the voice of some people. A large percentage of the American populace is represented by rap music today. By Lil Wayne, Ludacris, Snoop Dogg, 50 Cent, and all the rest. Americans like this. We produce it, we buy it, we want it. But does it speak to the people with a capital P? No, not at all. Even those people who buy the music will tell you, "No." This is not speaking to my political views or my spiritual socioeconomic, whatever. No. This is — I'm using this as an escape, this is my chance to bug out, this is my chance to just go free and happy and when the song is over I click it off and I get back to my serious life." So, and then the other part of the question?*

Mook: *Do you think that MCs today make the best use of technology available?*

KRS-One: *No. Next question.*

Mook: *Before we depart too far, I want to give Roca Dolla a chance to say one thing about hip hop in the university.*

Roca Dolla: *Well, not hip hop in the University. I just wanted to say that Dr. Westenberg teaches a hip hop 101 class at the Phoenix College, but I wanted to — I happened to be in one of her classes. I used to teach at Phoenix College but I also took one of her classes and I have some friends that came in, I think they call their group Fundamentals, is that what they call themselves? But what they do is they have — they educate youngsters. We were talking about hip hop as far as education. And using education they rap continents because it's easy for young kids to remember rap songs. So they rap about the continents and rap about math equations and various things and interject hip hop into the education and the education system. In a political system, in an educational system, in the streets. So I just wanted to add that.*

Mook: *I'm going to fold another layer into this. We have in the audience today a new music education professor here at ASU. One of the things that he studies is how students learn through* *hip hop music, and that's Evan Tobias. So now we have a school of education actually studying how hip hop teaches, and doing scholarship on that, which then informs teaching again. It's a layered thing. We're getting all tied up together.*

Q: [inaudible]

KRS-One: *You know, you raise several complex issues. One: the idea of virtue. Virtue and morality are opinions. If we constantly use the B-word, N-word, H-word, MF, blah blah, and you can even see, even as I think about my language I get happy. Now if I came into a University and I started speaking in my language, my coded language, when you say there are people who will not accept hip hop because of its language, that's the problem right there. We're not giving up our language. We will respect other people's wishes though, no doubt. We don't have to use the N-word around you. We don't have to use the B-word around you. But for us, these words don't have negative connotations. They're not negative at all in our culture. So again, I don't know that you can teach an authentic hip hop class in a University that doesn't respect its language. So that's the first part. I don't have an answer. I'm raising more problems to the questions you — I'm just raising more problems here. Because I would like to teach a class where I can use expletives, I can do things that may even be obscene, to teach. Go back to what you was mentioning about Lil Wayne and that. As long as that is the face of hip hop, academia will not respect it or bring it in for critical analysis.*

Martin Luther King, Dr. Martin Luther King Jr., had a concept called creative dissatisfaction. He spoke about it often. It was supposedly a part of the "I have a Dream" speech 'but it didn't make it. But he spoke about this thing called creative dissatisfaction that you are to express creatively your dissatisfaction. You are not to pick up a gun and go shoot. You're not to rob, steal, and kill to express your dissatisfaction. You are to express your dissatisfaction creatively. That's what Lil Wayne is. He is expressing the dissatisfaction that he feels with the United States of America. That's what all street culture really is. If the United States embraced the streets there would be no streets. There'd be no crack dealers and all this stuff. None of this would exist. But the more you ignore a population not only the stronger they get, but you yourself don't learn. And this is how we conquered the American mainstream of the 70s and 80s and 90s. When we first started our whole way of being was illegal. Rap music — I remember getting arrested in — not arrested, we weren't arrested, they just took our equipment and threw us out of the park. And we would go through this often because we didn't have permits to be in the park. We didn't even know we was supposed to have permits to be in the park. We just went out with our equipment, set it up in the park, we plugged into the light pole at the bottom. You break in to the light, and right away, that got the cops attention right there. There's a fuse in the light. You unscrew the fuse and you put in a — I don't know if you guys have seen this, it has a bulb and two outlets on the side. We used to get one of those, put it in to the light pole, and that's where we got power from. And I mention that because what if we teach today that that's what you should be doing to be hip hop.

Q: [inaudible]

KRS-One: *Hip hop is not misogynistic. Misogyny means hatred for women. It's a mental disease. Hip hop never ever in its thirty year history ever was misogynistic. There is no rap artist that will tell you that he hates women. Or even have participated in some sort of hatred toward women. No major rap — I wouldn't say anybody in hip hop is with that. The other part though —*

Q: *[inaudible]*

KRS-One: *True, but the images you see on television is what women are doing. And women are the ones who market promote and profit from hip hop. The biggest executives in hip hop are women. The one who produces the videos — women. The one who puts the short skirt on the other woman is a woman stylist. Women are in complete control of their destiny and of their image in hip hop — complete. It's women that are trying to compete with men that gives you the image that you see. If women in hip hop would be women, we wouldn't have this problem. But women are trying to be men. Or compete with men in hip hop. And so we're not even getting a female voice.*

Mook: *This is a very provocative comment that you're making I think because it sounds an awful lot like blaming the victim... Because we look at, or we hear the lyrics of many rap artists, yeah, it's pretty rough stuff.*

KRS-One: *Ever been to a strip club.*

Mook: *Well yeah, I see your point. No, I haven't, but I get the point. So I wanted to give you a chance to clarify what you're saying because I don't want to give our audience the impression that you're blaming a victim in this situation.*

KRS-One: *No, I thank you for that. This is a very collegiate conversation. We're tackling concepts that are controversial. And so let me try to be even more clear. We are not the victim, which is why I invite the criticism. By no means am I saying here that we are not at fault. We are. By no means am I saying that hip hop is perfect. It is not. But there is something to be said about our independence. And our right to exist. Just that. And that's the perspective that I come from. Not only that, a historical perspective as well. You're talking to a person that has seen hip hop from the beginning. Kool Herc, I lived across the street from Kool DJ Herc. 1972 he pulled his turntables out, at the request of his sister, by the way — Cindy. Cindy said Herc, bring your equipment out. I was right outside, me and my brother Kenny, we were right there. And we didn't know what we were listening to. We didn't know what anything was. But what we knew was: these people in this environment is our crew. This is our family. Take this, you might be able — not you — We might be able to understand this understanding how human beings in family, like the psychology of family is that my family does no wrong. I can criticize my family but you cannot. My family is crazy, no doubt, but it's my family and so I will defend it with my life. It's that psychology that I actually come from. I'm not saying that's even right, but I'm being honest about the way I feel.*

This is also, let me also put a disclaimer on it, this is how people join like the Nazi party, and justify it. This is how people join terrorist groups and justify it. This is how people join conservative parties, or democratic parties, or religious groups, even the police department if I may be so disrespectful. People join the police department and will defend it even though they know what's going on, even in their own precinct. But it's the fact that they're a cop and these are their boys and they understand. So the question then becomes in my mind: what is hip hop doing for itself internally, which is the judgment like: do you see us trying? Or are we just B-s, Hos, and N-s. "Accept us for who we are or don't listen to the music." We're not into that either. But what is the question — how do we live as ourselves?? We don't want to put another suit on. We don't want to put another hat on. We don't want to — we want to be ourselves. And that may mean starting our own institutions. I don't know that the University is worthy of hip hop.